Social Movements

This timely reader plays an important role in the field of social movements, filling a significant gap by covering a number of connected areas within social studies.

Responding to growing demand for interpretation and analysis of re-emerging social conflicts in the developed as well as the developing world, this timely collection is the outcome of the recent boost received by social movement studies since the spread of contention and collective action at international level and the growth of the 'antiglobalization' movement.

Ruggiero and Montagna have compiled key classic, as well as contemporary, works written by distinguished international experts, from a variety of disciplines. These address themes of conflict, social change, social movements and globalization. Intended not only as a comprehensive introduction for undergraduates and postgraduates studying social movements, this volume is also an incredibly valuable resource for more general courses on sociological theory, global sociology, the history of sociological thought, contemporary social theory, and international and globalization studies.

Vincenzo Ruggiero is Professor of Sociology at Middlesex University in London and at the University of Pisa in Italy. He is the author of *Crime and Markets*; *Movements in the City*; *Crime in Literature*; *Understanding Political Violence*; *Organised and Corporate Crime in Europe* and co-author of *Eurodrugs*. He co-edited *Western European Penal Systems* and *The New European Criminology*. **Nicola Montagna** is research fellow at Middlesex University. He is the editor of *I Movimenti Sociali e le Mobilitazioni Globali* (Milan: Franco Angeli), and is currently researching global social movements from a cognitive and organizational perspective.

Contributors include: Karl Marx, Frederick Engels, Emile Durkheim, Georg Simmel, Gustave Le Bon, Max Weber, Antonio Gramsci, Herbert Blumer, William Kornhauser, Neil J. Smelser, Mancur Olson, Anthony Oberschall, John D. McCarthy, Mayer M. Zald, Craig Jenkins, Gerard Marwell, Pamela Oliver, Sidney Tarrow, Sara Evans, Peter K. Eisinger, Hanspeter Kriesi, Dominique Wisler, Frances Fox Piven, Richard A. Cloward, Charles Tilly, Jürgen Habermas, Claus Offe, Alain Touraine, Alberto Melucci, Carol Mueller, Arturo Escobar, Sonia E. Alvarez, Bert Klandermans, David A. Snow et al., Mario Diani, Ron Eyerman, Andrew Jamison, Doug McAdam, Craig Calhoun, Arjun Appadurai, Marjorie Mayo, Jackie Smith, Sanjeev Khagram, James V. Riker, Kathryn Sikkink, Donatella della Porta, Nicola Montagna, Vincenzo Ruggiero.

Routledge Student Readers

Series Editor: Chris Jenks, Professor of Sociology, Goldsmiths College, University of London.

Already in this series:

Theories of Race and Racism: A Reader
Edited by Les Back and John Solomos

Gender: A Sociological Reader
Edited by Stevi Jackson and Sue Scott

The Sociology of Health and Illness: A Reader
Edited by Mike Bury and Jonathan Gabe

Social Research Methods: A Reader
Edited by Clive Seale

The Information Society Reader
Edited by Frank Webster

The Body: A Reader
Edited by Mariam Fraser and Monica Greco

Fashion Theory: A Reader
Edited by Malcolm Barnard

Emotions and Social Theory: A Reader
Edited by Monica Greco and Paul Stenner

Social Movements: A Reader
Edited by Vincenzo Ruggiero and Nicola Montagna

Social Movements

A Reader

**Edited by Vincenzo Ruggiero
and Nicola Montagna**

Routledge
Taylor & Francis Group

LONDON AND NEW YORK

First published 2008
by Routledge
2 Park Square, Milton Park, Abingdon, Oxon, OX14 4RN

Simultaneously published in the USA and Canada
by Routledge
270 Madison Avenue, New York, NY 10016

Routledge is an imprint of the Taylor & Francis Group, an informa business

Typeset in Perpetua by Keyword Group Ltd.
Printed and bound in Great Britain by The Cromwell Press, Trowbridge, Wiltshire

British Library Cataloguing in Publication Data
A catalogue record for this book is available from the British Library

Library of Congress Cataloging in Publication Data
A catalog record for this book has been requested

ISBN 10: 0–415–44582–5 pbk
ISBN 10: 0–415–44581–7 hbk

ISBN 13: 978–0–415–44582–5 pbk
ISBN 13: 978–0–415–44581–8 hbk

Contents

Series editor's preface   ix
Acknowledgements   xi
Biographies   xvii

Vincenzo Ruggiero and Nicola Montagna
INTRODUCTION   1

PART ONE
Conflict and collective action

1   Karl Marx and Frederick Engels
    THE COMMUNIST MANIFESTO   13

2   Karl Marx and Frederick Engels
    A CONTRIBUTION TO THE CRITIQUE OF POLITICAL ECONOMY   17

3   Karl Marx
    THE EIGHTEENTH BRUMAIRE OF LOUIS BONAPARTE   19

4   Emile Durkheim
    THE DIVISION OF LABOR IN SOCIETY   21

5   Emile Durkheim
    THE ELEMENTARY FORMS OF THE RELIGIOUS LIFE   25

6   Georg Simmel
    CONFLICT (ON INDIVIDUALITY AND SOCIAL FORMS)   29

7 Gustave Le Bon
THE CROWD   34

PART TWO
Hegemony and collective behaviour

8 Max Weber
THE CITY   47

9 Max Weber
CLASS, STATUS, PARTY   52

10 Antonio Gramsci
NOTES ON ITALIAN HISTORY   55

11 Antonio Gramsci
THE MODERN PRINCE   59

12 Herbert Blumer
SOCIAL MOVEMENTS   64

13 William Kornhauser
THE POLITICS OF MASS SOCIETY   73

14 Neil J. Smelser
THEORY OF COLLECTIVE BEHAVIOR   79

PART THREE
Resource mobilisation

15 Mancur Olson
THE LOGIC OF COLLECTIVE ACTION   93

16 Anthony Oberschall
SOCIAL CONFLICT AND SOCIAL MOVEMENTS   95

17 John D. McCarthy and Mayer N. Zald
RESOURCE MOBILIZATION AND SOCIAL MOVEMENTS: A PARTIAL THEORY   105

18 J. Craig Jenkins
RESOURCE MOBILIZATION THEORY AND THE STUDY OF SOCIAL MOVEMENTS   118

19 Gerard Marwell and Pamela Oliver
THE CRITICAL MASS IN COLLECTIVE ACTION   128

PART FOUR
Social movements and the political process

20 Sidney Tarrow
POWER IN MOVEMENT   145

21 Sara Evans
PERSONAL POLITICS
152

22 Peter K. Eisinger
THE CONDITIONS OF PROTEST BEHAVIOR IN AMERICAN CITIES
157

23 Hanspeter Kriesi and Dominique Wisler
SOCIAL MOVEMENTS AND DIRECT DEMOCRACY IN SWITZERLAND
163

24 Frances Fox Piven and Richard A. Cloward
POOR PEOPLE'S MOVEMENTS
170

25 Doug McAdam
POLITICAL PROCESS AND THE DEVELOPMENT OF BLACK INSURGENCY 1930–1970
177

26 Charles Tilly
SOCIAL MOVEMENTS AND NATIONAL POLITICS
186

PART FIVE
New social movements

27 Jürgen Habermas
NEW SOCIAL MOVEMENTS
201

28 Claus Offe
NEW SOCIAL MOVEMENTS: CHALLENGING THE BOUNDARIES
OF INSTITUTIONAL POLITICS
206

29 Alain Touraine
AN INTRODUCTION TO THE STUDY OF SOCIAL MOVEMENTS
212

30 Alberto Melucci
A STRANGE KIND OF NEWNESS: WHAT'S "NEW" IN NEW SOCIAL MOVEMENTS?
218

31 Carol Mueller
CONFLICT NETWORKS AND THE ORIGIN OF WOMEN'S LIBERATION
226

32 Arturo Escobar and Sonia E. Alvarez
THEORY AND PROTEST IN LATIN AMERICA TODAY
235

PART SIX
New directions

33 Bert Klandermans
MOBILIZATION AND PARTICIPATION: SOCIAL-PSYCHOLOGICAL EXPANSIONS
OF RESOURCE MOBILIZATION THEORY
247

34 David A. Snow et al.
FRAME ALIGNMENT PROCESSES, MICROMOBILIZATION,
AND MOVEMENT PARTICIPATION   255

35 Mario Diani
THE CONCEPT OF SOCIAL MOVEMENT   266

36 Ron Eyerman and Andrew Jamison
SOCIAL MOVEMENTS: A COGNITIVE APPROACH   272

37 Doug McAdam, John D. McCarthy and Mayer N. Zald
COMPARATIVE PERSPECTIVES ON SOCIAL MOVEMENTS   279

38 Craig Calhoun
PUTTING EMOTIONS IN THEIR PLACE   289

PART SEVEN
Globalisation and social movements

39 Arjun Appadurai
GRASSROOTS GLOBALIZATION   303

40 Marjorie Mayo
GLOBALIZATION AND GENDER: NEW THREATS, NEW STRATEGIES   307

41 Jackie Smith
GLOBALIZING RESISTANCE: THE BATTLE OF SEATTLE AND THE FUTURE OF SOCIAL
MOVEMENTS   316

42 Sanjeev Khagram, James V. Riker and Kathryn Sikkink
FROM SANTIAGO TO SEATTLE: TRANSNATIONAL ADVOCACY GROUPS
RESTRUCTURING WORLD POLITICS   327

43 Donatella della Porta and Sidney Tarrow
TRANSNATIONAL PROTEST AND GLOBAL ACTIVISM   339

44 Nicola Montagna
SOCIAL MOVEMENTS AND GLOBAL MOBILISATIONS   349

45 Vincenzo Ruggiero
DICHOTOMIES AND CONTEMPORARY SOCIAL MOVEMENTS   357

Index   367

Series Editor's Preface

I am pleased to welcome you to this the latest addition to our series of *Routledge Student Readers* in sociology. This set of major works is proving to be a very successful addition to the general fund of material that is already available to students of our discipline and not least because we have always focussed on topics that have a modern-day significance. The concept of a 'social movement' is just such a topic and as the editors Vincenzo Ruggiero and Nicola Montagna point out an address of this tradition of thinking is both timely and timeless; it provides an analytical vehicle that can transport us from the very origins of social theory to the cutting edge of contemporary social analysis.

Society is an incredibly difficult idea which, I would suggest, gets little easier even with experience in the field. Further the complexity of the idea is compounded by the exponential acceleration of time in modern history and the incontestable fact that commonality or even sharedness in culture, conventions, beliefs and standards of conduct is daily contested by war and conflict, discontinuity, dysfunctionality, misunderstanding or the wilful fragmentation of lifestyles and senses of a moral bond despite such totalizing notions as globalization – the new macro.

This apparent lack of consensus, usually juxtaposed with the view that such a consensus did once actually exist, has led some to the view that 'society' is no longer a viable way to view the collective life or indeed that in this post-modern world society (or indeed sociology) no longer has a substantive referent. Such positioning, I believe, demonstrates either a failure of nerve or an inability to think flexibly enough. The idea of a 'social movement' provides us with a ready solution; it offers a spectrum through which we can view material conflict in an industrial society and, equally well, view opinion, persuasion or disposition in a late-modern society. It also enables us to investigate the ideological differences or divergences of interest that allow separate formulations or paradigmatic positions to emerge.

In any time and at any historical moment there are vectors at work within collective life which enable us, either as social theorists or everyday actors, to understand and reconcile the uneven pressure of stasis and change that surrounds us. We do not give way to despair at the turbulence that threatens to engulf us, we make sense, we see movements, we analyse 'social movements'. The very idea of a movement links conflict with interest and change with purpose, so we may not agree but we can ascribe cause and consequence to action and thus save ourselves, individually or collectively, from chaos and randomness.

Social movements are integral to any sense of social structure, they cannot be understood in isolation from such overall, binding concepts. In this way if we trace the evolution of theories related to social movements we find that they are intimately entwined with theories concerning society's development. As our editors here demonstrate any analysis of the major body of work on social movements takes us through a taxonomy from collective behaviour theory, probably the most orthodox explanation; through resource mobilization theory; to new social movements interpretations to the most contemporary and innovative contribution of the action-identity approach. Such a trail takes us from Talcott Parsons to Touraine and Castells and also straddles both left and right wing political dispositions and a whole gamut of sociological interpretive perspectives. No one of these theoretical forms claims exclusive rights to full or accurate representation of their phenomena, all recognize the local and embedded nature of each. Clearly this is a highly contested zone which requires careful and explicit guidance, which is what I believe this text provides.

Both of our editors are experienced in this area of work and recognized for their contribution to its growth and significance in the sociological vocabulary. To this end they provide appropriate mentors in our quest to understand such an important area of study. Remember, when you are addressing class conflict at the turn of the 19th century, the Trades Union movement, feminism, 'green' politics or more recently our gathering concerns around climate change, these are all political stages, they are all 'social movements' and we can learn from their commonality but not be blinded to their significant differences. Remember too that the art of politics, particularly contemporary politics, is to successfully de-politicize the political and thus to normalize social movements.

I am sure that this book will provoke your interest in this topic and inspire your search for further reading.

Chris Jenks
Vice Chancellor and Professor of Sociology
Brunel University

Acknowledgements

The publishers would like to thank the following for permission to reprint their material:

Verso for permission to reprint extracts from Karl Marx and Frederick Engels, *The Communist Manifesto*, with an introduction by Eric Hobsbawn, London: Verso, 1987, 1998, pp 34–50 (edited extracts)

Lawrence and Wishart Ltd for permission to reprint extracts from Karl Marx and Frederick Engels, 'A Contribution to the Critique of Political Economy. Part One', from Karl Marx and Frederick Engels, *Collected Works, Volume 29*, London: Lawrence and Wishart, 1987, pp 262–264.

New Left Review for permission to reprint extracts from Karl Marx, 'The Eighteenth Brumaire of Louis Bonaparte', *Surveys from Exile: Political Writings, Volume 2*, Edited and Introduced by David Fernback, Penguin Books in association with *New Left Review*, 1992, pp 146–149.

Palgrave Macmillan for permission to reprint extracts from Emile Durkheim, 'The Forced Division of Labour', chapter 2 in *The Division of Labour in Society*, translated by George Simpson, The Free Press of Glencoe, Illinois, 1893; copyright © The Macmillan Company. Fourth printing, September 1960, USA, pp 374–381.

The Free Press / Simon & Schuster Adult Publishing Group for permission to reprint extracts from Emile Durkheim, 'The Forced Division of Labour', chapter 2 in *The Division of Labor in Society*, translated by George Simpson, The Free Press of Glencoe, Illinois, 1893, pp 374–381.

Taylor and Francis Books UK for permission to reprint extracts from Emile Durkheim, 'Origins of these beliefs', *The Elementary Forms of the Religious Life*, translated from the French by Joseph Ward Swain, London: George Allen and Unwin Ltd, 1912, pp 206–211.

The Free Press/Simon & Schuster Adult Publishing Group for permission to reprint extracts from Emile Durkheim, 'Origins of these beliefs', *The Elementary Forms of the Religious Life*, translated from the French by Joseph Ward Swain, London: George Allen and Unwin Ltd, 1912, pp 206–211.

The Free Press/Simon & Schuster Adult Publishing Group for permission to reprint extracts from Georg Simmel, '*Conflict*', chapter 6 in *The Sociology of Georg Simmel*, translated and edited by Kurt H. Wolff. Copyright © 1950 by The Free Press, pp 70–76.

The Free Press/Simon & Schuster Adult Publishing Group for permission to reprint extracts from Max Weber: 'The Patrician City' and 'The Plebeian City' from *The City*, translated and edited by Don Martindale and Gertrud Neuwirth, London: Heinemann, 1921, 1958, pp 122–129, 157–161.

Oxford University Press for permission to reprint extracts from Max Weber, 'Class, Status, Party' from *Max Weber: Essays in Sociology*, edited by Gerth, H.H and Wright Mills, C (OUP, 1958), by permission of Oxford University Press Inc.

Lawrence and Wishart for permission to reprint extracts from Antonio Gramsci, 'Notes on Italian History', in *Selections from the Prison Notebooks of Antonio Gramsci*, edited and translated by Quentin Hoare and Geoffrey Nowell Smith, London: Lawrence and Wishart, 1971, pp 52–61.

Lawrence and Wishart for permission to reprint extracts from Antonio Gramsci, 'The Modern Prince' in *Selections from the Prison Notebooks of Antonio Gramsci*, edited and translated by Quentin Hoare and Geoffrey Nowell Smith, London: Lawrence and Wishart, 1971, pp 128–153.

The Free Press/Simon & Schuster Adult Publishing Group for permission to reprint extracts from William Kornhauser, 'Mass Behaviour', from *The Politics of Mass Society*, The Free Press, 1959, pp 43–51.

Taylor and Francis Books UK for permission to reprint extracts from William Kornhauser: 'Mass Behaviour', from *The Politics of Mass Society*, London: Routledge and Kegan Paul, 1960, pp 43–51.

Taylor and Francis Books UK for permission to reprint extracts from Neil Smelser: Chapter I, 'Analyzing Collective Behaviour', pp 1-3, Chapter IX, 'The Norm Oriented Movement', pp 270-278 and Chapter X, 'The Value-Oriented Movement', pp 313–319, from *Theory of Collective Behaviour*, London and Henley: Routledge and Kegan Paul, 1962, reprinted 1976, © Neil J Smelser, 1962.

The Free Press/Simon & Schuster Adult Publishing Group for permission to reprint extracts from Neil Smelser: Chapter I, 'Analyzing Collective Behaviour', pp 1–3, Chapter IX, 'The Norm Oriented Movement', pp 270–278 and Chapter X, 'The Value-Oriented Movement', pp 313–319, from *Theory of Collective Behavior*, London and Henley: The Free Press, 1962.

Harvard University Press for permission to reprint Mancur Olson Jr., 'Introduction', pp 1–3, *The Logic of Collective Action: Public Goods and the Theory of Groups*, Cambridge, Mass: Harvard University Press, 1965, pp 1–3.

Pearson Education Inc. for permission to reprint extracts from Anthony Oberschall: Chapter 1 'The Sociological Study of Conflict, Social Movements, and Collective

Behaviour', 1973, p 1, pp 27–29; 'Mobilisation: the formation of Conflict Groups', pp 135–141; pp 162–165 in *Social Conflict and Social Movements*, New Jersey: Prentice Hall, Inc, 1973.

University of Chicago Press, Journals Division for permission to reprint extracts from John McCarthy and Mayer Zald, 'Resource Mobilisation and Social Movements: A Partial Theory', *American Journal of Sociology*, volume 8, no.6, 1977, pp 1212–1231.

Annual Reviews for kind permission to reprint extracts from J. Craig Jenkins, 'Resource Mobilisation Theory and the Study of Social Movements', *Annual Review of Sociology*, 1983, vol 9, pp 527–553.

Cambridge University Press for permission to reprint extracts from Gerard Marwell and Pamela Oliver, *The Critical Mass in Collective Action: A Micro-Social Theory*, Cambridge University Press, 1993, pp 1–11, 90–109, 186–193. Reproduced with permission. Reprinted with kind permission of the authors.

Cambridge University Press for permission to reprint extracts from Sidney Tarrow, 'Contentious Politics and Social Movements', in *Power in Movement: Social Movements and Contentious Politics*, 2nd edition, Cambridge: Cambridge University Press, pp 19–25. Reproduced with permission. Reprinted with kind permission of the author.

Sara Evans, Chapter 9, 'Personal Politics', in *Personal Politics: The Roots of Women's Liberation in the Civil Rights Movement and the New Left*, New York: Alfred A. Knopf, 1979, pp 212–222 (edited extracts).

Cambridge University Press for permission to reprint extracts from Peter K. Eisinger, 'The Conditions of Protest Behavior in American Cities', *American Political Science Review*, Vol 67, 1973, pp 11–15. ©The American Political Science Association, published by Cambridge University Press, reproduced with permission. Reprinted with kind permission of the author.

Blackwell Publishing Ltd for permission to reprint extracts from Hanspeter Kriesi and Dominique Wisler, 'Social Movements and Direct Democracy in Switzerland', *European Journal of Political Research*, 30, 19–40, July 1996 © 1996 Kluwer Academic Publishers, the Netherlands, pp 19–26, 40.

Frances Fox Piven and Richard A. Cloward, *Poor People's Movements: How they Succeed and How they Fail*, New York: Pantheon Books (Random House Inc New York, and Random House of Canada, Ltd, Canada), 1977, pp 6–7, 10–23, p 38 (edited extracts) © Frances Fox Piven (1932–) and Richard A Cloward, all rights reserved. ISBN 0-394-48840-7.

University of Chicago Press for permission to reprint extracts from Doug McAdam, 'The Political Process Model', *Political Process and the Development of Black Insurgency 1930–1970*, Chicago and London: University of Chicago Press, 1982, pp 36–50, 275–287. With permission of the author.

University of Michigan Press for permission to reprint extracts from Charles Tilly, 'Social Movements and National Politics' in *Statemaking and Social Movements: Essays in History and Theory*, edited by Charles Bright and Susan Hardine, Ann Arbor: The University of Michigan Press, 1984, pp 301–316. © University of Michigan Press 1984. Reprinted with permission of the author.

Telos for permission to reprint extracts from Jürgen Habermas: 'New Social Movements', *TELOS*, 49, 1981, pp 33–37.

Claus Offe, 'New Social Movements: Challenging the Boundaries of Institutional Politics', *Social Research*, Vol. 52, No. 4, (Winter 1985), pp 817–832 (edited extracts).

Alain Touraine, 'An Introduction to the Study of Social Movements', *Social Research*, Vol. 52, No. 4, (Winter 1985), pp 749–784 (edited extracts).

Temple University Press for permission to reprint extracts from Alberto Melucci, 'A Strange Kind of Newness: What's "New" in Social Movements?', in *New Social Movements: From Ideology to Identity*, edited by Enrique Laraña, Hank Johnston and Joseph Gusfield, Philadelphia: Temple University Press, 1994, pp 101–117, 126–129.

Temple University Press for permission to reprint extracts from Carol Mueller, 'Conflict Networks and the Origin of Women's Liberation', in *New Social Movements: From Ideology to Identity*, edited by Enrique Laraña, Hank Johnston and Joseph Gusfield, Philadelphia: Temple University Press, 1994, pp 243–262.

Westview Press for permission to reprint extracts from Arturo Escobar and Sonia Alvarez, 'Theory and Protest in Latin America Today', in *The Making of Social Movements in Latin America: Identity, Strategy, and Democracy*, Boulder, San Francisco, Oxford: Westview Press, 1992, pp 1–10. Reprinted by permission of Westview Press, a member of the Perseus Books Group.

American Sociological Association for permission to reprint extracts from Bert Klandermans 'Mobilisation and participation: Social-Psychological Expansions of Resource Mobilisation Theory', *American Sociological Review*, 1984, Vol. 49 (October: 583–600), pp 583–600. Also with permission of the author.

American Sociological Association for permission to reprint extracts from David A. Snow, E. Burke Rochford, Jr., Steven K. Worden and Robert D. Benford, 'Frame Alignment Processes, Micromobilisation and Movement Participation', *American Sociological Review*, 1986, Vol. 51 (August: 464-481) pp 464–481. Reprinted with kind permission of the authors.

Blackwell Publishing Ltd for permission to reprint extracts from Mario Diani, 'The Concept of Social Movement', *The Sociological Review*, Volume 40, No. 1, February 1992, pp 1–18. With permission of the author. © The Sociological Review, 1992, 0038-0261 92/4001-00 $3.00/1

Polity Press for permission to reprint extracts from Ron Eyerman and Andrew Jamison: 'Social Movements and Sociology', pp 42–44, and 'Dimensions of Cognitive Praxis', pp 78–93 in *Social Movements: A Cognitive Approach*, Cambridge: Polity Press, 1991.

Cambridge University Press for permission to reprint extracts from Doug McAdam, John McCarthy and Mayer Zald, 'Introduction', *Comparative Perspectives on Social Movements*, Cambridge University Press, 1996, pp 2–20. Reproduced with permission. With kind permission of the authors.

University of Chicago Press for permission to reprint extracts from Craig Calhoun, 'Putting Emotions in Their Place', in *Passionate Politics: Emotions and Social Movements*, edited by J. Goodwin, J.M. Jasper and F. Polletta, Chicago: University of Chicago Press, 2001, pp 48–57. Reprinted with permission of the author.

Duke University Press for permission to reprint extracts from Arjun Appadurai: 'Grassroots Globalisation' in *Fear of Small Numbers: An Essay on the Geography of Anger*, Public Planet Books, Durham and London: Duke University Press, 2006, pp 131–137.

Zed Books Limited for permission to reprint extracts from Marjorie Mayo, Chapter 7, 'Globalisation and Gender: New Threats, New Strategies' in *Global Citizens: Social Movements and the Challenge of Globalisation*, Canadian Scholars Press, Inc. Toronto/ London & New York: Zed Books, 2005, pp 133–152, 206–217. © Marjorie Mayo, 2005. Reprinted by permission of Zed Books, London and New York.

Rowman and Littlefield Publishers Inc. for permission to reprint extracts from Jackie Smith, 'Globalizing Resistance: The Battle of Seattle and the Future of Social Movements', Chapter 12 in *Globalization and Resistance*, edited by Jackie Smith and Hank Johnston, Lanham, Boulder, New York, Oxford: Rowman & Littlefield, 2002, pp 208–221.

University of Minnesota Press for permission to reprint extracts from Sanjeev Khagram, James V. Riker and Kathyn Sikkink, 'Santiago to Seattle: Transnational Advocacy Groups Restructuring World Politics', in *Restructuring World Politics: Transnational Social Movements, Networks and Norms*; Social Movements, Protest and Contention, Volume 14, Minneapolis & London: University of Minnesota Press, 2002, pp 1–20, pp 320–350.

Rowman and Littlefield Publishers, Inc. for permission to reprint extracts from Donatella Della Porta and Sidney Tarrow, 'Transnational Processes and Social Activism: An Introduction', in *Transnational Protest and Global Activism*, edited by D. della Porta and S. Tarrow, Lanham, Boulder, NY, Toronto, Oxford, Rowman and Littlefield Publishers, Inc., 2004, pp 1–10, pp 251–274.

Taylor and Francis Journals (UK) for kind permission to reprint extracts from Vincenzo Ruggiero, 'Dichotomies and Contemporary Social Movements', in *City*, Vol 9, No. 3, December 2005, pp 297–306.

The publishers have made every effort to contact authors/copyright holders of works reprinted in *Social Movements: A Reader*. This has not been possible in every case, however, and we would welcome correspondence from those individuals/companies whom we have been unable to trace.

Biographies

Part 1

Karl Marx (1818–1883) was a nineteenth-century philosopher, political economist and political revolutionary. Marx's analysis of the capitalist society has influenced millions of activists and thousands of scholars all over the world. The *Communist Manifesto* (1848), written with Frederick Engels, is the most influential political book ever written. *Capital* (1867) is Marx's major and more complete analysis of capitalism.

Émile Durkheim (1858–1917) was a French sociologist whose contributions were instrumental in the formation of sociology. His work and editorship of the first journal of sociology (*L'Année Sociologique*) helped establish sociology within the academic world as an accepted *social science*. Some of his major works are *The Division of Labour* (1983), *Rules of Sociological Methods* (1895) and *Suicide* (1897).

Georg Simmel (1858–1918) was one of the first generation of German sociologists. A key precursor of *social network* analysis, his studies pioneered the concept of social structure. He authored six books and more than seventy articles, many of which translated into English, French, Italian, Polish, and Russian. His most famous works today are *The Philosophy of Money* (1900), *The Metropolis and Mental Life* (1903) and *Sociology: Investigations on the Forms of Sociation* (1908).

Gustave Le Bon (1841–1931) was a French social psychologist, sociologist and amateur physicist. He is the author of several works hinging on theories of national character, racial superiority, herd behaviour and crowd psychology. His main works are *Les lois psychologiques de l'évolution des peuples* (*The Psychology of Peoples*, 1894), *The Crowd: A Study of the Popular Mind*, (1895, English translation 1896) and *L'homme et les sociétés* (*Man and Society*, 1881).

Part 2

Max Weber (1864–1920) is regarded as one of the founders of the modern study of society. He began his career at the University of Berlin, and later worked at the universities of Freiburg, Heidelberg, Vienna and Munich. His main interests ranged from the sociology of politics and government to the sociology of religion to economics. Some of his major works include *The Protestant Ethic and the Spirit of Capitalism* (1905) and *Economy and Society* (1914).

Antonio Gramsci (1891–1937) was an Italian political activist and theorist. A founding member and leader of the Communist Party of Italy, he was imprisoned by Mussolini's Fascist regime. His writings deal with the analysis of culture and political leadership and he is notable as a highly original and influential thinker within the Marxist tradition. His major work translated into English is *Selections from the Prison Notebooks* (1971).

Herbert Blumer (1900–1987) taught at the University of Chicago for 27 years and at the University of California-Berkeley. While developing the Sociology department at the University of California-Berkeley, Blumer worked on the theoretical aspects of racial prejudice, explored industrialization in traditional societies and oversaw a study of drug-usage by adolescents. Blumer's major works include *Movies and Conduct* (1933), *Movies, Delinquency, and Crime* (1933), *Human Side of Social Planning* (1935) and *Symbolic Interaction: Perspective and Method* (1969).

William Kornhauser (1925–2004) was Emeritus Professor of Sociology, at the University of California, Berkeley. A political sociologist and an expert in social movements, Kornhauser is known for his pioneering 1959 book *The Politics of Mass Society*. Over the years, he wrote dozens of scholarly articles and published another book, *Scientists in Industry: Conflict and Accommodation* (1962).

Neil J. Smelser is Emeritus Professor of Sociology at the University of California, Berkeley. His main research interests are sociological theory, economic sociology, collective behaviour, sociology of education, social change and comparative methods. In his long career as a sociologist he authored and edited many books, including *Economy and Society* (with Talcott Parsons, 1956), *Theory of Collective Behaviour* (1962), *The Sociology of Economic Life* (1963, second edition 1975) and *Sociological Theory: a Contemporary View* (1971). His most recent book is *The Faces of Terrorism* (2007).

Part 3

Mancur Olson (1932–1998) was one of the most influential political economists of the late twentieth century and worked at the University of Maryland. Mancur's two best-known works, *The Logic of Collective Action* (1971) and *The Rise and Decline of Nations* (1982), are seminal works in economics and political science. Each has been translated into ten languages.

Anthony Oberschall is Emeritus Professor of Sociology at the University of North Carolina. He has published five books and some 100 articles in scholarly journals, many of which deal with collective action, social conflict, group violence and conflict management. Recently he has researched and written about the break-up of Yugoslavia and post-war reconstruction and governance in the Balkans. His major books include *Social Conflict and Social Movements* (1973) and *Social Movements: Ideologies, Interests, and Identities* (1993).

Craig Jenkins is Professor of Sociology and Political Science, Ohio State University. His main research interests include political sociology, social movements and social conflict, political economy, American society, historical and comparative sociology, contemporary world societies and social change and development. His books include *The Politics of Social Protest: Comparative Perspectives on States and Social Movements* (co-edited with Bert Klandermans 1995) and *Identity Conflicts: Can Violence Be Regulated?* (co-edited with Esther Gottlieb 2007). He is also author of numerous articles including 'Political Opportunities and African-American Protest, 1948–1997' (with David Jacobs and Jon Agnone, 2003).

Gerald Marwell is Professor of Sociology at New York University. His main research interests are collective behaviour/social movements, religion and social psychology. His publications include 'Collective Action Theory and Social Movements Research' (with Pamela Oliver, 1984) and 'Social Networks and Collective Action: a Theory of the Critical Mass' (with Pamela E. Oliver and Ralph Prahl 1988).

Pamela Oliver is Professor at the Department of Sociology, University of Wisconsin. Her current research interests are collective action and social movements and the causes and consequences of racial disparity in imprisonment in the US. She has published a number of influential articles including 'The Coevolution of Social Movements' (2003) and 'Networks, Diffusion, and Cycles of Collective Action' (2004). She is also co-author of *The Critical Mass in Collective Action: A Micro-Social Theory* (with Gerald Marwell, 1993).

John McCarthy is Department Head and Professor of Sociology. His research and teaching interests include collective behaviour and social movements, policing of the public order, formal organizations and mass media processes. He is widely credited as one of the pioneers of the resource mobilization theoretical model. His main publications include *Social Movements in an Organizational Society* (with Mayer N. Zald 1987), 'The Channeling of Social Movements in the Modern American State' (with David W. Britt and Mark Wolfson, 1991) and 'The Enduring Vitality of the Resource Mobilization Theory of Social Movements' (with Mayer N. Zald, 2002).

Mayer Zald is Professor Emeritus of Sociology, Social Work and Business Administration at the University of Michigan. He is known for his contributions to the sociology of organizations and social movements. Some of his recent publications are *Political Opportunities, Mobilization and Framing: Comparative Studies in Social Movement Dynamics* (edited with Doug McAdam and John D. McCarthy, 1996), *Globalization and Social Movements: Culture, Power and the Transnational Public Sphere* (edited with John Guidry and Michael D. Kennedy, 2000), and 'The Enduring Vitality of the Resource Mobilization Theory of Social Movements' (with John McCarthy, 2002).

Part 4

Sidney Tarrow is Maxwell Upson Professor of Government and Sociology at Cornell University. His areas of interest include comparative politics, social movements, political parties, collective action and political sociology. His monograph *Democracy and Disorder* (1989) received the Best Book in Collective Action and Social Movements award from the American Sociological Association. His major book is *Power in Movement* (1998). Sydney Tarrow is also co-author, with Doug McAdam and Charles Tilly, of *Dynamics of Contention* (2001).

Doug McAdam is Professor of Sociology and Director of Urban Studies at Stanford University. His main research interests are political sociology and social movements. He is the author or co-author of over a dozen books and more than 50 articles, and is widely credited as one of the pioneers of the political process model in social movement analysis. His main books are *Freedom Summer* (1988), *Political Process and the Development of Black Insurgency, 1930–1970* (1999) and *Dynamics of Contention* (with Sidney Tarrow and Charles Tilly, 2001).

Peter K. Eisinger is Henry Cohen Professor of Political Science and Urban Studies, Milan School for Management and Urban Policy. His main research interests are urban politics and policy, state and local economic development, American politics, state politics and federalism. He is the author or co-author of seven books and nearly 60 articles on various aspects of urban politics and public policy including *The Patterns of Interracial Politics* (1976) and 'Understanding Urban Politics: a Comparative Perspective on the Nature of Urban Conflict' (1977).

Frances Fox Piven is Distinguished Professor of Political Science and Sociology at The Graduate Center, City University of New York, and is the current president of the American Sociological Association. Throughout her career, Piven has combined academic work with activism. She is the author of numerous books including *Poor People's Movements* (1977), *Why Americans Don't Vote* (2000), both co-authored with Richard Cloward and *Challenging Authority: How Ordinary People Change America* (2006).

Richard A. Cloward (1926–2001) was an American sociologist and political activist. He taught at Columbia University for 47 years. Cloward published numerous books, monographs and articles, including *Poor People's Movements: Why They Succeed, How they Fail* (1977) and *The Breaking of the American Social Compact* (1997), both co-authored with Frances Fox Piven.

Sara Evans is Regent Professor at the University of Minnesota. Her main research interests are gender analysis, family history, American women's history and social movements. Her most recent publications include *Born for Liberty: A History of American Women* (1989), *Tidal Wave: How Women Changed America at Century's End* (2003) and *Journeys That Opened Up the World: Women, Student Christian Movements, and Social Justice, 1955–75* (2003).

Hanspeter Kriesi is Professor at the Department of Political Science at the University of Zurich and directs the Swiss national research program on the 'Challenges to Democracy in the 21st Century' (NCCR Democracy). He is a specialist of Swiss direct democracy, but his wide-ranging research interests also include the study of social movements, political parties and interest groups, public opinion, the public sphere and the media. He recently co-edited (with David Snow and Sarah Soule) *The Blackwell Companion to Social Movements* (2004). Among his latest books is *Direct Democratic Choice: the Swiss Experience* (2005).

Dominique Wisler is a Consultant and Researcher. Her main research interests are protest and the policing of protest, police organization in Africa and the Balkans, and social movements. Her many publications include *A Conflict Early Warning System for Sudan* (co-edited with Eltayeb Haj Ateya, 2007) and 'Under the Spotlight: the Impact of Media Attention on Protest Policing' (with Marco Giugni, 1999).

Charles Tilly is Joseph L. Buttenwieser Professor of Social Science, Columbia University. His work focuses on large-scale social change and its relationship to contentious politics, especially in Europe since 1500. His most recent books are *The Politics of Collective Violence* (2003), *Contention and Democracy in Europe, 1650–2000* (2004), *Social Movements, 1768–2004* (2004), *Economic and Political Contention in Comparative Perspective* (co-edited with Maria Kousis, 2005), *Trust and Rule* (2005), *Popular Contention in Great Britain, 1758–1834* (2005, revised paperback edition of the 1995 book) and *Identities, Boundaries, and Social Ties* (2005). He is also author of the influential *From Mobilization to Revolution* (1978).

Part 5

Jürgen Habermas is a German philosopher and sociologist, and a contemporary representative of the critical theory tradition and American pragmatism. He is best known for his work on the public sphere and his theory of communicative action. His work has focused on the foundations of social theory and epistemology, the analysis of advanced capitalistic societies and democracy, the rule of law in a critical social-evolutionary context and contemporary politics, particularly German politics. His recent interests focus on cosmopolitan political order and on the relation between philosophy and religion. He has published dozens of books, some of which have been translated into many languages. Some of his major works include *The Structural Transformation of the Public Sphere* (1962) and *The Theory of Communicative Action* (1981). His most recent publications include *The Postnational Constellation* (1998), *Rationality and Religion* (1998), *The Future of Human Nature* (2003) and *The Divided West* (2006).

Claus Offe is Professor of Political Science at Humboldt University in Berlin. He is one of the world's leading political sociologist of Marxist orientation. His main fields of research include political sociology, social policy, democratic theory and transformation studies. Recent English language book publications include *The Varieties of Transition* (1996), *Modernity and the State: East and West* (with Charles Turner and Jeremy Gaines, 1998), *Institutional Design in Post-Communist Societies, Rebuilding the Ship at Sea* (with Jon Elster and Ulrich K. Preuss, 1998) and *Reflections on America: Tocqueville, Weber and Adorno in the United States* (2005).

Alain Touraine is one of the best known French sociologists. His work is based on a 'sociology of action' and on the notion that society shapes its future through its own social struggles. His main studies and books focus on social movements. In 1970 he founded the Centre for the Study of Social Movements, which attracted collaborators from many countries. Touraine is one of the leading authorities on issues around the formation, trajectory and fate of social movements around the world. He is the author of dozens of articles and some of the major books available on social movements, including *May Movement: Revolt and Reform* (1968, English translation, 1971),

The Voice of the Eye (1978, English translation, 1981) and *The Worker's Movement* (1984, English translation, 1987). Some of his most recent books are *Critique of Modernity* (1992, English translation 1995), *Pourrons nous vivre ensemble? Égaux et différents* (*Can we live together? Equal and Different*, 1997), and *Comment sortir du libéralisme?* (*Beyond Neo-Liberalism*, 1999).

Carol Mueller is Professor of Sociology at Arizona State University. Her main interests are social movements, globalization and violence against women. Her main recent publications include 'Feminism and the Women's Movement: a Global Perspective' (with Myra Ferree, 2004), *Repression and Mobilization* (co-edited with Christian Davenport and Hank Johnston, 2005) and 'Women's Movements' in *Encyclopaedia of Sociology* (2006).

Arturo V. Escobar is a Kenan Distinguished Professor in the Department of Anthropology at the University of North Carolina. His research interests are related to political ecology, the anthropology of development, social movements, Latin American development and politics. His most recent research is on Colombian social movements. He has published over twenty articles and has co-edited many books. His most recent books are *The World Social Forum: Challenging Empires* (co-edited with Jai Sen, Anita Anand and Peter Waterman, 2004), *World Anthropologies: Disciplinary Transformations in Contexts of Power* (co-edited with Gustavo Lins Ribeiro, 2005) and *Women and the Politics of Place* (co-edited with Wendy Harcourt, 2005).

Sonia E. Alvarez teaches Latin American Politics and Studies at the College of Social and Behavioral Science, University of Massachusetts Amherst. Her main research interests are Latin American politics, social movements and feminist movements. She is the author of numerous ground-breaking books and articles on feminism, social movements and democratization in Latin America, including *Engendering Democracy in Brazil: Women's Movements in Transition Politics* (1990) and *Cultures of Politics/Politics of Cultures: Re-visioning Latin American Social Movements* (co-edited with Evelina Dagnino and Arturo Escobar, 1998).

Alberto Melucci (1943–2001) was one of the leading analysts of contemporary social movements. He was an important pioneer in social movement studies and new social movements research. He authored over fifteen books in English and Italian on social movements, cultural change and personal and collective identity. These include *Nomads of the Present* (1989), *The Playing Self* (1996) and *Challenging Codes* (1996).

Part 6

David A. Snow is Professor of Sociology at the University of California, Irvine. His teaching and research interests include collective action and social movements, qualitative field methods, social psychology with an emphasis on self and identity from a symbolic interactionist perspective, changes in cognitive orientation and interpretive perspective, and socioeconomic inequality and marginality with an emphasis on homelessness and poverty. He is the author of 100 articles and chapters on these various topics, as well as a number of books, including *Down on their Luck: a Study of Homeless Street People* (with Leon Anderson, 1993), *Shakubuku: A Study of the Nichiren Shoshu Buddhist Movement in America, 1960–1975* (1993) and *The Blackwell Companion to Social Movements* (edited with Sarah Soule and Hanspeter Kriesi, 2004).

E. Burke Rochford, Jr. is Professor of Sociology at Middlebury College in Vermont, USA. His research over the past 25 years has focused on the Hare Krishna movement. He is the author of numerous articles addressing the development of this movement. He is the author of *Hare Krishna in America* (1985) and numerous journal articles dealing with aspects of ISKCON's North American development.

Steven Worden is Associate Professor at the University of Arkansas. His research interests include symbolic interactionism, religion, collective behaviour and social movements and theory. He is author of many articles including 'The Word on the Street: Homeless Men in Las Vegas' (2006).

Robert Benford is Professor of Sociology at the Southern Illinois University Carbondale. He has conducted research on social movement ideologies and grievances, how collective identities are formed, political discourse, interorganizational disputes and the cross-national diffusion of protest frames and tactics. He is co-author with David A. Snow of many leading articles including 'Framing processes and social movements: an overview and assessment' (2000), 'Ideology, Frame Resonance and Participant Mobilization' (1988) and 'Master Frames and cycles of protest' (1992).

Bert Klandermans is Professor of Applied Social Psychology at the Free University in Amsterdam. The emphasis in his work is on social psychological consequences of social, economic and political change. He has published extensively on the social psychology of participation in social movements and labour unions. His books include *From Structure to Action: Comparing Movement Participation across Cultures* (co-edited with Hans Peter Kriesi and Sidney Tarrow, 1988), *The Social Psychology of Protest* (1997), *The Social Psychology of Protest: Methods of Social Movement Research* (edited with Suzanne Staggenborg, 2002) and *Extreme Right Activists in Europe: Through the Magnifying Glass* (co-edited with Nonna Mayer, 2006).

Mario Diani is Professor of Sociology at the University of Trento and Visiting Research Professor at the University of Strathclyde in Glasgow. He has been the European editor of 'Mobilization', the international journal of theory and research on social movements and collective behaviour since 1997. He has written extensively on social movements and collective protest. His main publications include *Social Movements: An Introduction* (co-authored with Donatella della Porta, 1999, 2nd edition 2006), *Movimenti senza protesta?* (with Donatella della Porta, 2004) and *Social Movements and Networks* (co-edited with Doug McAdam, 2003).

Ron Eyerman is Professor of Sociology at Yale University and Co-Director of the Center for Cultural Sociology (CCS). His interests include cultural and social movement theory, critical theory, cultural studies and the sociology of the arts. He is the author of several recent books, including *Music and Social Movements: Mobilizing Tradition in the Twentieth Century* (1998), *Cultural Trauma: Slavery and the Formation of African-American Identity* (2002) and *Cultural Trauma and Collective Identity* (2004).

Andrew Jamison is Professor of Technology and Society at the Aalborg University. His main research interests are in the areas of politics of science, technology and the environment, social movements and cultural history. He has published widely on cultural aspects of social movements. His publications include *Music and Social Movements: Mobilizing Tradition in the Twentieth Century* (with Ron Eyerman, 1998), *The Making of Green Knowledge: Environmental Politics and Cultural Transformation* (2001) and *Hubris and Hybrids: A Cultural History of Technology and Science* (with Michael Hard, 2005).

Craig Calhoun is President of the Social Science Research Council and Professor of the Social Sciences at New York University. His empirical research has ranged from Britain and France to China and three different African countries. Some of his main publications are *Neither Gods Nor Emperors: Students and the Struggle for Democracy in China* (1994), *International Handbook of Sociology* (with Chris Rojek and Bryan Turner, 2005) and *Lessons of Empire?* (with Frederick Cooper and Kevin Moore, 2005).

Part 7

Arjun Appadurai is Senior Advisor for Global Initiatives and John Dewey Professor in the Social Sciences at the New School, New York City. His main areas of interest are historical anthropology, anthropology of globalization, ethnic violence, consumption, space and housing, international civil society and urban South Asia. His current research focuses on anthropology of global violence, Asian mega-cities, grassroots political activist networks in India and South Asia and cultural pluralism. He has published many books and articles in academic journals. His most recent books are *Globalization* (edited volume, 2001) and *Fear of Small Numbers: An Essay on the Geography of Anger* (2006).

Donatella della Porta is Professor of Sociology and Director of Studies, Department of Political and Social Sciences, European University Institute, Florence. She is widely known for her studies on social movements, political violence, terrorism, corruption, the police and policies of public order. On these issues she has conducted investigations in Italy, France, Germany and Spain. Currently she is involved in several comparative projects on citizenships and social movements. Some of her main recent books include *Social Movements: An Introduction* (with Mario Diani, 1999, 2nd edition 2006), *Transnational Protest and Global Activism* (with Sidney Tarrow, 2004) and *Globalization from Below* (with M. Andretta, L. Mosca and H. Reiter, 2006).

Sanjeev Khagram is Associate Professor of Public Affairs and International Studies at the Daniel J. Evans School of Public Affairs, University of Washington. His main research interests are transnational studies, global governance, civil society, corporate citizenship, human security and sustainable development. He has published widely including *Restructuring World Politics: Transnational Social Movements, Networks, and Norms* (co-edited with J. Riker and K. Sikkink, 2002) and *Dams and Development: Transnational Struggles for Water and Power* (2004).

Marjorie Mayo is Professor of Community Development and Head of 'Professional and Community Education' (PACE). Her research is concerned with community development and adult community education, with a current focus upon community participation in urban regeneration. Mayo's recent publications include *Cultures, Communities, Identities: Cultural Strategies for Participation and Empowerment* (2000), *Global Citizens. Social Movements and the Challenge of Globalization* (2005) and the journal articles 'The World Will Never Be the Same Again'? Reflecting on the Experiences of Jubilee' (2000), and 'Mobilizing Globally for the Remission of Unpayable Debts' (2005).

Nicola Montagna took his doctorate in 2005 on Italian Social Movements at Middlesex University in London, where he is currently Research Fellow. His main research interests are youth and urban movements, social movements and globalization, civil society, the third sector and migration. His recent publications on social movements include *La globalizzazione dei movimenti* (2007) and 'The Decommodification of Urban Space and the Occupied Social Centres in Italy' (2006).

James V. Riker is Director of 'Beyond the Classroom Living and Learning Program' at the University of Maryland. His main research interests are civic engagement, civil society, democracy and democratization, human rights, nonprofit leadership, social movements and transnational advocacy networks. On these issues he has published *Restructuring World Politics: Transnational Social Movements, Networks, and Norms* (co-edited with S. Khagram and K. Sikkink, 2002) and *Government–NGO Relations in Asia: Prospects and Challenges for People Centred Development* (co-edited with Noeleen Heyzer, James V. Riker and Antonio B. Quizon, 1995).

Vincenzo Ruggiero is Professor of Sociology at Middlesex University in London. His non-academic positions include research director for the United Nations. His has published extensively on social movements, urban issues, illicit drug markets, prison systems, comparative criminology, organized crime and political violence. Ruggiero's books include *Organised and Corporate Crime in Europe* (1996), *Crime and Markets* (2000), *Movements in the City* (2001), *Crime in Literature: Sociology of Deviance and Fiction* (2003) and *Understanding Political Violence* (2006). His work has been translated into several languages.

Kathryn Sikkink is the Arleen C. Carlson Professor of Political Science at the University of Minnesota. Her current research interests focus on the influence of international law on domestic politics, especially in the area of human rights, transnational social movements and networks, and the role of ideas and norms in international relations and foreign policy. Sikkink's publications include *Activists Beyond Borders: Advocacy Networks in International Politics* (co-authored with Margaret Keck, 1998) and *Restructuring World Politics: Transnational Social Movements, Networks, and Norms* (co-edited with J.V. Riker and K. Sikkink, 2002).

Jackie Smith is Associate Professor at the Department of Sociology at the Joan B. Kroc Institute for International Peace Studies at the University of Notre Dame. She is known for her research on the transnational dimensions of social movements, exploring ways in which global economic and political integration have influenced people's engagement in politics. She has co-edited three books on this subject: *Coalitions Across Borders: Transnational Protest in a Neoliberal Era* (with Joe Bandy, 2005); *Globalization and Resistance: Transnational Dimensions of Social Movements* (with Hank Johnston, 2002); and *Transnational Social Movements and Global Politics: Solidarity Beyond the State* (with Charles Chatfield and Ron Pagnucco, 1997).

Introduction

THE CONTRIBUTIONS COLLECTED in this reader address three intertwined themes: conflict, movements and social change. Such themes, it could be argued, constitute the major concerns of sociological theory in general, rather than the limited analytical interests of some sociological sub-discipline. Think of a founding father like Émile Durkheim, who posits that individuals may act for diverse subjective motives, but the outcome of their action possesses its own logic and cogency, and can be identified as a social fact. Action, in this sense, is the result of a conflict generated by a division of labour in society which is experienced as unjust. The outcome of action, as social fact, is change, namely a rearrangement of the division of labour that is felt to be more satisfactory by those acting. Of course, to a sociologist *avant la lettre* like Karl Marx conflict, movement and social change are the core, if not the exclusive, foci on which any theorising should be based. How to change, rather than just how to explain the status quo, is the Marxist task, in a world in which conflict (class struggle) is caused by the division between those holding the means of production and those possessing only their labour force. Change, however, does not automatically follow from increasingly polarised divisions in society, but may be produced when a 'class in itself' turns into a 'class for itself', that is to say when an objectively disadvantaged social condition forges a political awareness, a collective identity and a strategy for action: in our own jargon, when it becomes a social movement. Max Weber expresses a similar concept although in different words: disadvantage or lack of life chances by no means give rise to 'class action'. In his work *Class, Work, Party* Weber observes that collective action requires not only a distinctly recognisable condition of social injustice, but also an awareness that such injustice is unacceptable, because based on an arbitrary distribution of resources and power. Finally, Georg Simmel's notion of fluidity and movement describes a feeling of dizziness but also of perpetual change. In his *Philosophy of Money* one perceives a constant conflict between the objectivity of technological production and financial exchange and the subjectivity of individuals and groups making choices in their daily life.

In brief, the founders of traditional sociological thought are concerned with the variables and concepts which are central to the study of social movements. Following on from this tradition, it is useful to briefly look at the way in which conflict and social change are respectively conceptualised.

Social interactions may be characterised by harmony and cooperation as well as animosity and aversion. Mutual expectations and requirements provide a frame for social action. We will have a conflictual conduct when action is oriented against the expectations or requirements of another party. When there is disagreement over values, beliefs or notions of collective wellbeing, several possibilities present themselves. First, a clarification of the respective sets of values and notions may produce mutual understanding and tolerance. In this way, the parties involved will be led to accept their respective identities and recognise their right to co-exist. Second, when clarification, understanding and tolerance are hard to achieve, radical definitions of the disagreement and therefore of the contrasting identities will ensue. In such cases, general values might be mobilised and attempts to negotiate between the opposing groups holding them will be made. Third, when negotiation proves unfruitful, ultimate, rather than general, values will be expressed and, with communication between contrasting values becoming impossible, open conflict is likely to follow. Conflict may take the form of passive resistance, withdrawal or bargaining, with a view to altering the balance of power between the parties. In extreme cases, radical conducts may challenge the very legitimacy of the system against which they are addressed. Social movements use any of these single strategies or a combination thereof, thus implicitly alluding to the underlying conflict connoting their action.

Sociological theory has always been concerned with social order. But a thorough examination of such concern reveals a simultaneous interest in social change, particularly when order appears to be dangerously declining. We have already mentioned how Durkheim identifies in an unjust division of labour a potential for conflict and change leading to a more satisfactory social order. Social change and its consequences remain key themes for contemporary sociological theory, with debates and analyses inevitably drawing on previous conceptualisations and theories. Social change, for example, may be the unintended consequence of individual behaviour in the market place, as in the liberal tradition of thought. It may result from the purposive activities of groups aiming at the smooth and effective management of the economy, as in Durkheim's appreciative analysis of socialism. It may be inscribed in evolutionary processes leading societies from one stage to the next due to the conflictual nature of each stage, as in Marxist theory. Social change is associated with ideas and values shaping human action (Weber), or vice-versa it is social change which produces new ideas and values (Durkheim). Some groups pursuing social order may see change as the only viable strategy for the survival of a system, while others may interpret change as the product of action challenging and superseding that same system. Social movements express notions of social change that are detectable in their inception, strategy, vocabulary and the very type of contention in which they engage.

All contributions in this reader, while focused on collective behaviour, collective action or more explicitly on social movements, incorporate notions of conflict and social change that connote the philosophies or social theoretical affiliations of their authors. In this sense, it need not sound too extreme to argue that, by dealing with social movements, one is forced to deal with sociological thought as a whole. A celebrated contemporary author, Alain Touraine (1985), has stressed that the notion of social movement does not describe part of reality, but is an element of a specific mode of constructing social reality. In his view, sociological analysis should be organised less around the notions of society and social system than around that of social movement. Therefore, instead of analysing the social system as a set of norms and forms of organisation, the emphasis should be laid on the structural conflicts in a given society. In this approach, social actors are both culturally oriented and involved in structural conflicts.

Touraine is not alone in recognising the centrality of social movement in sociological studies. In his *Sociology Beyond Societies*, John Urry (2000) remarks that sociology has always attempted to make sense of collective desires, as those for example expressed by social movements, and it is unlikely that it will survive as a discipline unless it continues to embody the ever-emerging ambitions of social movements themselves. Pierre Bourdieu (2001) stresses that there is no meaningful change or even policy without movements capable of imposing them, hence the study of social processes and change coincides with that of social movements. To put the question in other terms, sociology survives best when it is engaged with public issues, and when it develops into social criticism. In this respect, Bryan Turner (2004) remarks that, without political and public commitments, sociology may turn into an esoteric, elitist and eccentric intellectual interest.

The present reader is organised around the notion that collective action responds to one of the fundamental questions posed by sociology: how can we live together? How do differentiated interests co-exist? When and how do grievances turn into collective action? When does the latter lead to social change? A classical sociologist such as Herbert Spencer, in this respect, distinguished between 'social statics', namely the social order, and 'social dynamics', that is the process of social change. Similarly, the authors we include in Part 1 of this reader attempt to explain the normative set up of society, which allows the functioning of a system, and at the same time the dynamics that may engender conflict and thus change in that system. The analysis of Karl Marx is very well known, and we offer a concise summary of it in three different excerpts. These should be read against the broad materialistic philosophy presented by Marx and Engels in a variety of their works. In *The German Ideology*, for example, the authors advocate a conception of history based on the understanding of material processes, on the production of life itself. It is from this material basis, they intimate, that the origin of the different forms of consciousness, religion, philosophy and ethics should be traced. Of course, throughout his major opus, *Capital*, Marx returns several times to the concept of historical materialism, which provides the backdrop to his analysis of the formation of the bourgeoisies and the attendant form of production.

In Part 1 we also include the classical Durkheimian analysis relating to the division of labour in society. In contrast to Marxist arguments, Durkheim does not see conflict as a permanent feature of societies based on class inequality. Rather, his notion of conflict is associated with that of transition, namely periods in which traditional forms of integration break down and new forms have not yet emerged. It is worth remarking that Durkheim's concept of anomie is consistent with this notion of conflict, as it denotes a transitional or exceptional condition, in contrast with subsequent functionalist analysis (see, for example, Robert Merton) which describes anomie as a permanent condition of modern societies. With Gustave Le Bon, whose contribution is also included in Part 1, we propose an understanding of social change which Marxist analysis would describe as idealistic, because produced by ideas rather than material conditions. In Le Bon, however, the crucial element explaining social movements is the breakdown of social arrangements and bonds: movements therefore add to situations of chaos by bringing their own dose of disruption. This part of the reader presents as a concluding extract a celebrated piece of work by Georg Simmel which vehemently highlights the central importance of conflict in human interactions.

Some forms of collective action lead to the establishment of a new social arrangement: this is the kernel of the excerpts from Max Weber and Antonio Gramsci we present in Part 2. Although the two authors focus on totally different historical periods, both underline the capacity of conflicting interests to promote social change. Whether such interests characterise confined professional groups or broadly identifiable social classes, they acquire maximum strength when supported by wide alliances, organisational ability and hegemonic values. In Weber and Gramsci we see some embryonic analytical elements which will shape future debates on social movements and their mobilising power. Analyses stressing the changing, if not evolutionary, nature of social systems are challenged by authors describing the attempt to establish new social orders as counterproductive, if not deleterious. Fear of mass participation in political action informs authors such as Kornhauser, who tends to see participants in social movements as susceptible to indoctrination or as victims of their own lack of ideas. Kornhauser's work chimes with the criticism expressed, for example, by Tönnies and Pareto towards social change and its human costs, and against optimistic accounts of progress which hide the formation of new types of domination. His arguments echo traditional positivist analysis of political offenders as fanatics needing to believe in something grand, 'neophiles' who embrace any doctrine because incapable of formulating one by themselves. Part 2 offers other contributions (by Blumer and Smelser) that shift attention from individual, psychological, motivations to collective, visible, action. Both authors are more interested in the specific dynamics guiding mobilisation than in their final outcomes in a general political sense. Some of their thoughts will be further developed into a structural-functionalist perspective that explains the emergence of social movements in terms of 'strains' related to uneven or dysfunctional developments within otherwise stable systems.

Resource mobilisation theory is regarded as a departure from the collective behaviour approach, its starting focus being less action per se than the organisational elements underpinning it. Part 3 of this reader gathers some of the most significant contributions produced by this school of thought, and is meant to convey the notion that social movements are pragmatic in their politics, self-controlled in their conduct and thoughtful about their goals. Resource mobilisation theorists are described as a new generation of social scientists who reject the view of social movements as irrational, retrograde and destructive forces. These theorists contend that, while in every society most people are unhappy with the status quo, only some discontented groups manage to join social movements and concretely express their grievance.

The tools, mechanisms, alliances, resources and organisational ability deployed by such groups are the central object of analysis characterising this perspective.

If mere access to resources is a key element explaining social movements, then groups bereft of resources, such as marginalised communities, may never be able to engage in a social movement or in any meaningful form of collective action. In response, some authors would suggest that, whether or not endowed with resources and functioning organisational structures, social movements are influenced by the surrounding political climate. This is the core of the political process approach, which posits that existing legislations, formal and informal ways of dealing with dissent and contrasting interests and ideas within the very elite account for the emergence and development of social movements. Part 4 is devoted to this school of thought, namely to the idea that it may be useless to identify some universal cause of collective action; rather, it is crucial to examine political structures and philosophies as incentives or obstacles to the formation of social movements. As John McCarthy *et al.* have remarked, when people join in collective action, they enter a complex social, political and economic environment. This environment has direct and indirect consequences for people's decisions as to how to define and pursue their own goals in particular and social change in general.

Paradigmatic shifts are the rule in social movement theory, at least until the 1960s and 1970s. Are we sure that social movements mobilise and are mobilised by resources, that they pursue material goods or aim at general, millenarian, change? The contributions of new social movement theorists, some of which we group in Part 5 of this reader, not only challenge the notion of actors rationally calculating the costs and benefits of their conduct, they also question the concept of class, which supposedly prompts goals and suggests avenues for change. New social movements are said to pursue post-materialist values and self-fulfilment, along with goals whose achievement is tremendously difficult to measure. They are depicted as the expression of post-industrial society, like old social movements were expressions of the now declining industrial society.

Part 6 testifies to the expansion of social movement studies and the growing necessity felt by scholars to explore new theoretical directions and/or to develop a comprehensive understanding of the subject matter. The contributions gathered in this part of the book appear to suggest that, while it is unlikely that a synthesis may be found between the different approaches, surely the proliferation of perspectives will benefit a field of study which may be too young to aspire to such a synthesis. Here we present the arguments for a social-psychological expansion of resource mobilisation theory, the efforts of applying Goffman's frame analysis to social movements, the attempts to view movements as cognitive praxis, a suggestion for a unifying concept of social movement, and a call for an analysis of emotions as core components of collective action.

Part 7 discusses the growing network of international organisations that could potentially function as a global civil society, a network which denounces the negative outcomes of extreme market liberalisation and unfettered economic globalisation. These organisations are formed by what Massimo De Angelis (2007) terms commoners, namely actors expressing alternative values to those centred on development and profit. Described as life-reclaiming forces, movements reacting to globalisation, in the analyses we present, forge international patterns of social solidarity, something resembling the reaction of Durkheim to WW1, when against the notion of obtuse nationalism, he called for international patriotism.

Yes, we start and end this conclusion with the classics. How could it be otherwise? Among the most original contemporary social theorists Jacques Rancière (2007) reiterates classical notions of conflict and social change, for example, remarking that we are far from the end of political divisions, social antagonisms and utopian projects. In his *On the Shores of Politics*, he smiles at the alacrity with which the elites attempt to persuade others that politics is over, an attempt made with a view to monopolising the political sphere undisturbed. Politics, in his view, is the art of suppressing the political, namely the art of convincing citizens to carry on with their lives rather than waste time with collective action. Similarly, Alain Badiou (2005) revisits notions of collective action and social change as opposed to the 'fiction of political representation'. In his opinion, what social movements keep showing is the weakness of every form of action bound to institutional politics. Meticulous 'unbinding' is the key concept he introduces, understood as a process whereby social groups empower themselves as collective entities. Echoing Simmel's conceptualisation of conflict and Durkheim's notion of 'the right of combat', Badiou stresses that, while official politics purports to be the expression of the existing plurality of opinions and interests, collective action demonstrates the possibility of breaking away from what exists and producing social change.

This reader on social movements is an attempt to link classical social theories with contemporary discourses on conflict and social change.

References

Badiou, A. (2005), *Metapolitics*, London/New York: Verso.

Bourdieu, P. (2001), *Contre-feux 2: Pour un Movement Social Européen*, Paris: Raisons D Agir.

De Angelis, M. (2007), *The Beginning of History*, London: Pluto.

Rancière, J. (2007), *On the Shores of Politics*, London/New York: Verso.

Touraine, A. (1985), 'An Introduction to the Study of Social Movements', *Social Research*, 52: 749–787.

Turner, B.S. (ed) (2004), *The Blackwell Companion to Social Theory*, Second Edition, Oxford: Blackwell.

Urry, J. (2000), *Sociology Beyond Societies*, London: Routledge.

PART ONE

Conflict and collective action

IN THE FIRST PART OF THIS BOOK we trace the concepts of conflict and collective action as elaborated by the founders of sociology. Although some of the authors mentioned below do not directly use the phrase 'social movement', their analysis of conflict, social change and political activity provides important pointers for future definitions elaborated by social movement theorists.

We are in the nineteenth century, when optimism about evolution and progress is widespread, with Darwinian theories suggesting that natural selection eliminates organisms unfit to survive while allowing the better fit to multiply. Applying such theories to human societies, early sociologists like Auguste Comte and Herbert Spencer, although in a different fashion, identify change with a relatively linear process leading to increasingly advanced stages of social organisation. In Comte (1953), for example, social change brings the collectivity through different stages: from a theological to a metaphysical and, finally, to a positive stage of consciousness. In the first, human thought is dominated by divinity, in the second by abstract philosophical principles, while in the third by factual, scientific knowledge (Noble, 2000). It is implicit in this vision that, once societies have reached their final stage of evolution, change is no longer possible, nor is conflict in any way justifiable. Thus, a fully developed industrial system of production, due to the highly cooperative arrangements such production requires, will make friction between employers and employees redundant. According to Comte, conflict and hostility belong to military, not to industrial societies.

Spencer (1873) sees evolution as a historical trajectory leading uniform human aggregations, with groups and individuals performing similar functions, towards differentiated aggregations, in which functions are diverse but complementary. Uniform societies are said to be organised in an authoritarian fashion, which makes cooperation compulsory, while in differentiated societies voluntary cooperation is said to predominate. The aim of Spencer is to demonstrate the superiority of liberal democratic systems and their ability to distribute resources and neutralise conflicts (Harrington, 2005). It is true, as Noble (2000) remarks, that the emphasis placed by Spencer on social harmony and integration does not warrant the inclusion of his ideas in the functionalist tradition. Nevertheless, his view that change and increasing integration are the result of the struggle for survival alludes to a final stage in which such struggle is meaningless and collaboration among groups and individuals harmonious and definitive. It is against this background that the contributions included in this section should be located.

Karl Marx incorporates both the notion of conflict and that of social change in the concept of class struggle. It may be controversial whether his philosophy still contains some of the evolutionary traits connoting his era. Even his view that social classes impose themselves by fighting against the dominant groups, until societies become totally cooperative aggregations, may be said to echo the evolutionary stages identified by positivists such as Comte. However, while Comte posits that industrialisation brings social energies together and makes collaboration inevitable, Marx sees the industrial productive system as a major contributor to social polarisation and institutional oppression. In his view, oppressors and oppressed, in every type of society, have always engaged in hidden or open fight. In *The Communist Manifesto* (1848), written with Frederick Engels, an analysis of such constant fight is provided in light of what is described as a progressive 'splitting up' of society into two great hostile formations: bourgeoisie and proletariat. Only rarely is the proletariat victorious, but the effect of labour conflicts is not measurable in terms of immediate results; rather, we are told, the outcome of struggles is found in the ever expanding political consciousness of workers and the growth of their organisations. Marx and Engels suggest that such growth is facilitated by the improved means of communication created by industry, which allow workers from different localities to establish contacts with one another. An echo of contemporary transnational social movements is conveyed by the authors in their claim that in England as in France, in America as in Germany, the proletariat has been stripped of every trace of national character. In another extract from Marx's work, *The Eighteenth Brumaire of Louis Bonaparte* (1852), the point is made that when the oppressed engage in the transformation of themselves and their material surroundings, they take inspiration from previous struggles and rebellions, adopting the language of their predecessors. As contemporary social movement theorists would put it, they draw on a repertoire of action established by those who have been oppressed before them, so that 'the resurrection of the dead serves to exalt the new struggles'. In his *Critique of Political Economy* (1859), Marx reiterates his view on how consciousness takes shape: it is not people's consciousness that determines their existence, but the latter that determines the former. This belief shapes his materialistic analysis of social change.

Spencer's concepts of evolution, differentiation and integration may be regarded as outdated and his writings read only for historical interest. These concepts, however, are developed into sophisticated and rigorous theories by subsequent authors. Émile Durkheim highlights the importance of social interdependence, and therefore solidarity, and his concepts of *mechanic* and *organic solidarity* echo Spencer's distinction between *militant* and *industrial* societies, the former characterised by authoritarian control, the second by self-control. In Durkheim, however, these concepts are suitable for the interpretation of both stability and change. The interdependence of individuals, within a widely accepted division of labour, generates strong social ties in the form of shared values and self-control. Here, we can still detect some traces of Spencer's notion that voluntary, rather than compulsory, cooperation tends to eliminate social conflicts. We can even liken Durkheim's analysis to Spencer's view that harmony and self-control are caused by a smooth differentiation of the individual functions performed. In Durkheim, nevertheless, self-control may collapse when the existing division of labour turns into differentiation. Durkheim warns that the two terms are not to be confused. The former brings vital forces together, whereas the latter causes disintegration, like microbes and cancer. 'Cancer and tuberculosis increase the diversity of organic tissues without bringing forth a new specialisation of biological functions'. In brief, if differentiation is seen by Spencer as a characteristic of advanced and harmonious societies, it is interpreted by Durkheim as dysfunctional or even socially lethal.

In a sense, the concept of anomie replicates the biological metaphor quoted above, in that it describes an exceptional situation hampering the normal functioning of society. But in Durkheim the polarisation between a condition of stability and one of anomie is only apparent because groups of individuals may challenge a specific form of stability without throwing the collectivity into a normless condition. The division of labour produces solidarity, he stresses, only if it is 'spontaneous' and not forced. The extract below is part of the chapter titled 'The Forced Division of Labour' in his classical book *The Division of Labour in Society* (1893). Durkheim mentions the notion of 'social force', a form of collective action for change in complex societies. Social change, in his perspective, takes place when there is an absolute equality in engaging in conflict and when the 'right of combat' is recognised. The second extract is taken from *The Elementary Forms of the Religious Life* (1912), where Durkheim elaborates concepts such as 'collective effervescence' and 'creative periods'. All communities, according to Durkheim, may experience 'magical moments', whereby individuals transcend themselves and prefigure a higher collective order. Collective effervescence leads individuals to integration into a superior unit, as the experience of action results in moments of communion. By acting above and beyond themselves, in concrete social practices, individuals achieve a form of solidarity typifying what Durkheim terms 'creative periods'. While new values are elaborated and egoistical interests are provisionally set aside, these periods, evanescent though they may be, remain in the memory of the collectivity as periods of 'supreme integration'. The extract proposed below focuses on the social function of religious beliefs, where Durkheim links the concept of 'effervescence' with those of moral and political authority as well as social action.

Politically a pragmatist who advocates social reform based on moral individualism, Durkheim is very much inspired by his fear of social disorder (Delanty, 2000). But is this his personal fear or does this belong to the broader concerns of sociology as an *engagé* discipline? True, the Franco-Prussian War, the Paris Commune, and the Dreyfus Affair are spectres threatening the fragile constitutional order of Europe, but Durkheim is not alone in hoping for social change leading to a new morality and, ultimately, a new social contract guaranteeing cooperation and stability. Durkheim advocates citizens' active participation, the creation of intermediary associations, that is, associations that occupy the space between the state and the individual, provide moral regulation of society, and mediate between the citizens and authorities.

'These heterogeneous community associations have been identified as an essential aspect of communal cohesiveness' (Turner, 2006: 95). These concerns, surely, are shared by all students of social aggregations who cherish justice and strive to find better ways of 'living together', even if 'collective effervescence' is included among such ways.

In the work of Gustave Le Bon, something similar to 'effervescence' seems to denote 'periods of transition and anarchy', when the power of crowds shapes events and the voice of the masses becomes preponderant. But this specific effervescence, in his view, cannot accomplish anything requiring a high degree of intelligence, because when the masses gather together it is not knowledge that they accumulate, but stupidity. In *The Crowd* (1895), Le Bon expresses his fears of mass participation in political activity, in a sense anticipating similar fears elicited by crowds and 'mobs' in the contemporary era. The crowd furnishes individuals with a collective mind, which makes them feel and think in a manner quite different from that in which each individual would otherwise feel and think. In total contrast with Marx's notion that consciousness and ideologies are determined by material conditions, Le Bon claims that behind important social events there are profound modifications in ideas: 'the memorable events of history are the visible effects of the invisible changes of human thought'. What is important to note here is that Le Bon's perspective is consonant with views of social movements as potentially dangerous collective behaviour which, if left unattended, might threaten established ways of life. His 'collective behaviour perspective' is to dominate the study of social movements until the late 1960s (Eyerman and Jamison, 1991: 12). We shall see later how, in opposition to this perspective, a 'collective action perspective' will develop.

In this respect, Simmel's work may seem ambiguous, as it echoes the fears of those who feel threatened by collective behaviour, but it also reminds us that such behaviour is action embedded in society, more specifically, in one of the fundamental aspects of our socialisation. Georg Simmel sees cities as characterised by varying degrees of instability and danger, as places of sudden 'extreme phenomena', spawned by an excessively rationalised and calculating environment. In *The Metropolis and Mental Life* (1903) he remarks that the excessive amount and variety of stimulations in the urban environment force us to assume a blasé attitude as a way of selecting and responding to them. The extract below is taken from *Conflict and the Web of Group-Affiliation* (1908). Here, Simmel stresses that urban life, which every day brings everybody in contact with innumerable others, would be impossible without some degree of aversion. His focus is on conflict, in his view the most vivid interaction which 'cannot possibly be carried out by one individual alone'. Engagement in conflict itself is a way of producing socialisation, rendered by Simmel with the term *sociation*. In Simmel's view, *sociation* entails the power and the right 'to rebel against tyranny, arbitrariness, moodiness, tactlessness'. Opposition and resistance give us 'inner satisfaction, distraction and relief'. The extract proposed below should be read in conjunction with his work on how identities are formed, where he stresses that identity is a field of tensions, a field determined by various sources and multifaceted experience. His notion of social movement, in sum, is linked to the idea that identities are shaped by the multiple relationships in which social actors engage (Diani, 2000). In Simmel's view, the social structure is the result of multiple linkages individuals establish with different primary and secondary groups. Social movements, in this perspective, develop their identity while diversifying their affiliation. In other words, where traditional movements establish loyalty, and therefore identity, through contacts provided by concentric circles of affiliation, in new social movements intersecting circles of affiliation prevail. We shall see later how important these reflections are for the development of contemporary theories of social movements.

References

Comte, A. (1953), *Cours de philosophie positive* (vol.VI), Paris: Gallimard.

Delanty, G. (2005), 'Modernity and Post-modernity', in Harrington, A. (ed), *Modern Social Theory*, Oxford: Oxford University Press.

Diani, M. (2000), 'Simmel to Rokham and Beyond: Towards a Network Theory of (New) Social Movements', *European Journal of Social Theory*, 3: 33–47.

Eyerman, R. and Jamison, A. (1991), *Social Movements: A Cognitive Approach*, Cambridge: Polity Press.

Harrington, A. (2005), 'Classical Social Theory: Contexts and Beginnings', in Harrington, A. (ed), *Modern Social Theory*, Oxford: Oxford University Press.

Noble, T. (2000), *Social Theory and Social Change*, Basingstoke: Macmillan.

Spencer, H. (1873), *The Study of Sociology*, London: Kegan Paul.

Turner, B. S. (2006), *Vulnerability and Human Rights*, University Park: Pennsylvania State University Press.

Chapter 1

Karl Marx and Frederick Engels

THE COMMUNIST MANIFESTO

[. . .]

1. Bourgeois and proletarians

THE HISTORY OF ALL HITHERTO existing society is the history of class struggles.

Freeman and slave, patrician and plebeian, lord and serf, guild-master and journeyman, in a word, oppressor and oppressed, stood in constant opposition to one another, carried on an uninterrupted, now hidden, now open fight, a fight that each time ended, either in a revolutionary reconstitution of society at large, or in the common ruin of the contending classes.

In the earlier epochs of history, we find almost everywhere a complicated arrangement of society into various orders, a manifold gradation of social rank. In ancient Rome we have patricians, knights, plebeians, slaves; in the Middle Ages, feudal lords, vassals, guild-masters, journey-men, apprentices, serfs; in almost all of these classes, again, subordinate gradations.

The modern bourgeois society that has sprouted from the ruins of feudal society has not done away with class antagonisms. It has but established new classes, new conditions of oppression, new forms of struggle in place of the old ones.

Our epoch, the epoch of the bourgeoisie, possesses, however, this distinctive feature: it has simplified the class antagonisms. Society as a whole is more and more splitting up into two great hostile camps, into two great classes directly facing each other: bourgeoisie and proletariat.

[. . .]

The proletariat goes through various stages of development. With its birth begins its struggle with the bourgeoisie. At first the contest is carried on by individual labourers, then by the workpeople of a factory, then by the operatives of one trade, in one locality, against the individual bourgeois who directly exploits them. They direct their attacks not against the bourgeois conditions of production, but against the instruments of production themselves; they destroy imported wares that compete with their labour, they smash to pieces machinery, they set factories ablaze, they seek to restore by force the vanished status of the workman of the Middle Ages.

At this stage the labourers still form an incoherent mass scattered over the whole country, and broken up by their mutual competition. If anywhere they unite to form more compact bodies, this is not yet the consequence of their own active union, but of the union of the bourgeoisie, which class, in order to attain its own political ends, is compelled to set the whole proletariat in motion, and is moreover yet, for a time, able to do so. At this stage, therefore, the proletarians do not fight their enemies, but the enemies of their enemies, the remnants of absolute monarchy, the landowners, the non-industrial bourgeois, the petty bourgeoisie. Thus the whole historical movement is concentrated in the hands of the bourgeoisie; every victory so obtained is a victory for the bourgeoisie.

But with the development of industry the proletariat not only increases in number; it becomes concentrated in greater masses, its strength grows, and it feels that strength more. The various interests and conditions of life within the ranks of the proletariat are more and more equalized, in proportion as machinery obliterates all distinctions of labour, and nearly everywhere reduces wages to the same low level. The growing competition among the bourgeois, and the resulting commercial crises, make the wages of the workers ever more fluctuating. The unceasing improvement of machinery, ever more rapidly developing, makes their livelihood more and more precarious; the collisions between individual workmen and individual bourgeois take more and more the character of collisions between two classes. Thereupon the workers begin to form combinations (trade unions) against the bourgeois; they club together in order to keep up the rate of wages; they found permanent associations in order to make provision beforehand for these occasional revolts. Here and there the contest breaks out into riots.

Now and then the workers are victorious, but only for a time. The real fruit of their battles lies, not in the immediate result, but in the ever expanding union of the workers. This union is helped on by the improved means of communication that are created by modern industry, and that place the workers of different localities in contact with one another. It was just this contact that was needed to centralize the numerous local struggles, all of the same character, into one national struggle between classes. But every class struggle is a political struggle. And that union, to attain which the burghers of the Middle Ages, with their miserable highways, required centuries, the modern proletarians, thanks to railways, achieve in a few years.

This organization of the proletarians into a class, and consequently into a political party, is continually being upset again by the competition between the workers themselves. But it ever rises up again, stronger, firmer, mightier. It compels legislative recognition of particular interests of the workers, by taking advantage of the divisions among the bourgeoisie itself. Thus the Ten Hours Bill in England was carried.[1]

Altogether, collisions between the classes of the old society further, in many ways, the course of development of the proletariat. The bourgeoisie finds itself involved in a constant battle; at first with the aristocracy; later on, with those portions of the bourgeoisie itself, whose interests have become antagonistic to the progress of industry; at all times, with the bourgeoisie of foreign countries. In all these battles it sees itself compelled to appeal to the proletariat, to ask for its help, and thus to drag it into the political arena. The bourgeoisie itself, therefore, supplies the proletariat with its own elements of political and general education, in other words, it furnishes the proletariat with weapons for fighting the bourgeoisie.

Further, as we have already seen, entire sections of the ruling classes are, by the advance of industry, precipitated into the proletariat, or are at least threatened in their conditions of existence. These also supply the proletariat with fresh elements of enlightenment and progress.

Finally, in times when the class struggle nears the decisive hour, the process of dissolution going on within the ruling class, in fact within the whole range of old society, assumes such a violent, glaring character, that a small section of the ruling class cuts itself adrift, and joins the revolutionary class, the class that holds the future in its hands. Just as, therefore, at an earlier period, a section of the nobility went over to the bourgeoisie, so now a portion of the bourgeoisie goes over to the proletariat, and in particular, a portion of the bourgeois ideologists, who have raised themselves to the level of comprehending theoretically the historical movement as a whole.

Of all the classes that stand face to face with the bourgeoisie today, the proletariat alone is a really revolutionary class. The other classes decay and finally disappear in the face of modern industry; the proletariat is its special and essential product.

The lower middle class, the small manufacturer, the shopkeeper, the artisan, the peasant, all these fight against the bourgeoisie, to save from extinction their existence as fractions of the middle class. They are therefore not revolutionary, but conservative. Nay more, they are reactionary, for they try to roll back the wheel of history. If by chance they are revolutionary, they are so only in view of their impending transfer into the proletariat, they thus defend not their present, but their future interests, they desert their own standpoint to place themselves at that of the proletariat.

The 'dangerous class',[2] the social scum, that passively rotting mass thrown off by the lowest layers of old society, may, here and there, be swept into the movement by a proletarian revolution; its conditions of life, however, prepare it far more for the part of a bribed tool of reactionary intrigue.

In the conditions of the proletariat, those of old society at large are already virtually swamped. The proletarian is without property; his relation to his wife and children has no longer anything in common with the bourgeois family relations; modern industrial labour, modern subjection to capital, the same in England as in France, in America as in Germany, has stripped him of every trace of national character. Law, morality, religion, are to him so many bourgeois prejudices, behind which lurk in ambush just as many bourgeois interests.

All the preceding classes that got the upper hand, sought to fortify their already acquired status by subjecting society at large to their conditions of appropriation. The proletarians cannot become masters of the productive forces of society, except by abolishing their own previous mode of appropriation, and thereby also every other previous mode of appropriation. They have nothing of their own to secure and to fortify; their mission is to destroy all previous securities for, and insurances of, individual property.

All previous historical movements were movements of minorities, or in the interest of minorities. The proletarian movement is the self-conscious, independent movement of the immense majority, in the interest of the immense majority. The proletariat, the lowest stratum of our present society, cannot stir, cannot raise itself up, without the whole superincumbent strata of official society being sprung into the air.

Though not in substance, yet in form, the struggle of the proletariat with the bourgeoisie is at first a national struggle. The proletariat of each country must, of course, first of all settle matters with its own bourgeoisie.

In depicting the most general phases of the development of the proletariat, we traced the more or less veiled civil war, raging within existing society, up to the point where that war breaks out into open revolution, and where the violent overthrow of the bourgeoisie lays the foundation for the sway of the proletariat.

Hitherto, every form of society has been based, as we have already seen, on the antagonism of oppressing and oppressed classes. But in order to oppress a class, certain conditions must be assured to it under which it can, at least, continue its slavish existence. The serf, in the period of serfdom, raised himself to membership in the commune, just as the petty bourgeois, under the yoke of feudal absolutism, managed to develop into a bourgeois. The modern labourer, on the contrary, instead of rising with the progress of industry, sinks deeper and deeper below the conditions of existence of his own class. He becomes a pauper, and pauperism develops more rapidly than population and wealth. And here it becomes evident that the bourgeoisie is unfit any longer to be the ruling class in society, and to impose its conditions of existence upon society as an overriding law. It is unfit to rule because it is incompetent to assure an existence to its slave within his slavery, because it cannot help letting him sink into such a state that it has to feed him, instead of being fed by him. Society can no longer live under this bourgeoisie, in other words, its existence is no longer compatible with society.

The essential condition for the existence, and for the sway of the bourgeois class, is the formation and augmentation of capital; the condition for capital is wage labour. Wage labour rests exclusively on competition between the labourers. The advance of industry, whose involuntary promoter is the bourgeoisie, replaces the isolation of the labourers, due to competition, by their revolutionary combination, due to association. The development of modern industry, therefore, cuts from under its feet the very foundation on which the bourgeoisie produces and appropriates products. What the bourgeoisie therefore produces, above all, are its own grave-diggers. Its fall and the victory of the proletariat are equally inevitable.

[. . .]

Notes

1   In 1846. See Engels's article 'The English Ten Hours Bill', Marx–Engels, *Articles on Britain*, Progress Publishers (Moscow 1971), pp. 96–108.

2   i.e. the lumpenproletariat of casual labourers and unemployed, which was very extensive in the cities of nineteenth-century Europe.

Chapter 2

Karl Marx and Frederick Engels

A CONTRIBUTION TO THE CRITIQUE OF POLITICAL ECONOMY

[...]

THE FIRST WORK which I undertook to dispel the doubts assailing me was a critical re-examination of the Hegelian philosophy of law; the introduction[1] to this work being published in the *Deutsch-Französische Jahrbücher* issued in Paris in 1844. My inquiry led me to the conclusion that neither legal relations nor political forms could be comprehended whether by themselves or on the basis of a so-called general development of the human mind, but that on the contrary they originate in the material conditions of life, the totality of which Hegel, following the example of English and French thinkers of the eighteenth century, embraces within the term "civil society"; that the anatomy of this civil society, however, has to be sought in political economy. The study of this, which I began in Paris, I continued in Brussels, where I moved owing to an expulsion order issued by M. Guizot.[2] The general conclusion at which I arrived and which, once reached, became the guiding principle of my studies can be summarised as follows. In the social production of their existence, men inevitably enter into definite relations, which are independent of their will, namely relations of production appropriate to a given stage in the development of their material forces of production. The totality of these relations of production constitutes the economic structure of society, the real foundation, on which arises a legal and political superstructure and to which correspond definite forms of social consciousness. The mode of production of material life conditions the general process of social, political and intellectual life. It is not the consciousness of men that determines their existence, but their social existence that determines their consciousness. At a certain stage of development, the material productive forces of society come into conflict with the existing relations of production or—this merely expresses the same thing in legal terms—with the property relations within the framework of which they have operated hitherto. From forms of development of the productive forces these relations turn into their fetters. Then begins an era of social revolution. The changes in the economic foundation lead sooner or later to the transformation of the whole immense superstructure. In studying such transformations it is always necessary to distinguish between the material transformation of the economic conditions of production, which can be determined with the precision of natural science, and the legal, political, religious, artistic or philosophic—in short, ideological forms in which men become conscious of this conflict and fight it out. Just as one does not judge an individual by what he thinks about himself, so one cannot judge such a period of transformation by its consciousness, but, on the contrary, this consciousness must be explained from the contradictions of material life, from the conflict existing between the social forces of production and the relations of production. No social formation is ever destroyed before all the productive forces for which it is sufficient have been developed, and new superior relations of production never replace older ones before the material conditions for their existence have matured within the framework of the old society. Mankind thus inevitably sets itself only such tasks as it is able to solve, since closer examination will always show that the problem itself arises only when the material conditions for its solution are already present or at least in the course of formation. In broad outline, the Asiatic, ancient, feudal and modern bourgeois modes of production may be designated as epochs marking progress in the economic development of society. The bourgeois relations of production are the last antagonistic form of the social process of production—antagonistic not in the sense of individual antagonism but of an antagonism that emanates from the individuals' social conditions of existence—but the productive forces developing within bourgeois society create also the material conditions for a solution of this antagonism. The prehistory of human society accordingly closes with this social formation.

[. . .]

Notes

1   See "Contribution to the Critique of Hegel's Philosophy of Law" and "Contribution to the Critique of Hegel's Philosophy of Law. Introduction".
2   On January 11, 1845.

Chapter 3

Karl Marx

THE EIGHTEENTH BRUMAIRE
OF LOUIS BONAPARTE

[. . .]

HEGEL REMARKS SOMEWHERE that all the great events and characters of world history occur, so to speak, twice. He forgot to add: the first time as tragedy, the second as farce, Caussidière in place of Danton, Louis Blanc in place of Robespierre, the Montagne of 1848–51 in place of the Montagne of 1793–5, the Nephew in place of the Uncle. And we can perceive the same caricature in the circumstances surrounding the second edition of the eighteenth Brumaire!

Men make their own history, but not of their own free will; not under circumstances they themselves have chosen but under the given and inherited circumstances with which they are directly confronted. The tradition of the dead generations weighs like a nightmare on the minds of the living. And, just when they appear to be engaged in the revolutionary transformation of themselves and their material surroundings, in the creation of something which does not yet exist, precisely in such epochs of revolutionary crisis they timidly conjure up the spirits of the past to help them; they borrow their names, slogans and costumes so as to stage the new world-historical scene in this venerable disguise and borrowed language. Luther put on the mask of the apostle Paul; the Revolution of 1789–1814 draped itself alternately as the Roman republic and the Roman empire; and the revolution of 1848 knew no better than to parody at some points 1789 and at others the revolutionary traditions of 1793–5. In the same way, the beginner who has learned a new language always retranslates it into his mother tongue: he can only be said to have appropriated the spirit of the new language and to be able to express himself in it freely when he can manipulate it without reference to the old, and when he forgets his original language while using the new one.

If we reflect on this process of world-historical necromancy, we see at once a salient distinction. Camille Desmoulins, Danton, Robespierre, Saint-Just and Napoleon, the heroes of the old French Revolution, as well as its parties and masses, accomplished the task of their epoch, which was the emancipation and establishment of modern *bourgeois* society, in Roman costume and with Roman slogans. The first revolutionaries smashed the feudal basis to pieces and struck off the feudal heads which had grown on it. Then came Napoleon. Within France he created the conditions which first made possible the development of free competition, the exploitation of the land by small peasant property, and the application of the unleashed productive power of the nation's industries. Beyond the borders of France he swept away feudal institutions so far as this was necessary for the provision on the European continent of an appropriate modern environment for the bourgeois society in France. Once the new social formation had been established, the antediluvian colossi disappeared along with the resurrected imitations of Rome – imitations of Brutus, Gracchus, Publicola, the tribunes, the senators, and Caesar himself. Bourgeois society in its sober reality had created its true interpreters and spokesmen in such people as Say, Cousin, Royer-Collard, Benjamin Constant and Guizot. The real leaders of the bourgeois army sat behind office desks while the fathead Louis XVIII served as the bourgeoisie's political head. Bourgeois society was no longer aware that the ghosts of Rome had watched over its cradle, since it was wholly absorbed in the production of wealth and the peaceful struggle of economic competition. But unheroic as bourgeois society is, it still required heroism, self-sacrifice, terror, civil war, and battles in which whole nations were engaged, to bring it into the world. And its gladiators found in the stern classical traditions of the Roman republic the ideals, art forms and self-deceptions they needed in order to hide from themselves the limited bourgeois content of their struggles and to maintain their enthusiasm at the high level appropriate to great historical tragedy. A century earlier, in the same way but at a different stage of development, Cromwell and the English people had borrowed for their bourgeois revolution the language, passions and illusions of the Old Testament. When the actual goal had been reached, when the bourgeois transformation of English society had been accomplished, Locke drove out Habakkuk.

In these revolutions, then, the resurrection of the dead served to exalt the new struggles, rather than to parody the old, to exaggerate the given task in the imagination, rather than to flee from solving it in reality, and to recover the spirit of the revolution, rather than to set its ghost walking again.

[. . .]

The social revolution of the nineteenth century can only create its poetry from the future, not from the past. It cannot begin its own work until it has sloughed off all its superstitious regard for the past. Earlier revolutions have needed world-historical reminiscences to deaden their awareness of their own content. In order to arrive at its own content the revolution of the nineteenth century must let the dead bury their dead. Previously the phrase transcended the content; here the content transcends the phrase.

[. . .]

Chapter 4

Emile Durkheim

THE DIVISION OF LABOR IN SOCIETY

I

IT IS NOT SUFFICIENT that there be rules, however, for sometimes the rules themselves are the cause of evil. This is what occurs in class-wars. The institution of classes and of castes constitutes an organization of the division of labor, and it is a strictly regulated organization, although it often is a source of dissension. The lower classes not being, or no longer being, satisfied with the role which has devolved upon them from custom or by law aspire to functions which are closed to them and seek to dispossess those who are exercising these functions. Thus civil wars arise which are due to the manner in which labor is distributed.

There is nothing similar to this in the organism. No doubt, during periods of crises, the different tissues war against one another and nourish themselves at the expense of others. But never does one cell or organ seek to usurp a role different from the one which it is filling. The reason for this is that each anatomic element automatically executes its purpose. Its constitution, its place in the organism, determines its vocation; its task is a consequence of its nature. It can badly acquit itself, but it cannot assume another's task unless the latter abandons it, as happens in the rare cases of substitution that we have spoken of. It is not so in societies. Here the possibility is greater. There is a greater distance between the hereditary dispositions of the individual and the social function he will fill. The first do not imply the second with such immediate necessity. This space, open to striving and deliberation, is also at the mercy of a multitude of causes which can make individual nature deviate from its normal direction and create a pathological state. Because this organization is more supple, it is also more delicate and more accessible to change. Doubtless, we are not, from birth, predestined to some special position; but we do have tastes and aptitudes which limit our choice. If no care is taken of them, if they are ceaselessly disturbed by our daily occupations, we shall suffer and seek a way of putting an end to our suffering. But there is no other way out than to change the established order and to set up a new one. For the division of labor to produce solidarity, it is not sufficient, then, that each have his task; it is still necessary that this task be fitting to him.

Now, it is this condition which is not realized in the case we are examining. In effect, if the institution of classes or castes sometimes gives rise to anxiety and pain instead of producing solidarity, this is because the distribution of social functions on which it rests does not respond, or rather no longer responds, to the distribution of natural talents.

[. . .]

The forced division of labor is, then, the second abnormal type that we meet. But the sense of the word "forced" must not be misunderstood. Constraint is not every kind of regulation, since, as we have just seen, the division of labor cannot do without regulation. Even when functions are divided in accordance with pre-established rules, this apportioning is not necessarily the result of constraint. This is what takes place even under the rule of castes, in so far as that is founded in the nature of the society. This institution is never arbitrary throughout, but when it functions in a society in regular fashion without resistance, it expresses, at least in the large, the immutable manner in which occupational aptitudes distribute themselves. That is why, although tasks are, in certain measure, divided by law, each organ executes its own automatically. Constraint only begins when regulation, no longer corresponding to the true nature of things, and, accordingly, no longer having any basis in customs, can only be validated through force.

Inversely, we may say that the division of labor produces solidarity only if it is spontaneous and in proportion as it is spontaneous. But by spontaneity we must understand not simply the absence of all express violence, but also of everything that can even indirectly shackle the free unfolding of the social force that each carries in himself. It supposes, not only that individuals are not relegated to determinate functions by force, but also that no obstacle, of whatever nature, prevents them from occupying the place in the social framework which is compatible with their faculties. In short, labor is divided spontaneously only if society is constituted in such a way that social inequalities exactly express natural inequalities. But, for that, it is necessary and sufficient that the latter be neither enhanced nor lowered by some external cause. Perfect spontaneity is, then, only a consequence and another form of this other fact, —absolute equality in the external conditions of the conflict. It consists, not in a state of anarchy which would permit men freely to satisfy all their good or bad tendencies, but in a subtle organization in which each social value, being neither over-estimated nor underestimated by anything foreign to it, would be judged at its true worth. It will be objected that, even under these conditions, there will still be conflict between the conquerors and the conquered, and that the latter will never accept defeat except when forced to do so. But this constraint does not resemble the other; they have only their name in common. What really constitutes constraint is the making of conflict itself impossible and refusing to admit the right of combat.

It is true that this perfect spontaneity is never met with anywhere as a realized fact. There is no society where it is unadulterated. If the institution of castes corresponds to the natural apportionment of capacities, it is, however, only in a very proximate and rough and ready manner. Heredity never acts with such precision that, even where it meets with most favorable conditions for its purpose, children can be identical with their parents. There are always exceptions to this rule, and, consequently, cases where the individual is not in harmony with the functions which are attributed to him. These discrepancies become more numerous as society develops, until, one day, the framework becomes too narrow and breaks down. When the regime of castes has lost juridical force, it survives by itself in customs, and, thanks to the persistance of certain prejudices, a certain distinction is attached to some individuals, a certain lack of distinction attached to others, independent of their merits. Finally, even where there remains no vestige of the past, hereditary transmission of wealth is enough to make the external conditions under which the conflict takes place very unequal, for it gives advantages to some which are not necessarily in keeping with their personal worth. Even today among the most cultivated peoples, there are careers which are either totally closed to or very difficult to be entered into by those who are bereft of fortune.

[. . .]

The progressive decline of castes, beginning from the moment the division of labor is established, is an historical law, for, as they are linked to the politico-familial organization, they necessarily regress along with this organization. The prejudices to which they have given rise and which they leave behind do not survive them indefinitely, but slowly become obliterated. Public office is more and more freely open to everybody with no question as to wealth. Finally, even this last inequality, which comes about through birth, though not completely disappearing, is at least somewhat attenuated. Society is forced to reduce this disparity as far as possible by assisting in various ways those who find themselves in a disadvantageous position and by aiding them to overcome it. It thus shows that it feels obliged to leave free space for all merits and that it regards as unjust any inferiority which is not personally merited. But what manifests this tendency even more is the belief, so wide-spread today, that equality among citizens becomes ever greater, and that it is just that this be so. A sentiment so general cannot be a pure illusion, but must express, in confused fashion, some aspect of reality. But as the progress of the division of labor implies, on the contrary, an ever growing inequality, the equality which public conscience thus affirms can only be the one of which we are speaking, that is, equality in the external conditions of conflict.

It is, moreover, easy to understand what makes this leveling process necessary. We have just seen that all external inequality compromises organic solidarity. There is nothing vexatious in this for lower societies where solidarity is assured pre-eminently by the community of beliefs and sentiments. However strained the ties which come from the division of labor, nevertheless, since they are not the ones which most strongly attach the individual to society, social cohesion is not menaced. The uneasiness which results from contrary aspirations is not enough to turn those who harbor them against the social order which is their cause, for they cling to this social order, not because they find in it the necessary field for the development of their occupational activity, but because it contains a multitude of beliefs and practices by which they live.

[. . .]

Then, as the collective conscience becomes weak, the anxieties which are thus produced can no longer be as completely neutralized. Common sentiments no longer have the same force to keep the individual attached to the group under any circumstances. Subversive tendencies, no longer having the same consequences, occur more frequently. More and more losing the transcendent character which placed it in a sphere higher than human interests, social organization no longer has the same force of resistance while it is breaking down. A work wholly human, it can no longer so well oppose human demands. When the flood becomes very violent, the dam which holds it in is broken down. It thus becomes more dangerous. That is why, in organized societies, it is indispensable that the division of labor be more and more in harmony with this ideal of spontaneity that we have just defined.

[. . .]

II

Equality in the external conditions of conflict is not only necessary to attach each individual to his function, but also to link functions to one another.

[. . .]

Chapter 5

Emile Durkheim

THE ELEMENTARY FORMS OF THE RELIGIOUS LIFE

[. . .]

IN A GENERAL WAY, it is unquestionable that a society has all that is necessary to arouse the sensation of the divine in minds, merely by the power that it has over them; for to its members it is what a god is to his worshippers. In fact, a god is, first of all, a being whom men think of as superior to themselves, and upon whom they feel that they depend. Whether it be a conscious personality, such as Zeus or Jahveh, or merely abstract forces such as those in play in totemism, the worshipper, in the one case as in the other, believes himself held to certain manners of acting which are imposed upon him by the nature of the sacred principle with which he feels that he is in communion. Now society also gives us the sensation of a perpetual dependence. Since it has a nature which is peculiar to itself and different from our individual nature, it pursues ends which are likewise special to it; but, as it cannot attain them except through our intermediacy, it imperiously demands our aid. It requires that, forgetful of our own interests, we make ourselves its servitors, and it submits us to every sort of inconvenience, privation and sacrifice, without which social life would be impossible. It is because of this that at every instant we are obliged to submit ourselves to rules of conduct and of thought which we have neither made nor desired, and which are sometimes even contrary to our most fundamental inclinations and instincts.

Even if society were unable to obtain these concessions and sacrifices from us except by a material constraint, it might awaken in us only the idea of a physical force to which we must give way of necessity, instead of that of a moral power such as religions adore. But as a matter of fact, the empire which it holds over consciences is due much less to the physical supremacy of which it has the privilege than to the moral authority with which it is invested. If we yield to its orders, it is not merely because it is strong enough to triumph over our resistance; it is primarily because it is the object of a venerable respect.

We say that an object, whether individual or collective, inspires respect when the representation expressing it in the mind is gifted with such a force that it automatically causes or inhibits actions, *without regard for any consideration relative to their useful or injurious effects*. When we obey somebody because of the moral authority which we recognize in him, we follow out his opinions, not because they seem wise, but because a certain sort of physical energy is imminent in the idea that we form of this person, which conquers our will and inclines it in the indicated direction. Respect is the emotion which we experience when we feel this interior and wholly spiritual pressure operating upon us. Then we are not determined by the advantages or inconveniences of the attitude which is prescribed or recommended to us; it is by the way in which we represent to ourselves the person recommending or prescribing it. This is why commands generally take a short, peremptory form leaving no place for hesitation; it is because, in so far as it is a command and goes by its own force, it excludes all idea of deliberation or calculation; it gets its efficacy from the intensity of the mental state in which it is placed. It is this intensity which creates what is called a moral ascendancy.

[. . .]

But a god is not merely an authority upon whom we depend; it is a force upon which our strength relies. The man who has obeyed his god and who, for this reason, believes the god is with him, approaches the world with confidence and with the feeling of an increased energy. Likewise, social action does not confine itself to demanding sacrifices, privations and efforts from us. For the collective force is not entirely outside of us; it does not act upon us wholly from without; but rather, since society cannot exist except in and through individual consciousnesses,[1] this force must also penetrate us and organize itself within us; it thus becomes an integral part of our being and by that very fact this is elevated and magnified.

There are occasions when this strengthening and vivifying action of society is especially apparent. In the midst of an assembly animated by a common passion, we become susceptible of acts and sentiments of which we are incapable when reduced to our own forces; and when the assembly is dissolved and when, finding ourselves alone again, we fall back to our ordinary level, we are then able to measure the height to which we have been raised above ourselves. History abounds in examples of this sort. It is enough to think of the night of the Fourth of August, 1789, when an assembly was suddenly led to an act of sacrifice and abnegation which each of its members had refused the day before, and at which they were all surprised the day after.[2] This is why all parties, political, economic or confessional, are careful to have periodical reunions where their members may revivify their common faith by manifesting it in common. To strengthen those sentiments which, if left to themselves, would soon weaken, it is sufficient to bring those who hold them together and to put them into closer and more active relations with one another. This is the explanation of the particular attitude of a man speaking to a crowd, at least if he has succeeded in entering into communion with it. His language has a grandiloquence that would be ridiculous in ordinary circumstances; his gestures show a certain domination; his very thought is impatient of all rules, and easily falls into all sorts of excesses. It is because he feels within him an abnormal over-supply of force which overflows and tries to burst out from him; sometimes he even has the feeling that he is dominated by a moral force which is greater than he and of which he is only the interpreter. It is by this trait that we are able to recognize what has often been called the demon of oratorical inspiration. Now this exceptional increase of force is something very real; it comes to him from the very group which he addresses. The sentiments provoked by his words come back to him, but enlarged and amplified, and to this degree they strengthen his own sentiment. The passionate energies he arouses re-echo within him and quicken his vital tone. It is no longer a simple individual who speaks; it is a group incarnate and personified.

Beside these passing and intermittent states, there are other more durable ones, where this strengthening influence of society makes itself felt with greater consequences and frequently even with greater brilliancy. There are periods in history when, under the influence of some great collective shock, social interactions have become much more frequent and active. Men look for each other and assemble together more than ever. That general effervescence results which is characteristic of revolutionary or creative epochs. Now this greater activity results in a general stimulation of individual forces. Men see more and differently now than in normal times. Changes are not merely of shades and degrees; men become different. The passions moving them are of such an intensity that they cannot be satisfied except by violent and unrestrained actions, actions of superhuman heroism or of bloody barbarism. This is what explains the Crusades,[3] for example, or many of the scenes, either sublime or savage, of the French Revolution.[4] Under the influence of the general exaltation, we see the most mediocre and inoffensive bourgeois become either a hero or a butcher.[5] And so clearly are all these mental processes the ones that are also at the root of religion that the individuals themselves have often pictured the pressure before which they thus gave way in a distinctly religious form. The Crusaders believed that they felt God present in the midst of them, enjoining them to go to the conquest of the Holy Land; Joan of Arc believed that she obeyed celestial voices.[6]

[. . .]

Notes

1   Of course this does not mean to say that the collective consciousness does not have distinctive characteristics of its own (on this point, see *Représentations individuelles et représentations collectives*, in *Revue de Métaphysique et de Morale*, 1898, pp. 273 ff.).

2   This is proved by the length and passionate character of the debates where a legal form was given to the resolutions made in a moment of collective enthusiasm. In the clergy as in the nobility, more than one person called this celebrated night the dupe's night, or, with Rivarol, the St. Bartholomew of the estates (see Stoll, *Suggestion und Hypnotismus in der Völkerpsychologie*, 2nd ed., p. 618, n. 2).

3   See Stoll, *op, cit.*, pp. 353 ff

4   *Ibid.*, pp. 619, 635.

5   *Ibid.*, pp. 622 ff.

6   The emotions of fear and sorrow are able to develop similarly and to become intensified under these same conditions. As we shall see, they correspond to quite another aspect of the religious life.

Chapter 6

Georg Simmel

CONFLICT (ON INDIVIDUALITY AND SOCIAL FORMS)

THE SOCIOLOGICAL SIGNIFICANCE of conflict (*Kampf*) has in principle never been disputed. Conflict is admitted to cause or modify interest groups, unifications, organizations. On the other hand, it may sound paradoxical in the common view if one asks whether irrespective of any phenomena that result from conflict or that accompany it, it itself is a form of sociation. At first glance, this sounds like a rhetorical question. If every interaction among men is a sociation, conflict—after all one of the most vivid interactions, which, furthermore, cannot possibly be carried on by one individual alone—must certainly be considered as sociation. And in fact, dissociating factors—hate, envy, need, desire—are the *causes* of conflict; it breaks out because of them. Conflict is thus designed to resolve divergent dualisms; it is a way of achieving some kind of unity, even if it be through the annihilation of one of the conflicting parties. This is roughly parallel to the fact that it is the most violent symptoms of a disease which represent the effort of the organism to free itself of disturbances and damages caused by them.

But this phenomenon means much more than the trivial "si vis pacem para bellum" [if you want peace, prepare for war]; it is something quite general, of which this maxim only describes a special case. Conflict itself resolves the tension between contrasts. The fact that it aims at peace is only one, an especially obvious, expression of its nature: the synthesis of elements that work both against and for one another.

This nature appears more clearly when it is realized that both forms of relation—the antithetical and the convergent—are fundamentally distinguished from the mere indifference of two or more individuals or groups. Whether it implies the rejection or the termination of sociation, indifference is purely negative. In contrast to such pure negativity, conflict contains something positive. Its positive and negative aspects, however, are integrated; they can be separated conceptually, but not empirically.

The sociological relevance of conflict

Social phenomena appear in a new light when seen from the angle of this sociologically positive character of conflict. It is at once evident then that if the relations among men (rather than what the individual is to himself and in his relations to objects) constitute the subject matter of a special science, sociology, then the traditional topics of that science cover only a subdivision of it: it is more comprehensive and is truly defined by a principle. At one time it appeared as if there were only two consistent subject matters of the science of man: the individual unit and the unit of individuals (society); any third seemed logically excluded. In this conception, conflict itself—irrespective of its contributions to these immediate social units—found no place for study. It was a phenomenon of its own, and its subsumption under the concept of unity would have been arbitrary as well as useless, since conflict meant the negation of unity.

A more comprehensive classification of the science of the relations of men should distinguish, it would appear, those relations which constitute a unit, that is, social relations in the strict sense, from those which counteract unity. It must be realized, however, that both relations can usually be found in every historically real situation. The individual does not attain the unity of his personality exclusively by an exhaustive harmonization, according to logical, objective, religious, or ethical norms, of the contents of his personality. On the contrary, contradiction and conflict not only precede this unity but are operative in it at every moment of its existence. Just so, there probably exists no social unit in which convergent and divergent currents among its members are not inseparably interwoven. An absolutely centripetal and harmonious group, a pure "unification" ("*Vereinigung*"), not only is empirically unreal, it could show no real life process. The society of saints which Dante sees in the Rose of Paradise may be like such a group, but it is without any change and development; whereas the holy assembly of Church Fathers in Raphael's *Disputa* shows if not actual conflict, at least a considerable differentiation of moods and directions of thought, whence flow all the vitality and the really organic structure of that group. Just as the universe needs "love and hate," that is, attractive and repulsive forces, in order to have any form at all, so society, too, in order to attain a determinate shape, needs some quantitative ratio of harmony and disharmony, of association and competition, of favorable and unfavorable tendencies. But these discords are by no means mere sociological liabilities or negative instances. Definite, actual society does not result only from other social forces which are positive, and only to the extent that the negative factors do not hinder them. This common conception is quite superficial. Society, as we know it, is the result of both categories of interaction, which thus both manifest themselves as wholly positive.

Unity and discord

There is a misunderstanding according to which one of these two kinds of interaction tears down what the other builds up, and what is eventually left standing is the result of the subtraction of the two (while in reality it must rather be designated as the result of their addition). The misunderstanding probably derives from the twofold meaning of the concept of unity. We designate as "unity" the consensus and concord of interacting individuals, as against their discords, separations, and disharmonies. But we also call "unity" the total group-synthesis of persons, energies, and forms, that is, the ultimate wholeness of that group, a wholeness which covers both strictly-speaking unitary relations and dualistic relations. We thus account for the group phenomenon which we feel to be "unitary" in terms of functional components considered *specifically* unitary; and in so doing, we disregard the other, larger meaning of the term.

This imprecision is increased by the corresponding twofold meaning of "discord" or "opposition." Since discord unfolds its negative, destructive character between particular individuals, we naïvely conclude that it must have the same effect on the total group. In reality, however, something which is negative and damaging between individuals if it is considered in isolation and as aiming in a particular direction, does not necessarily have the same effect within the total relationship of these individuals. For a very different picture emerges when we view the conflict in conjunction with other interactions not affected by it. The negative and dualistic elements play an entirely positive role in this more comprehensive picture, despite the destruction they may work on particular relations. All this is very obvious in the competition of individuals within an economic unit.

Conflict as an integrative force in the group

Here, among the more complex cases, there are two opposite types. First, we have small groups, such as the marital couple, which nevertheless involve an unlimited number of vital relations among their members. A certain amount of discord, inner divergence and outer controversy, is organically tied up with the very elements that ultimately hold the group together; it cannot be separated from the unity of the sociological structure. This is true not only in cases of evident marital failure but also in marriages characterized by a *modus vivendi* which is bearable or at least borne. Such marriages are not "less" marriages by the amount of conflict they contain; rather, out of so many elements, among which there is that inseparable quantity of conflict, they have developed into the definite and characteristic units which they are. Secondly, the positive and integrating role of antagonism is shown in structures which stand out by the sharpness and carefully preserved purity of their social divisions and gradations. Thus, the Hindu social system rests not only on the hierarchy, but also directly on the mutual repulsion, of the castes. Hostilities not only prevent boundaries within the group from gradually disappearing, so that these hostilities are often consciously cultivated to guarantee existing conditions. Beyond this, they also are of direct socio-logical fertility: often they provide classes and individuals with reciprocal positions which they would not find, or not find in the same way, if the causes of hostility were not accompanied by the *feeling* and the expression of hostility—even if the same objective causes of hostility were in operation.

The disappearance of repulsive (and, considered in isolation, destructive) energies does by no means always result in a richer and fuller social life (as the disappearance of liabilities results in larger property) but in as different and unrealizable a phenomenon as if the group were deprived of the forces of cooperation, affection, mutual aid, and harmony of interest. This is not only true for competition generally, which determines the form of the group, the reciprocal positions of its participants, and the distances between them, and which does so purely as a formal matrix of tensions, quite irrespective of its objective *results*. It is true also where the group is based on the attitudes of its members. For instance, the opposition of a member to an associate is no purely negative social factor, if only because such opposition is often the only means for making life with actually unbearable people at least possible. If we did not even have the power and the right to rebel against tyranny, arbitrariness, moodiness, tactlessness, we could not bear to have any relation to people from whose characters we thus suffer. We would feel pushed to take desperate steps—and these, indeed, would end the relation but do *not*, perhaps, constitute "conflict." Not only because of the fact (though it is not essential here) that oppression usually increases if it is suffered calmly and without protest, but also because opposition gives us inner satisfaction, distraction, relief, just as do humility and patience under different psychological conditions. Our opposition makes us feel that we are not completely victims of the circumstances. It allows us to prove our strength consciously and only thus gives vitality and reciprocity to conditions from which, without such corrective, we would withdraw at any cost.

Opposition achieves this aim even where it has no noticeable success, where it does not become manifest but remains purely covert. Yet while it has hardly any practical effect, it may yet achieve an inner balance (sometimes even on the part of *both* partners to the relation), may exert a quieting influence, produce a feeling of virtual power, and thus save relationships whose continuation often puzzles the observer. In such cases, opposition is an element in the relation itself; it is intrinsically interwoven with the other reasons for the relation's existence. It is not only a *means* for preserving the relation but one of the concrete functions which actually constitute it. Where relations are purely external and at the same time of little practical significance, this function can be satisfied by conflict in its *latent* form, that is, by aversion and feelings of mutual alienness and repulsion which upon more intimate contact, no matter how occasioned, immediately change into positive hatred and fight.

Without such aversion, we could not imagine what form modern urban life, which every day brings everybody in contact with innumerable others, might possibly take. The whole inner organization of urban interaction is based on an extremely complex hierarchy of sympathies, indifferences, and aversions of both the most short-lived and the most enduring kind. And in this complex, the sphere of indifference is relatively limited. Our psychological activity responds to almost every impression that comes from another person with a certain determinate feeling. The subconscious, fleeting, changeful nature of this feeling only *seems* to reduce it to indifference. Actually, such indifference would be as unnatural to us as the vague character of innumerable contradictory stimuli would be unbearable. We are protected against both of these typical dangers of the city by antipathy, which is the preparatory phase of concrete antagonism and which engenders the distances and aversions without which we could not lead the urban life at all. The extent and combination of antipathy, the rhythm of its appearance and disappearance, the forms in which it is satisfied, all these, along with the more literally unifying elements, produce the metropolitan form of life in its irresolvable totality; and what at first glance appears in it as dissociation, actually is one of its elementary forms of association.

Chapter 7

Gustave Le Bon

THE CROWD

Introduction: the era of crowds

THE GREAT UPHEAVALS which precede changes of civilisation, such as
the fall of the Roman Empire and the foundation of the Arabian Empire, seem at
first sight determined more especially by political transformations, foreign invasion,
or the overthrow of dynasties. But a more attentive study of these events shows that
behind their apparent causes the real cause is generally seen to be a profound modification in the ideas of the peoples. The true historical upheavals are not those which
astonish us by their grandeur and violence. The only important changes whence the
renewal of civilisations results, affect ideas, conceptions, and beliefs. The memorable
events of history are the visible effects of the invisible changes of human thought.
The reason these great events are so rare is that, there is nothing so stable in a race as
the inherited groundwork of its thoughts.

The present epoch is one of these critical moments in which the thought of
mankind is undergoing a process of transformation.

Two fundamental factors are at the base of this transformation. The first is the
destruction of those religious, political, and social beliefs in which all the elements
of our civilisation are rooted. The second is the creation of entirely new conditions of
existence and thought as the result of modern scientific and industrial discoveries.

The ideas of the past, although half destroyed, being still very powerful, and the
ideas which are to replace them being still in process of formation, the modern age
represents a period of transition and anarchy.

It is not easy to say as yet what will one day be evolved from this necessarily somewhat chaotic period. What will be the fundamental ideas on which the societies that are
to succeed our own will be built up? We do not at present know. Still it is already clear

that on whatever lines the societies of the future are organised, they will have to count with a new power, with the last surviving sovereign force of modern times, the power of crowds. On the ruins of so many ideas formerly considered beyond discussion, and to-day decayed or decaying, of so many sources of authority that successive revolutions have destroyed, this power, which alone has arisen in their stead, seems soon destined to absorb the others. While all our ancient beliefs are tottering and disappearing, while the old pillars of society are giving way one by one, the power of the crowd is the only force that nothing menaces, and of which the prestige is continually on the increase. The age we are about to enter will in truth be the ERA OF CROWDS.

Scarcely a century ago the traditional policy of European States and the rivalries of sovereigns were the principal factors that shaped events. The opinion of the masses scarcely counted, and most frequently indeed did not count at all. Today it is the traditions which used to obtain in politics, and the individual tendencies and rivalries of rulers which do not count; while, on the contrary, the voice of the masses has become preponderant. It is this voice that dictates their conduct to kings, whose endeavour is to take note of its utterances. The destinies of nations are elaborated at present in the heart of the masses, and no longer in the councils of princes.

The entry of the popular classes into political life—that is to say, in reality, their progressive transformation into governing classes—is one of the most striking characteristics of our epoch of transition. The introduction of universal suffrage, which exercised for a long time but little influence, is not, as might be thought, the distinguishing feature of this transference of political power. The progressive growth of the power of the masses took place at first by the propagation of certain ideas, which have slowly implanted themselves in men's minds, and afterwards by the gradual association of individuals bent on bringing about the realisation of theoretical conceptions. It is by association that crowds have come to procure ideas with respect to their interests which are very clearly defined if not particularly just, and have arrived at a consciousness of their strength. The masses are founding syndicates before which the authorities capitulate one after the other; they are also founding labour unions, which in spite of all economic laws tend to regulate the conditions of labour and wages. They return to assemblies in which the Government is vested, representatives utterly lacking initiative and independence, and reduced most often to nothing else than the spokesmen of the committees that have chosen them.

Today the claims of the masses are becoming more and more sharply defined, and amount to nothing less than a determination to utterly destroy society as it now exists, with a view to making it hark back to that primitive communism which was the normal condition of all human groups before the dawn of civilisation. Limitations of the hours of labour, the nationalisation of mines, railways, factories, and the soil, the equal distribution of all products, the elimination of all the upper classes for the benefit of the popular classes, etc., such are these claims.

Little adapted to reasoning, crowds, on the contrary, are quick to act. As the result of their present organisation their strength has become immense. The dogmas whose birth we are witnessing will soon have the force of the old dogmas; that is to say, the tyrannical and sovereign force of being above discussion. The divine right of the masses is about to replace the divine right of kings.

[. . .]

The mind of crowds: Chapter I

General characteristics of crowds—psychological law of their mental unity

In its ordinary sense the word "crowd" means a gathering of individuals of whatever nationality, profession, or sex, and whatever be the chances that have brought them together. From the psychological point of view the expression "crowd" assumes quite a different signification. Under certain given circumstances, and only under those circumstances, an agglomeration of men presents new characteristics very different from those of the individuals composing it. The sentiments and ideas of all the persons in the gathering take one and the same direction, and their conscious personality vanishes. A collective mind is formed, doubtless transitory, but presenting very clearly defined characteristics. The gathering has thus become what, in the absence of a better expression, I will call an organised crowd, or, if the term is considered preferable, a psychological crowd. It forms a single being, and is subjected to the *law of the mental unity of crowds*.

It is evident that it is not by the mere fact of a number of individuals finding themselves accidentally side by side that they acquire the character of an organised crowd. A thousand individuals accidentally gathered in a public place without any determined object in no way constitute a crowd from the psychological point of view. To acquire the special characteristics of such a crowd, the influence is necessary of certain predisposing causes of which we shall have to determine the nature.

The disappearance of conscious personality and the turning of feelings and thoughts in a different direction, which are the primary characteristics of a crowd about to become organised, do not always involve the simultaneous presence of a number of individuals on one spot. Thousands of isolated individuals may acquire at certain moments, and under the influence of certain violent emotions—such, for example, as a great national event—the characteristics of a psychological crowd. It will be sufficient in that case that a mere chance should bring them together for their acts to at once assume the characteristics peculiar to the acts of a crowd. At certain moments half a dozen men might constitute a psychological crowd, which may not happen in the case of hundreds of men gathered together by accident. On the other hand, an entire nation, though there may be no visible agglomeration, may become a crowd under the action of certain influences.

[. . .]

Among the psychological characteristics of crowds there are some that they may present in common with isolated individuals, and others, on the contrary, which are absolutely peculiar to them and are only to be met with in collectivities. It is those special characteristics that we shall study, first of all, in order to show their importance.

The most striking peculiarity presented by a psychological crowd is the following: Whoever be the individuals that compose it, however like or unlike be their mode of life, their occupations, their character, or their intelligence, the fact that they have been transformed into a crowd puts them in possession of a sort of collective mind which makes them feel, think, and act in a manner quite different from that in which each individual of them would feel, think, and act were he in a state of isolation.

There are certain ideas and feelings which do not come into being, or do not transform themselves into acts except in the case of individuals forming a crowd. The psychological crowd is a provisional being formed of heterogeneous elements, which for a moment are combined, exactly as the cells which constitute a living body form by their reunion a new being which displays characteristics very different from those possessed by each of the cells singly.

Contrary to an opinion which one is astonished to find coming from the pen of so acute a philosopher as Herbert Spencer, in the aggregate which constitutes a crowd there is in no sort a summing-up of or an average struck between its elements. What really takes place is a combination followed by the creation of new characteristics, just as in chemistry certain elements, when brought into contact—bases and acids, for example—combine to form a new body possessing properties quite different from those of the bodies that have served to form it.

It is easy to prove how much the individual forming part of a crowd differs from the isolated individual, but it is less easy to discover the causes of this difference.

To obtain at any rate a glimpse of them it is necessary in the first place to call to mind the truth established by modern psychology, that unconscious phenomena play an altogether preponderating part not only in organic life, but also in the operations of the intelligence. The conscious life of the mind is of small importance in comparison with its unconscious life. The most subtle analyst, the most acute observer, is scarcely successful in discovering more than a very small number of the unconscious motives that determine his conduct. Our conscious acts are the outcome of an unconscious substratum created in the mind in the main by hereditary influences. This substratum consists of the innumerable common characteristics handed down from generation to generation, which constitute the genius of a race. Behind the avowed causes of our acts there undoubtedly lie secret causes that we do not avow, but behind these secret causes there are many others more secret still which we ourselves ignore. The greater part of our daily actions are the result of hidden motives which escape our observation.

It is more especially with respect to those unconscious elements which constitute the genius of a race that all the individuals belonging to it resemble each other, while it is principally in respect to the conscious elements of their character—the fruit of education, and yet more of exceptional hereditary conditions—that they differ from each other. Men the most unlike in the matter of their intelligence possess instincts, passions, and feelings that are very similar. In the case of everything that belongs to the realm of sentiment—religion, politics, morality, the affections and antipathies, etc.— the most eminent men seldom surpass the standard of the most ordinary individuals. From the intellectual point of view an abyss may exist between a great mathematician and his bootmaker, but from the point of view of character the difference is most often slight or non-existent.

It is precisely these general qualities of character, governed by forces of which we are unconscious, and possessed by the majority of the normal individuals of a race in much the same degree—it is precisely these qualities, I say, that in crowds become common property. In the collective mind the intellectual aptitudes of the individuals, and in consequence their individuality, are weakened. The heterogeneous is swamped by the homogeneous, and the unconscious qualities obtain the upper hand.

This very fact that crowds possess in common ordinary qualities explains why they can never accomplish acts demanding a high degree of intelligence. The decisions affecting matters of general interest come to by an assembly of men of distinction, but specialists in different walks of life, are not sensibly superior to the decisions that would be adopted by a gathering of imbeciles. The truth is, they can only bring to bear in common on the work in hand those mediocre qualities which are the birthright of every average individual. In crowds it is stupidity and not mother-wit that is accumulated. It is not all the world, as is so often repeated, that has more wit than Voltaire, but assuredly Voltaire that has more wit than all the world, if by "all the world" crowds are to be understood.

If the individuals of a crowd confined themselves to putting in common the ordinary qualities of which each of them has his share, there would merely result the striking of an average, and not, as we have said is actually the case, the creation of new characteristics. How is it that these new characteristics are created? This is what we are now to investigate.

Different causes determine the appearance of these characteristics peculiar to crowds, and not possessed by isolated individuals. The first is that the individual forming part of a crowd acquires, solely from numerical considerations, a sentiment of invincible power which allows him to yield to instincts which, had he been alone, he would perforce have kept under restraint. He will be the less disposed to check himself from the consideration that, a crowd being anonymous, and in consequence irresponsible, the sentiment of responsibility which always controls individuals disappears entirely.

The second cause, which is contagion, also intervenes to determine the manifestation in crowds of their special characteristics, and at the same time the trend they are to take. Contagion is a phenomenon of which it is easy to establish the presence, but that it is not easy to explain. It must be classed among those phenomena of a hypnotic order, which we shall shortly study. In a crowd every sentiment and act is contagious, and contagious to such a degree that an individual readily sacrifices his personal interest to the collective interest. This is an aptitude very contrary to his nature, and of which a man is scarcely capable, except when he makes part of a crowd.

A third cause, and by far the most important, determines in the individuals of a crowd special characteristics which are quite contrary at times to those presented by the isolated individual. I allude to that suggestibility of which, moreover, the contagion mentioned above is neither more nor less than an effect.

To understand this phenomenon it is necessary to bear in mind certain recent physiological discoveries. We know to-day that by various processes an individual may be brought into such a condition that, having entirely lost his conscious personality, he obeys all the suggestions of the operator who has deprived him of it, and commits acts in utter contradiction with his character and habits. The most careful observations seem to prove that an individual immerged for some length of time in a crowd in action soon finds himself—either in consequence of the magnetic influence given out by the crowd, or from some other cause of which we are ignorant—in a special state, which much resembles the state of fascination in which the hypnotised individual finds himself in the hands of the hypnotiser. The activity of the brain being paralysed in the case of the hypnotised subject, the latter becomes the slave of all the unconscious activities of his spinal cord, which the hypnotiser directs at will. The conscious personality has entirely vanished; will and discernment are lost. All feelings and thoughts are bent in the direction determined by the hypnotiser.

Such also is approximately the state of the individual forming part of a psychological crowd. He is no longer conscious of his acts. In his case, as in the case of the hypnotised subject, at the same time that certain faculties are destroyed, others may be brought to a high degree of exaltation. Under the influence of a suggestion, he will undertake the accomplishment of certain acts with irresistible impetuosity. This impetuosity is the more irresistible in the case of crowds than in that of the hypnotised subject, from the fact that, the suggestion being the same for all the individuals of the crowd, it gains in strength by reciprocity. The individualities in the crowd who might possess a personality sufficiently strong to resist the suggestion are too few in number to struggle against the current. At the utmost, they may be able to attempt a diversion by means of different suggestions. It is in this way, for instance, that a happy expression, an image opportunely evoked, have occasionally deterred crowds from the most bloodthirsty acts.

We see, then, that the disappearance of the conscious personality, the predominance of the unconscious personality, the turning by means of suggestion and contagion of feelings and ideas in an identical direction, the tendency to immediately transform the suggested ideas into acts; these, we see, are the principal characteristics of the individual forming part of a crowd. He is no longer himself, but has become an automaton who has ceased to be guided by his will.

Moreover, by the mere fact that he forms part of an organised crowd, a man descends several rungs in the ladder of civilisation. Isolated, he may be a cultivated individual; in a crowd, he is a barbarian—that is, a creature acting by instinct. He possesses the spontaneity, the violence, the ferocity, and also the enthusiasm and heroism of primitive beings, whom he further tends to resemble by the facility with which he allows himself to be impressed by words and image—which would be entirely without action on each of the isolated individuals composing the crowd—and to be induced to commit acts contrary to his most obvious interests and his best-known habits. An individual in a crowd is a grain of sand amid other grains of sand, which the wind stirs up at will.

It is for these reasons that juries are seen to deliver verdicts of which each individual juror would disapprove, that parliamentary assemblies adopt laws and measures of which each of their members would disapprove in his own person. Taken separately, the men of the Convention were enlightened citizens of peaceful habits. United in a crowd, they did not hesitate to give their adhesion to the most savage proposals, to guillotine individuals most clearly innocent, and, contrary to their interests, to renounce their inviolability and to decimate themselves.

[. . .]

PART TWO

Hegemony and collective behaviour

SOME OF THE TEXTS COMPOSING this part offer clear examples of how social change is achieved through conflicts leading to the establishment of hegemonic social formations. In this respect it is useful to start from the formulation of social action proposed by Max Weber, according to whom action is 'social' insofar as individuals attach a subjective meaning to their behaviour while taking account of the behaviour of others. In his classical typology, *instrumentally rational* action is determined by expectations and calculated ends, *value-rational* action is generated by the belief in values for their own sake, *affective action* is the result of emotions, and *traditional action* of ingrained habits (Weber, 1968).

Max Weber's work *The City* (1921) focuses on the tensions and conflicting interests characterising the urban environment; without ever using the expression 'social movements', the author nevertheless analyses the social forces engaged in promoting transformation. In describing the patrician dominion in Venice, for example, Weber notes the long struggle between the nobility and the 'doge', who was supported by the Byzantine Empire and a large number of Eastern vassals. The nobility, however, thanks to an alliance formed with the artisans, was able to acquire some power so that 'the doge was formally demoted to the status of a salaried official'. Patricians in other Italian Communes are also described as constantly engaged in struggles for the control of resources and political influence. Finally, the notion of conflict receives specific analysis with the emergence of the 'popolo' as a revolutionary association: after the revolt of the Ciompi in Florence in 1378, groups of artisans not belonging to any official guild obtained a temporary share in government. The second extract, from *Economy and Society* (1922), exemplifies Weber's approach to the notions of class and status. Here, the emphasis is on class situation as ultimately 'market situation', and 'communal action' as a result of class interest.

Weber's texts presented below do not dwell on how culture, as a self-generating force, drives individuals and groups to action providing them with an orientation in the pursuit of their interests. The texts, therefore, should be read with a mind to other works in which the author illustrates how moral and metaphysical values forge material social models (Weber, 1930). Actors do not simply aim at maximising their advantages or satisfying their wants, while minimising losses or reducing their discomfort. Rather, they give meaning to their existence by embracing moral values and expressing passion (Cohen, 2000). Values add a degree of order to interest-led action. This process entails a first stage in which actors define themselves and the meaning of their behaviour, and to a degree they orient the behaviour of others. At a second stage, relationships are established whereby groups of actors orient the meaning of their collective action and of their shared values towards mutually beneficial ends. In this way, groups slowly acquire norms of conduct, prefigure a social system and forge its ethical content as well as its practical functioning. That system will achieve a form of legitimacy 'to the extent that at least some actors believe themselves to be duty-bound, emotionally compelled, or morally committed to follow its norms or rules' (ibid: 78).

Echoes of this process can be found in Gramsci's original and surprisingly enduring analysis of social change through the notion of hegemony. This notion links well with sociological work dealing specifically with how social change is brought by collective action. In the first extract, 'Notes on Italian History' (1935), Gramsci remarks that the unity of the ruling classes is realised in the State. Similarly, he suggests, the subaltern classes will be unable to unite until they are able to become a 'State', which can be achieved through the formulation of claims, the establishment of organisations or the affirmation of autonomous political programmes. As a case-study the author presents a brief history of the Action Party and its role in the process leading to the unification of Italy. Here, Gramsci provides a concrete example of how intellectual, moral and political hegemony, rather than pure material force, can bring social change. In the second extract, 'The Modern Prince' (1933), his analysis moves on to describe the characteristics of a political party, an organism which expresses a collective will. After clarifying that parties may exert their influence in an indirect way, for example, promoting and supporting general views rather than specific political ideas, he identifies the fundamental elements allowing a party to exist. His analysis is addressed to the formation of a new party supported by the subaltern classes producing social change.

The contributions by Weber and Gramsci reveal their contemporary value when examined in parallel with recent formulations by social movement theorists. For example, social movements can be interpreted as agents of change, within the city or within state institutions, when they target urban or institutional space and use them as resources for political mobilisation (Tonkiss, 2005). In the city as well as in state institutions, one way of measuring the success of social movements is to observe the space they occupy and control, through a physical but also a culturally hegemonic presence.

The other texts included in this part are important classics in which the concepts of social movement and collective behaviour are addressed within broader sociological discussions and analysis. Herbert Blumer's 'Social Movements' (1946) is a pioneering classification of general, specific and expressive social movements and of their respective characteristics. In a sense, Blumer's work on social movements fills a lacuna in the studies conducted by his colleagues of the Chicago school of sociology. While most of the research produced by this group of scholars hinges on excluded communities, deviant groups and dysfunctional enclaves, Blumer offers a theoretical framework which may explain how exclusion and marginalisation may be turned into collective efforts to generate social change. His work is better understood when located within the symbolic interactionist tradition established by Herbert Mead (1934). This tradition is concerned with how individuals develop an understanding of one another, establish a communicative relationship and adopt a specific role in that relationship. Mead noted that, through gestures and words, persons assume the attitude of their interlocutors, as well as calling out that attitude in them. In brief, human communication implies taking the role of the other person while being influenced by him or her. Mead's analysis has a particular significance in that it designates a structure of communicative relations between subjects that transcends the opposition between action determined by objective conditions and action resulting from individual choice (Joas, 1985). Against 'theories of imitation', Mead posits that the central character of social conduct is not 'that one individual does what others do, but that one's conduct stimulates others to perform a certain act, and that this act, again, becomes a stimulus to a certain reaction, and so on in ceaseless interaction' (Ruggiero, 2006: 109).

Blumer (1969) follows Mead in assuming that agents take on the role of the other in a way that makes them govern and guide their own conduct. Such conduct, however, may at times challenge social norms, values and institutions: in his view, while most sociologists study the social order and its constituents, sociologists of social movements study the ways in which a new social order comes into existence. Social movements are triggered by 'strains' related to expectations, and his concern is that such strains may give rise to social unrest (Crossley, 2002).

Blumer is criticised for 'his almost exclusively social psychological focus' and because his analysis of collective behaviour does not consider the context in which agents mobilise (ibid: 35). Kornhauser's text *The Politics of Mass Society* (1959) seems to us to be a better target for this type of criticism. The extract we present below focuses on mass behaviour, which in his view exhibits a number of characteristics. First, mass behaviour is said to address issues far removed from the personal experience and daily life of those involved. For this reason, it shows a limited sense of reality and responsibility. Second, mass behaviour adopts a direct mode of response to remote objects, and may employ various more or less coercive measures against those individuals and groups who resist them. Third, mass behaviour tends to be highly unstable and unpredictable. Fourth, it can become organised, thus acquiring a certain continuity shaping it into a mass movement. But continuity, commitment and long-term affiliation to a movement may be linked to practical, involuntary or otherwise, concerns and habits. Research conducted by Kornhauser (1962) on leaders of social movements attempted to reply to questions such as: why do some leaders continue to commit themselves even when evidence clearly shows that their political activity is going to be fruitless? Conversely, why do other leaders abandon the move-ment? His findings can be summarised in the following fashion: leaders remain in their position when their social relations are limited to the participants in the movement they lead, or when their income is mainly generated by their political activity. In short, the initial ideological motivations guiding movements and their leaders may wither away, but movements may carry on as they provide the only sources of socialisation and material support for participants and leaders alike. As for party leaders, 'the process of abandoning party positions and roles begins when commitments erode – when, for example, they have financial needs not met by the party and they take jobs unrelated to party role, or when they establish relations to persons not party members' (Stryker, 2000: 31).

Although Kornhauser, in the extract we propose below, also deals with the labour movement, which 'seeks to change only limited and specific aspects' of society in a 'constitutional manner', his main concern is addressed to 'totalitarian' movements and political activism, which threaten democracy with extreme forms of opposition. It has to be noted that a similar concern inspired Talcott Parsons' (1969) essay on the sociological aspects of fascist movements, although his emphasis was placed less on collective psychological dynamics than on 'the uneven effects of industrialisation, democratisation and cultural change on various social groups' (Eyerman and Jamison, 1991: 12).

Finally, from Neil's Smelser's *Theory of Collective Behaviour* (1962) we propose his typology of norm-oriented and value-oriented movements. Smelser follows in Parsons's footstep by rooting the emergence of collective action in spontaneous or planned responses to structural strains in society. Strain may stem from established cleavages which amount to social differentiation, and inevitably produce identity and at times resentment. Religious, but also ethnic, national, tribal and religious divisions are examples of such cleavages, which include division based on unequal allocation of wealth, prestige and power. Besides these established cleavages, hostility can emerge from divisions created by social movements themselves, which divide society into opposing camps, each defining the other as responsible for a variety of evils. Smelser implies that, while established cleavages are always conducive to hostility, due to their possessing long-term, well-functioning channels of expression and communication, new cleavages 'created' by social movements develop such channels only because agencies responsible for maintaining social order are unable, being weak, archaic or ineffective, to prevent the growth of hostility. It could be argued, on the contrary, that such channels, given the constant growth of communication networks, are increasingly available to all new and old movements, and that preventing some of these movements from accessing them could intensify rather than defuse hostility. Spread of beliefs, according to Smelser, is crucial for the development of social movements, and his emphasis is on communication preparing people for action through informal exchange of views or through organised propaganda and agitation. What is important in his view is not so much the power of images and beliefs exchanged, as the effectiveness of the established communication machinery utilised. This machinery will contribute to the actual mobilisation and organisation of conflictual outbursts, particularly when an efficacious and recognised leadership is provided. Contrary to Smelser's analysis, social movements may develop less thanks to highly motivated and daring leaders that to fractions of well-organised networks which act as informal and decentralised leaders of already aggrieved groups. We shall see later, in this respect, recent analyses of networks in social movement studies.

Smelser's theory of collective behaviour, particularly focused on strain, may leave little space to the variable 'agency', thus implying that structural variables are predominant in determining the emergence and development of collective action. His merit, however, consists in moving attention away from behaviour aimed at maintaining and reproducing social order onto non- or anti-institutional action. He is concerned with removing from collective action the stigma 'of being basically patho-logical and irrational, which is how it had been characterised by theories of mass psychology' (Joas, 1996:205). His related concern, however, seems to be of a political nature. The author is aware that discussions of social movements are distorted by polemics, hence his attempt to scientifically delineate types of events and the beliefs inspiring them. Riots and revolutions, he stresses, may be surprising, but they occur with regularity: they cluster in time and in certain cultural areas, they occur with more frequency among certain social groupings. 'This skewing in time and space invites explanation'. His effort, therefore, is addressed to reducing the indeterminacy that lingers in explanations of collective outbursts.

This section groups authors who could be characterised as 'breakdown theorists', in that they all (like Le Bon in the previous section) appear to see social movements as the effect of the breakdown of social arrangements and bonds, determined by, or aimed at producing, social change. A number of key concepts connote these theorists: strain, stress, mass society, emotion, irrationality, contagion, alienation, frustration and relative deprivation (Klandermans, 1997). Readers will find out by themselves whether the differences between the approaches presented below outweigh the similarities among them.

References

Blumer, H. (1968), *Symbolic Interactionism: Perspective and Method*, Berkeley: University of California Press.

Cohen, I.J. (2000), 'Theories of Action and Praxis', in Turner, B.S. (ed), *The Blackwell Companion to Social Theory*, Oxford: Blackwell.

Crossley, N. (2002), *Making Sense of Social Movements*, Buckingham: Open University Press.

Eyerman, R. and Jamison, A. (1991), *Social Movements: A Cognitive Approach*, Cambridge: Polity Press.

Joas, H. (1985), *G.H Mead: A Contemporary Re-Examination of his Thought*, Cambridge: Polity Press.

Joas, H. (1996), *The Creativity of Action*, Cambridge: Polity Press.

Klandermans, B. (1997), *The Social Psychology of Protest*, Oxford: Blackwell.

Kornhauser, W. (1962), 'Social Bases of Political Commitment: A Study of Liberals and Radicals', in Rose, A.M. (ed), *Human Behaviour and Social Process*, Boston: Houghton Mifflin.

Mead, H. (1934), *Mind, Self and Society*, Chicago: University of Chicago Press.

Parsons, T. (1969), *Politics and Social Structure*, New York: Free Press.

Ruggiero, V. (2006), *Understanding Political Violence*, Maidenhead/New York: Open University Press/McGraw-Hill.

Stryker, S. (2000), 'Identity Competition: Key to Differential Social Movement Participation?', in Stryker, S., Owens, T.J. and White, R.W. (eds), *Self, Identity and Social Movements*, Minneapolis: University of Minnesota Press.

Tonkiss, F. (2005), *Space, the City and Social Theory*, Cambridge: Polity Press.
Weber, M. (1930), *The Protestant Ethic and the Spirit of Capitalism*, London: Allen & Unwin.
Weber, M. (1968 [1922]), *Economy and Society*, New York: Bedminster Press.

Chapter 8

Max Weber

THE CITY

Monopolistically closed patrician dominion in Venice

THE DEVELOPMENT OF VENICE was initially determined by an increasing localization produced by the liturgical character of late Roman and Byzantine public economy. The policy also led to a localization of the recruitment of soldiers, beginning in Hadrian's reign. The soldiers of local garrisons were increasingly recruited from the resident population. In practice such soldiers were furnished by the estate owners out of their dependents *(coloni)*. The *tribunes* as commanders of the *numerus* were subordinates of the *dux*. The tribunate was a formal liturgical duty but simultaneously a privilege of the local estate-owning families from the circles of which they were supplied. The honor was in fact hereditary in certain families, while until the eighth century the *dux* was appointed by the Byzantine Empire.

It may be seen that families supplying *tribunes* constituted a military nobility. This military nobility formed the core of the oldest urban patriciate. With the decline of the money economy of the Mediterranian area and increasing militarization of the Byzantine Empire, the power of the tribunal nobility replaced that of the Roman *curia* and *defensores*. In a manner similar throughout Italy, the first revolution (726) which led Venice toward city formation was directed against the current iconoclastic government and its officials. The permanent victory won by this first revolutionary wave was the right of election of the *dux* by the tribunal nobility and the clergy. Soon after-wards the struggle began of the doge[1] with his adversaries: the nobility and patriarch.

The conflict was to last for three centuries during which time the doge attempted to establish a hereditary patrimonial city-kingdom. Both the nobility and the patriarch opposed his "taking ways" *("eigenkirchliche" Tendenzen)*, his attempt to consolidate power in his own hands.

However, the doge was supported by the empires of East and West. The acceptance of the son of the doge as co-regent, a device quite in accord with antique tradition, to disguise hereditary appropriation of the position, was favored by the Byzantine Empire. The dowry of Waldrada, niece of the German emperor, afforded the last *Candiano*[2] the means to enlarge the number of his foreign vassals and at the same time to augment the personal bodyguard upon which since 812 the regime of the doge was based. The thoroughly urban and at the same time royal patrimonial character of the rule of the doge stands out at the time in sharp relief.

The doge was simultaneously lord of a large manor and a great merchant; he monopolized the mail dispatch between the Orient and the Occident which passed through Venice; after 960 he also monopolized the slave trade because of the clerical censorship imposed on it. The doge dismissed and appointed patriarchs, abbots, and priests despite the protest of the church. He was head of jurisdiction, although restricted by the confederate principle of the *Ding*[3] which penetrated into Venice under Franconcian influence.

Still the doge as judicial superior was able to appoint judges and annul contestable verdicts. He conducted the administration through court officials and vassals and, in part, through the aid of the church. The help of the church was particularly desired by the doge as an instrument in Venetian foreign policy. The doge not only had disposition over his domain through nomination of a co-regent but in one case he also had disposition in his will over court property which was not separated from public property. He equipped the fleet out of his private means, entertained troops of soldiers, and disposed over villein labor which artisans owed the *Palatium*.[4] He even arbitrarily increased villein service at times, clearly, however, as a last resort due to growing pressures of foreign policy. That this was going a step too far is shown by the victorious revolt it occasioned in 1032.

The artisans' revolt against the doge in turn played into the hands of the nobility which was ever alert to opportunities to break down the power of the doge. As is always the case under conditions of military self-equipment, the doge was superior to every individual family and to most groups of families, but he was not superior to an alliance of them all. At the time, as today, the alliance held the last word. Thus, as soon as the doge approached the clans with increased financial demands he touched an interest sufficiently basic to bring the alliance about.

Thus the reign of the urban nobility residing in the *Rialto* began under rather democratic legal forms. Its first step was the prohibition of appointment of the doge's son as co-regent. Such a blow at hereditariness (as in Rome) might well have been described as the "first principle of the Republic." After an ambiguous ("standestaatliches") interim period during which rights and duties were distributed between the doge and the commune, as elsewhere between the sovereign and feudal lords, the terms of the elections settled the issue. The doge was formally demoted to the status of a salaried official, strictly controlled by restrictive formalities. His social position became one of *primus inter pares* in the corporation of noblemen. It is correctly observed by Lenel[5] that the power position of the doge which was formerly supported by his foreign contacts, was restricted by the new foreign policy. The Council of Sapientes (as indicated by events in 1141) gathered foreign policy into its own hands.

[. . .]

Patrician development in other Italian communes

[. . .]

The need for external closure and internal pacification of the nobility was not felt with the same intensity outside Venice. Nowhere else was the monopolization of trans-oceanic commercial opportunities so critically central to the very existence of the nobility as a whole as well as to the economic standing of the individual noble. As a consequence of feuds raging everywhere within the ranks of the patriciate even in the period of their unbroken rule the nobility was forced to grant consideration to the remaining strata outside the dignitaries. Furthermore the feuds between the families and deep mutual distrust of the large clans for each other excluded the creation of a rational administrative structure in the Venetian manner.

Thus, for centuries in other communes families which were especially wealthy in land and clientele confronted each other with alliances of numerous less wealthy families. Such "parties" attempted to exclude the opposing families and their allies from the offices and economic opportunities of the city administration. When possible they excluded their rivals from the city.

[. . .]

The revolutionary nature of the "popolo" as a political association

The manner in which the rule of patrician families was shattered shows strong parallels in the Middle Ages and Antiquity. These parallels are especially close if the large Italian cities are taken as characteristic for the Middle Ages, where the destruction of the patriciate was a development flowing from its own intrinsic nature—that is, it occurred without the interference of non-urban powers. In Italian cities after the origin of the *podesta* the next decisive stage in urban development was the emergence of the *popolo*.

Like the German guilds the *popolo* was economically composed of varied elements ranging from artisans to entrepreneurs. Initially the entrepreneurs led the fight against the noble families. While the entrepreneurs created and financed the sworn fraternities against the nobility the artisans' guilds provided the necessary manpower for battle. Once the revolution had succeeded the guild often established its own representative at the head of the commune to consolidate its gains. After the recalcitrant nobility had been exiled, Zürich (in 1335) was ruled by the knight Rudolf Brun and a council consisting of equal representatives of the remaining knights and constables, guilds of entrepreneurs, salt and cloth merchants, goldsmiths, and small tradesmen. The burghers of Zürich had consolidated into so solid a unity that they were able to withstand the siege of the Imperial Army.

In Germany the sworn confederation of guildsmen was ordinarily a temporary phenomenon. The city constitution was either transformed by the reception of the guild representatives into the council or by the absorption of the burghers including the nobility into the guild. The sworn confederation assumed permanent guild form only in some cities of Lower Germany and the Baltic region. However, even here it was of secondary importance compared to the professional association as shown by the composition of its board which was made up of the guild masters of separate associations. In Münster in the fifteenth century no one could be imprisoned without approval of the guild. The guild could, thus, function as a protective association against legal actions of the council. Furthermore, the council was assisted administratively by guild representatives either in all or in important matters. Nothing could be accomplished without consulting them. The protective association was comparatively more powerful in Italy than in the North.

Distribution of power among the social classes of the medieval Italian city

The Italian *popolo* was a political as well as an economic phenomenon. As a political sub-community it had its own official, finances, and military organization. In the truest sense it was a state within a state. At first it was a conscious, illegitimate, and revolutionary political association. It formed to counteract the presence of a settlement of families in the cities forming an urban nobility and practicing the knightly style of life based on an extensive development of economic and political power. The association of the *popolo* opposing them rested on the fraternization of professional associations (*arti* or *paratici*).

The *popolo* took form in a number of places at approximately the same time; Milano, 1198; Lucca, 1203; Lodi, 1206; Pavia, 1208; Siena, 1210; Verona, 1227; Bologna, 1228.

[. . .]

With the full success of the *popolo*, formally the nobility had only negative privileges, the offices of the commune were open to the populace; the offices of the *popolo* were not reciprocally open to the nobility. If insulted by the nobility, the populace was privileged in law suits. At times only the decisions of the *popolo* concerned the entire citizenry. Often the nobility was explicitly excluded from participation in communal administration either temporarily or permanently.

[. . .]

The basic social effect of the rise of the *popolo* was the fusion of resident urban families with the *popolo grasso*—strata distinguished by possession of university education or capital wealth. "*Popolo grasso*" was the name given the seven high ranking guilds embracing; judges, notaries, bankers, merchants of foreign cloth, merchants of Florentine woolens, silk-merchants, doctors, merchants of spices, and merchants of furs. Originally all officials of the city had to be elected from these groups into which, in the time of democratic crisis, the nobles entered. Eventually, after several additional revolutions the fourteen *arti minori* of the *popolo minuto* (small tradesmen) obtained some access to power. After the revolt of the *Ciompi* in 1378, artisan strata not belonging to the fourteen guilds obtained a temporary share in government. They did so as an independent guild association.

[. . .]

Notes

1   The change of name of the commune head from dux to doge marks the movement from Imperial Rome to the Middle Ages.
2   Doge Pietro Candiano IV (959–976).
3   Actually Dinggenossenschaft—The community as the whole group of legal associates.
4   The Palatine Hill in Rome on which Augustus had his house.
5   Walter Lenel, *Die Entstebung der Vorberschaft Venedigs an der Adria* (Strassburg: 1897) and *Venezianisch-Istrische Studien* (Strassburg: Trübner, 1911).

Chapter 9

Max Weber

CLASS, STATUS, PARTY

Determination of class-situation by market-situation

IN OUR TERMINOLOGY, 'classes' are not communities; they merely represent possible, and frequent, bases for communal action. We may speak of a 'class' when (1) a number of people have in common a specific causal component of their life chances, insofar as (2) this component is represented exclusively by economic interests in the possession of goods and opportunities for income, and (3) is represented under the conditions of the commodity or labor markets.

[. . .]

It is the most elemental economic fact that the way in which the disposition over material property is distributed among a plurality of people, meeting competitively in the market for the purpose of exchange, in itself creates specific life chances. According to the law of marginal utility this mode of distribution excludes the non-owners from competing for highly valued goods; it favors the owners and, in fact, gives to them a monopoly to acquire such goods. Other things being equal, this mode of distribution monopolizes the opportunities for profitable deals for all those who, provided with goods, do not necessarily have to exchange them. It increases, at least generally, their power in price wars with those who, being propertyless, have nothing to offer but their services in native form or goods in a form constituted through their own labor, and who above all are compelled to get rid of these products in order barely to subsist. This mode of distribution gives to the propertied a monopoly on the possibility of transferring property from the sphere of use as a 'fortune,' to the sphere of 'capital goods'; that is, it gives them the entrepreneurial function and all chances to share directly or indirectly in returns on capital. All this holds true within the area in which pure market conditions prevail. 'Property' and 'lack of property' are, therefore, the basic categories of all class situations. It does not matter whether these two categories become effective in price wars or in competitive struggles.

[. . .]

Communal action flowing from class interest

According to our terminology, the factor that creates 'class' is unambiguously economic interest, and indeed, only those interests involved in the existence of the 'market.' Nevertheless, the concept of 'class-interest' is an ambiguous one: even as an empirical concept it is ambiguous as soon as one understands by it something other than the factual direction of interests following with a certain probability from the class situation for a certain 'average' of those people subjected to the class situation. The class situation and other circumstances remaining the same, the direction in which the individual worker, for instance, is likely to pursue his interests may vary widely, according to whether he is constitutionally qualified for the task at hand to a high, to an average, or to a low degree. In the same way, the direction of interests may vary according to whether or not a *communal* action of a larger or smaller portion of those commonly affected by the 'class situation,' or even an association among them, e.g. a 'trade union,' has grown out of the class situation from which the individual may or may not expect promising results. (Communal action refers to that action which is oriented to the feeling of the actors that they belong together. Societal action, on the other hand, is oriented to a rationally motivated adjustment of interests.) The rise of societal or even of communal action from a common class situation is by no means a universal phenomenon.

The class situation may be restricted in its effects to the generation of essentially *similar* reactions, that is to say, within our terminology, of 'mass actions.' However, it may not have even this result. Furthermore, often merely an amorphous communal action emerges. For example, the 'murmuring' of the workers known in ancient oriental ethics: the moral disapproval of the work-master's conduct, which in its practical significance was probably equivalent to an increasingly typical phenomenon of precisely the latest industrial development, namely, the 'slow down' (the deliberate limiting of work effort) of laborers by virtue of tacit agreement. The degree in which 'communal action' and possibly 'societal action,' emerges from the 'mass actions' of the members of a class is linked to general cultural conditions, especially to those of an intellectual sort. It is also linked to the extent of the contrasts that have already evolved, and is especially linked to the *transparency* of the connections between the causes and the consequences of the 'class situation.' For however different life chances may be, this fact in itself, according to all experience, by no means gives birth to 'class action' (communal action by the members of a class). The fact of being conditioned and the results of the class situation must be distinctly recognizable. For only then the contrast of life chances can be felt not as an absolutely given fact to be accepted, but as a resultant from either (1) the given distribution of property, or (2) the structure of the concrete economic order. It is only then that people may react against the class structure not only through acts of an intermittent and irrational protest, but in the form of rational association. There have been 'class situations' of the first category (1), of a specifically naked and transparent sort, in the urban centers of Antiquity and during the Middle Ages; especially then, when great fortunes were accumulated by factually monopolized trading in industrial products of these localities or in foodstuffs. Furthermore, under certain circumstances, in the rural economy of the most diverse periods, when agriculture was increasingly exploited in a profit-making manner. The most important historical example of the second category (2) is the class situation of the modern 'proletariat.'

Types of 'class struggle'

Thus every class may be the carrier of any one of the possibly innumerable forms of 'class action,' but this is not necessarily so. In any case, a class does not in itself constitute a community. To treat 'class' conceptually as having the same value as 'community' leads to distortion. That men in the same class situation regularly react in mass actions to such tangible situations as economic ones in the direction of those interests that are most adequate to their average number is an important and after all simple fact for the understanding of historical events. Above all, this fact must not lead to that kind of pseudo-scientific operation with the concepts of 'class' and 'class interests' so frequently found these days, and which has found its most classic expression in the statement of a talented author, that the individual may be in error concerning his interests but that the 'class' is 'infallible' about its interests. Yet, if classes as such are not communities, nevertheless class situations emerge only on the basis of communalization.

[. . .]

The propertyless of antiquity and of the Middle Ages protested against monopolies, pre-emption, forestalling, and the withholding of goods from the market in order to raise prices. Today the central issue is the determination of the price of labor.

This transition is represented by the fight for access to the market and for the determination of the price of products. Such fights went on between merchants and workers in the putting-out system of domestic handicraft during the transition to modern times. Since it is quite a general phenomenon we must mention here that the class antagonisms that are conditioned through the market situation are usually most bitter between those who actually and directly participate as opponents in price wars. It is not the rentier, the share-holder, and the banker who suffer the ill will of the worker, but almost exclusively the manufacturer and the business executives who are the direct opponents of workers in price wars. This is so in spite of the fact that it is precisely the cash boxes of the rentier, the share-holder, and the banker into which the more or less 'unearned' gains flow, rather than into the pockets of the manufacturers or of the business executives. This simple state of affairs has very frequently been decisive for the role the class situation has played in the formation of political parties. For example, it has made possible the varieties of patriarchal socialism and the frequent attempts—formerly, at least—of threatened status groups to form alliances with the proletariat against the 'bourgeoisie.'

[. . .]

Chapter 10

Antonio Gramsci

NOTES ON ITALIAN HISTORY

History of the subaltern classes: methodological criteria

THE HISTORICAL UNITY OF THE RULING CLASSES is realised in the State, and their history is essentially the history of States and of groups of States. But it would be wrong to think that this unity is simply juridical and political (though such forms of unity do have their importance too, and not in a purely formal sense); the fundamental historical unity, concretely, results from the organic relations between State or political society and "civil society".

The subaltern classes, by definition, are not unified and cannot unite until they are able to become a "State": their history, therefore, is intertwined with that of civil society, and thereby with the history of States and groups of States. Hence it is necessary to study: 1. the objective formation of the subaltern social groups, by the developments and transformations occurring in the sphere of economic production; their quantitative diffusion and their origins in pre-existing social groups, whose mentality, ideology and aims they conserve for a time; 2. their active or passive affiliation to the dominant political formations, their attempts to influence the programmes of these formations in order to press claims of their own, and the consequences of these attempts in determining processes of decomposition, renovation or neo-formation; 3. the birth of new parties of the dominant groups, intended to conserve the assent of the subaltern groups and to maintain control over them; 4. the formations which the subaltern groups themselves produce, in order to press claims of a limited and partial character; 5. those new formations which assert the autonomy of the subaltern groups, but within the old framework; 6. those formations which assert the integral autonomy, ... etc.

The list of these phases can be broken down still further, with intermediate phases and combinations of several phases. The historian must record, and discover the causes of, the line of development towards integral autonomy, starting from the most primitive phases; he must note every manifestation of the Sorelian "spirit of cleavage". Therefore, the history of the parties of the subaltern groups is very complex too. It must include all the repercussions of party activity, throughout the area of the subaltern groups themselves taken globally, and also upon the attitudes of the dominant group; it must include as well the repercussions of the far more effective actions (effective because backed by the State) of the dominant groups upon the subaltern groups and their parties. Among the subaltern groups, one will exercise or tend to exercise a certain hegemony through the mediation of a party; this must be established by studying the development of all the other parties too, in so far as they include elements of the hegemonic group or of the other subaltern groups which undergo such hegemony.

[. . .]

The problem of political leadership in the formation and development of the nation and the modern State in Italy

The whole problem of the connection between the various political currents of the Risorgimento—of their relations with each other, and of their relations with the homogeneous or subordinate social groups existing in the various historical sections (or sectors) of the national territory—can be reduced to the following basic factual datum. The Moderates represented a relatively homogeneous social group, and hence their leadership underwent relatively limited oscillations (in any case, subject to an organically progressive line of development); whereas the so-called Action Party did not base itself specifically on any historical class, and the oscillations which its leading organs underwent were resolved, in the last analysis, according to the interests of the Moderates. In other words, the Action Party was led historically by the Moderates. The assertion attributed to Victor Emmanuel II that he "had the Action Party in his pocket", or something of the kind, was in practice accurate—not only because of the King's personal contacts with Garibaldi, but because the Action Party was in fact "indirectly" led by Cavour and the King.

The methodological criterion on which our own study must be based is the following: that the supremacy of a social group manifests itself in two ways, as "domination" and as "intellectual and moral leadership". A social group dominates antagonistic groups, which it tends to "liquidate", or to subjugate perhaps even by armed force; it leads kindred and allied groups. A social group can, and indeed must, already exercise "leadership" before winning governmental power (this indeed is one of the principal conditions for the winning of such power); it subsequently becomes dominant when it exercises power, but even if it holds it firmly in its grasp, it must continue to "lead" as well. The Moderates continued to lead the Action Party even after 1870 and 1876, and so-called "transformism" was only the parliamentary expression of this action of intellectual, moral and political hegemony. Indeed one might say that the entire State life of Italy from 1848 onwards has been characterised by transformism—in other words by the formation of an ever more extensive ruling class, within the framework established by the Moderates after 1848 and the collapse of the neo-Guelph and federalist utopias. The formation of this class involved the gradual but continuous absorption, achieved by methods which varied in their effectiveness, of the active elements produced by allied groups—and even of those which came from antagonistic groups and seemed irreconcilably hostile. In this sense political leadership became merely an aspect of the function of domination—in as much as the absorption of the 'enemies' *élites* means their decapitation, and annihilation often for a very long time. It seems clear from the policies of the Moderates that there can, and indeed must, be hegemonic activity even before the rise to power, and that one should not count only on the material force which power gives in order to exercise an effective leadership. It was precisely the brilliant solution of these problems which made the Risorgimento possible, in the form in which it was achieved (and with its limitations)— as "revolution" without a "revolution", or as "passive revolution".

[. . .]

In what forms, and by what means, did the Moderates succeed in establishing the apparatus (mechanism) of their intellectual, moral and political hegemony? In forms, and by means, which may be called "liberal"—in other words through individual, "molecular", "private" enterprise (i.e. not through a party programme worked out and constituted according to a plan, in advance of the practical and organisational action). However, that was "normal" given the structure and the function of the social groups of which the Moderates were the representatives, the leading stratum, the organic intellectuals.

For the Action Party, the problem presented itself differently, and different systems of organisation should have been adopted. The Moderates were intellectuals already naturally "condensed" by the organic nature of their relation to the social groups whose expression they were. (As far as a whole series of them were concerned, there was realised the identity of the represented and the representative; in other words, the Moderates were a real, organic vanguard of the upper classes, to which economically they belonged. They were intellectuals and political organisers, and at the same time company bosses, rich farmers or estate managers, commercial and industrial entrepreneurs, etc.) Given this organic condensation or concentration, the Moderates exercised a powerful attraction "spontaneously", on the whole mass of intellectuals of every degree who existed in the peninsula, in a "diffused", "molecular" state, to provide for the requirements, however rudimentarily satisfied, of education and administration. One may detect here the methodological consistency of a criterion of historico-political research: there does not exist any independent class of intellectuals, but every social group has its own stratum of intellectuals, or tends to form one; however, the intellectuals of the historically (and concretely) progressive class, in the given conditions, exercise such a power of attraction that, in the last analysis, they end up by subjugating the intellectuals of the other social groups; they thereby create a system of solidarity between all the intellectuals, with bonds of a psychological nature (vanity, etc.) and often of a caste character (technico-juridical, corporate, etc.). This phenomenon manifests itself "spontaneously" in the historical periods in which the given social group is really progressive—i.e. really causes the whole society to move forward, not merely satisfying its own existential requirements, but continuously augmenting its cadres for the conquest of ever new spheres of economic and productive activity. As soon as the dominant social group has exhausted its function, the ideological bloc tends to crumble away; then "spontaneity" may be replaced by "constraint" in ever less disguised and indirect forms, culminating in outright police measures and *coups d'état*.

The Action Party not only could not have—given its character—a similar power of attraction, but was itself attracted and influenced: on the one hand, as a result of the atmosphere of intimidation (panic fear of a terror like that of 1793, reinforced by the events in France of 1848–49) which made it hesitate to include in its programme certain popular demands (for instance, agrarian reform); and, on the other, because certain of its leading personalities (Garibaldi) had, even if only desultorily (they wavered), a relationship of personal subordination to the Moderate leaders. For the Action Party to have become an autonomous force and, in the last analysis, for it to have succeeded at the very least in stamping the movement of the Risorgimento with a more markedly popular and democratic character (more than that perhaps it could not have achieved, given the fundamental premisses of the movement itself), it would have had to counterpose to the "empirical" activity of the Moderates (which was empirical only in a manner of speaking, since it corresponded perfectly to the objective) an organic programme of government which would reflect the essential demands of the popular masses, and in the first place of the peasantry. To the "spontaneous" attraction of the Moderates it would have had to counterpose a resistance and a counter-offensive "organised" according to a plan.

[. . .]

Chapter 11

Antonio Gramsci

THE MODERN PRINCE

THE MODERN PRINCE, the myth-prince, cannot be a real person, a concrete individual. It can only be an organism, a complex element of society in which a collective will, which has already been recognised and has to some extent asserted itself in action, begins to take concrete form. History has already provided this organism, and it is the political party—the first cell in which there come together germs of a collective will tending to become universal and total. In the modern world, only those historico-political actions which are immediate and imminent, characterised by the necessity for lightning speed, can be incarnated mythically by a concrete individual. Such speed can only be made necessary by a great and imminent danger, a great danger which precisely fans passion and fanaticism suddenly to a white heat, and annihilates the critical sense and the corrosive irony which are able to destroy the "charismatic" character of the *condottiere* (as happened in the Boulanger adventure). But an improvised action of such a kind, by its very nature, cannot have a long-term and organic character. It will in almost all cases be appropriate to restoration and reorganisation, but not to the founding of new States or new national and social structures (as was at issue in Machiavelli's *Prince*, in which the theme of restoration was merely a rhetorical element, linked to the literary concept of an Italy descended from Rome and destined to restore the order and the power of Rome). It will be defensive rather than capable of original creation. Its underlying assumption will be that a collective will, already in existence, has become nerveless and dispersed, has suffered a collapse which is dangerous and threatening but not definitive and catastrophic, and that it is necessary to reconcentrate and reinforce it—rather than that a new collective will must be created from scratch, to be directed towards goals which are concrete and rational, but whose concreteness and rationality have not yet been put to the critical test by a real and universally known historical experience.

[. . .]

The political party

It has already been said that the protagonist of the new Prince could not in the modern epoch be an individual hero, but only the political party. That is to say, at different times, and in the various internal relations of the various nations, that determinate party which has the aim of founding a new type of State (and which was rationally and historically created for that end).

[. . .]

Although every party is the expression of a social group, and of one social group only, nevertheless in certain given conditions certain parties represent a single social group precisely in so far as they exercise a balancing and arbitrating function between the interests of their group and those of other groups, and succeed in securing the development of the group which they represent with the consent and assistance of the allied groups—if not out and out with that of groups which are definitely hostile. The constitutional formula of the king, or president of the republic, who "reigns but does not govern" is the juridical expression of this function of arbitration, the concern of the constitutional parties not to "unmask" the Crown or the president. The formulae stating that it is not the head of State who is responsible for the actions of the government, but his ministers, are the casuistry behind which lies the general principle of safeguarding certain conceptions—the unity of the State; the consent of the governed to State action—whatever the current personnel of the government, and whichever party may be in power.

[. . .]

Is political action (in the strict sense) necessary, for one to be able to speak of a "political party"? It is observable that in the modern world, in many countries, the organic and fundamental parties have been compelled by the exigencies of the struggle or for other reasons to split into fractions—each one of which calls itself a "party" and even an independent party. Hence the intellectual General Staff of the organic party often does not belong to any of these fractions, but operates as if it were a directive force standing on its own, above the parties, and sometimes is even believed to be such by the public. This function can be studied with greater precision if one starts from the point of view that a newspaper too (or group of newspapers), a review (or group of reviews), is a "party" or "fraction of a party" or "a function of a particular party". Think of the role of *The Times* in England; or that which *Corriere della Sera* used to have in Italy; or again of the role of the so-called "informational press" with its claim to be "apolitical"; or even of that of the sporting and technical press. Moreover, the phenomenon reveals interesting aspects in countries where there is a single, totalitarian, governing party. For the functions of such a party are no longer directly political, but merely technical ones of propaganda and public order, and moral and cultural influence. The political function is indirect. For, even if no other legal parties exist, other parties in fact always do exist and other tendencies which cannot be legally coerced; and, against these, polemics are unleashed and struggles are fought as in a game of blind man's buff. In any case it is certain that in such parties cultural functions predominate, which means that political language becomes jargon. In other words, political questions are disguised as cultural ones, and as such become insoluble.

But there is one traditional party too with an essentially "indirect" character— which in other words presents itself explicitly as purely "educative" moral, cultural. This is the anarchist movement. Even so-called direct (terrorist) action is conceived of as "propaganda" by example. This only further confirms the judgement that the anarchist movement is not autonomous, but exists on the margin of the other parties, "to educate them". One may speak of an "anarchism" inherent in every organic party. (What are the "intellectual or theoretical anarchists" except an aspect of this "marginalism" in relation to the great parties of the dominant social groups?) The "economists' sect" itself was an historical aspect of this phenomenon.

Thus there seem to be two types of party which reject the idea of immediate political action as such. Firstly, there is that which is constituted by an élite of men of culture, who have the function of providing leadership of a cultural and general ideological nature for a great movement of interrelated parties (which in reality are fractions of one and the same organic party). And secondly, in the more recent period, there is a type of party constituted this time not by an élite but by masses—who as such have no other political function than a generic loyalty, of a military kind, to a visible or invisible political centre. (Often the visible centre is the mechanism of command of forces which are unwilling to show themselves in the open, but only operate indirectly, through proxies and a "proxy ideology"). The mass following is simply for "manœuvre", and is kept happy by means of moralising sermons, emotional stimuli, and messianic myths of an awaited golden age, in which all present contradictions and miseries will be automatically resolved and made well.

To write the history of a political party, it is necessary in reality to confront a whole series of problems [. . .] in what will the history of a party consist? Will it be a simple narrative of the internal life of a political organisation? How it comes into existence, the first groups which constitute it, the ideological controversies through which its programme and its conception of the world and of life are formed? In such a case, one would merely have a history of certain intellectual groups, or even sometimes the political biography of a single personality. The study will therefore have to have a vaster and more comprehensive framework.

The history will have to be written of a particular mass of men who have followed the founders of the party, sustained them with their trust, loyalty and discipline, or criticised them "realistically" by dispersing or remaining passive before certain initiatives. But will this mass be made up solely of members of the party? Will it be sufficient to follow the congresses, the votes, etc., that is to say the whole nexus of activities and modes of existence through which the mass following of a party manifests its will? Clearly it will be necessary to take some account of the social group of which the party in question is the expression and the most advanced element. The history of a party, in other words, can only be the history of a particular social group. But this group is not isolated; it has friends, kindred groups, opponents, enemies. The history of any given party can only emerge from the complex portrayal of the totality of society and State (often with international ramifications too). Hence it may be said that to write the history of a party means nothing less than to write the general history of a country from a monographic viewpoint, in order to highlight a particular aspect of it. A party will have had greater or less significance and weight precisely to the extent to which its particular activity has been more or less decisive in determining a country's history.

We may thus see that from the way in which the history of a party is written there emerges the author's conception of what a party is and should be. The sectarian will become excited over petty internal matters, which will have an esoteric significance for him, and fill him with mystical enthusiasm. The historian, though giving everything its due importance in the overall picture, will emphasise above all the real effectiveness of the party, its determining force, positive and negative, in having contributed to bringing certain events about and in having prevented other events from taking place.

The problem of knowing when a party was actually formed, i.e. undertook a precise and permanent task, gives rise to many arguments and often too, unfortunately, to a kind of conceit which is absurd and dangerous [. . .]. It is true that one may say that a party is never complete and fully formed, in the sense that every development creates new tasks and functions, and in the sense that for certain parties the paradox is true that they are complete and fully-formed only when they no longer exist—i.e. when their existence has become historically redundant. Thus, since every party is only the nomenclature for a class, it is obvious that the party which proposes to put an end to class divisions will only achieve complete self-fulfilment when it ceases to exist because classes, and therefore their expressions, no longer exist. But here I wish to refer to a particular moment of this process of development, the moment succeeding that in which something may either exist or not exist—in the sense that the necessity for it to exist has not yet become "imperative", but depends to a great extent on the existence of individuals of exceptional will-power and of exceptional will.

When does a party become historically, necessary? When the conditions for its "triumph", for its inevitable progress to State power, are at least in the process of formation, and allow their future evolution—all things going normally—to be foreseen. But when can one say, given such conditions, that a party cannot be destroyed by normal means? To give an answer, it is necessary to develop the following line of reasoning: for a party to exist, three fundamental elements (three groups of elements) have to converge:

1.   A mass element, composed of ordinary, average men, whose participation takes the form of discipline and loyalty, rather than any creative spirit or organisational ability. Without these the party would not exist, it is true, but it is also true that neither could it exist with these alone. They are a force insofar as there is somebody to centralise, organise and discipline them. In the absence of this cohesive force, they would scatter into an impotent diaspora and vanish into nothing. Admittedly any of these elements might become a cohesive force, but I am speaking of them precisely at the moment when they are not this nor in any condition to become it—or if they are, it is only in a limited sphere, politically ineffectual and of no consequence.

2.   The principal cohesive element, which centralises nationally and renders effective and powerful a complex of forces which left to themselves would count for little or nothing. This element is endowed with great cohesive, centralising and disciplinary powers; also—and indeed this is perhaps the basis

for the others—with the power of innovation (innovation, be it understood, in a certain direction, according to certain lines of force, certain perspectives, even certain premisses). It is also true that neither could this element form the party alone; however, it could do so more than could the first element considered. One speaks of generals without an army, but in reality it is easier to form an army than to form generals. So much is this true that an already existing army is destroyed if it loses its generals, while the existence of a united group of generals who agree among themselves and have common aims soon creates an army even where none exists.

3. An intermediate element, which articulates the first element with the second and maintains contact between them, not only physically but also morally and intellectually. In reality, for every party there exist "fixed proportions" between these three elements, and the greatest effectiveness is achieved when these "fixed proportions" are realised.

[. . .]

Chapter 12

Herbert Blumer

SOCIAL MOVEMENTS

SOCIAL MOVEMENTS can be viewed as collective enterprises to establish a new order of life. They have their inception in a condition of unrest, and derive their motive power on the one hand from dissatisfaction with the current form of life, and on the other hand, from wishes and hopes for a new scheme or system of living. The career of a social movement depicts the emergence of a new order of life. In its beginning, a social movement is amorphous, poorly organized, and without form; collective behavior is primitive and the mechanisms of interaction are elementary and spontaneous. As a social movement develops, it takes on the character of a society. It acquires organization and form, a body of customs and traditions, established leadership, an enduring division of labor, social rules and social values – in short, a culture, a social organization, and a new scheme of life.

Our treatment of social movements will deal with three kinds – general social movements, specific social movements, and expressive social movements.

General social movements

New cultural trends

By general social movements we have in mind movements such as the labor movement, the youth movement, the women's movement, and the peace movement. Their background is constituted by gradual and pervasive changes in the values of people – changes that can be called cultural drifts. Such cultural drifts stand for a general shift in the ideas of people, particularly along the line of the conceptions people have of themselves and of their rights and privileges. Over a period of time many people may develop a new view of what they believe they are entitled to – a view largely made up of desires and hopes. It signifies the emergence of a new set of values, which influence people in the way in which they look upon their own lives. Examples of such cultural drifts in our own recent history are the increased value of health, the belief in free education, the extension of the franchise, the emancipation of women, the increasing regard for children, and the increasing prestige of science.

Indefinite images and behavior

The development of the new values that such cultural drifts bring forth involve some interesting psychological changes that provide the motivation for general social movements. They mean, in a general sense, that people have come to form new conceptions of themselves that do not conform to the actual positions that they occupy in their life. They acquire new dispositions and interests and, accordingly, become sensitized in new directions; conversely, they come to experience dissatisfaction where before they had none. These new images of themselves, which people begin to develop in response to cultural drifts, are vague and indefinite; and correspondingly, the behavior in response to such images is uncertain and without definite aim. It is this feature that provides a clue for the understanding of general social movements.

Characteristics of general social movements

General social movements take the form of groping and uncoordinated efforts. They have only a general direction, toward which they move in a slow, halting, yet persistent fashion. As movements they are unorganized, with neither established leadership nor recognized membership, and little guidance and control. Such a movement, as the women's movement, which has the general and vague aim of the emancipation of women, suggests these features of a general social movement. The women's movement, like all general social movements, operates over a wide range – in the home, in marriage, in education, in industry, in politics, in travel – in each area of which it represents a search for an arrangement that will answer to the new idea of status being formed by women. Such a movement is episodic in its career, with very scattered manifestations of activity. It may show considerable enthusiasm at one point and reluctance and inertia at another; it may experience success in one area, and abortive effort in another. In general, it may be said that its progress is very uneven with setbacks, reverses, and frequent retreading of the same ground. At one time the impetus to the movement may come from people in one place, at another time in another place. On the whole the movement is likely to be carried on by many unknown and obscure people who struggle in different areas without their striving and achievements becoming generally known.

A general social movement is usually characterized by a literature, but the literature is as varied and ill-defined as the movement itself. It is likely to be an expression of protest, with a general depiction of a kind of utopian existence. As such, it vaguely outlines a philosophy based on new values and self-conceptions. Such a literature is of great importance in spreading a message or view, however imprecise it may be, and so in implanting suggestions, awakening hopes, and arousing dissatisfactions. Similarly, the "leaders" of a general social movement play an important part – not in the sense of exercising directive control over the movement, but in the sense of being pace-makers. Such leaders are likely to be "voices in the wilderness," pioneers without any solid following, and frequently not very clear about their own goal. However, their example helps to develop sensitivities, arouse hopes, and break down resistances. From these traits one can easily realize that the general social movement develops primarily in an informal, inconspicuous, and largely subterranean fashion. Its media of interaction are primarily reading, conversations, talks, discussions, and the perception of examples. Its achievements and operations are likely to be made primarily in the realm of individual experience rather than by noticeable concerted action of groups. It seems evident that the general social movement is dominated to a large extent by the mechanisms of mass behavior. Especially in its earlier stages, general social movements are likely to be merely an aggregation of individual lines of action based on individual decisions and selections. As is characteristic of the mass and of mass behavior, general social movements are rather formless in organization and inarticulate in expression.

The basis for specific social movements

Just as cultural drifts provide the background out of which emerge general social movements, so the general social movement constitutes the setting out of which develop specific social movements. Indeed, a specific social movement can be regarded as the crystallization of much of the motivation of dissatisfaction, hope, and desire awakened by the general social movement and the focusing of this motivation on some specific objective. A convenient illustration is the antislavery movement, which was, to a considerable degree, an individual expression of the widespread humanitarian movement of the nineteenth century. With this recognition of the relation between general and specific social movements, we can turn to a consideration of the latter.

Specific social movements

Characteristics

The outstanding instances of this type of movement are reform movements and revolutionary movements. A specific social movement is one with a well-defined objective or goal. In this effort to reach this goal it develops an organization and structure, making it essentially a society. It develops a recognized and accepted leadership and a definite membership characterized by a "we-consciousness." It forms a body of traditions, a guiding set of values, a philosophy, sets of rules, and a general body of expectations. Its members form allegiances and loyalties. Within it there develops a division of labor, particularly in the form of a social structure in which individuals occupy status positions. Thus, individuals develop personalities and con- ceptions of themselves, representing the individual counterpart of a social structure.

A social movement, of the specific sort, does not come into existence with such a structure and organization already established. Instead, its organization and its culture are developed in the course of its career. It is necessary to view social movements from this temporal and developmental perspective. In the beginning a social movement is loosely organized and characterized by impulsive behavior. It has no clear objective; its behavior and thinking are largely under the dominance of restlessness and collective excitement. As a social movement develops, however, its behavior, which was originally dispersed, tends to become organized, solidified, and persistent. It is possible to delineate stages roughly in the career of a social movement that represent this increasing organization. One scheme of four stages has been suggested by Dawson and Gettys. These are the stage of social unrest, the stage of popular excitement, the stage of formalization, and the stage of institutionalization.

Stages of development

In the first of these four stages people are restless, uneasy, and act in a random fashion. They are susceptible to appeals and suggestions that tap their discontent, and hence in this stage, the agitator is likely to play an important role. The random and erratic behavior is significant in sensitizing people to one another and so makes possible the focusing of their restlessness on certain objects. The stage of popular excitement is marked even more by milling, but it is not quite so random and aimless. More definite notions emerge as to the cause of their condition and as to what should be done in the way of social change. So there is a sharpening of objectives. In this stage the leader is likely to be a prophet or a reformer. In the stage of formalization the movement becomes more clearly organized with rules, policies, tactics, and discipline. Here the leader is likely to be in the nature of a statesman. In the institutional stage, the movement has crystallized into a fixed organization with a definite personnel and structure to carry into execution the purposes of the movement. Here the leader is likely to be an administrator. In considering the development of the specific social movement our interest is less in considering the stages through which it passes than in discussing the mechanisms and means through which such a movement is able to grow and become organized. It is convenient to group these mechanisms under five headings: (1) agitation, (2) development of *esprit de corps*, (3) development of morale, (4) the formation of an ideology, and (5) the development of operating tactics.

The role of agitation

Agitation is of primary importance in a social movement. It plays its most significant role in the beginning and early stages of a movement, although it may persist in minor form in the later portions of the life-cycle of the movement. As the term suggests, agitation operates to arouse people and so make them possible recruits for the movement. It is essentially a means of exciting people and of awakening within them new impulses and ideas that make them restless and dissatisfied. Consequently, it acts to loosen the hold on them of their previous attachments, and to break down their previous ways of thinking and acting. For a movement to begin and gain impetus, it is necessary for people to be jarred loose from their customary ways of thinking and believing, and to have aroused within them new impulses and wishes. This is what agitation seeks to do. To be successful, it must first gain the attention of people; second, it must excite them, and arouse feelings and impulses; and third, it must give some direction to these impulses and feelings through ideas, suggestions, criticisms, and promises.

Agitation operates in two kinds of situations. One is a situation marked by abuse, unfair discrimination, and injustice, but a situation wherein people take this mode of life for granted and do not raise questions about it. Thus, while the situation is potentially fraught with suffering and protest, the people are marked by inertia. Their views of their situation incline them to accept it; hence the function of the agitation is to lead them to challenge and question their own modes of living. It is in such a situation that agitation may create social unrest where none existed previously. The other situation is one wherein people are already aroused, restless, and discontented, but where they are either too timid to act or else do not know what to do. In this situation the function of agitation is not so much to implant the seeds of unrest, as to intensify, release, and direct the tensions people already have.

[. . .]

The function of agitation, as stated above, is in part to dislodge and stir up people and so liberate them for movement in new directions. More specifically, it operates to change the conceptions people have of themselves, and the notions they have of their rights and dues. Such new conceptions, involving beliefs that one is justly entitled to privileges from which he is excluded, become of basic importance to the success of a social movement.

[. . .]

The development of esprit de corps

Agitation is merely the means of arousing the interest of people and thus getting them to participate in a movement. While it serves to recruit members, to give initial impetus, and to give some direction, by itself it could never organize or sustain a movement. Collective activities based on mere agitation would be sporadic, disconnected, and short-lived. Other mechanisms have to enter to give solidity and persistency to a social movement. One of these is the development of *esprit de corps*.

Esprit de corps might be thought of as the organizing of feelings on behalf of the movement. In itself, it is the sense that people have of belonging together and of being identified with one another in a common undertaking. Its basis is constituted by a condition of rapport. In developing feelings of intimacy and closeness, people have the sense of sharing a common experience and of forming a select group. In one another's presence they feel at ease and as comrades. Personal reserve breaks down and feelings of strangeness, difference, and alienation disappear. Under such conditions, relations tend to be of co-operation instead of personal competition. The behavior of one tends to facilitate the release of behavior on the part of others, instead of tending to inhibit or check that behavior; in this sense each person tends to inspire others. Such conditions of mutual sympathy and responsiveness obviously make for concerted behavior.

Esprit de corps is of importance to a social movement in other ways. Very significant is the fact that it serves to reinforce the new conception of himself that the individual has formed as a result of the movement and of his participation in it. His feeling of belonging with others, and they with him, yields him a sense of collective support.

In this way his views of himself and of the aims of the movement are maintained and invigorated. It follows that the development of *esprit de corps* helps to foster an attachment of people to a movement. Each individual has his sentiments focused on, and intertwined with, the objectives of the movement. The resulting feeling of expansion he experiences is in the direction of greater allegiance to the movement. It should be clear that *esprit de corps* is an important means of developing solidarity and so of giving solidity to a movement.

[. . .]

Esprit de corps may be regarded, then, as an organization of group feeling and essentially as a form of group enthusiasm. It is what imparts life to a movement. Yet just as agitation is inadequate for the development of a movement, so is mere reliance on *esprit de corps* insufficient. A movement that depends entirely on *esprit de corps* is usually like a boom and is likely to collapse in the face of a serious crisis. Since the allegiance it commands is based merely on heightened enthusiasm, it is likely to vanish with the collapse of such enthusiasm. Thus, to succeed, especially in the face of adversity, a movement must command a more persistent and fixed loyalty. This is yielded by the development of morale.

The development of morale

[. . .]

Morale seems to be based on, and yielded by, a set of convictions. In the case of a social movement these seem to be of three kinds. First is a conviction of the rectitude of the purpose of the movement. This is accompanied by the belief that the attainment of the objectives of the movement will usher in something approaching a millennial state. What is evil, unjust, improper, and wrong will be eradicated with the success of the movement. In this sense, the goal is always overvalued. Yet these beliefs yield to the members of a movement a marked confidence in themselves. A second conviction closely identified with these beliefs is a faith in the ultimate attainment by the movement of its goal. There is believed to be a certain inevitability about this. Since the movement is felt to be a necessary agent, for the regeneration of the world, it is regarded as being in line with the higher moral values of the universe, and in this sense as divinely favored. Hence, there arises the belief that success is inevitable, even though it may only be after a hard struggle. Finally, as part of this complex of convictions, there is the belief that the movement is charged with a sacred mission. Together, these convictions serve to give an enduring and unchangeable character to the goal of a movement and a tenacity to its effort. Obstructions, checks, and reversals are occasions for renewed effort instead of for disheartenment and despair, since they do not seriously impair faith in the rectitude of the movement nor in the inevitability of its success.

It is clear from this explanation that the development of morale in a movement is essentially a matter of developing a sectarian attitude and a religious faith. This provides a cue to the more prominent means by which morale is built up in a movement.

One of these is found in the emergence of a saint cult which is to be discerned in every enduring and persisting social movement. There is usually a major saint and a series of minor saints, chosen from the popular leaders of the movement. Hitler, Lenin, Marx, Mary Baker Eddy, and Sun Yat-sen will serve as convenient examples of major saints. Such leaders become essentially deified and endowed with miraculous power. They are regarded as grossly superior, intelligent, and infallible. People develop toward them attitudes of reverence and awe, and resent efforts to depict them as ordinary human beings. The pictures or other mementos of such individuals come to have the character of religious idols. Allied with the saints of a movement are its heroes and its martyrs. They also come to be regarded as sacred figures. The development of this whole saint cult is an important means of imparting what is essentially a religious faith to the movement and of helping to build up the kind of convictions spoken of above.

Similar in function is the emergence in the movement of a creed and of a sacred literature. These, again, are to be found in all persisting social movements. Thus, as has been said frequently, *Das Kapital* and *Mein Kampf* have been the bibles respectively, of the communist movement and of the National Socialist movement. The role of a creed and literature of this sort in imparting religious conviction to a movement should be clear.

Finally, great importance must be attached to myths in the development of morale in a social movement. Such myths may be varied. They may be myths of being a select group or a chosen people; myths of the inhumanity of one's opponents; myths about the destiny of the movement; myths depicting a glorious and millennial society to be realized by the movement. Such myths usually grow out of, and in response to the desires and hopes of the people in the movement and acquire by virtue of their collective character a solidity, a permanency, and an unquestioned acceptance. It is primarily through them that the members of the movement achieve their dogmatic adherence to their convictions, and seek to justify their actions to the rest of the world.

[. . .]

Reform and revolution

Mention has been made of the fact that specific social movements are primarily of two sorts: reform and revolutionary movements. Both seek to effect changes in the social order and in existing institutions. Their life-cycles are somewhat similar, and the development of both is dependent on the mechanisms we have just discussed. However, noteworthy differences exist between the two; some of these differences will now be indicated.

The two movements differ in the *scope of their objectives*. A reform movement seeks to change some specific phase or limited area of the existing social order; it may seek, for example, to abolish child labor or to prohibit the consumption of alcohol. A revolutionary movement has a broader aim; it seeks to reconstruct the entire social order.

This difference in objective is linked to a *different vantage paint of attack*. In endeavoring to change just a portion of the prevailing social order, the reform movement accepts the basic tenets of that social order. More precisely, the reform movement accepts the existing mores; indeed, it uses them to criticize the social defects it is attacking.

The reform movement starts with the prevailing code of ethics, and derives much of its support because it is so well grounded on the ethical side. This makes its position rather unassailable. It is difficult to attack a reform movement or reformers on the basis of their moral aims; the attack is usually more in the form of caricature and ridicule, and in characterizing reformers as visionary and impractical. By contrast, a revolutionary movement always challenges the existing mores and proposes a new scheme of moral values. Hence, it lays itself open to vigorous attack from the standpoint of existing mores.

A third difference between the two movements follows from the points already made. A reform movement has *respectability*. By virtue of accepting the existing social order and of orienting itself around the ideal code, it has a claim on existing institutions. Consequently, it makes use of these institutions such as the school, the church, the press, established clubs, and the government. Here again the revolutionary movement stands in marked contrast. In attacking the social order and in rejecting its mores, the revolutionary movement is blocked by existing institutions and its use of them is forbidden. Thus, the revolutionary movement is usually and finally driven underground; whatever use is made of existing institutions has to be carefully disguised. In general, whatever agitation, proselytizing, and maneuvers are carried out by revolutionary movements have to be done outside the fold of existing institutions. In the event that a reform movement is felt as challenging too seriously some powerful class or vested interests, it is likely to have closed to it the use of existing institutions. This tends to change a reform movement into a revolutionary movement; its objectives broaden to include the reorganization of the institutions that are now blocking its progress.

The differences in position between reform and revolutionary movements bring in an important distinction in their *general procedure and tactics*. A reform movement endeavors to proceed by developing a public opinion favorable to its aims; consequently, it seeks to establish a public issue and to make use of the discussion process considered above. The reform party can be viewed as a conflict group, opposed by interest groups and surrounded by a large inert population. The reform movement addresses its message to this indifferent or disinterested public in an effort to gain its support. In contradistinction, the revolutionary movement does not primarily seek to influence public opinion, but instead tries to make converts. In this sense it operates more like a religion.

[. . .]

Expressive movements

The distinctive feature of expressive movements

The characteristic feature of expressive movements is that they do not seek to change the institutions of the social order or its objective character. The tension and unrest out of which they emerge are not focused upon some objective of social change that the movement seeks collectively to achieve. Instead, they are released in some type of expressive behavior that, however, in becoming crystallized, may have profound effects on the personalities of individuals and on the character of the social order.

We shall consider two kinds of expressive movements: religious movements and fashion movements.

Religious movements

Religious movements begin essentially as cults; they have their setting in a situation that, psychologically, is like that of the dancing crowd. They represent an inward direction of unrest and tension in the form of disturbed feelings that ultimately express themselves in movement designed to release the tension. The tension does not then go over into purposive action but into expression. This characteristic suggests the nature of the situation from which religious movements emerge. It is a situation wherein people are upset and disturbed, but wherein they cannot act; in other words, a situation of frustration. The inability to release their tension in the direction of some actual change in the social order leaves as the alternative mere expressive behavior.

It is well to recall here the most prominent features of the dancing crowd. One of these is a feeling of *intense intimacy* and *esprit de corps*. Another is a heightened feeling of *exaltation* and ecstasy which leads individuals to experience personal expansion and to have a sense of being possessed by some transcendental spirit. Individuals feel inspired and are likely to engage in prophetic utterances. A third mark is the *projection of the collective feelings on outside objects* – persons, behavior, songs, words, phrases, and material objects – which thereby take on a sacred character. With the recurrence and repetition of this crowd behavior, the *esprit de corps* becomes strengthened, the dancing behavior formalized and ritualized, and the sacred objects reinforced. It is at this stage that the sect or cult appears.

[. . .]

Chapter 13

William Kornhauser

THE POLITICS OF MASS SOCIETY

Mass behavior

MASS BEHAVIOR is a form of collective behavior exhibiting the following characteristics. (a) The focus of attention is remote from personal experience and daily life. Remote objects are national and international issues or events, abstract symbols, and whatever else is known only through the mass media. Of course, not *any* concern for remote objects is a manifestation of mass behavior. Only when that concern leads to direct and activist modes of response can we speak of mass behavior. However, merely by virtue of the fact that mass behavior always involves remote objects certain consequences are likely to follow. Concern for remote objects tends to lack the definiteness, independence, sense of reality, and responsibility to be found in concern for proximate objects. The sphere of proximate objects consists of things that directly concern the individual:

> his family, his business dealings, his hobbies, his friends and enemies, his township or ward, his class, church, trade union or any other social group of which he is an active member—the things under his personal observation, the things which are familiar to him independently of what his newspaper tells him, which he can directly influence or manage and for which he

develops the kind of responsibility that is induced by a direct relation to the favorable or unfavorable effects of a course of action. (Schumpeter, 1947, pp. 258–9)

The sense of reality and responsibility declines as the object of concern becomes more remote:

> Now this comparative definiteness of volition and rationality of behavior does not suddenly vanish as we move away from those concerns of daily life in the home and in business which educate and discipline us. In the realm of public affairs there are sectors that are more within the reach of the citizen's mind than others. This is true, first, of local affairs. Even there we find a reduced power of discerning facts, a reduced preparedness to act upon them, a reduced sense of responsibility. . . . Second, there are many national issues that concern individuals and groups so directly and unmistakably as to evoke volitions that are genuine and definite enough. The most important instance is afforded by issues involving immediate and personal pecuniary profit to individual voters and groups of voters. . . . However, when we move still farther away from the private concerns of the family and the business office into those regions of national and international affairs that lack a direct and unmistakable link with those private concerns, individual volition, command of facts and method of inference soon [decline]. (Schumpeter, 1947, pp. 260–1).

(b) *The mode of response to remote objects is direct.* The lessening of the sense of reality and responsibility and effective volition with the greater remoteness of the focus of attention has particularly marked consequences when the mode of response is direct, rather than being mediated by several intervening layers of social relations. People act directly when they do not engage in discussion on the matter at hand, and when they do not act through groups in which they are capable of persuading and being persuaded by their fellows.

At times, people may act directly by grasping those means of action which lie immediately to hand. They may employ various more or less coercive measures against those individuals and groups who resist them (Heberle, 1951, p. 378). For example, when large numbers of people feel that taxes are intolerably high, they may engage in quite different types of action. On the one hand, they may seek to change the tax laws by financing lobbyists, electing representatives, persuading others of their views by means of discussion, and so forth. These types of action are mediated by institutional relations, and are therefore subject to rules concerning legitimate modes of political action. On the other hand, people may seek to prevent others from paying their taxes and forcibly impede officials from collecting taxes, as in the instance of the Poujadists in France. This is direct action.

> Mass behavior is associated with activist interpretations of democracy and with increasing reliance on force to resolve social conflict. . . . The breakdown of normal restraints, including internalized standards of right conduct, and established channels of action. . . . frees the mass to

engage in direct, unmediated efforts to achieve its goals and to lay hands upon the most readily accessible instruments of action. Ordinarily, even in countries having democratic constitutional systems, the population is so structured as to inhibit direct access to the agencies of decision. The electorate participates at specified times and in defined ways; it is not free to create *ad hoc* methods of pressure. The citizen, even when organized in a pressure group supporting, say, a farm lobby, can vote, write letters, visit his congressman, withhold funds, and engage in similar respectable actions. Other forms of activity are strange to him. But when this code has lost its power over him, he will become available for activist modes of intervention. (Selznick, 1952, pp. 293–4)

Political activism tends to be undemocratic because it abrogates institutional procedures intended to guarantee both majority choice and minority rights, and denies respect for principles of free competition and public discussion as the bases for compromising conflicting interests. When political activism is taken to the extreme, it is expressed in violence against opposition. This violence may be restricted to sporadic riots and mob action; or it may become embodied in the very principles of a mass movement. A philosophy of direct action was developed by Sorel (1950) in his idea of the general strike, an idea which influenced such mass movements as revolutionary syndicalism in France, as well as many totalitarian movements, such as fascism in Italy, nazism in Germany, and communism in Russia (Heberle, 1951, pp. 382–6). Totalitarian movements carry their activism to extremes, as indicated by the widespread use of violence on the part of the Fascists in post-war Italy, the Nazis in the Weimar Republic, and the Communists in all countries in which they have developed organizations. Violence also characterizes certain mass movements, like the I.W.W. and the K.K.K. Violence in word and deed is the hallmark of the mass movement uncommitted to institutional means. Mass behavior, then, involves direct, activist modes of response to remote symbols.

(c) Mass behavior also tends to be highly unstable, readily shifting its focus of attention and intensity of response. Activist responses are likely to alternate with apathetic responses. *Mass apathy* as well as mass activism is widespread in mass society. Mass apathy, like mass activism, is unstable and unpredictable, since it, too, is born of social alienation; and as an expression of resentment against the social order it can be transformed into extremist attacks on that order in times of crisis. In these respects, mass apathy differs from that indifference to public matters that is based on traditional conceptions of appropriate spheres of participation (for example, the indifference of women who believe that politics is a man's affair).

(d) When mass behavior becomes organized around a program and acquires a certain continuity in purpose and effort, it takes on the character of a *mass movement* (Blumer, 1951 p. 187). Mass movements generally have the following characteristics: their objectives are remote and extreme; they favor activist modes of intervention in the social order; they mobilize uprooted and atomized sections of the population; they lack an internal structure of independent groups (such as regional or functional units with some freedom of action). Totalitarian movements also possess these characteristics, but mass movements need not become totalitarian. The distinctive character of totalitarian movements lies in their effort to gain total control over their followers and over the whole society. Totalitarian movements are highly organized by an elite bent on total power, whereas mass movements tend to be amorphous collectivities, often without any stable leadership. The difference between the Communist movement and the I.W.W. is an example of the difference between a totalitarian movement and a mass movement.

Mass movements are miniature mass societies; totalitarian movements are miniature totalitarian societies. This parallelism implies the major similarity and the major difference between the two types of social movements: they both are based on atomized masses rather than on independent social groups, as are mass societies and totalitarian societies; on the other hand, the amorphous structure of the mass movement corresponds to the ease of access to elites in mass society, while the cadre organization of the totalitarian movement corresponds to the inaccessibility of the elite in totalitarian society.

Mass movements offer excellent opportunities for penetration by totalitarian groups. The Communist party, for example, deliberately creates cadres for the purpose of capturing mass movements.

> The Communist membership functions as the cadre of a wider mass movement. Each member has special training and ideally should be able to lead nonparty groups as they may from time to time become accessible. . . . In sum, the cadre party is a highly manipulable skeleton organization of trained agents; it is sustained by political combat and is linked to the mass movement as its members become leaders of wider groups in the community. (Selznick, 1952, p. 18)

Examples of mass movements which have been penetrated by the Communist party with varying success include anarchist and syndicalist movements in France, Italy, and Spain.

Since totalitarian movements typically are mass movements which have been captured by totalitarian cadres, we shall refer to totalitarian movements as "mass movements" in the present study when we wish to emphasize the contention that totalitarian movements are organizations of masses. This is not a matter of definition, but requires theoretical and empirical support. For there is a widely held theory that communism and fascism (the major cases of totalitarian movements) are essentially class movements, that is, expressions of specific class interests and forms of class organization bent on furthering these interests. It undoubtedly is true that not only some theorists but also many individual citizens (for example, in France) think in these class terms, and in the latter case express this belief by voting for a Communist (or Fascist) slate. The burden of the present study, however, is that large numbers of people do not respond to totalitarian movements primarily from the standpoint of economic calculus; but instead, they respond to the nihilistic tone of totalitarian movements, as an expression of their feelings of resentment against the present and hope for something completely new in the future. In Part III, we shall adduce considerable evidence to show that the strongest response to the totalitarian appeal is *not* to be found among those who are involved in class organization and class struggle; on the contrary, the strongest response comes from people with the weakest attachment to class organizations, or any other kind of social group. A totalitarian movement attracts socially isolated members of *all* classes.

Furthermore, whenever totalitarian groups gain power, they seek to smash all class organizations and to suppress all class interests. The inference is that movements which repeatedly have shown their contempt for class interests they are sometimes alleged to embody (and themselves sometimes claim to represent) can hardly be said to make their primary appeal to class interests.

What class analysis does not help to explain is the *extremism* of totalitarian movements: their appeal to the most extreme dispositions of individuals and their readiness to go to any extreme in the pursuit of their objectives. But it is precisely this quality of extremism which makes these movements so threatening to democratic politics and individual liberty.

> The extremist must be deeply alienated from the complex of rules which keep the strivings for various values in restraint and balance. An extremist group is an alienated group. This means that it is fundamentally hostile to the political order. It cannot share that sense of affinity to persons or the attachment to the institutions which confine political conflicts to peaceful solutions. Its hostility is incompatible with that freedom from intense emotion which pluralistic politics needs for its prosperity. (Shils, 1956, p. 231)

The present study is concerned with the fate of democracy insofar as it is affected by the opportunities provided for the growth of mass movements; and it seeks to analyze these opportunities with the aid of concepts of mass society.

Mass society is characterized by an abundance of mass movements. Other types of society are characterized by different kinds of social movements. Social movements which arise within communal society are characteristically traditional movements. For example, revival movements tend to be tradition-oriented, and manifest many of the features of the communal society within which they arise. Social movements which develop within pluralist societies are typically reform movements. For example, labor movements are reform movements when they seek to change only limited and specific aspects of working conditions, by developing a public opinion favorable to their aims in a constitutional manner. In totalitarian society, there is only one effective movement, and that is the totalitarian movement which supports the regime.

Mass movements may arise in non-mass societies, although they are not frequent in these societies. For example, millennial movements with mass characteristics arose at least as early as the Middle Ages. Mannheim has fixed the beginning of movements which combine the idea of a millennial kingdom on earth with the activism of large numbers of people in the "orgiastic chiliasm" of the Anabaptists: "the 'spiritualization of politics'. . . may be said to have begun at this turn in history" (1936, p. 191). The appearance of outbursts of social chiliasm in the Middle Ages should not obscure the fact that they were only sporadic occurrences which, though they may have engendered new sects, generally did not transform major institutions (Talmon, 1952, p. 9).

Mass behavior occurs at a low rate and in peripheral spheres in communal society, because the inaccessibility of elites inhibits mass behavior from above and the unavailability of non-elites inhibits it from below. In pluralist society, mass behavior also is located in peripheral areas, but the rate is higher because there are more remote symbols clamoring for attention (due to the accessibility of channels of communication).

In totalitarian society, the great power of the elite suppresses spontaneous behavior of masses, but that mass behavior that does occur tends to impinge on the vital centers of society (witness the rarity but the explosiveness of spontaneous mass actions in totalitarian societies, such as those which took place in East Berlin, Potsdam, and Budapest). In mass society, mass behavior occurs at a high rate and in central spheres of society; mass behavior is inhibited neither from above nor from below because mass society possesses both accessible elites and available non-elites.

[. . .]

References

Blumer, H. (1951), 'Collective Behavior', in A. M. Lee (ed.), *New Outlines of the Principles of Sociology*, New York: Barnes & Noble, 1951, pp.165–222.

Heberle, R. (1951), *Social Movements*, New York: Appleton-Century-Crofts.

Mannheim, K. (1936), *Ideology and Utopia*, London: Routledge and Kegan Paul.

Schumpeter, J. (1947), *Capitalism, Socialism and Democracy*, New York: Harper and Bros.

Selznick, P. (1952), *The Organizational Weapon*, New York: McGraw-Hill.

Shils, E.A. (1956), *The Torment of Secrecy*, Glencoe: The Free Press.

Sorel, G. (1950), *Reflections on Violence*, Glencoe: The Free Press.

Talmon, J.L. (1952), *The Rise of Totalitarian Democracy*, Boston: Beacon Press.

Chapter 14

Neil J. Smelser

THEORY OF COLLECTIVE BEHAVIOR

Introduction

The Problem. In all civilizations men have thrown themselves into episodes of dramatic behavior, such as the craze, the riot, and the revolution. Often we react emotionally to these episodes. We stand, for instance, amused by the foibles of the craze, aghast at the cruelties of the riot, and inspired by the fervor of the revolution.

The nature of these episodes has long excited the curiosity of speculative thinkers. In recent times this curiosity has evolved into a loosely defined field of sociology and social psychology known as collective behavior. Even though many thinkers in this field attempt to be objective, they frequently describe collective episodes as if they were the work of mysterious forces. Crowds, for instance, are "fickle," "irrational," or "spontaneous," and their behavior is "unanticipated" or "surprising." For all their graphic quality, such terms are unsatisfactory. They imply that collective behavior flows from sources beyond empirical explanation. The language of the field, in short, shrouds its very subject in indeterminacy.

Our aim in this study is to reduce this residue of indeterminacy which lingers in explanations of collective outbursts. Although wild rumors, crazes, panics, riots, and revolutions are surprising, they occur with regularity. They cluster in time; they cluster in certain cultural areas; they occur with greater frequency among certain social groupings—the unemployed, the recent migrant, the adolescent. This skewing in time and in social space invites explanation: Why do collective episodes occur *where* they do, *when* they do, and *in the ways* they do?

An Initial Clarification of Terminology. Our inquiry will cover the following types of events: (1) the panic response; (2) the craze response, including the fashion-cycle, the fad, the financial boom, the bandwagon, and the religious revival; (3) the hostile outburst; (4) the norm-oriented movement, including the social reform movement; (5) the value-oriented movement, including the political and religious revolution, the formation of sects, the nationalist movement, etc.

[. . .]

The most accurate term for encompassing the relevant classes of events would be an awkward one: "collective outbursts and collective movements." "Collective outbursts" would refer to panics, crazes, and hostile outbursts, which frequently (but not always) are explosive; "collective movements" would refer to collective efforts to modify norms and values, which frequently (but not always) develop over longer periods. For brevity we shall condense this awkward term into the conventional one, "collective behavior." The reader should remember that this chosen term is being used as a specific kind of shorthand, and that it has its own shortcomings.

[. . .]

The Norm-oriented movement

Introduction

Definition of a Norm-oriented Movement. A norm-oriented movement is an attempt to restore, protect, modify, or create norms in the name of a generalized belief. Participants may be trying either to affect norms directly (e.g., efforts of a feminist group to establish a private educational system for women) or induce some constituted authority to do so (e.g., pressures from the same group on a governmental agency to support or create a public co-educational system). Any kind of norm—economic, educational, political, religious—may become the subject of such movements. Furthermore, norm-oriented movements may occur on any scale—for instance, agitation by a group of nations to establish an international police force; agitation by groups of businessmen for tax legislation on the federal, state, or local level; agitation by the members of a local union to federate with other unions; agitation by a minority of members of a local chapter of the Society for the Prevention of Cruelty to Animals to amend the by-laws of the chapter. Finally, the definition includes movements of all political flavors—reactionary, conservative, progressive, and radical.

A normative innovation—a new law, custom, bureau, association, or segment of a political party—frequently appears as the result of a norm-oriented movement. Not all normative changes, however, are preceded by a movement with generalized beliefs. In fact, all normative changes could be located on a continuum from those routinely incorporated to those adopted as a result of an agitation based on a generalized belief.

[. . .]

Norm-oriented Movements and Other Collective Outbursts. A norm-oriented movement involves elements of panic (flight from existing norms or impending normative change), craze (plunge to establish new means), and hostility (eradication of someone or something responsible for evils). These lower-level components appear, explicitly or implicitly, in the beliefs that accompany norm-oriented movements.

Panic, craze, and hostility sometimes find open expression during the development of a norm-oriented movement. The armed uprising against state authorities in Massachusetts in 1786 known as Shay's rebellion, for instance, erupted from a norm-oriented agitation to reduce the state debt and to issue paper money. Violence in the Whiskey rebellion in Pennsylvania in 1794 was a manifestation of opposition to an excise tax on spirits. Personal attacks, property destruction, and other forms of hostility have accompanied suffragist and temperance movements. As we shall see, the degree of overt expression of these lower-level components in norm-oriented movements depends largely on the conditions of structural conduciveness and the behavior of agencies of social control.

Many norm-oriented movements occur independently of value-oriented movements, which call for more sweeping changes. The agitation for shorter hours of labor (a norm-oriented movement) in the United States, for instance, has been limited to demands for normative change; on the whole it has not been attached to movements which challenge the values of the capitalist system. In other contexts, however, the same movement may be an adjunct of a value-oriented movement. In England, continental Europe and Russia the movement for shorter hours was subordinated to socialistic aims of laboring groups in the late nineteenth century.

[. . .]

Norm-oriented Movements and More General Social Movements. Movements oriented to specific norms should be distinguished from those with more general programs. In general the latter possess neither sufficiently crystallized beliefs nor a sufficient degree of mobilization to fall in the category of collective outbursts. Rather they provide a backdrop from which many specific norm-oriented movements emanate.

Examples of general social movements include the following: (1) The labor movement is "an organized and continuous effort on the part of wage earners to improve their standards of living over a national area." From this general movement have flowed many specific agitations for normative change—shorter hours, higher wages, fringe benefits, legal protection, etc. (2) The peace movement is a general social movement which has been in existence since its beginning in England during the Revolutionary and Napoleonic Wars. During this period it has spawned many specific movements for international arbitration, codification of international law, disarmament, and finally the cessation of nuclear testing. (3) The humanitarian movement, also a product of the late eighteenth and early nineteenth centuries, lay behind a vast number of more specific reforms, not only in the field of international peace, but also with regard to the status of slaves, criminals, children, animals, and the insane. (4) Feminism, the general movement for women's rights, has manifested itself in numerous specific norm-oriented movements for the establishment of equal rights in education, economic opportunity, political participation, etc. (5) The "Country Life movement" refers to a general movement concerning "the cultural and social welfare of the rural population." Within this general movement many specific problems— health, town-country relations, education, home, religion, farm youth, farm income—have come up for consideration and projected reform.

[. . .]

Norm-oriented Movements and Types of Organizations. Frequently agitation in a norm-oriented movement is carried out by an organization, such as a political party, a pressure group, or a club—or any combination of these. The organizations associated with a movement, moreover, influence the movement's development and its success or failure.

[. . .]

Among these organizations a fundamental distinction is that between political parties and non-party organizations.

[. . .]

The Value-added Sequence of a Norm-oriented Movement. We shall analyze norm-oriented movements under the same set of categories we have already employed extensively—structural conduciveness, strain, generalized beliefs, precipitating factors, mobilization for action, and the response of agencies of social control. This treatment of the norm-oriented movement as a logical accumulation of determinants is similar to the study of the natural history of social movements. In this chapter, however, we are not interested primarily in the temporal accumulation of events; we are attempting to establish the conditions under which events become significant as determinants of a norm-oriented movement. The empirical succession of events may coincide with the analytic accumulation of determinants; for instance, conditions of structural conduciveness may arise first, conditions of strain next, and a generalized belief next. This coincidence need not be the case, however. A generalized belief may have lain dormant for a long time before any movement bearing its name arises; in order for this belief to become a determinant in such a movement it must be activated by conditions of conduciveness and strain. While we shall refer occasionally to temporal sequences of events, *we are not attempting to formulate generalizations about natural histories, but to generate a systematic account of the activation of events and situations as determinants.*

Structural conduciveness

The Structural Possibility of Demanding Normative Changes Alone. The most general condition of conduciveness concerns the possibility for demanding modifications of norms *without simultaneously appearing to demand a more fundamental modification of values.* If social arrangements permit these more limited kinds of demands, these arrangements are conducive to the development of norm-oriented movements; if social arrangements are such that all demands for normative change tend more or less immediately to generalize into conflicts over values, they are not conducive to the development of norm-oriented movements.

In specifying the kinds of social structures which meet these conditions of conduciveness we must distinguish between (1) the source of demands for normative change in the population and (2) the kind of reception that these demands receive at the political level.

[. . .]

The value-oriented movement

Introduction

Definition. A value-oriented movement is a collective attempt to restore, protect, modify, or create values in the name of a generalized belief. Such a belief necessarily involves all the components of action; that is, it envisions a reconstitution of values, a redefinition of norms, a reorganization of the motivation of individuals, and a redefinition of situational facilities.

Our definition encompasses the phenomena designated by the labels "nativistic movement," "messianic movement," "millenarian movement," "utopian movement," "sect formation," "religious revolution," "political revolution," "nationalistic movement," "charismatic movement," and many others. Given the inclusive character of our definition and given the complexity of any value-oriented movement, we must specify at the outset the principal aspects of these movements which we will attempt to explain.

Major Lines of Variability among Value-oriented Movements. Value-oriented beliefs may be composed of indigenous cultural items, of items imported from outside the culture, or—perhaps most frequently—a syncretism. Such beliefs may involve the restoration of past values, the perpetuation of present values, the creation of new values for the future, or any mixture of these.

We may also distinguish between religious and secular value-oriented beliefs.

[. . .]

Secular value-oriented beliefs include nationalism, communism, socialism, anarchism, syndicalism, and so on. Many beliefs display a mixture of religious and secular elements—for example, Christian Socialism in mid-nineteenth century Britain, or *Sarekat Islam*, the nationalist movement in Indonesia in the early twentieth century.

Value-oriented movements differ according to their outcome. Religious movements, for instance, may result in the following:

1   Religious revolution (e.g., the Protestant Reformation), in which the religious belief is the basis for challenging the legitimacy of established political authority. In any religious revolution, furthermore, the challenge may take the form of a secessionist movement (i.e., the attempt to set up a separate political unit)

or internal warfare (i.e., the attempt to overthrow forcibly and assume power from a government in the same political unit). Any given revolutionary movement may be classified according to the tactics it employs—terrorism, street fighting, guerrilla warfare, *coup d'état*, etc.

2   Formation of a more or less enduring collectivity *within a* political system, with no overt challenge to the legitimacy of existing political arrangements.

3   Disappearance, whether as a result of repression by authorities, internal decay, transformation into another kind of movement, or absorption into another kind of movement.

Similarly, secular value-oriented movements may result in the following:

1   Political revolution (e.g., the communist revolutions in Russia and China, the nationalist revolution in Indonesia), in which a secular belief is the basis for challenging the existing political authority. Like religious revolutions, these may be secessionist (e.g., anti-colonial revolutions, or the American Civil War), or they may be attempts to overthrow forcibly and assume power from a government (e.g., the French and Russian revolutions, or the German and Italian fascist revolutions). Finally, the political revolution, like the religious, may be classified according to the tactics employed by the revolutionary group.

2   Formation of a more or less enduring collectivity which may remain revolutionary in principle but which is contained within the political system. Examples are the Communist parties of Britain, Holland, Belgium, and Scandinavia, and political sects, clubs, or societies like the anarchists or socialists.

3   Disappearance.

Thus many outcomes are possible for a given value-oriented movement. Our task in this chapter is to ask and attempt to answer the following questions: What are the determinants of value-oriented movements in general? Why, among value-oriented movements, are some religious and others secular? Why do some value-oriented beliefs eventuate in revolutionary movements, others in peaceful sects or political parties? To answer these questions we shall rely on the variables of structural conduciveness, strain, generalized beliefs, precipitating factors, mobilization for action, and social control as these variables combine in a value-added process.

[. . .]

Let us now clarify several frequently confused relations: the relations among value-oriented movements on the one hand, and religious change, revolutions and violence on the other.

Value-oriented Movements and Religious Change. Not all religious movements are value-oriented. We have seen that revivalism in evangelical Protestantism conforms to the typical craze process, and that reform movements within the church (e.g., the Social Gospel movement) are analyzable as norm-oriented movements. Furthermore, the mere diffusion of new rituals into a religion does not necessarily require a full-fledged value-oriented movement. In order for a religious movement to be termed a value-oriented movement it must possess a distinctive generalized belief and proceed through a definite value-added process.

Value-oriented Movements and Revolution. The term "revolution" frequently refers not only to challenges to the legitimacy of a ruling power, but also to rapid social change of any sort—e.g., the industrial Revolution, the scientific revolution, the managerial revolution.

[. . .]

Examples of value-oriented revolutions are the British, French, and Russian revolutions, the fascist revolutions in Italy and Germany; the modern nationalistic revolutions directed against colonial domination, such as the Indonesian, Chinese, Indo-Chinese, and so on.

Value-oriented Movements and Violence. Because of the hostile component in the beliefs of all value-oriented movements, the *potential* for violence is always present in such movements. Violence has actually accompanied revolutionary movements throughout history. But not all revolutionary overthrows are violent, as when the ruling power submits without a struggle. Furthermore, many non-revolutionary value-oriented movements (e.g., scattered millenarian protests) never show open hostility toward the ruling authorities, even though this hostility appears in fantasy.

[. . .]

PART THREE

Resource mobilisation

CONFLICT MAY BE A CONSTANT feature of all societies and contexts, but its overt manifestation may require more than contrasting interests among individuals and groups. We have seen so far how social change is triggered by contentious politics and collective action, and how processes of change require that emerging groups gain some degree of moral and cultural hegemony. We have also seen some of the characteristics of collective behaviour, the dynamics through which it evolves, along with the potential outcomes it may generate. The question we pose in this section is: assuming that conflicting interests are a permanent trait of social settings, why do these turn into collective action in some contexts and not in others? Behind this question lies a fundamental sociological dilemma: do groups always act in their common self-interest? Self-interested behaviour is deemed the rule, at least when material goods are at stake, and particularly if rational calculus is thought to lead choices. With *The Logic of Collective Action* (1965) we present Mancur Olson's argument that, unless coercion or other types of devises are used, rational self-interested individuals and groups will not act to achieve their common interests. Action is, therefore, potential, and group-oriented behaviour is latent, until separate and selective incentives will stimulate collective action and help formulate demands. Many groups, like for instance consumers or migrant workers, are not organised, while others, like for example unionised labourers and farmers, rely on some degree of organisation. The latter, according to Olson, develop significant lobbying power when they are also organised for some *other* purpose. In brief, active and powerful groups develop their strength because they perform some function which supplements their pursuit of collective interests. Such groups, therefore, have the capacity to 'mobilise' latent action by means of selective incentives, for example delivering services or goods to members, or by exercising some form of legitimate coercion. Olson refers, here, to organisations with a policy of compulsory membership. Among such organisations the author discusses the labour unions, which abandoned general political struggle and became strong lobbying organisations after making membership compulsory, and professional associations, described as 'miniature governments', where membership may not be a legal requirement, but is advisable at least for the benefits it entails.

The originality of Olson's analysis can hardly be denied, in that it runs counter to the prevailing view that groups spontaneously and rationally purse their collective goals: for Olson, groups rationally chose to 'free-ride', namely to enjoy the benefits of collective action while abstaining from participating in it. Moreover, there is something inherently innovative in his argument, whereby collective action is not just the result of frustration and discontent, but predominantly of strength and capacity to mobilise. Olson, in this respect, analyses the most powerful lobbies, those characterised by 'special interests' situated in the business community. The role of government in promoting political pressure is then focused upon, and again the notion is implicitly put forward that lobbying power is determined by institutions making resources available and inducing groups and individuals to mobilise. After an analysis of 'non-economic lobbies', Olson deals with the forgotten groups, those who suffer in silence, the disadvantaged who would have all reasons to mobilise but fail to do so due to lack of resources: these groups cannot be expected to organise or act simply because the gains from group action would exceed the costs.

Resource mobilisation theory takes its distinctive shape after the groundbreaking analysis of Olson is reckoned with and partly critiqued for its (supposed) excessive reliance on rational actor theory (Laver, 1997; Elster, 1989). In *Social Conflict and Social Movements* (1973), Anthony Oberschall, after remarking that to write about the antecedents of theories of conflict and social movements is tantamount to writing the history of sociological thought itself, notes that sociologists dealing with conflict and social change have developed an approach one may refer to as a 'resource management' approach. By resource one may mean anything from material things such as income, savings, material goods and services, to non-material items such as authority, moral commitment, trust, skills or camaraderie. Mobilisation is a process by which an aggrieved group marshals and utilises resources for the pursuit of its specific set of goals. In this book, Oberschall offers a case study showing how a shared culture, but also national sentiments and historical tradition, can also constitute resources for mobilisation. The uprisings taking place in Hungary in 1956 are thus presented as the outcomes of the accumulation of such resources, which include the establishment of leaderships and the development of ideological components. In the excerpt below, however, the focus is placed upon participants and the way in which they are recruited by social movements. In what the author terms 'hypothesis 4', participants in collective action are primarily those individuals who are all well integrated and active in a collectivity. Throughout the revolutionary period in France, he remarks, the working people who mobilised against the shortage of bread were already politically conscious, active and organised. Resources, in this case, may be likened to previously deployed practices and established antagonistic networks. Obeschall then moves on to analyse the conditions favourable to the initiation of mobilisation, noting that often conflict is catalysed 'from the outside', namely through the activities of elite groups within the ruling classes themselves. The divisions among the upper-status groups, in other words, determine the mobilisation of lower-status sections of the population whose support is sought by the conflicting groups. We shall see in the next part of this book how this view is severely criticised. Oberschall, however, notes that the activities carried out by groups within the ruling elite determine a loosening of social control addressed to the underprivileged thereby favouring their mobilisation. Initiation of mobilisation finds another favourable condition in apparently successful protest movements operating at some 'focal point' in the national or international system. Focal points, it is argued, act as exemplars, thus inspiring the action of contentious groups in other areas or countries. In sum, mobilisation in one point creates precipitating conditions for mobilisation elsewhere. This excerpt ends with an examination of the risks and rewards associated with social movement activity and with a set of hypothetical points on how the degree of openness found in systems determines collective mobilisation.

Resource mobilisation theory, therefore, moves away from previous analyses of social movements as the mere result of frustration and grievances experienced by groups. In reiterating some concepts and propositions of this theory, McCarthy and Zald emphasise the variety of resources on which movements base their action, and focus on the relationship between movements, the media, authorities and official political parties. Their analysis leads to the identification of three levels of collective action, respectively linked to the social movement sector, the social movement industry and social movement organisation. The authors, therefore, do not limit their contribution to a more or less detailed sketch of the emerging perspective, but in discussing the merits of such perspective add a number of concepts and discreet variables with a view to clarifying its specific features. A social movement is defined as a set of opinions and beliefs in a group (or sector of society) which represents preferences for changing some elements of the social structure. A social movement organisation, we are told, is a complex, or formal, organisation which identifies its goals with the preferences of a social movement and attempts to implement those goals. A social movement industry, finally, includes all the organisations attempting to implement the goals of a social movement.

As can be easily noticed, the jargon used by these scholars is borrowed from the vocabulary of economics (sector, industry, organisation), and is particularly suitable for the depiction of social movements as rational entities carefully weighing costs and benefits of their action (Savage, 2000; Jasper, 1997). In another section of this book the criticism levelled at this approach will be presented. The analysis of McCarthy and Zald, however, becomes more nuanced when, within and around social movements, the authors identify a number of figures such as constituents, adherents, bystanders and opponents. Their task is then to discuss how the respective resources held by the figures identified can shift to the advantage or disadvantage of a social movement. For example, adherents may be converted into constituents or bystanders into adherents. Moreover, potential beneficiaries of a social movement may be turned into participants, and so on. In conclusion, their contribution emphasises the interaction between resource availability, the pre-existing organisation of preference structures, and entrepreneurial attempts to meet preference demand.

The word 'entrepreneurial' may make participants in, and students of, social movement uncomfortable, in that it conveys a notion of cold calculus applied to social action which, instead, is often inspired by ideals and passion. But this is exactly the notion that resource mobilisation theorists intend to convey, namely that social movements do not result from relative deprivation, structural strain or rapid social change (Butler and Savage, 1995). In other words, they are not propelled by transitory discontent, they are not sharply different from institutionalised action, and participants are not irrational actors. The article by Jenkins proposed below could not be clearer in this respect. Resource mobilisation theory posits that movement actions are rational, adaptive responses to the costs and benefits associated with different optional conducts. While conflicts of interest among social groups are ubiquitous, only some conflicts of interest give rise to mobilisation of movements, which therefore depend on resources, organisations and opportunities for action. Jenkins provides an overview of resource mobilisation theory while underlying the validity of the 'entrepreneurial model', for example, in the study of 'public interest movements', which pursue the goals of disorganised collectivities who are unlikely to mobilise without the initiative of entrepreneurs. Similarly, the movements of deprived groups, such as farm workers and welfare recipients, are said to owe their mobilisation to specific 'entrepreneurs', namely the cadres who have gained political consciousness and skills in previous struggles. Deprived groups, Jenkins argues, have limited resources, rudimentary political experience and little prior organisation, a circumstance that makes outside organisers critical in their mobilisation. Hence the emphasis on the significance of outside contribution and the cooptation of institutional resources by social movements. After a critical re-examination of Olson's pioneering work on social action and 'selective incentives', Jenkins elaborates a notion of social movement as a fusion of interest pursuit and identity formation. Here, some variables which will be fully developed by new social movement theorists appear to slowly take shape. The author argues that participants in social movements act both in pursuit of their interests as well as by virtue of their internalised values and sentiments. Mobilisation, therefore, may well be determined by the strength of pre-existing organisations, networks and resources, but it is certainly also propelled by collective solidarity, ideological commitment and shared identity. The excerpt presented here, in brief, constitutes a transitional piece vaguely alluding to future theoretical developments, and in its concluding part deals with the yet unresolved dilemma of whether movements benefit in greater measure from a centralised bureaucratic or a decentralised informal type of organisation.

The idea of critical mass is central to the understanding of collective action. People and resources are necessary to spread ideas, attract participants and persuade sympathisers. Collective action is more likely to take place when participants feel the strength of others participating. In *The Critical Mass in Collective Action* (1993), Marwell and Oliver focus on interdependence among actors, heterogeneity within groups and the role of mobilising agents. The authors assume that, in most instances, collective action is produced by a relatively small group of highly motivated individuals, who hold sufficient resources to gather a 'critical mass' and direct it towards the achievement of goals. The authors critique Olson's theorising of the 'free-rider problem' because they feel that it is based on the assumption that individuals in an interest group act in total isolation. Their emphasis on interdependence, instead, posits that individual behaviour takes account of the effect of one's participation in collective action on the participation of others. They proceed with an analysis of models of decisions and models of information, which leads them to the formulation of a typology of social networks and cliques, their density and centralisation. A distinction between subjective interests and purposive incentives clarifies Marwell and Oliver's distance from Olson's formulations, while a final statement signals how the authors do not share the ambition to 'solve' the dilemma of the free-rider and the relation between individual and group interests. In their view, attempts to generalise are misguided, and potential solutions to the dilemma can only derive from an appreciation of the different nature of collective interests and goods, and of the different situations within which people make interdependent choices.

It is hard to deny the importance of resource mobilisation theory, nor is it easy to dismiss its conceptual framework when dealing with contemporary issues around movements and change. Political debates, at least among certain groups of activists, are still centred on the conditions that lead to mobilisation and contentious action, and opinions still differ as to what exactly triggers protest: is it total despair, deprivation and exclusion or, on the contrary, opportunity, awareness of one's strength, previously accumulated skills, pre-established networks, minimum leaving standard? In conclusion, echoes of this dilemma are found in discussions whether collective action takes place in worsening social condition or, by contrast, in improving ones.

References

Butler, T. and Savage, M. (eds) (1995), *Social Change and the Middle Classes*, London: UCL Press.

Elster, J. (1989), *Nuts and Bolts for the Social Science*, Cambridge: Cambridge University Press.

Jasper, J. (1997), *The Art of Moral Protest*, Chicago: University of Chicago Press.

Laver, M. (1997), *Private Desires, Political Action*, London: Sage.

Savage, M. (2000), *Class Analysis and Social Transformation*, Buckingham: Open University Press.

Chapter 15

Mancur Olson

THE LOGIC OF COLLECTIVE ACTION

Introduction

IT IS OFTEN TAKEN FOR GRANTED, at least where economic objectives are involved, that groups of individuals with common interests usually attempt to further those common interests. Groups of individuals with common interests are expected to act on behalf of their common interests much as single individuals are often expected to act on behalf of their personal interests. This opinion about group behavior is frequently found not only in popular discussions but also in scholarly writings. Many economists of diverse methodological and ideological traditions have implicitly or explicitly accepted it. This view has, for example, been important in many theories of labor unions, in Marxian theories of class action, in concepts of "countervailing power," and in various discussions of economic institutions. It has, in addition, occupied a prominent place in political science, at least in the United States, where the study of pressure groups has been dominated by a celebrated "group theory" based on the idea that groups will act when necessary to further their common or group goals. Finally, it has played a significant role in many well-known sociological studies.

The view that groups act to serve their interests presumably is based upon the assumption that the individuals in groups act out of self-interest. If the individuals in a group altruistically disregarded their personal welfare, it would not be very likely that collectively they would seek some selfish common or group objective. Such altruism, is, however, considered exceptional, and self-interested behavior is usually thought to be the rule, at least when economic issues are at stake; no one is surprised when individual businessmen seek higher profits, when individual workers seek higher wages, or when individual consumers seek lower prices. The idea that groups tend to act in support of their group interests is supposed to follow logically from this widely accepted premise of rational, self-interested behavior. In other words, if the members of some group have a common interest or objective, and if they would all be better off if that objective were achieved, it has been thought to follow logically that the individuals in that group would, if they were rational and self-interested, act to achieve that objective.

But it is *not* in fact true that the idea that groups will act in their self-interest follows logically from the premise of rational and self-interested behavior. It does *not* follow, because all of the individuals in a group would gain if they achieved their group objective, that they would act to achieve that objective, even if they were all rational and self-interested. Indeed, unless the number of individuals in a group is quite small, or unless there is coercion or some other special device to make individuals act in their common interest, *rational, self-interested individuals will not act to achieve their common or group interests*. In other words, even if all of the individuals in a large group are rational and self-interested, and would gain if, as a group, they acted to achieve their common interest or objective, they will still not voluntarily act to achieve that common or group interest.

[. . .]

If the members of a large group rationally seek to maximize their personal welfare, they will *not* act to advance their common or group objectives unless there is coercion to force them to do so, or unless some separate incentive, distinct from the achievement of the common or group interest, is offered to the members of the group individually on the condition that they help bear the costs or burdens involved in the achievement of the group objectives. Nor will such large groups form organizations to further their common goals in the absence of the coercion or the separate incentives just mentioned. These points hold true even when there is unanimous agreement in a group about the common good and the methods of achieving it.

The widespread view, common throughout the social sciences, that groups tend to further their interests, is accordingly unjustified, at least when it is based, as it usually is, on the (sometimes implicit) assumption that groups act in their self-interest because individuals do. There is paradoxically the logical possibility that groups composed of either altruistic individuals or irrational individuals may sometimes act in their common or group interests. But, as later, empirical parts of this study will attempt to show, this logical possibility is usually of no practical importance. Thus the customary view that groups of individuals with common interests tend to further those common interests appears to have little if any merit.

None of the statements made above fully applies to small groups, for the situation in small groups is much more complicated. In small groups there may very well be some voluntary action in support of the common purposes of the individuals in the group, but in most cases this action will cease before it reaches the optimal level for the members of the group as a whole. In the sharing of the costs of efforts to achieve a common goal in small groups, there is however a surprising tendency for the "exploitation" of the *great* by the *small*.

[. . .]

Chapter 16

Anthony Oberschall

SOCIAL CONFLICT AND SOCIAL MOVEMENTS

Introduction

UNTIL WELL INTO THE NINETEENTH CENTURY, theories of social conflict at the macrosocietal level were part and parcel of the basic writings of political theorists, political economists, and philosophers on society, the social order, and social change. To write about the antecedents of macrotheories of social conflict and social movements would be tantamount to writing the history of sociological thinking itself, starting with Marx and Tocqueville. This has been done interestingly and capably by a number of writers and need not be repeated here. The works of the classical theorists are now routinely taught at both the undergraduate and graduate levels of instruction. None of the great classical theorists, however, with the exception of Simmel, dealt systematically with middle-range and microlevel aspects of conflict (i.e., the group bases of social conflict and its psychological and social psychological foundations, including such topics as public opinion, crowds, sects, riots, and social movements).

The foundations of present-day theories of group conflict, collective behavior, and social movements were laid by the eighteenth-century *philosophes* and moral philosophers, by the late nineteenth-century French social scientists, social Darwinists, and historians who specialized in the French Revolution and in the history of the socialist and labor movements.

[. . .]

Oberschall, Anthony, *Social Conflict and Social Movements*, 1ˢᵗ edition, © 1973, pp 27–29, 135–141, 162–165. Reprinted by permission of Pearson Education, Inc., Upper Saddle River, NJ.

Recent contributions

Within the past few years, a number of sociologists dealing with change and conflict processes have developed an approach that one might refer to as the "resource management" approach.

[. . .]

The basic idea is that of resource. This can be anything from material resources—jobs, income, savings, and the right to material goods and services—to nonmaterial resources—authority, moral commitment, trust, friendship, skills, habits of industry, and so on. In ordinary everyday activity, at work, in family life, and in politics, people manage their resources in complex ways: they exchange some resources for other resources; they make up resource deficits by borrowing resources; they recall their earlier investments. Resources are constantly being created, consumed, transferred, assembled and reallocated, exchanged, and even lost. At any given time some resources are earmarked for group ends and group use, not just individual use. All of these processes can be referred to as "resource management."

Group conflict in its dynamic aspects can be conceptualized from the point of view of resource management. Mobilization refers to the processes by which a discontented group assembles and invests resources for the pursuit of group goals. Social control refers to the same processes, but from the point of view of the incumbents or the group that is being challenged. Groups locked in conflict are in competition for some of the same resources as each seeks to squeeze more resources from initially uncommitted third parties. When one party to the conflict succeeds in obtaining some hitherto unallocated resources, these resources are no longer available to the opposition. The terms mobilization and social control are relative, since both sides seek to mobilize further resources from their supporters and to control resources that are already allocated to their side. But from a societal perspective, from the perspective of conflict and change that result in major shifts of resources from positively privileged to negatively privileged groups, mobilization in the broad sense refers to processes by which an opposition assembles resources for challenging the incumbents, and social control to the processes by which incumbents seek to protect their vested interests. The social system of conflict is an open system, since groups initially outside the conflict, sometimes even foreigners and other countries, may be progressively drawn into the conflict and commit some resources to one or the other side. Demobilization processes can also be analyzed from the resource management perspective, since groups and individuals recall and reallocate to other private or group pursuits the resources they have earlier committed to the conflict and to the pursuit of group ends. In all this the individuals who are faced with resource management decisions make rational choices based on the pursuit of their selfish interests in an enlightened manner. They weigh the rewards and sanctions, costs and benefits, that alternative courses of action represent for them. In conflict situations, as in all other choice situations, their own prior preferences and history, their predispositions, as well as the group structures and influence processes they are caught up in, determine their choices. Indeed, many are bullied and coerced into choices that are contrary to their predispositions. The resource management approach can account for these processes in a routine way.

Although we do not know enough about the precise nature of resource creation, exchange, allocation, consumption, and conversion to be able to express relationships in a quantitative manner, enough is known about them to provide a start for a qualitative analysis of conflict processes.

[. . .]

Social structures can be analyzed from the point of view of how resources, including leadership, are managed and allocated and the manner in which these resources can be converted to the pursuit of group goals. The theory of mobilization described below rests on such an analysis. The problem that negatively privileged groups have had in assembling their meager resources for the pursuit of their collective goals and the extent to which outside support can make up their resource deficits are described most fully in the chapter dealing with the civil rights and black power movement. How a shared culture, national sentiments, and historical tradition can be rapidly converted into a resource base for conflict, even in the face of an authoritarian regime, is described in greatest detail in the section devoted to the Hungarian revolution of 1956. Participation and leadership in social movements can also be analyzed from the point of view of cost-benefit and resource allocation; so can the ideological component in conflict be viewed as a matter of resources and competition for resources. The strategies of social control utilized by incumbents in the face of growing unrest, in particular also the loosening of social control produced by reform responses, can be usefully viewed from the point of view of the allocation and competition for resources by the conflict groups.

[. . .]

A hypothesis about participants

Although mass society theorists and some writers on modernization stress the social isolation and atomization of participants in mass movements and in violent protests this point of view is too simple and is contrary to much available evidence. Hypothesis 4, in opposition to such views, is

> Hypothesis 4, Participants in popular disturbances and activists in opposition organizations will be recruited primarily from previously active and relatively well-integrated individuals within the collectivity, whereas socially isolated, atomized, and uprooted individuals will be under-represented, at least until the movement has become substantial.

For weakly organized collectivities such as the black urban slums of the 1960s in the U.S., the most comprehensive studies have shown that active participants in riots represent a cross-section of the male population living in them and do not draw disproportionately from among the disorganized, unemployed, and criminal element. Similarly, the work of Soboul, Rudé, Tonensson, and other historians of the French Revolution concerned with popular participation in revolutionary demonstrations, popular disturbances, and patriotic associations confirms hypothesis 4, as recently summarized by Tilly (1964: 114–15): "The findings imply very little participation in either ordinary political activity or revolutionary outbursts by misfits, outcasts, nomads, the truly marginal, the desperately poor." Although questions of subsistence, in particular the provision of an ample and cheap supply of bread and price controls, were a central concern of the Paris working people throughout the revolutionary period, "the shortage of bread mobilized a population already politically conscious, active, and organized." Rudé's research extends these patterns of participation for a wide class of riots, demonstrations, and popular disturbances in the late eighteenth century and first half of the nineteenth century in Western Europe. Just as important for mobilization theory is Tilly's emphasis on the mobilizing potential in Paris of the still viable social organization and solidarity within small shops and the traditional crafts binding masters and apprentices, small employers and their employees, in a neighborhood setting in which competition for local leadership by "outside" bourgeois elements was absent (Tilly, 1964: 115–16). This neighborhood setting in revolutionary Paris is another example of a segmented structure that favors the emergence of both solidary sentiments and inside protest leadership. Such a pattern was also found in Saskatchewan by Lipset, in Schleswig-Holstein by Heberle, and during the Montgomery bus boycott. In Montgomery, since the black community was segregated and the black churches controlled from within, black leadership centered on these churches did not have to overcome competition by outside white leaders in their endeavor to mobilize the black population. In Saskatchewan, because the farmers were geographically isolated in communities with little internal stratification and because the small-town professional and business groups were still linked to and identified with the farmers through kinship ties and economic bonds, no other competing outside groups were available to head the school boards, marketing agencies, and local government that constituted the organizational base of the later CFF.

Hypothesis 4 is not confined to working- or lower-class movements. Crane Brinton (1930:50–64) has shown that throughout France the Jacobins came from a predominantly bourgeois rather than working-class background, drawing heavily from the notables and substantial citizens and property owners in provincial towns and cities—lawyers, teachers, physicians, ex-priests, shopkeepers, merchants, and officers. These certainly cannot be called the less successful members of the bourgeoisie, let alone be designated as an outcast, marginal, uprooted element. In his later comparative study of revolutions, Brinton (1952:100–105) confirmed a similar pattern for other revolutions so far as the social origin of middle-level revolutionaries staffing revolutionary bodies and associations is concerned. Nor are these findings surprising from the point of view of the theory of mobilization, since hypothesis 1 implies that those who are already participants in premovement networks of association become activated in the movement as these associations and leaders merge into the movement.

Conditions favorable to the initiation of mobilization: the loosening of social control

The initiation of mobilization of conflict groups often takes place from the outside through the activities of upper-status groups in opposition to the government or ruling groups. Brinton (1952: chapter 2) has long ago emphasized the importance of divisions among the old ruling class, one faction of which initiates opposition and resistance to the government and, in the course of these events, starts mobilizing popular support for its struggle against the authorities. The "aristocratic revolution" before the outbreak of the French Revolution of 1789 and the campaign of banquets led by the Republican parliamentary opposition in France just prior to 1848 illustrates this process. These groups, of course, very rapidly lose control over the popular movement they helped to create and that soon turns against them after the *ancien régime* has been toppled. By stressing division among the upper class, Crane Brinton put his finger on the very general and widespread pattern of the loosening of social control preceding mobilization. In Hungary before 1956, it was division within the Communist party hierarchy, in particular the desertion of the writers and intellectuals, that eventually led to mobilization of wider circles as the social control apparatus of the party and especially the secret police were seriously weakened and immobilized due to indecision within both the Hungarian and Soviet Communist leadership on how much and what kind of reforms and liberalization to allow under the new policy of destalinization.

The Mexican revolution was precipitated by President Diaz's announced intention in 1908 not to seek reelection in 1910, which was later reversed, Madero's imprisonment on the eve of the election when he refused to withdraw his candidacy in opposition to Diaz, and the subsequent Madero movement to stop Diaz. In Morelos, the district where the Zapata rebellion broke out, intense political activity took place with the help of Mexico City political clubs in the campaign for governor in 1909 after Diaz's announced retirement. All political factions sought to elect their candidate in anticipation of the end of the Diaz era. When Diaz reversed himself and imposed his own and the large plantation owners' candidate upon Morelos, the unpopular Escandon who had few local ties, Diaz managed to antagonize all the remaining groups who continued to mobilize their supporters in opposition to Diaz and Escandon despite repression. Mobilization was further helped by Escandon's ineptitude and partiality to the planters.

In Rwanda, the Belgian administration reversed its previous policy on Tutsi-Hutu relations in 1959 by initiating a purge of Tutsi elements from the police and the administration in preparation for Rwanda independence. It also gave tacit approval to the January 1961 coup against Tutsi rule. It is these events, initiated or encouraged by the colonial power, that resulted in loosening social controls and set the stage for the subsequent revolution.

The importance of freedom of association, speech, and, in general, of oppositional activity based on civil liberties, cannot be overemphasized in a theory of mobilization.

[. . .]

In the U.S., the 1954 Supreme Court school desegregation decision marks a far-reaching reversal on race relations: it is considered the most convenient starting date of the civil rights movement. In all these instances, the actions of the authorities or some groups within the ruling class legitimize the demands of the protesters while at the same time they loosen social control and allow mobilization of the protest group to proceed. Prolonged or unsuccessful wars also result in a loosening of social control by the mere fact of exhausting the resources an authoritarian regime can raise to suppress opposition.

Conditions favorable to the initiation of mobilization: focal points

There is a class of precipitating conditions of protest movements that signal hope of success and the weakness of existing social control mechanisms with the success of a protest movement occurring at some focal point in the national or international system. In 1848, revolutions broke out in Vienna, Berlin, Budapest, and other cities shortly after the news of the successful toppling of the Orleanist regime in Paris. In 1960, military coups d'état took place within a week in Turkey, Korea, Peru, and somewhat later in other Latin American countries. In 1956, the Hungarian revolution followed shortly upon the successes of Gomulka and the anti-Stalinists in Poland. In the U.S. urban riots of the 1960s, major riots not only occurred each summer in rapid succession, but set off smaller disturbances in adjoining cities and suburbs where no precipitating incident involving a policeman and residents occurred. Again in the 1960s, student unrest on campuses seemed to spread swiftly within a country and also across national boundaries. These instances are to be distinguished from the case of coordinated, simultaneously planned, and centrally led outbreaks led by highly organized groups such as the 1948 Communist risings in Southeast Asia following shortly upon a conference at which these risings had been planned. Social contagion, with its unfortunate connotation of an emotional and irrational process, is a poor term to describe this phenomenon.

Rather, what happened in all these instances is that prior to the outbreaks there had grown up a complex and often international system of orientation, communication, and social control with focal points. Both the potential participants in conflict groups and the social control agencies had learned to focus their expectations on and take cues from these focal points. Thus in 1848, and ever since the French Revolution, the eyes of revolutionary and reactionary groups alike were focused on Paris. Paris had the most highly developed liberal and radical clubs and circles. European liberals and radicals everywhere in Europe were taking their ideas and fixing their hopes and expectations on Paris. Events there were bound to be repeated elsewhere. Similarly, within Germany itself, Prussia and Berlin were secondary focal points. When the king of Prussia made certain concessions and promised reforms as a result of popular disturbances, the other kings and princes in the German states followed his lead, even where large-scale riots were not taking place. When the king was successful in repressing the popular movement, other states followed his lead. In quite the same way, in 1956, the Kremlin's reaction to destalinization efforts in Poland was the crucial factor in the timing of opposition efforts elsewhere in Eastern Europe. The Hungarians were encouraged by Gomulka's success in Poland and the Soviet reception of the Polish changes. In the nationalist movements in Africa, the constitutional developments in Ghana and Ghana's independence stimulated hope of success elsewhere in the British colonies, since it was correctly assumed that Britain would have no more cause to repress nationalism elsewhere than it had in Ghana. The military coups d'état that follow each other in quick succession actually all have a focal point in the U.S. State Department, whose reactions to the first coup d'état are carefully weighed: does the State Department merely voice the usual platitudes about a return to civilian government at some future unspecified date, or is it applying stronger pressures against the regime by cutting off military and other aid and withholding recognition of the new military regime for an unusual length of time? In these illustrations, Paris and Berlin in 1848, the Kremlin, the British Foreign Office, the U.S. State Department, are focal points for an international system of social control that conditions the responses of both regime opponents and the agents of social control located at peripheral points. Successes of insurgents at the focal point signal the loosening and weakening of social control at its center of greatest strength, and therefore provide the hope of success for protesters and a clear-cut precipitating occasion on which all attention is centered. The outbreak of protest movements and their initial success at focal points is therefore another condition favoring the initiation of mobilization elsewhere.

Conditions favoring mobilization: the relations between city and countryside

Many protest movements among peasants, agricultural workers, and rural peoples receive urban-based support for mobilization. The activities of urban professionals and intellectuals in mobilizing rural people into nationalist movements in Africa have already been commented upon, as well as the socialist-backed creation of peasant leagues in Sicily. Even some famous rural risings during the Middle Ages received some support from townsmen. Pirenne (1958:196) reports that the rising of western Flanders from 1323 to 1328 "was excited and supported by the craftsmen of Ypres and Bruges," and that the English insurrection of 1381 was the common work of townspeople and those of the countryside.

[. . .]

In Morelos just before the outbreak of the Zapatista movement, the Mexico City based Organizing Club of the Democratic Party and the Leyvista Liberal Political Club and other urban political groups helped mobilize the anti-Diaz forces in the cities, small towns, and villages against the Diaz-sponsored candidate for governor in Morelos. Later on, the Zapatistas received the services of urban radicals to help create a revolutionary administration in Morelos, to draw up new laws, to institute land reforms, and to negotiate with the central government. The ill-fated "La Violencia" period in rural Colombia, precipitated by the 1948 assassination of Gaitan, the popular leader of the radical reform wing of the Liberals, followed upon disturbances that were egged on initially by national leaders in the capital as Conservatives initiated a nationwide purge of Liberals upon their return to power. These leaders soon lost control over the rural bosses, their followers, and the rural people as a vicious cycle of reprisals and a bloodbath killing at least two hundred thousand was started for the next decade. Elsewhere in Latin America, [studies] have shown from election returns the radicalizing impact of miners and other organized left-wing groups upon the surrounding traditionally conservative rural population in a context of strong class divisions and a weakening feudal order headed by landowners. As in the case of Japan, no doubt kinship ties and the occupational mobility between agricultural proletariat and miners facilitated the establishment of direct lines of influence. In Morocco, short-lived and frequent rebellions among the desert tribes have resulted from the extension of political links and patronage ties from an urban-based, rival political leadership into the rural hinterland, each faction aligned with competing rural factions and each calling for a demonstration of local support in connection with tests of strength in the capital.

The rural-urban interchange in mobilization is not, however, completely one-sided. In France and Italy there exist rural areas with a tradition of anticlericalism and political radicalism from which population migration takes place into cities for industrial employment. These dechristianized rural population centers provide a reservoir and recruiting base for the Communist party in the cities as the newly arrived "preradicalized" migrants get fully drawn into the network of Communist party associations and subculture. Because migrants frequently return to their villages of origin at election time, at least in the south of Italy, and because they influence their kinsmen and fellow villagers, the transfer of manpower from rural areas to the cities has increased the Communist vote more rapidly in the countryside than in the cities.

One should not underestimate the crucial role of a peasantry in making for success of an urban-based movement, especially of a revolutionary movement.

[. . .]

The fastest way to produce high rates of social movement participation is to lower risks and increase rewards *simultaneously*. A previously authoritarian or repressive regime may create a dangerous situation for itself when introducing far-reaching democratic reforms all at once by allowing both civil liberties and opposition rights and by establishing political offices that opposition leaders can compete for. On the other hand, the gradual relaxation of either dimension followed by a gradual relaxation of the other, but not both at the same time, will probably result in a slower emergence of opposition movements and a greater capacity of the incumbents to control it and to relinquish their monopoly of power in graduated steps while still remaining firmly in the saddle. An especially alert government will want to make certain that it opens up opportunities and channels of social and occupational ascent to able and ambitious individuals in potential opposition groups, and only then introduce greater freedom of expression, civil liberties, and tolerance for opposition, since it will then be able to keep the rewards of opposition participation relatively low compared to the opportunities it is able to provide, and thus can proceed safely to lower the risk dimension. The principle of co-optation of unruly and vocal elements in situations where a government or incumbents are unable to raise the risks of opposition essentially involves their manipulation of the reward dimension, the only other alternative. By lowering the rewards of opposition relative to the rewards and opportunities they are willing to provide through institutionalized means, they manipulate a dangerous situation by moving it from the high probability of participation region to one with medium or fairly low participation probability. Nevertheless, it often happens that an authoritarian regime will bar students and other youth from civil service jobs and other opportunities for making a living if they have at any time engaged in opposition activity. It thereby creates a situation in which the rewards of protest and of opposition involvement remain high for these groups since the rewards from other types of legal activity remain very low. Even if the regime keeps cracking down—that is, moving risks from the lower end to the higher end of the dimension—it can at best move these groups from a high to a medium probability of participation. Thus, it can look forward to years of fluctuating unrest on the part of activists who at some point might establish leadership of a larger social movement of opposition when social strata and classes in the population experience increased hardship.

The approach described here can now be applied to the explanation of previously described high rates of participation of free professionals, students, and intellectuals in opposition leadership, and the low rates of participation and relative absence of businessmen and members of the most deprived social categories.

Members of the free professions, especially lawyers, journalists, artists, writers, professors, physicians, and students who are training to become professionals, have frequently taken the initiative and most active role in opposition and protest movements. Aside from possessing intellectual and organizational skills by virtue of their education and an initial economic resource base that can be drawn upon, these groups can build up a following from their clientele upon whose welfare their own social status and economic standing depends. In a segmented society, their rise to the top of their profession and to the top of the society might be blocked because of ascriptive factors and discrimination. If a certain amount of open opposition is allowed, these groups can gain a lot by achieving high political office at relatively low risk— low risk because they have the skills and means of legal defense and the regime cannot muzzle them without a trial and without publicity, as it might ordinary people. If these groups are repressed and have to go underground, their means of livelihood, their access to their clientele is cut off, and they have little choice but to continue in opposition. The rewards of opposition are now even higher when compared to any other alternative. One thing that repression cannot do is to take away their intellectual and organizational skills on which their leadership potential rests. In difficult times, because their relatives and friends usually do come from among the well-to-do, they can frequently fall back upon assistance from their kin and associates who for a time can afford to support them. If they are prosecuted, punishment will not be as harsh as for ordinary people because professionals are usually members of associations and of organized bodies that will rise up in defense of their members. Thus, the risk/reward ratio for professionals in many situations is such as to favor their active involvement in opposition when compared to the situation that other social strata are normally faced with.

Business groups are in a far more vulnerable position since they have fixed, nonmovable assets, and the gains or rewards of active protest involvement are relatively small compared to their usual expected economic gains. Care must be taken to distinguish larger from smaller businessmen. Owners and managers of large indus- trial enterprises, substantial merchants, and so on, are seldom in the position of being severely deprived or lacking access to the centers of power of their society. Therefore, one would expect them to show up with low frequency in the ranks of opposition groups and movements. Rather than engage directly in politics, large businessmen make the more rational decision when they influence the elites and the authorities through economic lobbies and other similar means. Faced with an opposition social movement that grows in strength, businessmen may well wish to reach an accommodation with it no matter how distasteful the goals and the ideology of the movement are to them, and this often entails making financial contributions to the social movement as well as to other political groups as an insurance policy.

[. . .]

References

Brinton, C. (1930), *The Jacobins*, New York: Macmillan.
Brinton, C. (1952), *The Anatomy of Revolution*, New York: Vintage Books.
Pirenne, H. (1958), *Economic and Social History of Medieval Europe*, New York: Harvest Books.
Tilly, C. (1964), 'Reflections on the Revolution of Paris', *Social Problems*, 12, pp. 99–121.

Chapter 17

John D. McCarthy and Mayer N. Zald

RESOURCE MOBILIZATION AND SOCIAL MOVEMENTS: A PARTIAL THEORY

RECENTLY A NUMBER OF SOCIAL SCIENTISTS have begun to articulate an approach to social movements, here called the resource mobilization approach, which begins to take seriously many of the questions that have concerned social movement leaders and practical theorists. Without attempting to produce handbooks for social change (or its suppression), the new approach deals in general terms with the dynamics and tactics of social movement growth, decline, and change. As such, it provides a corrective to the practical theorists, who naturally are most concerned with justifying their own tactical choices, and it also adds realism, power, and depth to the truncated research on and analysis of social movements offered by many social scientists.

The resource mobilization approach emphasizes both societal support and constraint of social movement phenomena. It examines the variety of resources that must be mobilized, the linkages of social movements to other groups, the dependence of movements upon external support for success, and the tactics used by authorities to control or incorporate movements. The shift in emphasis is evident in much of the work published recently in this area (J. Wilson 1973; Tilly 1973, 1975; Tilly, Tilly, and Tilly 1975; Gamson 1975; Oberschall 1973; Lipsky 1968; Downs 1972; McCarthy and Zald 1973). The new approach depends more upon political sociological and economic theories than upon the social psychology of collective behavior.[1]

This paper presents a set of concepts and propositions that articulate the resource mobilization approach. It is a partial theory because it takes as given, as constants, certain components of a complete theory. The propositions are heavily based upon the American case, so that the impact of societal differences in development and political structure on social movements is unexplored, as are differences in levels and types of mass communication. Further, we rely heavily upon case material concerning organizations of the left, ignoring, for the most part, organizations of the right.

The main body of the paper defines our central concepts and presents illustrative hypotheses about the social movement sector (SMS), social movement industries (SMI), and social movement organizations (SMO). However, since we view this approach as a departure from the main tradition in social movement analysis, it will be useful first to clarify what we see as the limits of that tradition.

Perspectives emphasizing deprivation and beliefs

Without question the three most influential approaches to an understanding of social movement phenomena for American sociologists during the past decade are those of Gurr (1970), Turner and Killian (1972), and Smelser (1963).[2] They differ in a number of respects. But, most important, they have in common strong assumptions that shared grievances and generalized beliefs (loose ideologies) about the causes and possible means of reducing grievances are important preconditions for the emergence of a social movement in a collectivity. An increase in the extent or intensity of grievances or deprivation and the development of ideology occur prior to the emergence of social movement phenomena. Each of these perspectives holds that discontent produced by some combination of structural conditions is a necessary if not sufficient condition to an account of the rise of any specific social movement phenomenon. Each, as well, holds that before collective action is possible within a collectivity a generalized belief (or ideological justification) is necessary concerning at least the causes of the discontent and, under certain conditions, the modes of redress. Much of the empirical work which has followed and drawn upon these perspectives has emphasized even more heavily the importance of understanding the grievances and deprivation of participants. (Indeed, scholars following Gurr, Smelser, and Turner and Killian often ignore structural factors, even though the authors mentioned have been sensitive to broader structural and societal influences, as have some others.)[3]

Recent empirical work, however, has led us to doubt the assumption of a close link between preexisting discontent and generalized beliefs in the rise of social movement phenomena.[4] A number of studies have shown little or no support for expected relationships between objective or subjective deprivation and the outbreak of movement phenomena and willingness to participate in collective action (Snyder and Tilly 1972; Mueller 1972; Bowen et al. 1968; Crawford and Naditch 1970). Other studies have failed to support the expectation of a generalized belief prior to out-breaks of collective behavior episodes or initial movement involvement (Quarantelli and Hundley 1975; Marx 1970; Stallings 1973). Partially as a result of such evidence, in discussing revolution and collective violence Charles Tilly is led to argue that these phenomena flow directly out of a population's central political processes instead of expressing momentarily heightened diffuse strains and discontents within a population (Tilly 1973).

Moreover, the heavy focus upon the psychological state of the mass of potential movement supporters within a collectivity has been accompanied by a lack of emphasis upon the processes by which persons and institutions from outside of the collectivity under consideration become involved; for instance, Northern white liberals in the

Southern civil rights movement, or Russians and Cubans in Angola. Although earlier perspectives do not exclude the possibilities of such involvement on the part of outsiders, they do not include such processes as central and enduring phenomena to be used in accounting for social movement behavior.

The ambiguous evidence of some of the research on deprivation, relative deprivation, and generalized belief has led us to search for a perspective and a set of assumptions that lessen the prevailing emphasis upon grievances. We want to move from a strong assumption about the centrality of deprivation and grievances to a weak one, which makes them a component, indeed, sometimes a secondary component in the generation of social movements.

We are willing to assume (Turner and Killian [1972] call the assumption extreme) "… that there is always enough discontent in any society to supply the grass-roots support for a movement if the movement is effectively organized and has at its disposal the power and resources of some established elite group" (p. 251). For some purposes we go even further: grievances and discontent may be defined, created, and manipulated by issue entrepreneurs and organizations.

We adopt a weak assumption not only because of the negative evidence (already mentioned) concerning the stronger one but also because in some cases recent experience supports the weaker one. For instance, the senior citizens who were mobilized into groups to lobby for Medicare were brought into groups only after legislation was before Congress and the American Medical Association had claimed that senior citizens were not complaining about the medical care available to them (Rose 1967). Senior citizens were organized into groups through the efforts of a lobbying group created by the APL-CIO. No doubt the elderly needed money for medical care. However, what is important is that the organization did not develop directly from that grievance but very indirectly through the moves of actors in the political system. Entertaining a weak assumption leads directly to an emphasis upon mobilization processes. Our concern is the search for analytic tools to account adequately for the processes.

Resource mobilization

The resource mobilization perspective adopts as one of its underlying problems Olson's (1965) challenge: since social movements deliver collective goods, few individuals will "on their own" bear the costs of working to obtain them. Explaining collective behavior requires detailed attention to the selection of incentives, cost-reducing mechanisms or structures, and career benefits that lead to collective behavior (see, especially, Oberschall 1973).

Several emphases are central to the perspective as it has developed.[5] First, study of the aggregation of resources (money and labor) is crucial to an understanding of social movement activity. Because resources are necessary for engagement in social conflict, they must be aggregated for collective purposes. Second, resource aggregation requires some minimal form of organization, and hence, implicitly or explicitly, we focus more directly upon social movement organizations than do those working within the traditional perspective. Third, in accounting for a movement's successes and failures there is an explicit recognition of the crucial importance of involvement on the part of individuals and organizations from outside the collectivity which a social movement represents. Fourth, an explicit, if crude, supply and demand model is sometimes applied to the flow of resources toward and away from specific social movements. Finally, there is a sensitivity to the importance of costs and rewards in explaining individual and organizational involvement in social movement activity. Costs and rewards are centrally affected by the structure of society and the activities of authorities.

We can summarize the emerging perspective by contrasting it with the traditional one as follows:

1. Support base
    A. Traditional. Social movements are based upon aggrieved populations which provide the necessary resources and labor. Although case studies may mention external supports, they are not incorporated as central analytic components.
    B. Resource mobilization. Social movements may or may not be based upon the grievances of the presumed beneficiaries. Conscience constituents, individual and organizational, may provide major sources of support. And in some cases supporters—those who provide money, facilities, and even labor—may have no commitment to the values that underlie specific movements.
2. Strategy and tactics
    A. Traditional. Social movement leaders use bargaining, persuasion, or violence to influence authorities to change. Choices of tactics depend upon prior history of relations with authorities, relative success of previous encounters, and ideology. Tactics are also influenced by the oligarchization and institutionalization of organizational life.
    B. Resource mobilization. The concern with interaction between movements and authorities is accepted, but it is also noted that social movement organizations have a number of strategic tasks. These include mobilizing supporters, neutralizing and/or transforming mass and elite publics into sympathizers, achieving change in targets. Dilemmas occur in the choice of tactics, since what may achieve one aim may conflict with behavior aimed at achieving another. Moreover, tactics are influenced by inter-organizational competition and cooperation.
3. Relation to larger society
    A. Traditional. Case studies have emphasized the effects of the environment upon movement organizations, especially with respect to goal change, but have ignored, for the most part, ways in which such movement organizations can utilize the environment for their own purposes (see Perrow 1972). This has probably been largely a result of the lack of comparative organizational focus inherent in case studies. In analytical studies emphasis is upon the extent of hostility or toleration in the larger society. Society and culture are treated as descriptive, historical context.
    B. Resource mobilization. Society provides the infrastructure which social movement industries and other industries utilize. The aspects utilized include communication media and expense, levels of affluence, degree of access to institutional centers, preexisting networks, and occupational structure and growth.

Theoretical elements

Having sketched the emerging perspective, our task now is to present a more precise statement of it. In this section we offer our most general concepts and definitions. Concepts of narrower range are presented in following sections.

A *social movement* is a set of opinions and beliefs in a population which represents preferences for changing some elements of the social structure and/or reward distribution of a society. A *countermovement* is a set of opinions and beliefs in a population opposed to a social movement. As is clear, we view social movements as nothing more than preference structures directed toward social change, very similar to what political sociologists would term issue cleavages. (Indeed, the process we are exploring resembles what political scientists term interest aggregation, except that we are concerned with the margins of the political system rather than with existing party structures.)

The distribution of preference structures can be approached in several ways. Who holds the beliefs? How intensely are they held? In order to predict the likelihood of preferences being translated into collective action, the mobilization perspective focuses upon the preexisting organization and integration of those segments of a population which share preferences. Oberschall (1973) has presented an important synthesis of past work on the preexisting organization of preference structures, emphasizing the opportunities and costs for expression of preferences for movement leaders and followers. Social movements whose related populations are highly organized internally (either communally or associationally) are more likely than are others to spawn organized forms.

A *social movement organization* (SMO) is a complex, or formal, organization which identifies its goals with the preferences of a social movement or a countermovement and attempts to implement those goals. If we think of the recent civil rights movement in these terms, the social movement contained a large portion of the population which held preferences for change aimed at "justice for black Americans" and a number of SMOs such as the Student Non-Violent Coordinating Committee (SNCC), the Congress of Racial Equality (CORE), the National Association for the Advancement of Colored People (NAACP), and Southern Christian Leadership Conference (SCLC). These SMOs represented and shaped the broadly held preferences and diverse subpreferences of the social movement.

All SMOs that have as their goal the attainment of the broadest preferences of a social movement constitute a *social movement industry* (SMI) —the organizational analogue of a social movement.

[. . .]

Definitions of the central term, social movement (SM), typically have included both elements of preference and organized action for change. Analytically separating these components by distinguishing between an SM and an SMI has several advantages. First, it emphasizes that SMs are never fully mobilized. Second, it focuses explicitly upon the organizational component of activity. Third, it recognizes explicitly that SMs are typically represented by more than one SMO. Finally, the distinction allows the possibility of an account of the rise and fall of SMIs that is not fully dependent on the size of an SM or the intensity of the preferences within it.

Our definitions of SM, SMI, and SMO are intended to be inclusive of the phenomena which analysts have included in the past. The SMs can encompass narrow or broad preferences, millenarian and evangelistic preferences, and withdrawal preferences. Organizations may represent any of these preferences.

[. . .]

Given our task, the question becomes how to group SMOs into SMIs. This is a difficult problem because particular SMOs may be broad or narrow in stated target goals. In any set of empirical circumstances the analyst must decide how narrowly to define industry boundaries. For instance, one may speak of the SMI which aims at liberalized alterations in laws, practices, and public opinion concerning abortion. This SMI would include a number of SMOs. But these SMOs may also be considered part of the broader SMI which is commonly referred to as the "women's liberation movement" or they could be part of the "population control movement." In the same way, the pre-1965 civil rights movement could be considered part of the broader civil liberties movement.

[. . .]

Let us now return to the resource mobilization task of an SMO. Each SMO has a set of *target goals*, a set of preferred changes toward which it claims to be working. Such goals may be broad or narrow, and they are the characteristics of SMOs which link them conceptually with particular SMs and SMIs. The SMOs must possess resources, however few and of whatever type, in order to work toward goal achievement. Individuals and other organizations control resources, which can include legitimacy, money, facilities, and labor.

Although similar organizations vary tremendously in the efficiency with which they translate resources into action (see Katz 1974), the amount of activity directed toward goal accomplishment is crudely a function of the resources controlled by an organization. Some organizations may depend heavily upon volunteer labor, while others may depend upon purchased labor. In any case, resources must be controlled or mobilized before action is possible.

From the point of view of a SMO the individuals and organizations which exist in a society may be categorized along a number of dimensions. For the appropriate SM there are adherents and nonadherents. *Adherents* are those individuals and organizations that believe in the goals of the movement. The *constituents* of a SMO are those providing resources for it.

At one level the resource mobilization task is primarily that of converting adherents into constituents and maintaining constituent involvement. However, at another level the task may be seen as turning nonadherents into adherents. Ralph Turner (1970) uses the term bystander public to denote those nonadherents who are not opponents of the SM and its SMOs but who merely witness social movement activity. It is useful to distinguish constituents, adherents, bystander publics, and opponents along several other dimensions. One refers to the size of the resource pool controlled; and we shall use the terms mass and elite to describe crudely this dimension. Mass constituents, adherents, bystander publics, and opponents are those individuals and groups controlling very limited resource pools. The most limited resource pool which individuals can control is their own time and labor. Elites are those who control larger resource pools.

Each of these groups may also be distinguished by whether or not they will benefit directly from the accomplishment of SMO goals. Some bystander publics, for instance, may benefit directly from the accomplishment of organizational goals, even though they are not adherents of the appropriate SM. To mention a specific example, women who oppose the preferences of the women's liberation movement or have no relevant preferences might benefit from expanded job opportunities for women pursued by women's groups. Those who would benefit directly from SMO goal accomplishment we shall call *potential beneficiaries.*

In approaching the task of mobilizing resources a SMO may focus its attention upon adherents who are potential beneficiaries and/or attempt to convert bystander publics who are potential beneficiaries into adherents. It may also expand its target goals in order to enlarge its potential beneficiary group. Many SMOs attempt to present their goal accomplishments in terms of broader potential benefits for ever-wider groupings of citizens through notions of a better society, etc. (secondary benefits). Finally, a SMO may attempt to mobilize as adherents those who are not potential beneficiaries. *Conscience adherents* are individuals and groups who are part of the appropriate SM but do not stand to benefit directly from SMO goal accomplishment. *Conscience constituents* are direct supporters of a SMO who do not stand to benefit directly from its success in goal accomplishment.[6]

[. . .]

A SMOs potential for resource mobilization is also affected by authorities and the delegated agents of social control (e.g., police). While authorities and agents of control groups do not typically become constituents of SMOs, their ability to frustrate (normally termed social control) or to enable resource mobilization are of crucial importance. Their action affects the readiness of bystanders, adherents, and constituents to alter their own status and commitment. And they themselves may become adherents and constituents.

[. . .]

Conclusion

The resource mobilization model we have described here emphasizes the interaction between resource availability, the preexisting organization of preference structures, and entrepreneurial attempts to meet preference demand. We have emphasized how these processes seem to operate in the modern American context. Different historical circumstances and patterns of preexisting infrastructures of adherency will affect the strategies of SMO entrepreneurial activity in other times and places. Our emphasis, however, seems to be useful in accounting for parallel activity in different historical contexts, including peasant societies, and in explaining the processes of growth and decline in withdrawal movements as well.

The history of the Bolshevik SMO (Wolfe 1955) shows how important stable resource flows are to the competitive position of a SMO. The Bolsheviks captured the resource flow to the Russian Social Revolutionary movement and, at certain points in their history, depended heavily upon isolated conscience constituents. Free media are probably necessary to mass isolated constituent involvement in resource flows, so isolated adherents with control over large resource pools are probably more important to SMI growth in societies without mass media. Leites and Wolf (1970) make a similar analysis of the revolutionary SMI in its relationship to the constant rewards of participation by the peasants in Vietnam. Of course, the extent of discretionary resources varies considerably between that case and the modern American case, but so did the ability of authorities to intervene in the manipulation of costs and rewards of individual involvement in the revolutionary SMO. The flow of resources from outside South Vietnam was important in the SMO's ability to manipulate these costs and rewards. Extranational involvement in the American SMS seems almost nonexistent.

Moreover, Oberschall (1973) has shown how important communal associations may be for facilitating mobilization in tribal and peasant societies. Although the number of SMOs and hence the size of the SMI may be smaller in peasant societies, resource mobilization and SM facilitation by societal infrastructure issues are just as important.

Withdrawal movements are typically characterized primarily by the way in which constituents are bound to the SMO (Kanter 1972). But SMOs in withdrawal SMs also encounter difficulties in developing stable resource flows, and they use a variety of strategies similar to those of other SMOs in response to their difficulties. The recent behavior of the Unification Church of America (led by the Rev. Sun Myung Moon) in the United States illustrates processes close to those we have focused upon for modern reform movements: heavy use of advertising and emphasis upon stable resource flows in order to augment the development of federated constituencies. The Father Divine Peace Mission (Cantril 1941) utilized rather different strategies of resource mobilization, including a heavier dependence upon the constituents themselves, but the importance of maintaining flows for continued viability was recognized in both of these withdrawal movements.

Our attempt has been to develop a partial theory; we have only alluded to, or treated as constant, important variables—the interaction of authorities, SMOs, and bystander publics; the dynamics of media involvement; the relationship between SMO workers and authorities; the impact of industry structure; the dilemmas of tactics. Yet, in spite of the limitations of our brief statement of the resource mobilization perspective, we believe it offers important new insights into the understanding of social movement phenomena and can be applied more generally.

Notes

1   One reflection of this change has been discussion of the appropriateness of including the study of social movements within the social psychology section of the American Sociological Association (see the *Critical Mass Bulletin* 1973–74). The issue is whether or not social movement research should consist largely of individual social psychological analysis (e.g., value, attitudes, and grievances of participants).

2   We are responding here to the dominant focus. Some analysts, most notably Rudolf Heberle (1951, 1968) among American-based sociologists, have viewed social movements from a distinctly structural perspective. Of course, structural approaches have remained dominant in Europe.

3   For example, see Levy 1970. For an early attempt to move beyond a simple grievance model see Morrison (1971): this article attempts to explain recruitment in social movement organizations rather than the attitudes of movement support of isolated individuals. Gurr's own empirical studies have led him to emphasize institutional-structural factors more heavily, as he has found that the structural characteristics of dissident groups are important factors in accounting for both violent and nonviolent civil strife (Gurr 1972).

4   For a full and balanced review of research and theory about social movements during the past decade, see Marx and Wood (1975).

5   Other contributors to the research mobilization perspective, aside from those already noted, are James Q. Wilson (1973), Breton and Breton (1969), Leites and Wolf (1970), Etzioni (1968), Jenkins and Perrow (1977), Salisbury (1969), Strickland and Johnston (1970), and Tullock (1966).

6   We have borrowed this term from Harrington (1968, p. 291), who uses it to refer to middle-class liberals who have demonstrated strong sympathies for the interests of underdog groups. Our use broadens the meaning of the term.

References

Bailis, L. 1974. *Bread or Justice*. Springfield, Mass.: Heath-Lexington.

Bain, J. S. 1959. *Industrial Organization*. New York: Wiley.

Blumer, H. 1946. "Collective Behavior." Pp. 167–219 in *A New Outline of the Principles of Sociology*, edited by A. M. Lee. New York: Barnes & Noble.

Bowen, D., E. Bowen, S. Gawiser, and L. Masotti. 1968. "Deprivation, Mobility, and Orientation toward Protest of the Urban Poor." Pp. 187–200 in *Riots and Rebellion: Civil Violence in the Urban Community*, edited by L. Masotti and D. Bowen. Beverly Hills, Calif.: Sage.

Bradburn, N., and D. Caplovitz. 1964. *Reports on Happiness*. Chicago: Aldine.

Breton, A., and R. Breton. 1969. "An Economic Theory of Social Movements." *American Economic Review. Papers and Proceedings of the American Economic Association*, 59, no. 2 (May).

Brown, L. 1970. "Hunger U.S.A.: The Public Pushes Congress." *Journal of Health and Social Behavior* 11 (June): 115–25.

Campbell, A., P. E. Converse, W. E. Miller, and D. E. Stokes. 1960. *The American Voter*. New York: Wiley.

Cantril, H. 1941. *The Psychology of Social Movements*. New York: Wiley.

———. 1965. *The Pattern of Human Concern*. New Brunswick, N.J.: Rutgers University Press.

Cicchetti, C. J., A. M. Freeman III, R. H. Haveman, and J. L. Knetsch, 1971. "On the Economics of Mass Demonstrations: A Case Study of the November 1969 March on Washington." *American Economic Review* 61, no. 4 (September): 719–24.

Clark, P. B., and J. Q. Wilson. 1961. "Incentive Systems: A Theory of Organizations." *Administrative Science Quarterly* 6 (September): 129–66.

Connolly, W. E. 1969. *The Bias of Pluralism*. New York: Atherton.

Converse, P. E. 1969. "Of Time and Partisan Stability." *Comparative Political Studies* 2, no. 2 (July): 139–71.

Crawford, T. J., and M. Naditch. 1970. "Relative Deprivation, Powerlessness and Militancy: The Psychology of Social Protest." *Psychiatry* 33 (May): 208–23.

Critical Mass Bulletin. 1973–74. Vol. 1. University of Tennessee.

Downs, A. 1972. "Up and Down with Ecology—the Issue Attention Cycle." *Public Interest* 28 (Summer): 38–50.

Etzioni, A. 1968, *The Active Society*. New York: Free Press.

Freeman, J. 1975. *The Politics of Women's Liberation*. New York: McKay.

Gamson, W. A. 1968. *Power and Discontent*. Homewood, Ill.: Dorsey.

———. 1975. *The Strategy of Protest*. Homewood, Ill.: Dorsey.

Gerlach, L., and V. Hines. 1970. *People, Power and Change: Movements of Social Transformation*. Indianapolis: Bobbs-Merrill.

Gurr, T. R. 1970. *Why Men Rebel*. Princeton, N.J.: Princeton University Press.

———. 1972. *Politimetrics: An Introduction to Quantitative Macropolitics*. Engle-wood Cliffs, N.J.: Prentice-Hall.

Halloron, R. 1971. "The Idea that Politics Is Everybody's Business." *New York Times*. (March 7), sec. 4, p. 3.

Harrington, M. 1968. *Toward a Democratic Left: A Radical Program for a New Majority*. New York: Macmillan.

Heberle, R. 1951. *Social Movements: An Introduction to Political Sociology*. New York: Appleton-Century.

———. 1968. "Types and Functions of Social Movements." Pp. 438–44 in *International Encyclopedia of the Social Sciences*, vol. 14, edited by David Sills. New York: Macmillan.

Hentoff, N. 1963. *Peace Agitator: The Story of A. J. Muste*. New York: Macmillan.

Hubbard, H. 1968. "Five Long Hot Summers and How They Grew." *Public Interest* 12 (Summer): 3–24.

Jenkins, C., and C. Perrow. 1977. "Insurgency of the Powerless: Farm Workers Movements (1946–72)." *American Sociological Review*.

Jonas, G. 1971. *On Doing Good: The Quaker Experiment*. New York: Scribner's.

Kahn, S, 1970. *How People Get Power: Organizing Oppressed Communities for Action*. New York: McGraw-Hill.

Kanter, R. M. 1972. *Commitment and Community: Communes and Utopias in Sociological Perspective*. Cambridge, Mass.: Harvard University Press.

Katz, H. 1974. *Give! Who Gets Your Charity Dollar?* Garden City, N.Y.: Doubleday.

Killian, L. 1972. "The Significance of Extremism in the Black Revolution." *Social Problems* 20 (Summer): 41–48.

Leites, N., and C. Wolf, Jr. 1970. *Rebellion and Authority*. Chicago: Markham.

Levy, S, 1970. "The Psychology of Political Activity." *Annals* 391 (September): 83–96.

Lin, N. 1974–75. "The McIntire March: A Study of Recruitment and Commitment." *Public Opinion Quarterly* 38 (Winter): 562–73.

Lipset, S. M., and E. Raab. 1970. *The Politics of Unreason: Right-Wing Extremism in America, 1790–1970*. New York: Harper & Row.

Lipsky, M. 1968. "Protest as a Political Resource." *American Political Science Review* 62:1144–58.

Lowi, T. J. 1971. *The Politics of Disorder*. New York: Basic.

McCarthy, J. D., and M. N. Zald. 1973. *The Trend of Social Movements in America: Professionalization and Resource Mobilization.* Morristown, N.J.: General Learning Press.

———. 1974. "Tactical Considerations in Social Movement Organizations." Paper delivered at the meeting of the American Sociological Association, August, Montreal.

Martin, G. T. 1971. "Organizing the Underclass: Findings on Welfare Rights." Working Paper no. 17. Human Side of Poverty Project, Department of Sociology, State University of New York at Stony Brook.

———. 1974. "Welfare Recipient Activism: Some Findings on the National Welfare Rights Organization." Paper presented at the annual meeting of the Midwest Political Science Association, Chicago, April 26.

Marx, G. T. 1970, "Issueless Riots." *Annals* 391 (September): 21–33.

———. 1974. "Thoughts on a Neglected Category of Social Movement Participant: The Agent Provocateur and the Informant." *American Journal of Sociology* 80 (September): 402–42.

Marx, G. T., and M. Useem. 1971. "Majority Involvement in Minority Movements: Civil Rights, Abolition, Untouchability." *Journal of Social Issues* 27 (January): 81–104.

Marx, G. T., and J. Wood. 1975. "Strands of Theory and Research in Collective Behavior." *Annual Review of Sociology* 1:363–428.

Meier, A., and E. Rudwick. 1973. *CORE: A Study in the Civil Rights Movement, 1942–1968.* New York: Oxford University Press.

———. 1976. "Attorneys Black and White. A Case Study of Race Relations within the NAACP." *Journal of American History* 62 (March): 913–46.

Miller, W. E., and T. E. Levitin. 1976. *Leadership and Change: The New Politics and the American Electorate.* Cambridge, Mass.: Winthrop.

Morgan, J. N., R. F. Dye, and J. H. Hybels. 1975. *A Survey of Giving Behavior and Attitudes: A Report to Respondents.* Ann Arbor, Mich.: Institute for Social Research.

Morris, B. 1975. "Consumerism Is Now a Luxury Item." *Washington Star* (October 28), pp. 1, 7.

Morrison, D. E. 1971. "Some Notes toward Theory on Relative Deprivation. Social Movements, and Social Change." *American Behavioral Scientist* 14 (May/June): 675–90.

Mueller, E. 1972. "A Test of a Partial Theory of Potential for Political Violence." *American Political Science Review* 66 (September): 928–59.

New York Times. 1974. "Social Action Hit by Financial Woes." (November 8), sec. 1 p. 20.

Oberschall, A. 1973. *Social Conflict and Social Movements.* Englewood Cliffs, N.J.: Prentice-Hall.

Olson, M., Jr. 1965. *The Logic of Collective Action.* Cambridge, Mass.: Harvard University Press.

Organizer's Manual Collective. 1971. *The Organizer's Manual.* New York: Bantam.

Orum, A. M., and K. L. Wilson. 1975. "Toward a Theoretical Model of Participation in Political Movements. I. Leftist Movements." Unpublished paper. Department of Sociology, University of Texas at Austin.

Perrow, C. 1970. "Members as Resources in Voluntary Organizations." Pp. 93–116 in *Organizations and Clients,* edited by W. R. Rosengren and M. Lefton. Columbus, Ohio: Merrill.

———. 1972. *Complex Organizations: A Critical Essay.* Glenview, Ill.: Scott, Foresman.

Pombeiro, B. G. 1975. "Recession Cripples Social Aid Groups." *Philadelphia Inquirer* (October 12), pp. 1–2.

Quarantelli, E. L., and J. R. Hundley. 1975. "A Test of Some Propositions about Crowd Formation and Behavior." Pp. 317–86 in *Readings in Collective Behavior*, edited by R. R. Evans. 2nd ed. Chicago: Rand McNally.

Rose, A. 1967. *The Power Structure*. New York: Oxford University Press.

Ross, D. K. 1973. *A Public Citizen's Action Manual*. New York: Grossman.

Ross, R. 1975. "Generational Change and Primary Groups in a Social Movement." Unpublished paper. Clark University, Worcester, Mass.

Sale, K. 1973. *SDS*. New York: Random House.

Salisbury, R. H, 1969. "An Exchange Theory of Interest Groups." *Midwest Journal of Political Science* 13 (February): 1–32.

Samuelson, P. 1964. *Economics: An Introductory Analysis*. New York: McGraw-Hill.

Smelser, N. 1963. *Theory of Collective Behavior*. New York: Free Press.

Snyder, D., and C. Tilly. 1972. "Hardship and Collective Violence in France." *American Sociological Review* 37 (October): 520–32.

Stallings, R. A. 1973. "Patterns of Belief in Social Movements: Clarifications from Analysis of Environmental Groups." *Sociological Quarterly* 14 (Autumn): 465–80.

Stinchcombe, A. L. 1965. "Social Structure and Organizations." Pp. 142–93 in *Handbook of Organizations*, edited by James March. Chicago: Rand-McNally.

Stouffer, S. 1955. *Communism, Conformity and Civil Liberties*. Garden City, N.Y.: Doubleday.

Strickland, D. A., and A. E. Johnston. 1970. "Issue Elasticity in Political Systems." *Journal of Political Economy* 78 (September/October): 1069–92.

Tilly, C. 1973. "Does Modernization Breed Revolution?" *Comparative Politics* 5 (April): 425–47.

———. 1975. "Revolution and Collective Violence." Pp. 483–555 in *Handbook of Political Science*, edited by F. Greenstein and N. Polsky. Vol. 3. *Macro Political Theory*. Reading, Mass.: Addison-Wesley.

Tilly, C., L. Tilly, and R. Tilly. 1975. *The Rebellious Century: 1830–1930*. Cambridge, Mass.: Harvard University Press.

Tullock, G. 1966. "Information without Profit." Pp. 141–60. In *Papers on Non-Market Decision Making*, edited by G. Tullock. Charlottesville: University of Virginia, Thomas Jefferson Center for Political Economy.

Turner, R. H. 1969. "The Public Perception of Protest." *American Sociological Review* 34 (December): 815–31.

———. 1970. "Determinants of Social Movement Strategies." Pp. 145–64 in *Human Nature and Collective Behavior: Papers in Honor of Herbert Blumer*, edited by Tamotsu Shibutani. Englewood Cliffs, N.J.: Prentice-Hall.

Turner, R. N., and L. Killian. 1972. *Collective Behavior*. 2d ed. Englewood Cliffs, N.J.: Prentice-Hall.

U.S. Treasury Department. 1965. *Report on Private Foundations*. Washington, D.C.: Government Printing Office.

Von Eschen, D., J. Kirk, and M. Pinard. 1969. "The Disintegration of the Negro Nonviolent Movement." *Journal of Peace Research* 3:216–34.

———. 1971. "The Organizational Sub-Structure of Disorderly Politics." *Social Forces* 49 (June): 529–43.

Walzer, M. 1971. *Political Action: A Practical Guide to Movement Politics*. Chicago: Quadrangle.

Wilkinson, P. 1971. *Social Movements*. New York: Praeger.

Wilson, J. 1973. *Introduction to Social Movements*. New York: Basic.

Wilson, J. Q. 1973. *Political Organisations*. New York: Basic.

Wolfe, B. 1955. *Three Who Made a Revolution*. Boston: Beacon.

Wootton, G. 1970. *Interest Groups*. Englewood Cliffs, N.J.: Prentice-Hall.

Zald, M. N., and R. Ash. 1966. "Social Movement Organizations: Growth, Decline and Change." *Social Forces* 44 (March): 327–40.

Zald, M. N., and D. Jacobs. 1976. "Symbols into Plowshares: Underlying Dimensions of Incentive Analysis." Unpublished paper. Vanderbilt University, Nashville, Tenn.

Zald, M. N., and J. D. McCarthy. 1974. "Notes on Cooperation and Competition amongst Social Movement Organizations." Unpublished paper. Vanderbilt University, Nashville, Tenn.

———. 1975. "Organizational Intellectuals and the Criticism of Society." *Social Service Review* 49 (September): 344–62.

Chapter 18

J. Craig Jenkins

RESOURCE MOBILIZATION THEORY AND THE STUDY OF SOCIAL MOVEMENTS

The emergence of resource mobilization theory

OF THE WIDE-RANGING EFFECTS that the social movements of the 1960s had on sociology, one of the more significant was the reorientation of the study of social movements. Traditionally the central problem in the field had been explaining individual participation in social movements. The major formulations— mass society theory, relative deprivation, collective behavior theory—pointed to sudden increases in individual grievances generated by the "structural strains" of rapid social change. While specific hypotheses varied, these traditional theories shared the assumptions that movement participation was relatively rare, discontents were transitory, movement and institutionalized actions were sharply distinct, and movement actors were arational if not outright irrational. The movements of the 1960s dramatically challenged these assumptions. By providing a rich array of experience and enlisting the active sympathies of an enlarged pool of analysts, the movements stimulated a shift in theoretical assumptions and analytic emphases that eventually became formalized in the resource mobilization theory of social movements.

[. . .]

These new perspectives emphasized the continuities between movement and institutionalized actions, the rationality of movement actors, the strategic problems confronted by movements, and the role of movements as agencies for social change.

Adapted and reprinted, with permission, from the *Annual Review of Sociology*, Volume 9 © 1983 by Annual Reviews www.annualreviews.org

In specific, these analysts argued that: *(a)* movement actions are rational, adaptive responses to the costs and rewards of different lines of action; *(b)* the basic goals of movements are defined by conflicts of interest built into institutionalized power relations; *(c)* the grievances generated by such conflicts are sufficiently ubiquitous that the formation and mobilization of movements depend on changes in resources, group organization, and opportunities for collective action; *(d)* centralized, formally structured movement organizations are more typical of modern social movements and more effective at mobilizing resources and mounting sustained challenges than decentralized, informal movement structures; and *(e)* the success of movements is largely determined by strategic factors and the political processes in which they become enmeshed.

[. . .]

Sources of contention: resource mobilization vs traditional approaches

The clash between resource mobilization theory and traditional approaches, especially collective behavior theories, has stemmed in large part from different conceptions of social movements. Traditional definitions have included any set of noninstitutionalized collective actions consciously oriented towards social change (or resisting such changes) and possessing a minimum of organization. Social movements are traditionally seen as extensions of more elementary forms of collective behavior and as encompassing both movements of personal change (e.g. religious sects, cults, and communes) and those focused on institutional changes (e.g. legal reforms and changes in political power). Resource mobilization theorists have, in contrast, seen social movements as extensions of institutionalized actions and have restricted their focus to movements of institutional change that attempt to alter elements of social structure and/or the reward distribution of society, organize previously unorganized groups against institutional elites or represent the interests of groups excluded from the polity.

[. . .]

The formation of social movements

The sine qua non of the study of social movements has traditionally been the question of why movements form. Traditional explanations have emphasized sudden increases in short-term grievances created by the "structural strains" of rapid social change (Gusfield 1968). In contrast, resource mobilization theorists have argued that grievances are secondary. Tilly (1978), Jenkins & Perrow (1977), and Oberschall (1978) have argued that grievances are relatively constant, deriving from structural conflicts of interest built into social institutions, and that movements form because of long-term changes in group resources, organization, and opportunities for collective action. While grievances are necessary for movement formation, they are explained either by changes in power relations or by structural conflicts of interest. McCarthy & Zald (1973, 1977) have taken a slightly different direction, arguing for an entrepreneurial theory of movement formation in which the major factor is the availability of resources, especially cadres and organizing facilities. Grievances are either structurally given or, increasingly in the contemporary setting, manufactured by the mobilizing efforts of movement entrepreneurs. As McCarthy & Zald formulate it, "the definition of grievances will expand to meet the funds and support personnel available" (1973:13).

The debate touched off by these formulations, especially the McCarthy–Zald version, has produced support for both formulations as well as a refined theory of grievances. The strongest support for the McCarthy–Zald theory has come from studies of the "public interest" movement that came to prominence in the 1970s.

[. . .]

These movements pursued goals linked to the interests of broad, diffuse, disorganized collectivities such as the general public or middle-class consumers who were unlikely to mobilize without the initiative of entrepreneurs.

The entrepreneurial model has also received support from movements of deprived groups such as farm workers and welfare recipients. In these cases, the entrepreneurs had branched out after being cadres in the civil rights and student movements. Both were also centered among deprived groups with few resources, minimal political experience, and little prior organization, making outside organizers critical in the formation of a movement. In fact, such cadre diversification was also critical in launching a wide array of movements among less deprived groups such as women's liberation, radical ecology, and neighborhood and general citizen organizing. In other words, the entrepreneurial model appears most relevant for movements among deprived groups and broad disorganized collectivities. The entrepreneurs are typically generated by the factionalization of previous movements. Significantly, however, major movements do not appear to emerge from the de novo manufacture of grievances by entrepreneurs. As McCarthy & Zald (1973:28) argue, entrepreneurs are more successful by seizing on major interest cleavages and redefining long-standing grievances in new terms.

Recent studies have also demonstrated the significance of increased grievances generated by sudden and major threats to the interests of cohesive and moderately resourceful groups.

[. . .]

Studies have also confirmed the argument that long-term changes in the organization, resources, and opportunities of groups give rise to movement formation. Industrial conflicts are more likely among ecologically concentrated workers in large factories and densely populated urban neighborhoods. Likewise, the emergence of the civil rights movement in the 1950s stemmed from the urbanization of the southern black population, increased numbers of middle-class and working-class blacks, growing black college enrollments, and the organizational expansion of black churches. These changes simultaneously freed blacks from traditional paternalistic social controls, increased levels of black organization and resources, and placed the black voter in a strategic location in national politics.

[. . .]

The process of mobilization

Mobilization is the process by which a group secures collective control over the resources needed for collective action. The major issues, therefore, are the resources controlled by the group prior to mobilization efforts, the processes by which the group pools resources and directs these towards social change, and the extent to which outsiders increase the pool of resources.

Little agreement exists on the types of resources that are significant. Several analysts have offered classificatory schemes based upon the usefulness of particular resources in controlling the actions of targets distinguishing *instrumental* resources used in actual influence attempts from *infra*-resources that condition the use of instrumental resources. Similarly, Jenkins (1982a) has distinguished *power* resources that provide the means for controlling the actions of targets from *mobilizing* resources such as facilities that provide for mobilizing power resources.

The problem with schemes based on uses, however, is that most resources have multiple uses. Any scheme that ignores the intrinsic features of resources is therefore of limited value. In response, most analysts have simply listed the assets that are frequently mobilized by movements: money, facilities, labor, and legitimacy; land, labor, capital, and technical expertise. Freeman (1979:172–5) has offered a more useful scheme, distinguishing *tangible* assets such as money, facilities, and means of communication from the *intangible* or "human" assets that form the central basis for movements. Intangible assets include both specialized resources such as organizing and legal skills, and the unspecialized labor of supporters.

The most distinctive contribution of resource mobilization theory has been to emphasize the significance of outside contributions and the cooptation of institutional resources by contemporary social movements. Traditionally, analysts have assumed that resources come from the direct beneficiaries of the social changes pursued and that, since movements lie outside institutionalized politics, they derive their resources from noninstitutional sources. McCarthy & Zald (1973, 1977), however, have argued that the movements of the 1960s and 1970s mobilized a "conscience constituency" of the wealthy and the affluent middle class (including college students) and coopted institutional resources from private foundations, social welfare institutions, the mass media, universities, governmental agencies, and even business corporations. Social movements have therefore shifted from classical social movement organizations (or classical SMOs) with indigenous leadership, volunteer staff, extensive membership, resources from direct beneficiaries, and actions based on mass participation, towards professional social movement organizations (or professional SMOs) with outside leadership, full-time paid staff, small or nonexistent membership, resources from conscience constituencies, and actions that "speak for" rather than involve an aggrieved group.

[. . .]

While McCarthy & Zald are correct that professional SMOs and the cooptation of institutional resources increased in the 1960s, these features hardly explain the mobilization of generalized political turmoil in that period. Most of the movements were not professional SMOs and did not rely on external resources for their crucial victories. Contributors of external resources were largely reactive, not initiatory, and were not consistently beneficial. The civil rights movement was indigenously led by black clergy and students, mobilized resources chiefly through local community networks, and tapped "conscience constituents" only after generalized turmoil had already been mobilized. Moreover, most of the external resources were mobilized by the moderate wing of the movement after it had successfully entered the polity and begun institutionalizing the gains of the Civil Rights Acts of 1964 and 1965. Ironically, the militant wing was more dependent on external resources and, partially because of conflicts over the use of these resources, became increasingly radical, eventually turning against their "conscience constituents" and destroying the organizations. Nor is the McCarthy-Zald theory fully satisfactory in explaining the middle-class and student involvement in the various movements of the 1960s. By focusing exclusively on economic changes that facilitated involvement (discretionary income and time schedules, social reform careers, institutional "slack"), the theory ignores changing cultural values and elite actions that led to an interest in movement politics. The middle-class "participation revolution" was rooted in the shift towards "postmaterialist" values emphasizing self-fulfillment that supported demands for direct participation in political decisions and moral concern for the plight of others. When elites challenged these values by manipulative acts and outright rejection, the middle class rallied around the movements.

The McCarthy-Zald theory does, however, identify significant aspects of recent social movements. The student and antiwar movements did rely heavily on the mobilization of transitory teams through coopting the mass media. Additionally, the welfare rights movement, farm worker movement, and "older wing" of the women's movement were initiated by movement entrepreneurs who relied heavily on institutional resources. Moreover, the environmental, consumer rights and general "public interest" movements of the 1970s have fit the professional SMO model quite closely. Finally, professional SMOs such as Mobilization for Youth and the Community Action Program did function as social control devices, "diffusing the radical possibilities of dissent ... by applying large amounts of resources ... in ameliorative directions" (McCarthy & Zald 1973:26).

If direct beneficiaries have been the major contributors to recent movements, how have they been mobilized? Because of its rationalistic assumptions, the major debate has been over the usefulness of Mancur Olson's theory of collective action. According to Olson, rational self-interested individuals will not contribute to securing "collective goods" because of the superior rationality of "riding free". Mobilization occurs only if "selective benefits" (i.e. distinct divisible benefits) are offered, the group is sufficiently small that benefits to individuals are greater than the costs of securing the collective good, or the group is "privileged" (i.e. contains individuals sufficiently endowed that the marginal costs of securing the collective good are less than their individual benefit).

All three of Olson's solutions to the problem of collective goods have come under critical attack. The major target has been the "by-product" theory of mobilization based on selective incentives. According to the theory, movement entrepreneurs motivated by the selective incentives of career opportunities offer selective incentives to members for their contributions, creating an expanding cycle of collective actions and further mobilization.

[. . .]

The Olson theory, however, cannot be dismissed. One case that supports it is the National Welfare Rights Organization experience (Bailis 1974). The NWRO was initiated by professional organizers who used the selective incentive of assistance in securing special cash benefits to mobilize welfare recipients. When organizers shifted to nonmaterial incentives, few prospective members were receptive. In line with Olson's theory, as soon as members learned how to secure the welfare benefits for themselves, contributions to the NWRO trailed off, leaving behind a core of activists motivated largely by the selective benefits of social recognition. When welfare administrators abolished the cash benefit program, the NWRO virtually collapsed.

The Olson theory correctly identifies a major problem but fails to offer an adequate solution. Olson is correct that movements cannot be mobilized around collective material benefits and that free-riding is potentially a major problem. The strongest evidence comes from Walsh (1981) study of residents surrounding the Three Mile Island nuclear plant disaster. Free-riding was pervasive; only 13% of those opposed to the restart contributed. Free-riding was largely due to ignorance and calculations of personal interest. Almost half (48%) of the free-riders were unaware of the oppostion effort or had not been contacted by movement organizers. The remainder cited personal constraints (24%), distaste for protest tactics and movement leaders (11%), or pessimism about their own political efficacy (5%). In other words, free-riding is probably widespread in natural settings and, while organizing efforts can reduce its frequency, personal calculations of costs and rewards are significant considerations.

How, then, do successful movements overcome the problem? The major method is the development of programs that offer the *collective incentives* of group solidarity and commitment to moral purpose. Group solidarity and purposive incentives are collective in that they entail the fusion of personal and collective interests. Movement supporters, like all socialized actors, act in terms of internalized values and sentiments as well as calculations of self-interest. The major task in mobilization, then, is to generate solidarity and moral commitments to the broad collectivities in whose name movements act.

The mobilization potential of a group is largely determined by the degree of preexisting group organization. Groups sharing strong distinctive identities and dense interpersonal networks exclusive to group members are highly organized and hence readily mobilized. By providing prior solidarities and moral commitments, these identities and networks provide a basis for the operation of collective incentives. The "bloc recruitment" of preexisting solidary groups is the most efficient form of recruitment and appears to be typical of large-scale institutional change movements. Conversely, groups with weak identities, few intragroup networks, and strong ties to outsiders are less likely to mobilize. As Foster (1974) found among English industrial workers, communities with strong intraclass networks based on intermarriage and involvement in recreational activities mobilized more readily and more extensively than those with weak networks and/or strong ties outside of their class. Similarly, Jenkins (1982) found that seasonal farm workers who were immune to the paternalistic ties of their employers and enmeshed in cohesive work and kinship networks were more readily mobilized than either migrants who lacked intragroup ties or permanent hands who were subject to employer controls.

Recruitment strategies follow the same basic principles. Campaigns centered around purposive and solidary incentives, focused on preexisting or "natural" groups, and linking the vision of change to the preexisting group culture are more effective. Farm worker unions that emphasized "bread and butter" gains were less successful than those that organized solidary events and inaugurated ideological training programs (Jenkins 1982). Similarly, individual recruitment requires greater resource investments and is much slower than bloc recruitment. Likewise, organizers who draw on the cultural symbols of the target population are more sucessful than those emphasizing abstract ideologies.

Differential recruitment follows essentially the same outlines. Recruitment tends to select individuals who are more enmeshed in interpersonal networks, active in political organizations that support social change, ideologically committed to social change, and structurally available for participation. Differential recruitment also changes as movements expand. Early recruits to the student movement came from higher socioeconomic backgrounds, attended elite universities, were more active in political organizations, and were more committed to social change ideologies than later recruits. Likewise, social classes appear to respond to different incentives. In general, more secure middle- and upper-class groups are more receptive to purposive incentives, while less secure, lower-class groups respond to selective incentives and collective solidarity. Similarly, differential participation tends to follow receptiveness to different incentives.

Note that the preceding discussion has ignored the major emphasis in classic studies of differential recruitment—namely, the role of personality characteristics. While personality differences undoubtedly play a role in differential recruitment, existing studies have been inconclusive as to which personality traits are significant and, more importantly, have been methodologically unable to demonstrate that these traits are independent of the social characteristics that lead to differential recruitment and participation.

The organization of social movements

The major debate over the organization of movements has been between proponents of a centralized bureaucratic model and those arguing for a decentralized informal model. The former argue that a formalized structure with a clear division of the labor maximizes mobilization by transforming diffuse commitments into clearly defined roles and that a centralized decision-making structure increases combat readiness by reducing internal conflicts (Gamson 1975: 89–109). In contrast, Gerlach & Hine (1970:34–56) have argued that decentralized movements with a minimum division of labor and integrated by informal networks and an overarching ideology are more effective. A segmented, decentralized structure maximizes mobilization by providing extensive interpersonal bonds that generate solidarity and reinforce ideological commitments. In addition, such a structure is highly adaptive, encouraging tactical experimentation, competition among subgroups, and lessened vulnerability to suppression or cooptation by authorities.

This debate, however, has been seriously derailed by several misinterpretations. Some analysts have assumed that the debate centers around identifying the single typical form of movement organization. As Zald & Ash (1966) argued sometime ago, movements adopt different forms depending on their goals. Personal change movements tend to adopt decentralized structures and exclusive membership rules while institutional change movements are typically centralized and inclusive. Moreover, analysts have ignored the distinction between social movements (or SMs) defined by broad goals and/or interests, and social movement organizations (or SMOs) defined by particular organizational structures. Since social movements are typically characterized by multiple SMOs, a multi-organizational model allowing the coexistence of diverse types is generally more appropriate in gauging the organization of a single social movement. Finally, commentators have often taken these formulations as descriptions rather than ideal-typical extremes. Current research indicates that there are also intermediary forms of SMOs: centralized structures with semi-autonomous locals and autonomous locals loosely coordinated through federative structures.

[. . .]

The broadest treatment of movement organization has been the analysis of the modernization of collective action by Charles Tilly (1978) and his associates. Building on the classic distinction between communal and associational organization, they have documented the broad shift over the past four centuries from short reactive actions by small-scale informal solidary groups (or communities) to long proactive actions mounted by large-scale special purpose associations. The shift broadly conforms to that from decentralized, informally structured communal movements to centralized, formally structured SMOs. The major sources of this shift have been linked to the broad contours of social development. The growth of industrial capitalism and the building of modern states destroyed the autonomy of small solidary groups and forced claimants to compete in a larger national political arena in which large numbers and bureaucratic structures were keys to success. Furthermore, urbanization and the growth of the mass media reduced the costs of large-scale mobilization, making bureaucratized associations more feasible. Finally, the institutionalization of liberal democracy, especially mass electoral participation, furnished an environment well suited to movement organizations that could mobilize large numbers of supporters. As the traditional communal group gave way to the modern bureaucratized association, the goals and forms of action shifted. Communal actors were "instinctive radicals," treating outside intrusions as fundamental violations, while associations were more moderate, maximizing gains within a given political environment. The former adopted a relatively fixed repertoire borrowed from existing structures of authority while the latter were more flexible, experimenting with different forms of action and, at least in liberal democracies, adopting the mass demonstration because of its advantages in signalling numerical support.

[. . .]

Yet despite this broad shift, decentralized movements have continued to emerge. Often decentralized structures are a product of deliberate choices by redemptive or personal-change movements attempting to embody ideals in the hope that these will serve as models for emulation. The student movement adopted a decentralized "leaderless" model of democratic structure in order to maximize the values of direct participation and communal involvement and to avoid the dangers of oligarchy and cooptation. Decentralized structures can also evolve from ecological constraints and inherited models.

[. . .]

Within a basic framework, the organizational structures of movements can still evolve. Contrary to the classic Weber–Michels theory, however, change is not inevitably in the direction of greater bureaucratization. As the National Organization for Women expanded in the mid-1970s to become the major organization in the women's movement, it became more internally diverse and developed a more decentralized structure composed of special task forces to accommodate the diverse ideologies and interests of its rapidly growing membership. The growth of the welfare rights movement in the late 1960s produced a multi-organizational field of informally coordinated organizations, providing the movement with the advantages of a decentralized structure. While this created strains because of internal competition for resources, decentralization also reduced factionalist tendencies by allowing activists to pursue diverse concerns. The same could be argued for the multi-organizational civil rights movement during its expansionary phase. Likewise, movement organizations can preserve their decentralized communal structures by adopting restrictions on size, using mutual criticism to restrain core activists, remaining economically marginal, relying strictly on internal financing, and attempting to reduce knowledge differentials among participants.

[. . .]

The future of resource mobilization theory

The future of resource mobilization theory lies in two directions; extending the basic polity model to deal with a broader variety of regimes, and refining the basic mobilization model by developing a more sophisticated social psychology of collective action. The central concern of the polity model is the link between regime changes and opportunities for political access. Research has been confined largely to liberal democratic regimes, linking movement access to changing electoral alignments, governing coalitions, and the institutional structure of the state. The development of neocorporatism offers the most provocative thesis for future analysis. Will neocorporatism allow governing elites to deflect and selectively coopt movements or force challengers into broader third party coalitions? Where neocorporatism is weakly developed (as in the United States), will partisan coalitions and alliances with polity members continue to regulate the access of single-issue reform movements? The largest vacuum lies in the analysis of authoritarian and one-party regimes. Are liberal democracies actually more permeable? Do elite cleavages within these regimes play the same role as partisan clashes in opening or closing access? Do corporatist devices have the same implications as in liberal democracies?

The central concern of the mobilization model is the link between collective interests and the pooling of resources. Collective interests are assumed to be relatively unproblematic and to exist prior to mobilization, instead of being socially constructed and created by the mobilization process. The critique of the Olson theory, however, suggests that collective interests are often emergent. How are such collective identities formed? Is resocialization central? Is there a logic of emergence that governs the content of such collective identities? Calhoun (1982), for example, has argued that "radical" definitions emerge only among densely connected informal communities that perceive threats as effecting their complete way of life. Paige (1975), in contrast, argues that this is because of the underlying zero-sum conflict of interests prevalent in traditional agrarian production systems. How indeterminant are such collective redefinitions of interests?

Once resource mobilization theory has expanded its scope in these two directions, it will have served its major purpose, linking the study of social movements to a comparative political sociology of states and regimes and to a more sophisticated social psychology of collective action.

References

Bailis, L. 1974. *Bread or Justice*. Lexington, MA: Heath. 254 pp.

Calhoun, C. 1982. *The Question of Class Struggle*. NY: Oxford Univ. Press. 182 pp.

Foster, J. 1974. *Class Struggle in the Industrial Revolution*. NY: St. Martins Press. 338 pp.

Freeman, J. 1979. Resource mobilization and strategy. In *The Dynamics of Social Movements*, ed. M. N. Zald, J. M. McCarthy, pp. 167–89. Cambridge, MA: Winthrop. 274 pp.

Gamson, W. 1975. *The Strategy of Social Protest*. Homewood, IL: Dorsey. 217 pp.

Gerlach, L., Hine, V. 1970. *People, Power, Change*. NY: Bobbs-Merrill. 257 pp.

Gusfield, J. R. 1982. Social movements and social change. *Res. Soc. Movem., Confl. Change* 4:283–316

Jenkins, J. C. 1982. The transformation of a constituency into a movement. In *The Social Movements of the 1960s and 1970s*, ed. J. Freeman. NY: Longmans. 397 pp.

Jenkins, J. C., Perrow, C. 1977. Insurgency of the powerless. *Am. Sociol. Rev.* 42:249–68

McCarthy, J., Zald, M. N. 1973. *The Trend of Social Movements*. Morristown, NJ: General Learning. 30 pp.

McCarthy, J. D., Zald, M. N. 1977. Resource mobilization and social movements. *Am. J. Sociol.* 82:1212–41

Oberschall, A. 1978. Theories of social conflict. *Ann. Rev. Sociol.* 4:291–315

Paige, J. 1975. *Agrarian Revolution*. NY: Free Press. 435 pp.

Tilly, C. 1978. *From Mobilization to Revolution*. Reading, MA: Addison-Wesley. 349 pp.

Walsh, E. J. 1981. Resource mobilization and citizen protest in communities around Three Mile Island. *Soc. Probl.* 26:1–21

Zald, M. N., Ash, R. 1966. Social movement organizations. *Soc. Forces* 44:327–41

Chapter 19

Gerald Marwell and Pamela Oliver

THE CRITICAL MASS IN COLLECTIVE ACTION

The critical mass and the problem of collective action

The idea of the *critical mass* is central to many understandings of collective action. Social movement activists, community leaders, and fund-raisers use the term when they talk about getting together enough resources to accomplish some goal. They express the understanding that it takes some minimum number of people or some minimum accumulation of seed money to draw in the participation and contributions of others. The phenomenon can also be seen in other, less intentional forms of collective action. Lynchings, wildcat strikes, and riots proceed when people become convinced that enough others are participating. Detailed observational studies of spontaneous collective action show incipient "organizers" calling to others to join their action, and they show potential participants talking to each other and reaching a common agreement about who will act.

[. . .]

The term *collective action* is understood by most social scientists today to be an abstraction that encompasses a staggeringly broad array of empirical phenomena: from raising an army to raising a barn; from building a bridge across a gulf separating states to building a faith community that spans the gulf between races; from organizing a business cartel to organizing a small partnership to compete in a crowded market; from the food riots of revolutionary France to the progressive dinners of charitable New York. As we will explain more carefully, the elements common to these disparate phenomena are mutual interests and the possibility of benefits from coordinated action. Given this variety, it is no surprise that over the past two decades most of the social sciences have shown an accelerating interest in understanding the process by which collective action comes to occur.

Our theory of the critical mass is a contribution to the tradition of studying collective action in the abstract. It differs from previous theory primarily in its focus on interdependence among actors, heterogeneity within groups, and the role of mobilizing agents. We assume that in most instances collective action is produced by a relatively small cadre of highly interested and resourceful individuals, rather than by the efforts of the "average" group member. Our major objective is to delineate the structural conditions under which such a "critical mass" of individuals and resources will be accumulated and directed toward the achievement of a collective goal.

We offer a general framework and a series of specific theoretical analyses. Our specific analyses address only a subset of the possibilities suggested by our general framework. We do not provide a comprehensive, "one size fits all" theory of collective action. To the contrary, we will show that there is no unitary phenomenon of "collective action" that can be described by a simple set of theoretical propositions. We will attempt to show the futility of posing general questions such as "Is collective action rational?" or "Do people free-ride?" Instead, we will lay out the dimensions of the field of collective action, then focus in on small parts of the field and provide detailed analysis of what we find in those small pots.

[. . .]

Background

Beginnings: free riding and the logic of collective action

For us, as for most social scientists, Mancur Olson's treatise *The Logic of Collective Action* (1965) served as an exciting introduction to the field of public goods and to the problem of collective action. Much of Olson's impact results from his strongly worded three-page introduction, in which he asserts that "rational, self-interested individuals will not act to achieve their common or group interests" (1965, p. 2). The reason for this claim is that, when interests are shared, rational actors should prefer to free-ride, that is, let others pay the costs of goods that will benefit everyone. The rationale for this assertion is explicated in the first, widely cited part of Olson's book. The rest of the book surveys the history of labor unions, classes and the state, interest groups, and pressure groups, defending Olson's thesis that collective action is always accompanied by private (selective) incentives to reward contributors or to punish noncontributors.

[. . .]

Economists had long argued that economically rational individuals will not voluntarily contribute money to pay for public goods such as armies, legislatures, parks, public schools, or sewage systems. Olson's important contribution was to argue that all group goals or group interests were subject to the same dilemma.

[. . .]

Olson defined a *collective good* as any good in which a group of individuals is *interested* (i.e., from which each thinks he will benefit) and which, if provided to one member of the group, cannot be withheld from any other member. For example, a park is a collective good for the "group" of park-loving city residents if none of them can be prevented from enjoying it. This is true even if the park were wholly purchased and built through private contributions to a park fund or, in the extreme, by a single private benefactor. If its use cannot be – or in practice is not – restricted to contributors, the park is a collective good.

In this conception, any and all activity aimed, at the provision of a collective good is defined as *collective action*.

[. . .]

Olson argues that because of the "free-rider problem," collective goods such as parks will generally *not* be provided through voluntary contributions. "Free riders," in this context, are people who do not contribute to the provision of a good but consume it (or, in the case of parks, use it) anyway.

[. . .]

The free-rider problem is a classic expression of the conflict that often arises between individual and group "rationality." The emergence of collective action in groups is not simply a matter of the group "realizing" its collective needs and therefore acting to meet them. Groups cannot be reified. In Olson's formulation, they simply consist of a number of individuals who share an interest in a good. They do not have explicit organization or institutions. They are *interest groups*, such as social classes or occupational categories, or parents whose children share a similar disease. Any "collective action" by such a group must be understood as the aggregated behavior of its individual members.

[. . .]

Notice that, contrary to a common misunderstanding, Olson does *not* argue or prove that individuals participate in collective action out of self-interest. Rather, he argues that self-interest implies that individuals will not participate in collective action. One perfectly reasonable conclusion to deduce from Olson's logic is that only *irrational* motives can explain collective action. The argument readily supports scholars who claim that solidarity or altruism or some other motive besides self-interest is particularly important for collective action.

[. . .]

Although we are ultimately critical of some of Olson's theorizing, the importance of Olson's argument to the history of social science cannot be overstated. Before Olson, almost all social scientists assumed that people would instinctively or naturally act on common interests, and that *inaction* needed to be explained. After Olson, most social scientists treat collective action as problematic.

[. . .]

Providing collective goods: theories and research

Free riding is a real problem. And yet collective goods are everywhere provided. Most real societies have armies, parks, and some form of public works. More important, voluntary action is widespread. People often make large personal sacrifices for social movements for diffuse collective goods such as freedom for everyone. Unions are organized. Ordinary people are brave in the face of repression. Charities are funded, sometimes by rich donors, but sometimes by the small gifts of thousands of individual donors responding in their own homes to appeals received through the mail. Any reasonable theory must account for these phenomena, as well as for the equally obvious fact that many collective goods ardently desired by some group, or even a whole population, never come to pass.

Of course, the obvious source of many collective goods is coercion by government. The classic analysis of the reason for government is precisely that armies, parks, and sewer systems require taxation, impressment, and the right to back up these processes with force. To Olson, however, coercion is only one instance, albeit possibly the most important, of a broader class of phenomena he calls "selective incentives." These include "social status and social acceptance" (p. 61) and monetary incentives that are privately delivered for participation in the collective action. The fundamental example of the latter is the salaries paid some individuals to work for organizations engaged in collective action.

[. . .]

Development

[. . .]

Our key difference with Olson's formulation (although not our only difference) is that we do not assume that the individuals in an interest group are acting in total isolation. Instead, we assume *interdependence* among actors, where interdependence may be defined most generally as behavior that takes account of the effect of one's participation in collective action on the participation of others. The structural conditions for interdependent behavior are that the effect on the collective good of one actor's choice varies depending on the choices of others, and that actors have at least some information about each other's actions.

Interdependence is certainly common in the empirical world of collective action. An urbanite considering joining in a riot may assume that the risk of any one individual being arrested declines with larger numbers of rioters; an office worker may consider the possibility that her contribution to United Way will increase the social pressures on others to contribute as well; a participant in a wildcat strike may also expect his presence on the line to embolden others to participate. People join groups involved in collective pursuits not only out of perceived common interests, but also because they regard the groups or individuals organizing the action as in some sense efficacious. Belief in the efficacy of a group may be based on a record of previous successes at stated goals, on the endorsement of a friend or relative who is already involved in the group, or even on lip service by authorities to the goals of the group. For most people, however, the most prominent and convincing evidence of a group's efficacy is probably the group's size and command over resources. Groups that are large and rich are likely to be seen as powerful. Growth itself is often seen as further evidence of potency and tends to attract still more contributions; groups that are stagnant or shrinking are likely to be seen as ineffective, accelerating their loss of membership. In this simple fashion, the decisions of individuals who come into contact with a group or its organizer are clearly interdependent with the decisions of others.

It is important to note that although assumptions of interdependence complicate formal models of collective campaigns, they in no way invalidate a basic decision-theoretic approach.

[. . .]

Group heterogeneity and the critical mass

[. . .]

Having realized the importance of the critical mass in mobilizing others, we turned a great deal of our attention to developing an explicit theory of organizing. We developed a model of organizer-centered mobilizations and discovered that there were very interesting results that followed from this model concerning the effects of social networks, information levels, and recruitment strategies.

Models of decisions and models of information

We develop our theory using an instrumentalist cost–benefit metatheory. We use this metatheory not as true believers who think that all decisions are or should be made "rationally," but because it gives us a fairly simple set of assumptions about individuals that permit us to gain a great deal of purchase in our understanding of groups. However, we do find this to be a plausible metatheory for collective action when collective action is *resource constrained*. Economics is often referred to as the science of behavior under conditions of scarcity. While we certainly do not think that our sociological theories can be reduced to economics, we do think that people contemplating collective action are usually operating in conditions of scarcity. If they are not, our theory will not apply. But when they have limited time and money, as most people do, they have to make choices about how they will allocate their time and money, and we believe they will somehow attempt to weigh costs and benefits. We do *not* assume that only material costs and benefits matter, but we do assume that subjective concerns are somehow balanced by people in a way that can be captured as a comparison of costs and benefits. To the extent that our assumption fits a particular situation, our models ought to apply. When the assumption is simply wrong, then the situation falls outside the scope of our theory.

Our models are all within the school of bounded rationality. That is, we assume that people are weighing not the universe of all logically possible actions, but the very limited set of cognitively available choices. At some points in the analysis, we assume perfect information about these limited choices, not because we believe information is ever perfect, but to provide a solid baseline for analysis. Later in the analysis, the degree of information itself becomes a variable.

[. . .]

In general, the problem of collective action is one of getting some relatively small subset of a group interested in the provision of a public good to make contributions of time, money, or other resources toward the production of that good. This subset is the critical mass needed to begin any collective action.

Social networks: density, centralization, and cliques

[. . .]

The core of our model of simultaneous coordinated action is the assumption that there is a single organizer who contacts all possible actors and absorbs all the costs of organizing the action.

[. . .]

The organizer is conceived as asking others to participate in a risk-free agreement to make contributions if enough others also agree. Group members will agree to contribute if the total benefit they would experience from the "contract" exceeds their own share of the cost. Our single organizer is usually thought of as one person, but the model would also apply to any small group whose members have decided to pool their resources and act in concert, as if they were one complex person.

[. . .]

We make no claim that all collective actions are organizer-centered or can be approximated by the organizer-centered model. But we do believe that organizer-centered mobilizations are an extremely common form of collective action and probably the most common source of simultaneous coordinated actions.

We investigate the ways in which the structure of social networks in a group promotes or hinders the prospects for organizer-centered mobilizations in that group. Our analysis is focused on the group level, on the group characteristics that give rise to organizers, not on the individual characteristics of organizers. In our analysis, we give every group member an analytic "chance" to be the organizer, and the dependent variables are whether any such organizer emerges and the highest level of action that could be achieved in that particular group.

The social structure of an interest group of moderate or large size is usually marked by a complex network of social ties that differentiate the relationships among the individual members. Any given organizer is usually in easy and ready communication with some group members but would find it difficult to deal with others. She might not even know that particular individuals actually have an interest in the good.

[. . .]

That social ties are important for collective action is a commonplace observation in the literature. For example, it is widely agreed that participants in social movement organizations are usually recruited through preexisting social ties, and that mobilization is more likely when the members of the beneficiary population are linked by social ties than when they are not. But exactly how and why social ties are important is less well established. What kinds of ties are most important for collective action? What features of social ties are especially relevant? Are social ties important because they make mobilization less costly or because they connect more people? And how can we distinguish these explanations?

[. . .]

Variables

[. . .]

The dependent variable is the amount of resources contributed toward the collective action. The major independent variables, which require further discussion, are density, centralization, organization costs, and group heterogeneity in interests and resources.

Density

[. . .]

In terms of our example, density is best imagined as varying between cities. Since the affected employees in each city need to have a clause passed by their own council, they constitute separate, isolated, and comparable interest groups. Consider the cities Alpha and Beta. Alpha is fairly isolated, and most of its affected employees live in a single suburb, Centauri. They attend Centauri's churches, send their children to Centauri's public schools, and belong to Centauri chapters of social and service clubs; and all are served by the same local telephone exchange. In contrast, Beta is part of an ethnically diverse two-state megalopolis, and its affected employees are scattered across a dozen different suburbs in two states and four counties. They rarely see one another after work. They go to different churches, send their children to different schools, read four or five different newspapers, and pay toll charges for telephone calls between many of the suburbs.

We would find virtual unanimity among social scientists in predicting that the employees in Alpha are more likely than those in Beta to organize collective action. Other things being equal, the large number of social interconnections in Alpha provides a solid basis for interdependence, while their virtual absence in Beta is surely a hindrance. We have noted that it is practically a truism among social movement theorists that social networks are important for recruiting participants and these theorists are supported by a fair amount of empirical evidence.

[. . .]

The basic argument was even important to Marx, who reasoned that employees who are in regular contact with one another will develop a "habit of cooperation," and be more likely to act collectively than will employees who work in isolation.

Centralization

But there is more to know about an interest group's social ties than simply how many there are. We also need to know how they are structured. In the present analysis, the aspect of structure on which we shall focus is the extent to which the ties are *centralized* or concentrated in a few individuals rather than being spread more evenly across the whole group. In contrast to density, whose effects on collective action are both important and obvious, the effects of network centralization have been little explored in the literature and appear to be quite complex.

To illustrate, consider the cities Delta and Epsilon. The affected employees of Delta have the same total number or density of social ties as the employees of Epsilon. However, these ties are distributed quite differently. Delta has annexed all its potential suburbs. Its affected employees are therefore not suburbanites, but residents of Delta's "exurbs," lightly sprinkled around a sparsely settled rural fringe. They shop in the city's many shopping centers and attend city churches. In fact, they share only one important local institution – the county primary and secondary schools, which serve the entire rural area. The one affected city employee, who is on the county school board, therefore accounts for a very high proportion (let us say 50%) of all the ties among affected employees.

Social ties among affected employees in Epsilon are much less centralized. Epsilon is the central city of a small metropolis, and affected employees live in a number of contiguous suburbs with diffuse and indistinct social and economic boundaries. There are a few dozen churches that serve larger or smaller catchments depending on the denomination. Service clubs have loose geographical bases and draw in residents of adjacent suburbs. There are eight municipalities, four school districts, and three suburban newspapers with distinct, but partially overlapping territories. Different employees see each other in different contexts.

To make a prediction about the prospects for Delta and Epsilon, we have to assess the effect of the different levels of centralization of network ties. We have to decide whether collective actions are more likely to thrive where a small number of people know many others (while most know almost no one) or where many people each know some others (but no one knows a large number). The centralization around the school board in Delta suggests the possibility of efficient coordination of action by the affected employee who knows everyone else. But it also means that if the school board member is incompetent, or is just not interested in spearheading the collective action, no alternative affected employee has much of a chance to get things going. On the other hand, the crisscrossing social ties and overlapping memberships in Epsilon evoke images of more diffuse potential loci for action. If one person doesn't show initiative, perhaps another one will. The problem in Epsilon is that no one person is in a social network position to efficiently gather together some major proportion of all the affected workers. There are advantages and disadvantages in either situation, and in the absence of good theory, it is not obvious how these will balance out.

[. . .]

Organizing cost

Our third independent variable is organizing *cost*, that is, the cost of using one of the social ties for some purpose, such as asking the person to participate in a collective action. This variable is often confounded with network density in work on social ties. To some extent we committed this confounding in our comparison of Alpha and Beta. Factors that make it cheaper to communicate across social ties, such as free local versus costly message-unit telephone rates, may also help determine whether such ties exist at all. Empirically, the two are often correlated. However, a *theoretical* distinction between the presence or absence of ties and the cost of using them is needed, because each factor may have a different effect on the prospects for collective action.

To illustrate this issue, we need a three-way comparison, such as among cities Mu, Sigma, and Rho. Suppose Mu's affected employees average ten ties to other affected employees and generally have to pay message unit charges for calls to one another. Sigma's employees also average ten ties, but all the suburban areas are in the same extended calling area. Finally, Rho's employees average fifteen ties but have the same message unit charges as Mu's. Clearly, we would expect the prospects for collective action to be worse in Mu than in either Sigma or Rho. But what prediction do we have about the prospects for success in Sigma compared with those in Rho? Another way of asking this is, if one were in Mu, would there be a bigger effect of increasing the number of employees who know each other or of devising a cheaper mode of communication among those who already have social ties? A real group of employees might have to decide if its efforts to generate collective action would be helped more by social gatherings and other efforts to increase the group's density of social ties or by finding ways to reduce the cost of communication among people who already know each other, perhaps by printing a directory of home addresses and telephone numbers. This is really a question about comparative rates of change, and it does not have an obvious answer.

[. . .]

Interest and resource heterogeneity

In the current analysis, we expect the effects of the network variables to interact with the degree of resource and interest heterogeneity in the interest group. Remember that although all present employees who live outside the city share an interest in an exemption, they differ in the magnitude of that interest, depending on such factors as how easy it would be for them to get another job, whether they own or rent their home, and whether their spouse is employed. They may also vary in the amount of time and money (i.e., resources) objectively available to them.

[. . .]

Further issues

What kind of further analysis might prove most useful? We hope that others will contribute fresh perspectives and fresh ideas, but to help we suggest in this section two areas of inquiry that are important but that do not flow directly from what we have written here.

Organizing costs and incentive structures

Mancur Olson claimed to prove that collective action was irrational, that is, that it could not arise from selfish individuals' interest in collective goods. He could have concluded from this that collective action, when it occurred, must have arisen from unselfish or irrational motives, but he did not. Instead, he argued that collective action always required *selective incentives*, private (i.e., excludible) goods that would reward contributors and punish noncontributors. Olson believed that private incentives were necessary and sufficient for collective action. Subsequent analysts critiqued both necessity and sufficiency. Incentives were shown not to be necessary for collective action, because collective action is not always irrational. There are many critiques in this vein, which essentially shows that jointness of supply, interdependence, or other factors define broad classes of situations in which contributions are noticeable and individual benefits exceed individual costs. Incentives were also shown not to be sufficient for collective action, because the provision of an incentive system is, itself, a nonexcludible collective good that may be subject to the very dilemma of collective action described by Olson.

Although they are neither necessary nor sufficient for collective action, selective incentives are nevertheless a very important component of collective action in many situations. There is a great potential for future formal theorizing in analyzing them. Only a little of this work has been done.

[. . .]

We distinguish between inclusive incentives, that is, the social reinforcement that all participants give to and receive from each other by virtue of their coparticipation, and exclusive incentives, the prestige and honor that only a few can be given for their special roles or contributions.

Purposive incentives are basically attitudes. They are feelings of self-worth and self-approval for doing the right thing (or self-reproach for doing the wrong thing). Since they are both attitudinal, it can be empirically difficult to distinguish between a subjective interest in a collective good and purposive incentive, but there is an analytic distinction. The subjective interest in the collective good is the value you attach to getting world peace or racial equality or whatever, while the purposive incentive is the value you attach to knowing that *you* helped to accomplish the goal, or at least gave outward expression to your concerns.

[. . .]

Dynamic models

All of the models we have analyzed are essentially static, in that we take as givens the factors that affect individuals' decisions. This assumption is clearly false. It does not lead us to abandon our results, because we believe they provide us with useful baselines and insights. But we do feel that there is great promise in developing dynamic models that build on our work.

[. . .]

One last exhortation

[. . .]

The most important determinants of collective action in our models are the interest and resource (or contribution size) levels relative to the cost of contributing. Expensive actions that provide no noticeable benefit are predicted never to occur, no matter what the other variables are. Conversely, when individual benefits are greater than individual costs, we predict that people will act. We say little about these effects because we consider them to be obvious and, therefore, theoretically uninteresting. But if you imagine running a regression on the universe of possible collective action situations, the effect coefficients for the total or average levels of resources, benefits, and costs would dwarf any of the other factors we discuss.

[. . .]

Thus, contrary to some published citations to our work, there is nothing anywhere in our analysis that "solves" the collective dilemma, that explains away the problem of the relation between individual and group interests. What we do say is that the dilemma is not the same for everything denoted by the definition of collective goods or collective action, and that attempts to make sweeping generalizations about collective action are misguided. Instead, what we show is that the specifics of the problem and the nature of potential solutions can vary greatly depending on the nature of the collective good and the social structural situations within which people make interdependent choices.

[. . .]

PART FOUR

Social movements and the political process

AGGRIEVED POPULATIONS, frustrated intellectuals or marginal workers who do not adapt to rapid changes do not necessarily engage in collective protest or social movement action. At times protest and collective action are not attempts to resist social change, but to promote it, through cultural and political innovation or the experimentation with new forms of life. We have seen that social movements rely on previously accumulated resources such as pre-existing networks, and that organisational skills, solidarity, tactics and strategies have an important role in determining collective action.

The *political process* approach we present in this section, like a number of other approaches discussed in this book, is based on a rational choice model whereby actors pursue goals while calculating the possible outcomes. Political process developed simultaneously with resource mobilisation theory and can be viewed as both an alternative and an integration of the latter. However, while resource mobilisation emphasises the organisational aspects internal to movements, *political process* focuses on external variables such as the political and institutional environment (Della Porta and Diani, 1999). Broadly speaking, the concept of *political process* refers to the degree of openness or closure of a political system in a way that might facilitate or discourage the rise of social movements (Neveu, 2001). This idea was first developed by Alexis de Tocqueville more than a century ago. In *Democracy in America* Tocqueville established a close relationship between political institutions and collective action (Tarrow, 1998). In his analysis and comparison between France and America, he argued that centralised and strong states weaken civil society and incite violence and confrontation when collective movements erupt. Conversely, weak states encourage the development of civil society and therefore facilitate peaceful forms of participation in organised action. Although Toqueville's emphasis on the difference between the French and American states was slightly overstated, his analysis of the relationship between state and civil society, along with his idea that the strength or weakness of states affects social movements' action and strategies, has been largely influential in social movement studies (Della Porta and Diani 1999: 197).

In his seminal work on protest in American cities in the sixties (*The Conditions of Protest Behaviour in American Cities*), Peter Eisinger (1973) uses the 'structure of political opportunities' as an explanatory tool for the variation in number and intensity of protest cycles. He distinguishes protest against local government targets from other forms of political behaviour including collective violence. Protest, he stresses, is a type of collective action which is disruptive in nature and is designed to maximise benefits while minimising costs. Protest, moreover, provides participants with bargaining power in political contention. On the basis of this conceptual and empirical definition, Eisinger finds an interaction between the political environment, its openings, barriers and resources, and protest cycles, which vary according to the systems they confront. Open political systems are likely to offer incentives for action to powerless people. He thus concludes that 'protest is neither a viable nor a fruitful strategy in extremely closed systems (...) protest seems an activity which marks the political life of contemporary American cities at a stage when they are becoming more, not less, responsive to minority demands. Protest is a sign that the opportunity structure is flexible and vulnerable to the political assaults of excluded groups' (1973: 28).

Since this initial formulation, several other variables have been introduced to address the meaning of political process. In their book on poor people's movements in America in the 1930s and 1960s (*Poor People's Movements*), Cloward and Piven (1977) identify political instability and other concepts as key tools for explaining cycles of protest. To the question of why protest arises and 'the poor do become defiant' in some circumstances and not in others, Cloward and Piven reply arguing that for protest to arise major social and political transformations have to occur. Such transformations are exceptional and sporadic, so that people usually conform to the institutional arrangements regulating their daily life. The status quo appears to be the only viable arrangement, and in ordinary times activists feel that they can do very little to change things or create new opportunities for action. The eruption of discontent, on the other hand, is determined by institutional changes affecting the structure of everyday life, and by the consequent, growing, perception that deprivation can be fought and redressed. Political opportunities and institutional arrangements not only open the way to protest, they also shape its characteristics. The political system shapes the expression and the very patterns of defiance, while the forms of political protest are forged by the institutional context in which it takes place. Political discontent may first be expressed through the electoral system and then develop into other forms of protest depending on the specific environment inspiring them. This may explain why industrial workers protest by striking or by slowing down the rhythm of the assembly line, why the unemployed engage in street riots, and why students organise demonstrations, rallies and sit-ins at universities.

The emergence of social movements may also result from the activity of specific actors who promote and encourage organised collective action. Such actors, in other words, may utilise the political opportunities offered by the system, and at the same time pave the way for the creation of new opportunities. In her *Personal*

Politics: The Roots of Women's Liberation in the Civil Rights Movement and the New Left, Evans (1978) relates the consciousness raising practices among the first women's liberation groups to the action of the civil rights movement and the New Left in the USA. Liberating practices and movements create yet other, new, opportunities for action. These are linked with the political context as a whole, its openness or closure, but the resulting movements act as models of action, displaying repertoires of contention that can inspire other movements and an increasing variety of protests. In other words, social movements create an ideologically and socially favourable environment for new social groups to mobilise: for example, their challenge to traditional authorities may be replicated by those who are intimidated by authority, and their new ideas may spread in unpredictable directions. The North American case shows that, on the one hand, the civil rights movements and the New Left provided models for action to groups such as the women 'consciousness raising' groups, in which women could rely on mutual trust and share their intimate experiences, views and feelings. On the other hand, the women's participation in the southern civil rights movement and in the northern New Left allowed them to gain a new awareness of their oppression and to develop a different set of expectations regarding their mobilisation and their future. The growth of social movements, in brief, created new social spaces of communication and new ideological and theoretical arenas of debate within which women could reinterpret their own experience and develop new forms of identity. At the same time, as Evans shows, the feminist movement affected the external environment. Feminism spread into the advertising and publishing industry, transforming language and communication images, and into mainstream institutions such as higher education and party politics, imposing new legislations and establishing new rights.

As McAdam (1982) (*Political Process and the Development of Black Insurgency 1930–1970*) argues, the political process model represents an alternative to, but also an integration of, the resource mobilisation perspective. In his view, social movements are *political phenomena* that cannot be analysed in relation to particular phases of their existence, but should be examined in their specific history, from inception through to decline. The perspective offered by McAdam combines an analysis of the elite with aspects of Marxist analysis of power. He sets off with the premise that wealth and power are concentrated in the hands of an elite and that social movements are rational attempts of the excluded to revert this condition. He then asserts that such a condition is not ineluctable and can be changed through subjective efforts leading to a new condition. While emphasising subjectivity, McAdam also focuses on the structure of political opportunities, which are described as flexible and constantly evolving: wars, industrialisation processes, international political instability, and changing alliance systems are some examples of what such opportunities might be. While classical theorists such as Kornhauser (1959) saw a direct link between these events and political insurgency, analysts adopting the political process model only see an indirect relation between them, a relation that becomes visible over a longer period of time. Events and opportunities may lead to insurgency when a certain degree of organisational strength is acquired. This implies that two necessary conditions are in place. First, resources must be available to social movements capable of using them. Political opportunities must be 'converted' into organised campaigns through collective action undertaken by an aggrieved population. However, political opportunities and organisation alone do not produce social movements or political insurgency. Therefore, the second condition is that the subjectivity of actors makes resources usable and collective action viable. Therefore, the *political process* approach assumes that social movements result from the transformation and development of political consciousness among significant sectors of aggrieved populations. Such consciousness, it is argued, will help actors and groups to frame their situation as unjust and liable to change.

Charles Tilly, throughout his long career as a social analyst and social historian, has offered a variety of persuasive conceptualisations of political opportunities and processes. In his influential article (*Social Movements and National Politics, 1984*) that we propose below, as well as in many of his books and other scientific contributions, he argues that national social movements constitute a quite recent phenomenon and that their development is concomitant with the rise of nation states and modern democracies. He defines social movements as organised, sustained, self-conscious challenges to an existing authority, and roots his analysis in space and time. Therefore, social movements are historically specific forms of action that try to influence governments and challenge their power. Social movements differ from the popular uprisings and the street rebellions of the past; rather, they should be located within the framework of the social and political changes that made other forms of political action possible. These include the growth of national electoral politics and the proliferation of associations and groups as vehicles of action. Social movements back their demands with specific repertoires of action, which were unknown to the outbursts of the past, and such repertoires have a central position in the study of social movements and contention. According to Tilly, changes in repertoires of action occur simultaneously with the alterations in the structure of power. His examples of the forms of protest in France, from the Fronde in the seventeenth century to the Revolution of 1848, from tax rebellions to demonstrations and strikes in later periods, show a decline in contentious politics at the local community level and the growing centrality of national political action.

A similar approach is adopted by Sidney Tarrow. In his work on Italian social movements *Democracy and Disorder* (1989) he further develops the concept of political opportunities. Tarrow distinguishes between structural changes and changes in political opportunities. While the former only create the potential for social mobilisation, the latter translate this potential into action. In the excerpt from *Power in Movement* (1998) we propose below, the author attempts to formulate a synthesis of various theoretical models. His analysis addresses opportunities and constraints, seen less as fixed and rigid entities than as a set of changing and external resources that encourage or discourage people to take part in contentious politics. Political opportunities and constraints are said to shape the repertoires of contention adopted by social movements. Forms of action are chosen on the basis of the institutional context and the goals pursued, but also against the background of established contentious traditions and resources available. Moreover, collective action depends on a number of other variables that fall into the domain of subjectivity. 'Ideology', to use a traditional terminology, or 'framing work', in a more contemporary vocabulary, are among them. Social movements are guided by framing processes that define social reality, shape grievances, and turn them into broader claims justifying and dignifying discontent while prompting collective action (1998: 21). We will return to these processes in Part 6 of this book with the analysis of 'frame alignment'.

In Tarrow, 'framing work' not only shapes social reality, but also defines the enemy and builds boundaries between 'us' and 'them'. Collective action, finally, requires the availability of mobilising or connective structures and social networks which make possible face-to-face relations and the circulation of information among activists or potential allies. To sum up, contentious politics is possible when political opportunities broaden. However, contention turns into a social movement when connective structures, framing processes and repertoires of contention are present.

In their essay (*Social Movements and Direct Democracy in Switzerland*) Kriesi and Wisler offer an empirical example of the political process approach by examining the impact of direct democratic institutions on social movements repertoires. More specifically, the authors compare social movements in the Germanic and the Neo-Latin areas of the Swiss confederation and test the hypothesis that the degree of openness or closure of institutions affect action repertoires. Adopting an approach very similar to that of Tilly's, who argues that repertoires of action are historical creations situated in specific political contexts, Kriesi and Wisler suggest that repertoires are shaped by the institutions of a given political system and that the availability of direct-democratic institutions has a decisive impact on social movement forms of mobilisation. They conclude that the availability of direct-democratic institutions has a moderating effect on social movement and action repertoires, channelling protest into more conventional forms.

References

Della Porta, D. and Diani, M. (1999), *Social Movements. An Introduction*, Oxford: Blackwell Publishers.

Kornhauser, A. (1959), *The Politics of Mass Society*, Glencoe: Free Press.

Neveu, E. (2001), *I movimenti sociali*. Bologna: Il Mulino.

Tarrow, S. (1989), *Democracy and Disorder: Protest and Politics in Italy 1965–1975*, Oxford: Clarendon Press.

Tarrow, S. (1998), *Power in Movement. Social Movements, Collective Action and Politics*, New York/Cambridge: Cambridge University Press.

Chapter 20

Sidney Tarrow

POWER IN MOVEMENT

Toward a synthesis

THE MOST FORCEFUL ARGUMENT of this study will be that people engage in contentious politics when patterns of political opportunities and constraints change and then, by strategically employing a repertoire of collective action, create new opportunities, which are used by others in widening cycles of contention. When their struggles revolve around broad cleavages in society, when they bring people together around inherited cultural symbols, and when they can build on or construct dense social networks and connective structures, then these episodes of contention result in sustained interactions with opponents–specifically, in social movements.

Political opportunities and constraints

By political opportunities, I mean consistent – but not necessarily formal, permanent, or national – dimensions of the political struggle that encourage people to engage in contentious politics. By political constraints, I mean factors – like repression, but also like authorities, capacity to present a solid front to insurgents – that discourage contention. There is no simple formula for predicting when contentious politics will emerge, both because the specification of these variables varies in different historical and political circumstances, and because different factors may vary in opposing directions. As a result, the term "political opportunity structure" should not be understood as an invariant model inevitably producing social movements, but as a set of clues for when contentious politics will emerge, setting in motion a chain of causation that may ultimately lead to sustained interaction with authorities and thence to social movements.

The concept of political opportunity emphasizes resources *external* to the group. Unlike money or power, these can be taken advantage of by even weak or disorganized challengers but in no way "belong" to them. I argue that contentious politics emerges when ordinary citizens, sometimes encouraged by counter elites or leaders, respond to opportunities that lower the costs of collective action, reveal potential allies, show where elites and authorities are most vulnerable, and trigger social networks and collective identities into action around common themes.

Like Hanspeter Kriesi and his collaborators (1995), I argue that both state structures and political cleavages create relatively stable opportunities. The most obvious of these are forms of access to institutions and capacity for repression. *Changing* opportunities and constraints, however, provide the openings that lead resource-poor actors to engage in contentious politics. Whether contention ripens into social movements depends on how people act collectively, on how consensus is mobilized around common claims, and on the strength and location of mobilizing structures.

The repertoire of contention

People do not simply "act collectively." They petition, assemble, strike, march, occupy premises, obstruct traffic, set fires, and attack others with intent to do bodily harm. No less than in the case or religious rituals or civic celebrations, contentious politics is not born in organizers' heads but is culturally inscribed and socially communicated. The learned conventions of contention are part of a society's public culture. Social movements are repositories of knowledge of particular routines in a society's history, which help them to overcome the deficits in resources and communication typically found among the poor and disorganized (Kertzer 1988: 104–108).

Because social movements seldom neither possess selective incentives or constraints over followers, nor are bound by institutional routines, leadership has a creative function in selecting forms of collective action. Leaders invent, adapt, and combine various forms of contention to gain support from people who might otherwise stay at home. Albert Hirschman had something like this in mind when he complained that Olson regarded collective action *only* as a cost – when to many it is a benefit (1982: 82–91). For people whose lives are mired in drudgery and desperation, the offer of an exciting, risky, and possibly beneficial campaign of collective action may be a gain.

Forms of contention are inherited or rare, habitual or unfamiliar, solitary or part of concerted campaigns. They can be linked to themes that are either inscribed in the culture or invented on the spot or – more commonly – blend elements of convention with new frames of meaning. Protest is a resource, according to political scientist Michael Lipsky (1968), and the forms of contention are themselves a collective incentive to mobilization and a challenge to opponents.

Particular groups have a particular history – and memory – of contentious forms. Workers know how to strike because generations of workers struck before them; Parisians build barricades because barricades are inscribed in the history of Parisian contention; peasants seize the land carrying the symbols that their fathers and grandfathers used in the past.

[. . .]

Consensus mobilization and identities

The coordination of collective action depends on the trust and cooperation that are generated among participants by shared understandings and identities – or, to use a broader category, on the collective action *frames* that justify, dignify, and animate collective action. Ideology, as David Apter wrote in his classic essay in *Ideology and Discontent*, dignifies discontent, identifies a target for grievances, and forms an umbrella over the discrete grievances of overlapping groups (1964: ch. 1).

But "ideology" is a rather dry way of describing what moves people to action. In recent years, students of social movements have begun to use terms like cognitive frames, ideological packages, and cultural discourses to describe the shared meanings that inspire people to collective action. Whatever the terminology, rather than regarding ideology as either a superimposed intellectual category or as the automatic result of grievances, these scholars agree that movements do passionate "framing work": shaping grievances into broader and more resonant claims (Snow and Benford 1988) and stimulating what William Gamson calls "hot cognitions" around them (1992).

Framing not only relates to the generalization of a grievance, but defines the "us" and "them" in a movement's conflict structure. By drawing on inherited collective identities and shaping new ones, challengers delimit the boundaries of their prospective constituencies and define their enemies by real or imagined attributes and evils (Hardin 1995: ch. 4). As much as through the content of their ideological messages, they do this through the images they project of both enemies and allies. This means paying attention to the "costumes" collective actors don as they appear on the public stage as well as to the ideological framing of their claims.

Although movement organizers actively engage in framing work, not all framing takes place under their control. In addition to building on inherited cultural understandings, they compete with the media, which transmit messages that movements must attempt to shape and influence. As sociologist Todd Gitlin found, much of the communication that helped shape the American New Left in the 1960s passed through the medium of the media, in the place of what would have had to be organizational efforts in earlier periods (1980).

States are also constantly framing issues, both in order to gain support for their policies and to contest the meanings placed in public space by movements. In the struggle over meanings in which movements are constantly engaged, it is rare that they do not suffer a disadvantage in competition with states, which not only control the means of repression but have at their disposal important instruments for meaning construction. The struggle between states and movements takes place not only in the streets but in contests over meaning (Melucci 1996; Rochon 1998).

Mobilizing structures

Although it is individuals who decide whether or not to take up collective action, it is in their face-to-face groups, their social networks, and the connective structures between them that it is most often activated and sustained. This has been made clear through recent research both in the laboratory and in the real world of movement mobilization.

In the early collective behavior approach, there was a tendency to see isolated, deprived individuals as the main actors in collective action. But by the 1980s, scholars were finding that, it is life within groups that transforms the potential for action into social movements (Hardin 1995: ch. 2). For example, Doug McAdam's work on the Freedom Summer campaign showed that – far more than their social background or ideologies – it was the social networks in which Freedom Summer applicants were embedded that played a key role in determining who would participate in this campaign and who would stay at home (1986, 1988).

Institutions are particularly economical "host" settings in which movements can germinate. This was particularly true in estate societies like prerevolutionary France, where the provincial parliaments provided institutional spaces where liberal ideas could germinate (Egret 1977). But it is also true in America today. For instance, sociologist Aldon Morris showed that the origins of the civil rights movement were bound up with the role of the black churches (1984). And political scientist Mary Katzenstein found that the internal structures of the Catholic world were unwitting accomplices in the formation of networks of dissident religious women (1998; also see Levine 1990; Tarrow 1988).

The role of social networks and institutions in stimulating movement participation helps us to put Mancur Olson's thesis that large groups will not support collective action in perspective. For when we look at the morphology of movements, it becomes clear that they are only "large" in an arithmetic sense: they are really much more like an interlocking network of small groups, social networks, and the connections between them. Collective action may arise only among the best-endowed or most courageous members of these groups, but the connections between them affect the likelihood that one actor's action will incite another.

To summarize what will have to be shown in detail in later chapters: contentious politics is produced when political opportunities broaden, when they demonstrate the potential for alliances, and when they reveal the opponents' vulnerability. Contention crystallizes into a social movement when it taps embedded social networks and connective structures and produces collective action frames and supportive identities able to sustain contention with powerful opponents. By mounting familiar forms of contention, movements become focal points that transform external opportunities into resources. Repertoires of contention, social networks, and cultural frames lower the costs of bringing people into collective action, induce confidence that they are not alone, and give broader meaning to their claims. Together, these factors trigger the dynamic processes that have made social movements historically central to political and social change.

The dynamics of movement

The power to trigger sequences of collective action is not the same as the power to control or sustain them. This dilemma has both an internal and an external dimension. Internally, a good part of the power of movements comes from the fact that they activate people over whom they have no control. This power is a virtue because it allows movements to mount collective action without possessing the resources that would be necessary to internalize a support base. But the autonomy of their supporters also disperses a movement's power, encourages factionalization, and leaves it open to defection, competition, and repression.

Externally, movements are affected by the fact that the same political opportunities that have created them and diffuse their influence also affect others – either complementary, competing, or hostile. Particularly if collective action succeeds, these opportunities produce broader cycles of contention that spread from movement activists to those they oppose, to ordinary interest groups and political parties, and, inevitably, to the state. As a result of this dynamic of diffusion and creation, movements succeed or fail as the result of forces outside their control.

Cycles of contention

As opportunities widen and information spreads about the susceptibility of a polity to challenge, not only activists but ordinary people begin to test the limits of social control. Clashes between early challengers and authorities reveal the weak points of the latter and the strengths of the former, inviting even timid social actors to align themselves on one side or another. Once triggered by a situation of generally widening opportunities, information cascades outward and political learning accelerates. As Hill and Rothchild write,

> As protests and riots erupt among groups that have long histories of conflict, they stimulate other citizens in similar circumstances to reflect more often on their own background of grievance and mass action. (1992: 193)

During such periods, the opportunities created by early risers provide incentives for new movement organizations. Even conventional interest groups are tempted by unconventional collective action. Alliances are formed, often across a shifting boundary between challengers and members of the polity (Tilly 1978: ch. 2). New forms of contention are experimented with and diffused. Political information and uncertainty spread, and a dense and interactive "social movement sector" appears in which organizations cooperate and compete (Garner and Zald 1985).

The process of diffusion in cycles of contention is not merely one of "contagion," though a good deal of such contagion occurs. It also results from rational decisions to take advantage of opportunities that have been demonstrated by other groups' actions: it occurs when groups make gains that invite others to seek similar outcomes; when someone's ox is gored by demands made by insurgent groups; and when the predominance of an organization or institution is threatened and it responds by adopting collective action.

As the cycle widens, movements create opportunities for elites and opposition groups too. Alliances form between participants and challengers, oppositional clues make demands for changes that would have seemed foolhardy earlier; governmental forces respond either with reform, repression, or a combination of the two. The widening logic of collective action leads to outcomes in the sphere of institutional politics, where the challengers who began the cycle have less and less leverage over its outcomes.

At the extreme end of the spectrum, cycles of contention give rise to revolutions. Revolutions are not a single form of collective action; nor are they wholly made up of popular collective action. As in the cycles to which they are related, collective action in revolutions forces other groups and institutions to take part, providing the bases and frameworks for new social movements, unhinging old institutions and the networks that surround them, and creating new ones out of the forms of collective action with which insurgent groups begin the process.

The difference between movement cycles and revolutions is that, in the latter, multiple centers of sovereignty are created, turning the conflict between challengers and members of the polity into a struggle for power (Tilly 1993). This difference – which is substantial – has led to an entire industry of research on "great" revolutions, which are usually compared only with one another. This specialization on great revolutions is understandable, but it has squandered the possibility of comparing revolutions with lesser conflagrations, making it impossible to isolate those factors in the dynamic of a cycle which lead it down the path to revolutions and those which lead it to collapse.

Outcomes of movements

These arguments about the interactions within a cycle of protest suggest that it will not be particularly fruitful to examine the outcomes of single social movements on their own. In general cycles of contention, policy elites respond not to the claims of any individual group or movement but to the degree of turbulence and to the demands made by elites and opinion groups, which only partially correspond to the demands of those they claim to represent. Regarding the outcomes of social movements, the important point is that, although movements usually conceive of themselves as outside of and opposed to institutions, acting collectively inserts them into complex policy networks, and thus within the reach of the state. If nothing else, movements try to enunciate demands in terms of frames of meaning comprehensible to a wider society; they use forms of collective action drawn from an existing repertoire; and they develop types of organization that often mimic the organizations of those they oppose.

We can begin to study social movements as isolated confrontations between single social actors and their opponents, but – particularly when we examine their outcomes – we quickly arrive at the more complex and less tractable networks of politics. It is through the political opportunities seized and created by challengers, movements, and their allies and enemies that major cycles of contention begin. They, in turn, create opportunities for elites and counterelites, and actions that begin in the streets are resolved in the halls of government or by the bayonets of the army. Movements – and particularly the waves of movement that are the main catalysts of social change – are part of national struggles for power. Let us begin by turning to how that struggle first produced national social movements in the modern history of the West.

Bibliography

Apter D. (1964) *Ideology and Discontent*, Glencoe, Ill.: Free Press.
Egret J. (1977) *The French Pre-revolution 1787–1788*, Chicago: University of Chicago Press.

Gamson W. (1992) "The Social Psychology of Collective Action", in A. Morris and C. McClurg Mueller (eds.) *Frontiers in Social Movement Theory*, Yale University Press, New Haven, pp. 53–56.

Garner R.A. and Zald M.N. (1985) "The Political Economy of Social Movement Sectors", in Gerald Suttles and Mayer N. Zald (eds.) *The Challenge of Social Control: Citizenship and Institution Building in Modern Society: Essays in Honor of Morris Janowitz*, Norwood, N.J.: Ablex, pp. 119–45.

Gitlin T. (1980) *The Whole World Is Watching: Mass Media in the Making and Unmaking of the New Left*, Berkeley: University of California Press.

Hardin R. (1995) *One for All: The Logic of Group Conflict*, Princeton, NJ.: Princeton University Press.

Hill S., Rothchild D. (1992) "The Impact of Regime on the Diffusion of Political Conflict," in M. Midlarsky (ed.), *The Internationalization of Communal Conflict*, London and New York: Routledge, pp. 189–206.

Hirschman A. (1982) *Shifting Involvement: Private Interest and Public Action*, Princeton: Princeton University Press.

Katzenstein M. (1998) *Faithful and Fearless: Moving Feminist Protest Inside The Church and Military*, Princeton: Princeton University Press.

Kertzer, D. (1988) *Ritual Politics and Power*, New Haven: Yale University Press.

Kriesi, H., Koopman, R., Duyvendak, J.W. and Giugni, M. (1995) *New Social Movements in Western Europe: A Comparative Analysis*, Minneapolis: University of Minnesota Press.

Levine D.H. (1990) "Popular Groups, Popular Culture, and Popular Religion", *Comparative Studies in Society and History*, 32(4): pp. 718–764.

Lipsky M. (1968) "Protest As a Political Resource" *American Political Science Review*, 62: pp. 1144–58.

McAdam D. (1986) "Recruitment to High-Risk Activism: The Case of Freedom Summer", *American Journal of Sociology*, 92: pp. 64–90.

McAdam D. (1988) *Freedom Summer*, Chicago: University of Chicago Press.

Melucci A. (1996) *Challenging Codes: Collective Action in the Information Age*, Cambridge: Cambridge University Press.

Morris A. (1984) *The Origins of the Civil Rights Movement: Black Communities Organising for Change*, New York: Free Press.

Rochon T.R. (1998) *Mobilizing for Peace: The Antinuclear Movements in Western Europe*, Princeton: Princeton University Press.

Snow, D.A., Benford, R. (1988) "Ideology, Frame Resonance and Participant Mobilization", in Klandermans B., Kriesi H., Tarrow S. (eds.), *From Structure to Action*, Greenwich: JAI Press, pp. 197–218.

Tarrow S. (1988) "Old Movements in New Cycles of Protest: The Career of an Italian Religious Community", in B. Klandermans, H. Kriesi & S. Tarrow (eds.) *From Structure to Action: Comparing Social Movement Research Across Cultures*, International Social Movement Research, vol. 1 Greenwich, Conn.: JAI, pp. 281–304.

Tilly C. (1978) *From Mobilization to Revolution*, Reading, London: Addison-Wesley.

Tilly C. (1993) *European Revolutions, 1492–1992*, Oxford: Blackwell.

Chapter 21

Sara Evans

PERSONAL POLITICS

BY THE LATE 1960S it was dramatically apparent that most American women's lives bore no relation to the happy housewife image of the 1950s. And like the proverbial child who pointed out that the emperor had no clothes, it was America's youth who first heralded the discrepancy between myth and reality. Young women from the new left had torn away with intrepid zeal and directness the shrouds of ambiguity and mystification surrounding women's roles. Kathie Sarachild compared their new examination of personal experience with the seventeenth-century struggle against the scholastics and dogmatists who clung to ancient texts on anatomy despite the very different facts revealed by dissection: "So they'd deny what they saw in front of their eyes, because Galen didn't say it was there." Thus the women's liberation movement was initiated by women in the civil rights movement and the new left who dared to test the old assumptions and myths about female nature against their own experience and discovered that something was drastically wrong. And they dared because within these movements they had learned to respect themselves and to know their own strength. They could do so because the new left provided an egalitarian ideology, which stressed the personal nature of political action, the importance of community and cooperation, and the necessity to struggle for freedom for the oppressed. They had to dare because within the same movement that gave them so much they were simultaneously thrust into subservient roles—as secretary, sex object, housekeeper, "dumb chick."

The feminine mystique of the 1950s had blinded American women to the realities of their experience. It had depicted happiness where there was frustration. It projected the idea of pleasant housework where that often meant the additional burden of another full-time job. The mystique drew on centuries of tradition and specifically on the separation between the home and work spheres in the modern economy. Yet industrial capitalism, which once had pushed women to the periphery of the paid economy and remodeled the family into a private enclave, now drew women back into the labor force. While the expansion of government and the service sector of the economy pulled women into jobs outside the home, such workers still found themselves performing subservient tasks. And they received in the public sphere, as they had in the private, a low evaluation of their work and worth—this time expressed in the form of low pay and job discrimination. As the public and private spheres interpenetrated, the inherited roles proved less and less adequate as sources of identity and self-esteem. Traditional definitions could not encompass, explain, or help women to cope with the new realities of their lives. Thus, only a movement that simultaneously challenged their roles in both the home and the outside workplace could have tapped the pain and anger of most women and moved them to action.

[. . .]

The experiences of the first few women's liberation groups were repeated hundreds of times over. Young women's instinctive sharing of their personal experiences soon became a political instrument called "consciousness-raising." The models for consciousness-raising ranged from the earliest SNCC meetings, to SDS's "Guatemala Guerrilla" organizing approach, to the practice of "speaking bitterness" in the Chinese revolution. It evolved into a kind of phenomenological approach to women's liberation. Kathie Sarachild advocated that women should junk all the old theories and start from scratch, relying on their own experience: "In our groups, let's share our feelings and pool them. Let's let ourselves go and see where our feelings lead us. Our feelings will lead us to ideas and then to actions." Thus consciousness-raising became both a method for developing theory and a strategy for building up the new movement.

Consciousness-raising exemplified both the frontal assault on sex roles and the personalized approach to politics that soon became hallmarks of the proliferating new feminist groups. The radical democracy of the new left carried over into an unequivocal assertion of sexual equality and an impatience with any belief that women should be treated or expected to act differently from men. The notion that women were different but equal, argued by biological determinists, sounded to the new movement like the "separate but equal" rhetoric of southern segregationists. And their demands led beyond equal *rights*, in formal terms, to a demand for equality of power. Thus they inspired a thorough critique of personal life and of the subtleties of an oppression that was at once internal and external.

The focus on the personal experience of oppression, moreover, led to the creation of small groups within which women could share with mutual trust the intimate details of their lives. Formed almost instinctively at first as radical women gathered in each others' living rooms to discuss their needs, these small groups quickly became the primary structure of the women's revolt. They provided a place, a "free space," in which women could examine the nature of their own oppression and share the growing knowledge that they were not alone. The qualities of intimacy, support, and virtual structurelessness made the small group a brilliant tool for spreading the movement. Anyone could form a group anywhere: an SDS women's caucus, a secretarial pool, a friendship circle, a college dorm, a coffee klatsch.

Each small group—and soon there were thousands—created a widening impact among the families, friends, and co-workers of its members. Soon the radical ideas and cooperative forms of the women's movement were reshaping the more conservative, tightly structured "women's rights" branch of the movement. Within a few years NOW had strengthened its positions on issues like abortion and lesbianism and had considerably changed its style. In several cities NOW became the chief instigator of new consciousness-raising groups. Individual leaders responded as well, for the new movement awakened them to the broader aspects of their feminism. For instance, theologian Mary Daly advocated "women's rights" in the Church when she wrote *The Church and the Second Sex* in 1968. Several years later she had become a leading exponent of a feminist theology that challenged patriarchal images of God.

As feminist ideas and rebellions spread into mainstream institutions—business offices, churches, and the mass media—the advertising and publishing industries, quick to perceive a shift in public mood, tried to make the best of it.

[. . .]

The combined impact of women's liberation and the women's rights branches of the new feminism rocked institutions of higher education. Women in the New University Conference, a new left group, joined with a large constituency of professional women, many already active in NOW, to form women's caucuses within academic professions. Normally staid professional meetings began to ring with acrimony as women cried "foul" about hiring, admissions, and promotion practices. Then exercising the intellectual tools of their disciplines on the substance of the disciplines themselves, they criticized the male biases involved in the treatment of women and sex roles. Thus armed with new questions and mutually supportive organizations, women generated an outpouring of scholarly studies on the sociology of family and sex roles, female psychology, women's history and literature by and about women. Women's studies programs encouraged interdisciplinary cross-fertilization and provided points of intersection with the women's movement itself.

The dramatic growth of feminism—a term that itself signaled the blurring lines between women's liberation and women's rights—affected political institutions as well. The women's rights movement had first coalesced around support for the Equal Rights Amendment and Title VII of the Civil Rights Act. Younger radical women pushed hardest for the issues that they felt struck closer to women's fundamental oppression—abortion and child care. As imaginative public presentations, mass demonstrations, and widespread publicity reinforced their lobbying, liberal politicians leaped on the bandwagon and for a moment all the bulwarks seemed to be crumbling. In 1972, after more than fifty years of sporadic debate, Congress passed the Equal Rights Amendment and sent it to the states for ratification. The EEOC and HEW stopped treating discrimination against women as a joke. The Supreme Court ruled that abortion in the first three months of pregnancy was a medical problem to be settled privately between patient and doctor. A bill for massive federal funding of child care found heretofore unheard of support in Congress. For a time it seemed that the power of an aroused, united mass movement of women was irresistible.

Within a few years the women's liberation movement had spread through many layers of American society. Where the public ideology of groups like NOW had originally focused on legal inequities and formal rights, the newer revolt made a critique of family and personal life the very cornerstone of its existence. Without such a critique there would likely have been a strong feminist lobby, for the severe pressures on professional women ensured that they would participate in the reform impetus of the sixties. But there would have been no mass insurgency. For most American women only a movement that addressed the oppression at the core of their identity could have generated the massive response that in fact occurred. Women from the new left had been able to penetrate to the essence of their roles because of their specific experiences in the 1960s, which facilitated the emergence of an insurgent group consciousness.

The issue of consciousness-formation has been posed most often by theoreticians writing from a Marxist perspective. Marxists have distinguished between the concept of a class in itself (one that exists according to objective criteria) and a class for itself (one with a self-conscious collective identity, able to act on its own behalf). Yet despite the Marxist concern with class, the question of how class consciousness develops remains virtually unexamined. The sociologist Neil Smelser posits the growth of a "generalized belief" which explains a collective situation and points to a solution. His theory applies most clearly, however, to crowd and panic forms of collective behavior. When used to explain social movements, the theory implies that social protest is based on an inherently irrational leap from a generalized questioning of values or norms to specific sources of social strain.

[. . .]

Examining the social roots of feminism in the fifties and sixties, I would suggest that the essential preconditions for an insurgent collective identity include:

(1) social spaces within which members of an oppressed group can develop an independent sense of worth in contrast to their received definitions as second-class or inferior citizens;
(2) role models of people breaking out of patterns of passivity;
(3) an ideology that can explain the sources of oppression, justify revolt, and provide a vision of a qualitatively different future;
(4) a threat to the newfound sense of self that forces a confrontation with the inherited cultural definitions—in other words, it becomes impossible for the individual to "make it on her own" and escape the boundaries of the oppressed group; and finally
(5) a communication or friendship network through which a new interpretation can spread, activating the insurgent consciousness into a social movement.

These preconditions evolved as young women participated in the southern civil rights movement, particularly SNCC, and in the northern new left, particularly ERAP.

Women from the new left explained the sources of their new awareness by pointing to the discrepancy between the movement's egalitarian ideology and the oppression they continued to experience within it. What they failed to perceive, however, was the fact that the new left did more than simply perpetuate the oppression of women. Even more importantly, it created new arenas—social space—within which women could develop a new sense of self-worth and independence; it provided new role models in the courage and capability of southern black women and female community leaders; and having heightened women's self-respect, it also allowed them to claim the movement's ideology for themselves. The point at which they did so came when the movement that had opened for them a new sense of their own potential simultaneously thrust them into menial domestic roles. Feminism was born in that contradiction—the threatened loss of new possibility.

Moreover, as conditions within the new left permitted young women to reexamine and reinterpret their own experiences, their situation also proved parallel to that of millions of American women far beyond the enclaves of the left. Indeed, it represented in microcosm the dilemma of most American women, trapped in an obsolete domestic role while new realities generated an unarticulated sense of greater potential. Although women's liberation was shocking and alienating to many, especially as seen through the magnifying lens of a hostile media, the reactions to the outcry on behalf of women's equality indicated that feminism had tapped a vein of enormous frustration and anger. The Harris Survey found in 1971 that 62 percent of American women believed that women had to "speak up" in order to accomplish anything, although most of them disapproved the tactics of picketing and protest and did not support "efforts to strengthen and change women's status in society." Nearly five years later, after the intervening upsurge of activism, 65 percent endorsed such efforts. Previously, ambivalence and fear of change had made women even less likely than men to advocate greater sexual equality. But by 1975 a new sense of rights and possibilities had led women to assert their belief in equal rights and opportunities for females in greater numbers and with greater intensity than men. Similarly, on specific issues such as abortion, child care, and the Equal Rights Amendment, opinion polls recorded a steady shift in public opinion toward the endorsement of feminist programs. By the bicentennial year, 1976, the *Reader's Digest* conceded: "Women's Liberation has changed the lives of many Americans and the way they look at family, job and sexual equality." Nearly a decade after the women's movement began, the confused response of most American women would be: "I'm not a women's Libber, but ... I believe women ought to be equal."

Within the context of such massive shifts of opinion, as millions of women readjusted their view of themselves and of the world, many thousands also moved to activism and into the burgeoning women's liberation movement. But success was not without its problems: neither the leaders nor the organizational structures could maintain a unified movement. And at the same time that the issue of sexual equality had become a subject of dinner conversation in households across the nation, the new revolt suffered from internal weaknesses inherited from the new left.

[...]

Chapter 22

Peter K. Eisinger

THE CONDITIONS OF PROTEST BEHAVIOR IN AMERICAN CITIES

Political environment and protest

THE COMPLEX INTERRELATIONSHIP between political environment variables on the one hand and political behavior on the other has been a persistent concern of analysts of urban politics. The purpose of this paper is to begin an exploration of various environmental conditions associated with the incidence of political protest activities directed toward urban institutions, agencies, and officials in American cities.

Political environment is a generic term used variously in the literature of political science to refer to, among other things, aspects of formal political structure, the climate of governmental responsiveness, social structure, and social stability. Scholarly efforts have generally been directed toward examination of the extent to which specific configurations of environmental variables and distinctive patterns of local politics occur together. Treating environmental elements as independent variables,[1] students have shown relationships, for example, between reformed municipal institutions and low voting turnout,[2] reform government and high spending and tax policies,[3] centralization of local power and urban renewal success,[4] and less representative councilmanic institutions and the incidence of race riots.[5]

This type of analysis has depended on the use of data on macro-level, or community, characteristics for its independent variables. The linkages between these diverse characteristics and patterns of political behavior and those among the environmental variables themselves have seldom been made explicit theoretically.

Such research efforts take on theoretical coherence, however, if it is understood the first instance that the environmental variables are related to one another in the sense that they establish a *context* within which politics takes place.[6] Furthermore, the possible linkages between this context and the patterns of political behavior become evident if the elements of the context are conceived as components of the particular *structure of political opportunities* of a community. That is to say, such factors as the nature of the chief executive, the mode of aldermanic election, the distribution of social skills and status, and the degree of social disintegration, taken individually or collectively, serve in various ways to obstruct or facilitate citizen activity in pursuit of political goals. Other environmental factors, such as the climate of governmental responsiveness and the level of community resources, help to establish the chances of success of citizen political activity. In short, elements in the environment impose certain constraints on political activity or open avenues for it. The manner in which individuals and groups in the political system behave, then, is not simply a function of the resources they command but of the openings, weak spots, barriers, and resources of the political system itself. There is, in this sense, interaction, or linkage, between the environment, understood in terms of the notion of a structure of political opportunities, and political behavior.

By measuring these environmental factors, the analyst develops a means to judge the nature of the biases which groups in a political system must confront. Such judgments lead to conclusions about the ease with which people can get what they want from the political system through collective action. Where the structure of government is potentially more responsive to an electorate by providing opportunities of formal representation for distinct segments of the population (blacks, for example) or where the government is demonstrably responsive to citizen needs and demands, the structure of opportunities is relatively open. There exist chances for diverse groups to exercise influence through delegates on representative bodies and influence appears to elicit government action.

Where formal or informal power appears to be concentrated and where government is not responsive, the opportunities for people to get what they want or need through political action are limited. The opportunity structure is relatively closed.

[. . .]

Reformed local government structure, whose rationale is to eliminate "politics" and partiality from municipal administration, restricts the opportunities which minority and outgroups have for success through political action. Not only is it likely that minorities will experience difficulty in gaining representation or even access in reform systems, but their needs often cannot be met using the criterion of efficient management. Reform governments attempt to institutionalize efficient management at the expense of recognizing particularistic and often costly interests.[7] This may lead to intense frustration on the part of excluded groups. Lieberson and Silverman find evidence to support their hypothesis that the less direct the relationship between the voter and his alderman (measured on a continuum which ranges from extensive at-large electoral systems to small district ward systems); the more likely it will be that race riots will occur.[8] Small districts provide access for more people and offer the possibility of minority representation, both of which serve to enlarge or open up the structure of opportunities. Similarly, it would seem reasonable to suspect that the incidence of protest, one manifestation of political frustration or impatience, is related to the nature of the opportunity structure.

Several studies have attempted to demonstrate linkages between aspects of what I have called the opportunity structure and the incidence of mass ghetto violence. Their results have been uniformly negative. Downes and Spilerman independently found that the incidence of ghetto riots was essentially related to nothing more than the numerical size of a city's black population, while Palley and Palley discovered that objective indicators of the degree of black social and economic deprivation were unreliable predictors of ghetto violence.

If one were to follow the notion of a number of scholars that ghetto violence is simply a form of protest,[9] a more virulent extension of what is essentially the same political activity, then this inquiry could stop here. There would be little reason to believe that "peaceful" protest and ghetto "revolts" are related to substantially different sets of conditions.

I would contend, however, that protest against local government targets and collective ghetto violence are two forms of political expression which may be distinguished conceptually and empirically. The conceptual distinctions—which I believe apply to protest directed against *any* target and to most forms of collective political violence—simply suggest that protest and violence are so different in their basic dynamics that the likelihood that the conditions associated with one will also be associated with the other is not a foregone conclusion. Some of the empirical distinctions suggest explicitly that the more narrow categories of behavior with which we are concerned here are reactions to different stimuli. That is, protest against local government targets is likely to be related to the nature of local politics, while ghetto violence is not.

Let us examine some conceptual distinctions first. The term "protest" may be used either generically to refer to any form of verbal or active objection or remonstrance or it may be used technically to refer to a conceptually distinctive set of behaviors. I shall use it in the latter sense.

Protest refers to a host of types of collective manifestations, disruptive in nature, designed to provide "relatively powerless people" with bargaining leverage in the political process. It may be distinguished from other forms of verbal objection and politically inspired collective violence by the following characteristics.

1   Protest is a collective act, carried out by those concerned with the issue and not by their representatives. The vehement congressman who declares that he "protests" an action is not in fact relying on the forces, or resources, which protest, understood in the technical sense, brings into play. While the solitary congressman relies on his status to lend his objection impact, protest is a mass action which relies on the resources which groups of people can command, in this case resources involving the ability of relatively unpredictable masses to disrupt and inspire fear. Only as a mass participatory action are such forces brought into play.

2   Protest is a device by which actors making demands in the political system attempt to maximize the impact of their meager resources while at the same time they strive to minimize the costs which they might incur by such demand making.

Efforts to Control Costs Distinguish Protest from Political Violence.

Those who pursue violent political strategies are also attempting to maximize the impact of relatively insubstantial resources, but by their action they are also exposing themselves to the possibility that the costs of such behavior will be maximized, if death, serious physical injury, and loss of freedom and legitimacy are taken as maximum costs. Protestors on the other hand seldom must make such expenditures.

Protest is a product, then, of a cost-benefit calculation; violent actors in contrast have essentially thrown cost considerations to the winds.

3   Political protest may also be distinguished from political violence by the fact that those who pursue the former rely for their impact largely on the *implicit* threat of violence, while those who pursue the latter are *explicit* in their intention to do physical harm in that they either make open threats or actually engage in violence. What is implicitly threatening in a protest is not only the socially unconventional display by crowds of people, which offends and frightens norm-abiding observers, but the visions which bystanders and targets conjure up about what such obviously angry behavior could lead to. Participants, targets, and third-parties have come to understand that the protest confrontation provides a relatively fertile matrix for the outbreak of violence. Indeed, the society may react to protest by resorting to pre-emptive violence. That protest may lead to violence, then, is undeniable; that the latter is simply an extension of the former does not follow, however.

The implicit-explicit dividing line is crucial. Protest harnesses aggressive impulses by controlling and, to some extent, masking them, while violence gives free reign to these impulses. The strategy of controlling aggression by basing behavior on the unacknowledged threat of violence follows from the cost-benefit calculation. The advantages to the protestors of such a strategy are manifold. Fear is an important motive force, but the costs of acknowledging the manipulation of threat to produce fear are high. Once actors acknowledge the potential violence which underlies their behavior, the goals sought in the action become secondary in the conflict. Target actors—those against whom the protest is directed—may then refuse to debate the issues which gave rise to the protest. They may turn instead to the issue of the legitimacy of the means by which the demand is put.

As long as protestors do not manipulate the threat of violence explicitly, they enjoy a slim legality, even, occasionally, legitimacy. Once they employ their threat openly, however, they open the way for authorities to suppress their movement or action.

Protest, then, is a device by which groups of people manipulate fear of disorder and violence while at the same time they protect themselves from paying the potentially extreme costs of acknowledging such a strategy.

Protest and violence may also be distinguished empirically to some extent. One obvious point is that the ghetto violence of recent years mobilized primarily blacks as demand-makers, while urban protests have appealed to both races. More important, several recent empirical efforts have suggested that the ghetto violence of the last decade can be viewed as a response to certain *national* forces which cut across or transcend city lines: Spilerman cites vacillatory federal action, the development of black consciousness, and the suggestive impact of the national news media, particularly television.[10] Protest against local government targets on the other hand, judging from the present data, is stimulated by specific grievances related to particular local agencies or officials. Whether or not protest occurs in a city, then, is more likely to be a function to some degree of the nature of the local political system, while the likelihood of violence is not (witness the riots in the "model" cities of New Haven and Detroit).

In addition, certain correlates of one form of behavior are not present with the other. For example, while Downes, Spilerman, and the data collected for this present inquiry all show strong relationship between the incidence of violence and the size of a city's black population, my data show no relationship between the frequency of black protest and the size of the black population. Second, my data indicate the violence, prompted either by the police or the protestors, did not occur in the vast number of cases of protest, leading the observer to suspect that implicit threat manipulation and explicit threat manipulation are two distinct forms of political expression. And finally, a number of scholars argue that recent ghetto violence while politically motivated, was largely expressive in nature,[11] while some preliminary survey evidence shows that most actors who engage in protest activities, conventionally defined, do so for instrumental purposes.[12]

In short, the study of protest has an integrity all its own. The lessons of the studies of mass violence in the nation's cities are not likely to be fully applicable to this enterprise.

The concern of this study is to explore the notion that the incidence of protest is in part function of the nature of a city's political opportunity structure.

There appear to be two plausible hypotheses. One is that protest occurs most frequently in unresponsive and unrepresentative political systems—in other words, in cities in which the opportunity as structure is relatively closed. Protest may be viewed in this situation primarily as a frustrated response by groups unable to gain access to decision-making councils by conventional means.[13] Groups which find or consider themselves deprived of political representation or which cannot elicit favorable policy decisions.

Notes

1   John H. Kessel, "Governmental Structure and Political Environment," *American Political Science Review*, 56 (Sept., 1962), 615–620; Leo Schnore and Robert Alford, "Forms of Government and Socio-Economic Characteristics of Suburbs." *Administrative Science Quarterly*, 8 (June, 1963), 1–17; Robert Alford and Harry Scoble, "Political and Socio-Economic Characteristics of American Cities," *Municipal Yearbook 1965* (Chicago: International City Managers' Association, 1965), 82–97; and Raymond Wolfinger and John Osgood Field, "Political Ethos and the Structure of City Government," *American Political Science Review*, 60 (June, 1966), 306–326.

2   Robert Alford and Eugene Lee, "Voting Turnout in American Cities," *American Political Science Review*, 62 (September, 1968), 796–813.

3   Edgar L. Sherbenou, "Class, Participation, and the Council-Manager Plan," *Public Administration Review*, 21 (Summer, 1961), 131–135.

4   Amos H. Hawley, "Community Power and Urban Renewal Success," *American Journal of Sociology*, 68 (January, 1963), 422–431.

5   Stanley Lieberson and Arnold R. Silverman, "The Precipitants and Underlying Conditions of Race Riots," *American Sociological Review*, 30 (December, 1965), 887–898.

6   Robert Lineberry, "Approaches to the Study of Community Politics," in *Community Politics*, ed. Charles Bonjean, Terry N. Clark, and Robert Lineberry (New York: The Free Press, 1971), p. 20.

7   This view of reform government is most cogently put in Edward Banfield and James Q. Wilson, *City Politics* (Cambridge, Massachusetts: Harvard and MIT Presses, 1963), pp. 40 ff.

8   Lieberson and Silverman, p. 896.

9   See, for example, Robert Fogelson, *Violence as Protest* (New York: Doubleday, 1971); Ralph Turner, "The Public Perception of Protest," *American Sociological Review*, 34 (December, 1969), 816–830; and Edward Banfield, *The Unheavenly City* (Boston: Little, Brown, and Co., 1970). Banfield speaks of "demonstrations" as a form of "rioting." See Chapter 9, esp. p. 191.

10   Spilerman, pp. 1–2.

11   See Peter Lupsha, "On Theories of Urban Violence," *Urban Affairs Quarterly*, 4 (March, 1969), 275.

12   Peter K. Eisinger, "Protest Behavior and the Integration of Urban Political Systems," *Journal of Politics*, 33 (November, 1971), 989–990.

13   Ted Gurr, *Why Men Rebel* (Princeton, New Jersey).

Chapter 23

Hanspeter Kriesi and Dominique Wisler

SOCIAL MOVEMENTS AND DIRECT DEMOCRACY IN SWITZERLAND

Introduction

[. . .]

Our study focuses on Switzerland, which is the European country where direct-democratic procedures are most developed. Such procedures exist on all three levels – federal, cantonal and local – of the Swiss federal state. In general, the two most important direct-democratic institutions available to social movements in Switzerland are the 'optional referendum' and the 'initiative'. On the federal level, the *optional legislative referendum* against bills of parliament was first introduced at the time of the adoption of the constitution of 1874: today, if 50,000 citizens ask for it by signing the referendum, a bill of parliament has to be submitted to a popular vote which decides about its fate. A simple majority of the citizens then decides whether the bill is approved or rejected. In the course of this century, several other forms of referendum have been introduced on the federal level, but for our purposes, the optional legislative referendum is the most important one. From the point of view of social movements, it provides a possibility to veto a bill that has been adopted by the political elite.

The *popular initiative* exists on the federal level since 1891. It allows 100,000 citizens, by signing a formal proposition, to demand a constitutional amendment as well as to propose the alteration or removal of an existing provision. The proposition can be expressed in a precise amendment, or in general terms upon which the Federal Assembly can make a formal proposition. Contrary to the referendum, which intervenes at the end of a decision making process, the initiative forms its point of departure. The initiative opens up the *opportunity to give an impulse*, to put a problem on the political agenda. Contrary to a petition, which has no binding force at all, the initiative obliges the political elite to deal with the problem in question. After deposition, the initiative is discussed by the government and by parliament, which may make a counter-proposal. Initiatives and possible counter-proposals are then submitted to a popular vote. If accepted, they become part of the constitution. As with all constitutional changes, acceptance requires majorities of both the individual voters and the cantons. The Swiss initiative is sometimes called 'indirect' to distinguish it from the 'direct' initiative of the OS member states, which is submitted to the popular vote without intervention of parliament. On the federal level, the Swiss initiative applies only to modifications of the constitution. On the cantonal and local levels, there is also a *legislative initiative*, which provides the citizens with the opportunity to submit a proposal for a legislative bill to the cantonal parliament. Quite generally, the direct democratic instruments are more elaborate on the cantonal and local levels of the Swiss federal system. Most notably, there are also various forms of compulsory financial and administrative referendum on these levels.

Our analysis is essentially based on *two data sets on 'protest events'* that have been collected by Kriesi and his collaborators (1981, 1992, 1995). The first data set has been collected for a study of mobilization in Swiss politics during the period 1945 to 1978, the second one has been collected for an internationally comparative study of mobilization in France, Germany, the Netherlands and Switzerland during the period 1975 to 1989. Both sets are based on systematic analyses of newspapers, but the internationally comparative study only covers Monday issues, while the Swiss study is based on issues of the whole week. The notion of 'protest event' employed by the authors is quite broad and includes an extensive list of various forms of unconventional political action, as well as some conventional ones such as direct democratic procedures.

Unfortunately, the definitions used by the two studies are not exactly critical. Thus, a series of conventional events and strikes have not been included in the second study. This is why we have dropped them altogether from our analysis. More seriously, the definition of direct-democratic events and the reliability of the data concerning these events varies from one study of the other: both data sets contain information on the events launching direct-democratic campaigns and on the presentation of the signatures to the authorities which is typically staged as a media event. Given that these events usually take place during the week, they are likely to be underestimated for the more recent period. The first data set was completed by a systematic survey of cantonal referenda and initiatives. The more recent data set tried to make up for its unreliable information on direct-democratic events by a systematic collection of the popular votes on referendum and initiatives which are always taking place over the weekend and are, therefore, reported in the Monday issues. That is, contrary to the data on the previous period, the data covering the period 1975–1989 include campaigns linked to a popular vote on referendum and initiatives among the 'protest events'. In spite of the fact that the two data-sets are not strictly comparable, we shall present analogous results for both of them. Given the lack of strict comparability, we shall be less interested in the development over time than in the general pattern of relationships.

Let us, finally, add that although we are performing secondary analyses on two datasets that have already been analyzed before, the results presented in this paper are quite original.

Action repertories

The POS approach assumes that social movements are strategic actors who make use of institutional opportunities. Other things being equal, direct democratic procedures first of all *facilitate* their access to the political system. They *lower the costs* of grassroots' individual participation in collective action. Signing an optional referendum or an initiative is an easy and entirely conventional act, which does not cost the individual participant very much. For the social movement organization, direct-democratic access is attractive because it does not entail any risk of repression. In general, a direct-democratic campaign can count on official toleration by the authorities. Of course, collecting enough signatures to meet the legal requirements for qualification for the ballot, may be quite costly – at least in terms of time, money and organizational resources. In other words, for the social movement organization (SMO), launching a direct-democratic procedure is likely to imply important *opportunity costs*: the resources invested in a direct-democratic campaign cannot be employed for other activities. That is, the action repertory of an SMO engaging in a direct-democratic campaign is likely to be considerably restricted by that choice. This is pointed out by Epple-Gass (1998, 1991) with respect to the initiative in particular. Epple adds that the campaign for the collection of signatures of an initiative or a referendum gives rise to a number of additional conventional events appealing to the public and drawing attention to the campaign. He maintains, however, that more direct forms of action tend to be neglected as a result of the availability of direct-democratic procedures. In line with Tilly's (1978: 156ff.) more general argument about the impact of the accumulated experience with prior collective action, he also suggests that the availability of direct-democratic procedures exercises a socializing effect on movement activists. Once they have learnt how to use these procedures, they will go on using them, independently of the substantive success they achieve. Finally, he maintains that the initiative reinforces the centralization and bureaucratization of a challenging movement, which also has a disciplining effect on its grass-root members. These considerations suggest that the direct-democratic access has a moderating effect on the action repertory of social movements.

We arrive at the same conclusion if we take into account the *chances of success* – another crucial factor linking the institutional structure to the strategic choice of the movement actors (see Koopmans 1992). The availability of direct-democratic procedures does not guarantee a substantive impact, but it certainly implies a procedural one. From the point of view of the movement's mobilization capacity, it has a multiplicative effect. If the campaign succeeds in collecting the required number of signatures, not only the political elite, but the entire voting public will be confronted with the issue raised by the social movement and will have to take a position on it. This makes direct-democratic procedures attractive for movement activists, even if they do not make any substantive impact, and might explain why they continue to use such procedures in the absence of more far-reaching forms of success. Finally, the availability of direct-democratic forms of access raises the costs of other, more radical forms of collective action. Such forms tend to become illegitimate for the authorities as well as for the general public. The direct-democratic opening puts a heavy pressure on social movements to moderate their action repertory, to develop their organizations and to become regular, institutionalized participants in the political process. In other words, if chances of success of direct-democratic forms of action are uncertain, more radical forms of action are almost certainly doomed to failure in a context where direct-democratic institutions provide open access to the political system.

The comparison of the action repertories of Swiss social movements with their counterparts in Germany, France and the Netherlands which is presented in Kriesi et al. (1995) confirms that the protest repertory of Swiss movements is more moderate than the corresponding repertories in the other three countries. Thus, the Swiss not only use the direct-democratic instruments which are unavailable in the other countries, they also make much more frequent use of petitions than the French, the Germans and the Dutch. Moreover, another very moderate form of action – political festivals – also proves to be quite popular in Switzerland – especially with the regional movements in the Jura. By contrast, confrontational and violent actions together account for only a quarter (26 percent) of the Swiss protest events, compared to more than half (56 percent) in France. France constitutes the opposite case of a country with a rather radical action repertory. The Dutch and the German action repertories are neither particularly moderate nor particularly radical.

These differences between the action repertories of the social movements in the four countries can, of course, not exclusively be attributed to the availability or absence of direct-democratic procedures. As Banaszak (1991) has pointed out, the functioning of direct democratic procedures should always be put into the political context in which they occur. Thus, the Swiss institutional structure and the prevailing strategy of the Swiss authorities provide a greater number of access points than the French political system, independently of the direct democratic institutions: the federal structure of the country, its proportional electoral system, and the integrative overall strategy of its authorities with respect to outsiders all contribute to the opening of the system and contrast with the French situation. In order to strengthen the case of the argument maintaining that direct-democratic procedures have a moderating effect on the action repertories of social movements, we would now like to show the extent to which variations with respect to direct-democratic access *within* the Swiss federal state have an impact on the action repertory of Swiss movements.

The fact that the Swiss cantons – the member states of the Swiss Confederation – determine the details of direct-democratic rights of their citizens on their own provides us with the unique opportunity to study the impact of variations in direct-democratic access on the utilisation of the direct-democratic channel by social movements. Table 1 provides an overview over the 'entry price' of direct-democratic institutions in the Swiss cantons and four large cities. It lists the number of signatures required for constitutional initiatives, legislative initiatives and optional referenda as a percentage of the electorate, and it gives the maximum number of days available for collecting the required number of signatures for each one of these three institutions. In addition, it also provides some information about the electoral systems of the various cantons. As the table makes fairly clear, we can distinguish between two sets of cantons which correspond more or less to German-speaking Switzerland, on the one hand, and French- and Italian-speaking Switzerland, on the other. The German-speaking cantons are, on the whole, more open than the Latin ones. With respect to direct-democratic access, they impose lower ratios for the required number of signatures and they accord more time to collect them. In the electoral arena, they

Table 1 The 'entry price' of direct democracy in the Swiss cantons and four cities[a]

Canton	Number of signatures required (as percentage of electorate)			Maximum number of days for collecting the signatures			Electoral system
	Constitut. initiative	Legislative initiative	Optional referendum	Constitut. initiative	Legislative initiative	Optional referendum	
Glarus	0.00	0.00	–	–	–	–	P
Appenzell-AI	0.01	0.01	2.03	–	–	30	M
Appenzell-AR	0.18	0.18	–	–	–	–	M
Aargau	0.83	0.83	0.83	360	360	90	P
Basel-Country	0.87	0.87	0.87	–	–	56	P
Uri	1.19	1.19	1.19	–	–	90	M
Zürich	1.31	1.31	0.66	180	180	45	P
Zurich-City	1.74	1.74	1.74	180	180	20	P
Lucerne	1.78	1.78	1.33	360	360	60	P
Solothurn	1.85	1.85	0.93	540	540	90	P
Schaffhausen	2.08	2.08	2.08	–	–	90	P
Berne	2.24	2.24	1.50	180	180	90	P
Obwalden	2.40	0.01	0.48	–	–	30	P
Schwyz	2.56	2.56	2.56	–	–	30	P
St. Gallen	2.88	1.44	1.44	180	90	30	P
Thurgau	2.97	2.97	1.48	180	180	90	P
Basel-City	3.07	3.07	1.53	–	–	42	PQ (5%)
Basel-City	1.6	1.6	0.8	–	–	30	PQ (5%)
Vaud	3.38	3.38	3.38	90	90	40	PQ (5%)
Lausanne[b]	*	*	7.69	*	*	40	PQ (5%)

[a] '–' implies no particular constraints; P = proportional system; M = majority system; PQ = proportional system with quorum (the level is indicated between parentheses).

[b] In Lausanne, the two forms of initiatives do not exist.

Source for cantonal direct-democratic institutions: Research and Documentation Center on Direct Democracy (C2D) of the University of Geneva.

Table 2 Forms taken by protest events in German-speaking and Latin Switzerland for cantonal and local events only (in %)

Form of action	1945–1978		1975–1989	
	German-speaking	Latin	German-speaking	Latin
Referendum	14.0	8.8	12.9	11.6
Initiative	42.8	12.6	48.5	27.7
Direct-democratic	56.8	21.4	61.4	39.3
Petitions	16.4	43.1	3.6	3.6
Demonstrations	12.7	11.5	16.8	38.3
Confrontative	8.8	12.5	8.5	11.6
Violent	5.3	11.5	9.6	7.3
Total	100.0	100.0	100.0	100.0
N	(1783)	(1352)	(1128)	(303)

do not impose a threshold for obtaining a seat in parliament, while all but two Latin cantons – Vaud, Valais Fribourg, Genève, Neuchâtel, but not Jura and the Italian-speaking Ticino – have a threshold. Similar differences can be observed between the two German-speaking cities – Zurich and Basel, on the one hand, and the two French-speaking cities – Lausanne and Geneva, on the other.

Given the greater closure of the Latin cantons, we would, following our previous reasoning, expect that the social movements mobilizing in these parts of the country make less use of direct-democratic institutions and that their action repertory is more radical. A closer inspection of the action forms taken by regional and local protest events in the two parts of the country confirms this expectation. As is shown by Table 2, direct-democratic institutions are, indeed, more frequently used in the German-speaking regions. The difference is small for the referenda, but very strong for popular initiatives. As a consequence, the action repertory of the social movements in the Latin regions turns out to be more radical than that of their counterparts in German-speaking Switzerland. Although the two data sets used are not strictly comparable, they give the same general results. There are some differences, however: in the earlier period, the lack of access to direct-democratic instruments in the Latin regions is mainly compensated by a more intensive use of petitions, another very moderate form of action. Only more recently has this lack of direct-democratic access given rise to a much more intensive use of demonstrations in these parts of the country. Without going into any more details of the table, we may conclude that this intra-national comparison confirms the international comparison drawn by Kriesi et al. (1995): if direct-democratic institutions are readily available, they are used by the social movements, which leads to a general moderation of their action repertory. The comparison between the different Swiss regions makes this general result more specific by pointing out that the institutional details of the direct-democratic opening are critically important for the overall moderating direct.

References

Banaszak, L.A. (1991). The influence of the initiative on the Swiss and American women's suffrage movements, *Annuaire suisse de science politique* 31: 187–207.

Epple-Gass, R. (1991). Neue Formen politischer Mobilisierung: (k)eine Herausforderung der schweizerischen Demokratie?, *Annuaire suisse de science politique* 31: 150–171.

Epple-Gass, R. (1998). *Friedensbewegung und direkte Demokratie in der Schweiz*. Frankfurt: Haag + Herchen.

Koopmans, R. (1992). *Democracy from below: New social movements and the political system in West Germany*. PhD Thesis, University of Amsterdam.

Kriesi, H., Koopmans, R., Duyvendak, J.W. & Giugm, M.G. (eds.), (1995). *The politics of new social movements in Western Europe: A comparative analysis*. Minneapolis: University of Minnesota Press.

Kriesi, H., Koopmans, R., Duyvendak, J.W. & Giugni, M.G. (1992). New social movements and political opportunities in Western Europe, *European Journal of Political Research* 22: 219–244.

Kriesi, H., Levy, R., Ganguillet, G. & Zwicky, H. (eds.). (1981). *Politische Aktivierung in der Schweiz, 1945–78*. Diessenhofen: Rugger.

Linder, W. (1994). *Swiss democracy: Possible solutions to conflict in multicultural societies*. London: St. Martin's Press.

Tilly, C. (1978). *From mobilization to revolution*. Reading, MA: Addison-Wesley.

CHAPTER 24

Frances Fox Piven and Richard A. Cloward

POOR PEOPLE'S MOVEMENTS

Institutional limits on the incidence of mass insurgency

ARISTOTLE believed that the chief cause of internal warfare was inequality, that the lesser rebel in order to be equal. But human experience has proved him wrong, most of the time. Sharp inequality has been constant, but rebellion infrequent. Aristotle underestimated the controlling force of the social structure on political life. However hard their lot may be, people usually remain acquiescent, conforming to the accustomed patterns of daily life in their community, and believing those patterns to be both inevitable and just. Men and women till the fields each day, or stoke the furnaces, or tend the looms, obeying the rules and rhythms of earning a livelihood; they mate and bear children hopefully, and mutely watch them die; they abide by the laws of church and community and defer to their rulers, striving to earn a little grace and esteem. In other words most of the time people conform to the institutional arrangements which enmesh them, which regulate the rewards and penalties of daily life, and which appear to be the only possible reality.

[. . .]

Sometimes, however, the poor do become defiant. They challenge traditional authorities, and the rules laid down by those authorities. They demand redress for their grievances. American history is punctuated by such events, from the first uprisings by freeholders, tenants, and slaves in colonial America, to the postrevolutionary debtor rebellions, through the periodic eruptions of strikes and riots by industrial workers, to the ghetto riots of the twentieth century. In each instance, masses of the poor were somehow able, if only briefly, to overcome the shame bred by a culture which blames them for their plight; somehow they were able to break the bonds of conformity enforced by work, by family, by community, by every strand of institutional life; somehow they were able to overcome the fears induced by police, by militia, by company guards.

When protest does arise, when masses of those who are ordinarily docile become defiant, a major transformation has occurred. Most of the literature on popular insurgency has been devoted to identifying the preconditions of this transformation (often out of a concern for preventing or curbing the resulting political disturbances). Whatever the disagreements among different schools of thought, and they are substantial, there is general agreement that the emergence of popular uprisings reflects profound changes in the larger society. This area of agreement is itself important, for it is another way of stating our proposition that protest is usually structurally precluded. The agreement is that only under exceptional conditions will the lower classes become defiant—and thus, in our terms, *only under exceptional conditions are the lower classes afforded the socially determined opportunity to press for their own class interests.*

[. . .]

Ordinary life for most people is regulated by the rules of work and the rewards of work which pattern each day and week and season. Once cast out of that routine, people are cast out of the regulatory framework that it imposes. Work and the rewards of work underpin the stability of other social institutions as well. When men cannot earn enough to support families, they may desert their wives and children, or fail to marry the women with whom they mate. And if unemployment is longlasting entire communities may disintegrate as the able-bodied migrate elsewhere in search of work.

[. . .]

Thus it is not only that catastrophic depression in the 1930s and modernization and migration in the 1960s led to unexpected hardships; massive unemployment and the forced uprooting of people and communities had other, perhaps equally traumatic effects on the lives of people. The loss of work and the disintegration of communities meant the loss of the regulating activities, resources, and relationships on which the structure of everyday life depends, and thus the erosion of the structures that bound people to existing social arrangements. Still, neither the frustrations generated by the economic change, nor the breakdown of daily life, may be sufficient to lead people to protest their travails. Ordinarily, when people suffer such hardships, they blame God, or they blame themselves.

For a protest movement to arise out of these traumas of daily life, people have to perceive the deprivation and disorganization they experience as both wrong, and subject to redress. The social arrangements that are ordinarily perceived as just and immutable must come to seem both unjust and mutable. One condition favoring this transvaluation is the scale of distress. Thus in the 1930s, and again in the postwar years, unemployment reached calamitous proportions. Large numbers of people lost their means of earning a livelihood at the same time. This was clearly the case in the 1930s when unemployment affected one-third of the work force. But among blacks the experience in the post-World War II period was equally devastating, for millions were forced off the land and concentrated in the ghettos of the cities. Within these central city ghettos, unemployment rates in the 1950s and 1960s reached depression levels. The sheer scale of these dislocations helped to mute the sense of self-blame, predisposing men and women to view their plight as a collective one, and to blame their rulers for the destitution and disorganization they experienced.

This transvaluation is even more likely to take place, or to take place more rapidly, when the dislocations suffered by particular groups occur in a context of wider changes and instability, at times when the dominant institutional arrangements of the society, as people understand them, are self-evidently not functioning. When the mammoth industrial empires of the United States virtually ground to a halt in the early 1930s and the banks of the country simply closed their doors, the "American Way" could not be so fully taken for granted by the masses of impoverished workers and the unemployed. Similarly, while the institutional disturbances that preceded the black movements of the 1960s were not dramatically visible to the society as a whole, they were to the people who were uprooted by them. For blacks, changes in the southern economy meant nothing less than the disintegration of the *ancien régime* of the feudal plantation, just as the subsequent migratory trek to the cities meant their wrenching removal into an unknown society.

Finally, as these objective institutional upheavals lead people to reappraise their situation, elites may contribute to that reappraisal, thus helping to stimulate mass arousal—a process that has often been noted by social theorists. Clearly, the vested interest of the ruling class is usually in preserving the status quo, and in preserving the docility of the lower orders within the status quo. But rapid institutional change and upheaval may affect elite groups differently, undermining the power of some segments of the ruling class and enlarging the power of other segments, so that elites divide among themselves. This dissonance may erode their authority, and erode the authority of the institutional norms they uphold. If, in the ensuing competition for dominance, some among the elite seek to enlist the support of the impoverished by naming their grievances as just, then the hopes of the lower classes for change will be nourished and the legitimacy of the institutions which oppress them further weakened.

[. . .]

The patterning of insurgency

Just as quiescence is enforced by institutional life, and just as the eruption of discontent is determined by changes in institutional life, the forms of political protest are also determined by the institutional context in which people live and work. This point seems self-evident to us, but it is usually ignored, in part because the pluralist tradition defines political action as essentially a matter of choice. Political actors, whoever they may be, are treated as if they are not constricted by a social environment in deciding upon one political strategy or another; it is as if the strategies employed by different groups were freely elected, rather than the result of constraints imposed by their location in the social structure. In this section, we turn, in the most preliminary way, to a discussion of the ways in which the expression of defiance is patterned by features of institutional life.

The electoral system as a structuring institution

In the United States the principal structuring institution, at least in the early phases of protest, is the electoral-representative system. The significance of this assertion is not that the electoral system provides an avenue of influence under normal circumstances. To the contrary, we shall demonstrate that it is usually when unrest among the lower classes breaks out of the confines of electoral procedures that the poor may have some influence, for the instability and polarization they then threaten to create by their actions in the factories or in the streets may force some response from electoral leaders. But whether action emerges in the factories or the streets may depend on the course of the early phase of protest at the polls.

Ordinarily defiance is first expressed in the voting booth simply because, whether defiant or not, people have been socialized within a political culture that defines voting as the mechanism through which political change can and should properly occur. The vitality of this political culture, the controlling force of the norms that guide political discontent into electoral channels, is not understood merely by asserting the pervasiveness of liberal political ideology in the United States and the absence of competing ideologies, for that is precisely what has to be explained. Some illumination is provided by certain features of the electoral system itself, by its rituals and celebrations and rewards, for these practices help to ensure the persistence of confidence in electoral procedures. Thus it is significant that the franchise was extended to white working-class men at a very early period in the history of the United States, and that a vigorous system of local government developed. Through these mechanisms, large proportions of the population were embraced by the rituals of electoral campaigns, and shared in the symbolic rewards of the electoral system, while some also shared in the tangible rewards of a relatively freely dispensed government patronage. Beliefs thus nurtured do not erode readily.

Accordingly, one of the first signs of popular discontent in the contemporary United States is usually a sharp shift in traditional voting patterns. In a sense, the electoral system serves to measure and register the extent of the emerging disaffection. Thus, the urban working class reacted to economic catastrophe in the landslide election of 1932 by turning against the Republican Party to which it had given its allegiance more or less since 1896. Similarly, the political impact of the forces of modernization and migration was first evident in the crucial presidential elections of 1956 and 1960. Urban blacks, who had voted Democratic in successively larger proportions since the election of 1936, began to defect to Republican columns or to stay away from the polls.

But when people are thus encouraged in spirit without being appeased in fact, their defiance may escape the boundaries of electoral rituals, and escape the boundaries established by the political norms of the electoral-representative system in general. They may indeed become rebellious, but while their rebellion often appears chaotic from the perspective of conventional American politics, or from the perspective of some organizers, it is not chaotic at all; it is structured political behavior. When people riot in the streets, their behavior is socially patterned, and within those patterns, their actions are to some extent deliberate and purposeful.

Social location and forms of defiance

In contrast to the effort expended in accounting for the sources of insurgency, relatively little attention has been given to the question of why insurgency, when it does occur, takes one form and not another. Why, in other words, do people sometimes strike and at other times boycott, loot, or burn? Perhaps this question is seldom dealt with because defiant behavior released often appears inchoate to analysts, and therefore not susceptible to explanation, as in the nineteenth-century view of mental illness. Thus Parsons characterizes reactions to strain as "irrational"; Neil Smelser describes collective behavior as "primitive" and "magical"; and Kornhauser attributes unstable, extremist, and antidemocratic tendencies to mass movements. Many defiant forms of mass action that fall short of armed uprisings are thus often simply not recognized as intelligent political behavior at all.

The common but false association of lower-class protest with violence may also be a residue of this tradition and its view of the mob as normless and dangerous, the barbarian unchained. Mass violence is, to be sure, one of many forms of defiance, and perhaps a very elemental form, for it violates the very ground rules of civil society. And lower-class groups do on occasion resort to violence—to the destruction of property and persons—and perhaps this is more likely to be the case when they are deprived by their institutional location of the opportunity to use other forms of defiance. More typically, however, they are not violent, although they may be militant. They are usually not violent simply because the risks are too great; the penalties attached to the use of violence by the poor are too fearsome and too overwhelming. (Of course, defiance by the lower class frequently *results* in violence when more powerful groups, discomfited or alarmed by the unruliness of the poor, use force to coerce them into docility. The substantial record of violence associated with protest movements in the United States is a record composed overwhelmingly of the casualties suffered by protestors at the hands of public or private armies.)

Such perspectives have left us with images which serve to discredit lower-class movements by denying them meaning and legitimacy, instead of providing explanations. While the weakening of social controls that accompanies ruptures in social life may be an important precondition for popular uprisings, it does not follow either that the infrastructure of social life simply collapses, or that those who react to these disturbances by protesting are those who suffer the sharpest personal disorientation and alienation. To the contrary it may well be those whose lives are rooted in some institutional context, who are in regular relationships with others in similar straits, who are best able to redefine their travails as the fault of their rulers and not of themselves, and are best able to join together in collective protest. Thus while many of the southern blacks who participated in the civil rights movement were poor, recent migrants to the southern cities, or were unemployed, they were also linked together in the southern black church, which became the mobilizing node of movement actions.

Just as electoral political institutions channel protest into voter activity in the United States, and may even confine it within these spheres if the disturbance is not severe and the electoral system appears responsive, so do other features of institutional life determine the forms that protest takes when it breaks out of the boundaries of electoral politics. Thus, it is no accident that some people strike, others riot, or loot the granaries, or burn the machines, for just as the patterns of daily life ordinarily assure mass quiescence, so do these same patterns influence the form defiance will take when it erupts.

First, people experience deprivation and oppression within a concrete setting, not as the end product of large and abstract processes, and it is the concrete experience that molds their discontent into specific grievances against specific targets. Workers experience the factory, the speeding rhythm of the assembly line, the foreman, the spies and the guards, the owner and the paycheck. They do not experience monopoly capitalism. People on relief experience the shabby waiting rooms, the overseer or the caseworker, and the dole. They do not experience American social welfare policy. Tenants experience the leaking ceilings and cold radiators, and they recognize the landlord. They do not recognize the banking, real estate, and construction systems. No small wonder, therefore, that when the poor rebel they so often rebel against the overseer of the poor, or the slumlord, or the middling merchant, and not against the banks or the governing elites to whom the overseer, the slumlord, and the merchant also defer. In other words, it is the daily experience of people that shapes their grievances, establishes the measure of their demands, and points out the targets of their anger.

Second, institutional patterns shape mass movements by shaping the collectivity out of which protest can arise. Institutional life aggregates people or disperses them, molds group identities, and draws people into the settings within which collective action can erupt. Thus factory work gathers men and women together, educates them in a common experience, and educates them to the possibilities of cooperation and collective action. Casual laborers or petty entrepreneurs, by contrast, are dispersed by their occupations, and are therefore less likely to perceive their commonalities of position, and less likely to join together in collective action.

Third, and most important, institutional roles determine the strategic opportunities for defiance, for it is typically by rebelling against the rules and authorities associated with their everyday activities that people protest. Thus workers protest by striking. They are able to do so because they are drawn together in the factory setting, and their protests consist mainly in defying the rules and authorities associated with the workplace. The unemployed do not and cannot strike, even when they perceive that those who own the factories and businesses are to blame for their troubles. Instead, they riot in the streets where they are forced to linger, or storm the relief centers, and it is difficult to imagine them doing otherwise.

It is our second general point, then, that the opportunities for defiance are structured by features of institutional life. Simply put, people cannot defy institutions to which they have no access, and to which they make no contribution.

The limited impact of mass defiance

If mass defiance is neither freely available nor the forms it takes freely determined, it must also be said that it is generally of limited political impact. Still, some forms of protest appear to have more impact than others, thus posing an analytical question of considerable importance. It is a question, however, that analysts of movements, especially analysts of contemporary American movements, have not generally asked. The literature abounds with studies of the social origins of protestors, the determinants of leadership styles, the struggles to cope with problems of organizational maintenance. Thus protest seems to be wondered about mainly for the many and fascinating aspects of social life which it exposes, but least of all for its chief significance: namely, that it is the means by which the least-privileged seek to wrest concessions from their rulers.

[. . .]

Chapter 25

Doug McAdam

POLITICAL PROCESS AND THE DEVELOPMENT OF BLACK INSURGENCY 1930–1970

THE POLITICAL PROCESS MODEL represents an alternative to the classical and, resource mobilization perspectives. The term "political process" has been taken from an article by Rule and Tilly entitled "Political Process in Revolutionary France, 1830–1832" (1975: 41–85). It should, however, be emphasized that the model advanced by Rule and Tilly is compatible but not synonymous with the perspective outlined here. The name has been adopted, not because the two models are identical, but because the term "political process" accurately conveys two ideas central to both perspectives. First, in contrast to the various classical formulations, a social movement is held to be above all else a *political* rather than a psychological phenomenon. That is, the factors shaping institutionalized political processes are argued to be of equal analytic utility in accounting for social insurgency. Second, a movement represents a continuous *process* from generation to decline, rather than a discrete series of developmental stages. Accordingly, any complete model of social insurgency should offer the researcher a framework for analyzing the entire process of movement development rather than a particular phase (e.g., the emergence of social protest) of that same process.

The political process model and institutionalized politics

A point stressed repeatedly in this work is that theories of social movements always imply a more general model of institutionalized power. Thus, in Chapter 1, it was argued that the classical view of social movements is best understood as a theoretical extension of the pluralist model. By contrast, it was suggested, in Chapter 2, that the resource mobilization perspective implies adherence to the elite model of the American political system. The political process model is also based on a particular conception of power in America. In many respects this conception is consistent with the elite model. Like the latter, the perspective advanced here rests on the fundamental assumption that wealth and power are concentrated in America in the hands of a few groups, thus depriving most people of any real influence over the major decisions that affect their lives. Accordingly, social movements are seen, in both perspectives, as rational attempts by excluded groups to mobilize sufficient political leverage to advance collective interests through noninstitutionalized means.

Where this perspective diverges from the elite model is in regard to the extent of elite control over the political system and the insurgent capabilities of excluded groups. While elite theorists display a marked diversity of opinion on these issues, there would seem to be a central tendency evident in their writings. That tendency embodies a perception of the power disparity between elite and excluded groups that would seem to grant the former virtually unlimited power in politico-economic matters. Excluded groups, on the other hand, are seen as functionally powerless in the face of the enormous power wielded by the elite. Under such conditions, the chances for successful insurgency would seem to be negligible.

By contrast, on both these counts, the political process model is more compatible with a Marxist interpretation of power. Marxists acknowledge that the power disparity between elite and excluded groups is substantial but hardly regard this state of affairs as inevitable. Indeed, for orthodox Marxists, that which is inevitable is not the retention of power by the elite but the accession to power by the masses. One need not accept the rigidity of this scenario, to conclude that it represents an improvement over elite theory insofar as it embodies a clear understanding of the latent political leverage available to most segments of the population. The insurgent potential of excluded groups comes from the "structural power" that their location in various politico-economic structures affords them.

[. . .]

A second Marxist influence on the model outlined here concerns the importance attributed to subjective processes in the generation of insurgency. Marxists, to a much greater extent than elite theorists, recognize that mass political impotence may as frequently stem from shared perceptions of powerlessness as from any objective inability to mobilize significant political leverage. Thus, the subjective transformation of consciousness is appreciated by Marxists as a process crucial to the generation of insurgency. The importance of this transformation is likewise acknowledged in the political process model.

[. . .]

The generation of insurgency

The political process model identifies three sets of factors that are believed to be crucial in the generation of social insurgency. The first is the level of organization within the aggrieved population; the second, the collective assessment of the prospects for successful insurgency within that same population; and third, the political alignment of groups within the larger political environment. The first can be conceived of as the degree of organizational "readiness" within the minority community; the second, as the level of "insurgent consciousness" within the movement's mass base; and the third, following Eisinger, as the "structure of political opportunities" available to insurgent groups (Eisinger, 1973: 11). Before the relationships between these factors are outlined, each will be discussed in turn.

Structure of political opportunities

Under ordinary circumstances, excluded groups, or challengers, face enormous obstacles in their efforts to advance group interests. Challengers are excluded from routine decision-making processes precisely because their bargaining position, relative to established polity members, is so weak. But the particular set of power relationships that define the political environment at any point in time hardly constitute an immutable structure of political life.

[. . .]

The opportunities for a challenger to engage in successful collective action do vary greatly over time. And it is these variations that are held to be related to the ebb and flow of movement activity. As Eisinger has remarked, "protest is a sign that the opportunity structure is flexible and vulnerable to the political assaults of excluded groups" (1973: 28).

Still unanswered, however, is the question of what accounts for such shifts in the "structure of political opportunities." A finite list of specific causes would be impossible to compile. However, Eisinger suggests the crucial point about the origin of such shifts: "protest signifies changes not only among previously quiescent or conventionally oriented groups but also *in the political system itself*" (1973: 28; emphasis mine). The point is that *any* event or broad social process that serves to undermine the calculations and assumptions on which the political establishment is structured occasions a shift in political opportunities. Among the events and processes likely to prove disruptive of the political status quo are wars, industrialization, international political realignments, prolonged unemployment, and widespread demographic changes.

It is interesting to note that classical theorists have also described many of these same processes as productive of mass protest. In particular, industrialization and urbanization have been singled out as forces promoting the rise of social movements (Kornhauser, 1959: 143–58). The difference between the two models stems from the fact that classical theorists posit a radically different causal sequence linking these processes to insurgency than is proposed here. For classical theorists the relationship is direct, with industrialization/urbanization generating a level of strain sufficient to trigger social protest.

In contrast, the political process model is based on the idea that social processes such as industrialization promote insurgency only indirectly through a restructuring of existing power relations. This difference also indexes a significant divergence between the two models in terms of the time span during which insurgency is held to develop.

The classical sequence of disruption/strain depicts insurgency as a function of dramatic changes in the period immediately preceding movement emergence. By contrast, the perspective advanced here is based on the notion that social insurgency is shaped by broad social processes that usually operate over a longer period of time. As a consequence, the processes shaping insurgency are expected to be of a more cumulative, less dramatic nature than those identified by proponents of the classical model.

[. . .]

Regardless of the causes of expanded "political opportunities," such shifts can facilitate increased political activism on the part of excluded groups either by seriously undermining the stability of the entire political system or by increasing the political leverage of a single insurgent group. The significance of this distinction stems from the fact that the former pattern usually precipitates widespread political crisis while the latter does not.

Generalized political instability destroys any semblance of a political status quo, thus encouraging collective action by *all* groups sufficiently organized to contest the structuring of a new political order.

[. . .]

It remains only to identify the ways in which favorable shifts in the structure of political opportunities increase the likelihood of successful insurgent action. Two major facilitative effects can be distinguished. Most fundamentally, such shifts improve the chances for successful social protest by reducing the power discrepancy between insurgent groups and their opponents. Regardless of whether the broad social processes productive of such shifts serve to undermine the structural basis of the entire political system or simply to enhance the strategic position of a single challenger, the result is the same: a net increase in the political leverage exercised by insurgent groups. The practical effect of this development is to increase the likelihood that insurgent interests will prevail in a confrontation with a group whose goals conflict with those of the insurgents. This does not, of course, mean that insurgent interests will inevitably be realized in all conflict situations. Even in the context of an improved bargaining position, insurgent groups are likely to be at a distinct disadvantage in any confrontation with an established polity member. What it does mean, however, is that the increased political strength of the aggrieved population has improved the bargaining position of insurgent groups and thus created new opportunities for the collective pursuit of group goals.

Second, an improved bargaining position for the aggrieved population raises significantly the costs of repressing insurgent action. Unlike before, when the powerless status of the excluded group meant that it could be repressed with relative impunity, now the increased political leverage exercised by the insurgent group renders it a more formidable opponent. Repression of the group involves a greater risk of political reprisals than before and is thus less likely to be attempted even in the face of an increased threat to member interests. For, as Gamson notes in summarizing the evidence from his survey of challenging groups, insurgents "are attacked not merely because they are regarded as threatening—all challenging groups are threatening to some vested interest. They are threatening *and* vulnerable" (1975: 82). To the extent, then, that shifting political conditions increase the power of insurgent groups, they also render them less vulnerable to attack by raising the costs of repression. Or to state the matter in terms of the insurgent group, increased political power serves to encourage collective action by diminishing the risks associated with movement participation.

Indigenous organizational strength

A conducive political environment only affords the aggrieved population the opportunity for successful insurgent action. It is the resources of the minority community that enable insurgent groups to exploit these opportunities. In the absence of those resources the aggrieved population is likely to lack the capacity to act even when granted the opportunity to do so. Here I am asserting the importance of what Katz and Gurin have termed the "conversion potential" of the minority community (1969: 350). To generate a social movement, the aggrieved population must be able to "convert" a favorable "structure of political opportunities" into an organized campaign of social protest.

Conditioning this conversion is the extent of organization within the minority community. That indigenous structures frequently provide the organizational base out of which social movements emerge has been argued by a number of theorists. Oberschall, for instance, has proposed a theory of mobilization in which he assigns paramount importance to the degree of organization in the minority community. If no networks exist, he contends, the aggrieved population is capable of little more than "short-term, localized, ephemeral outbursts and movements of protest such as riots" (Oberschall, 1973: 119).

[. . .]

Members. If there is anything approximating a consistent finding in the empirical literature, it is that movement participants are recruited along established lines of interaction. This remains true in spite of the numerous attempts to explain participation on the basis of a variety of individual background or psychological variables. The explanation for this consistent finding would appear to be straightforward: the more integrated the person is into the minority community, the more readily he/she can be mobilized for participation in protest activities. The work of Gerlach and Hine supports this interpretation. They conclude, "no matter how a typical participant describes his reasons for joining the movement, or what motives may be suggested by a social scientist on the basis of deprivation, disorganization, or deviancy models, it is clear that the original decision to join required some contact with the movement" (Gerlach and Hine, 1970: 79). The significance of indigenous organizations—informal ones no less than formal—stems from the fact that they render this type of facilitative contact more likely, thus promoting member recruitment. This function can be illustrated by reference to two patterns of recruitment evident in empirical accounts of insurgency.

First, individuals can be recruited into the ranks of movement activists by virtue of their involvement in organizations that serve as the associational network out of which a new movement emerges. This was true, as Melder notes, in the case of the nineteenth-century women's rights movement, with a disproportionate number of the movement's recruits coming from existing abolitionist groups (1964). Curtis and Zurcher have observed a similar phenomenon in connection with the rise of two contempory antipornography groups. In their study, the authors provide convincing data to support their contention that recruits were overwhelmingly drawn from the broad "multi-organizational fields" in which both groups were embedded (Curtis and Zurcher, 1973).

Second, indigenous organizations can serve as the primary source of movement participants through what Oberschall has termed "bloc recruitment" (1973: 125). In this pattern, movements do not so much emerge out of established organizations as they represent a merger of such groups. Hicks, for instance, has described how the Populist party was created through a coalition of established farmers' organizations (1961). The rapid rise of the free-speech movement at Berkeley has been attributed to a similar merger of existing campus organizations (Lipset and Wolin, 1965). Both of these patterns, then, highlight the indigenous organizational basis of much movement recruitment, and they support Oberschall's general conclusion: "mobilization does not occur through recruitment of large numbers of isolated and solitary individuals. It occurs as a result of recruiting blocs of people who are already highly organized and participants" (1973: 125).

Established Structure of Solidary Incentives. A second resource available to insurgents through the indigenous organizations of the minority community are the "established structures of solidary incentives" on which these organizations depend. By "structures of solidary incentives," I am simply referring to the myriad interpersonal rewards that provide the motive force for participation in these groups. It is the salience of these rewards that helps explain why recruitment through established organizations is generally so efficient. In effect, these established "incentive structures" solve the so-called "free-ride problem."

First discussed by Mancur Olson (1965), the "free-rider problem" refers to the difficulties insurgents encounter in trying to convince participants to pursue goals whose benefits they would derive even if they did not participate in the movement. The fact is, when viewed in the light of a narrow economic calculus, movement participation would indeed seem to be irrational. Even if we correct for Olson's overly rationalistic model of the individual, the "free rider" mentality would still seem to pose a formidable barrier to movement recruitment. The solution to this problem is held to stem from the provision of selective incentives to induce the participation that individual calculation would alone seem to preclude (Gamson, 1975: 66–71; Olson, 1965).

In the context of existent organizations, however, the provision of selective incentives would seem unnecessary. These organizations already rest on a solid structure of solidary incentives which insurgents have, in effect, appropriated by defining movement participation as synonymous with organizational membership. Accordingly, the myriad of incentives that have heretofore served as the motive force for participation in the group are now simply transferred to the movement. Thus, insurgents have been spared the difficult task of inducing participation through the provision of new incentives of either a solidary or material nature.

Communication Network. The established organizations of the aggrieved population also constitute a communication network or infrastructure, the strength and breadth of which largely determine the pattern, speed, and extent of movement expansion. Both the failure of a new movement to take hold and the rapid spread of insurgent action have been credited to the presence or absence of such an infrastructure. Freeman has argued that it was the recent development of such a network that enabled women in the 1960s to create a successful feminist movement where they had earlier been unable to do so:

> The development of the women's liberation movement highlights the salience of such a network precisely because the conditions for a movement existed *before* a network came into being, but the movement didn't exist until afterward. Socioeconomic strain did not change for women significantly during a 20-year period. It was as great in 1955 as in 1965. What changed was the organizational situation. It was not until a communications network developed among like-minded people beyond local boundaries that the movement could emerge and develop past the point of occasional, spontaneous uprising (Freeman, 1973:804).

[. . .]

Leaders. All manner of movement analysts have asserted the importance of leaders or organizers in the generation of social insurgency. To do so requires not so much a particular theoretical orientation as common sense. For in the context of political opportunity and widespread discontent there still remains a need for the centralized direction and coordination of a recognized leadership.

The existence of established organizations within the movement's mass base insures the presence of recognized leaders who can be called upon to lend their prestige and organizing skills to the incipient movement. Indeed, given the pattern of diffusion discussed in the previous section, it may well be that established leaders are among the first to join a new movement by virtue of their central position within the community. There is, in fact, some empirical evidence to support this. To cite only one example, Lipset, in his study of the Socialist C.C.F. party, reports that "in Saskatchewan it was the local leaders of the Wheat Pool, of the trade-unions, who were the first to join the C.C.F." His interpretation of the finding is that "those who are most thoroughly integrated in the class through formal organizations are the first to change" (1950: 197). Regardless of the timing of their recruitment, the existence of recognized leaders is yet another resource whose availability is conditioned by the degree of organization within the aggrieved population.

Existent organizations of the minority community, then, are the primary source of resources facilitating movement emergence. These groups constitute the organizational context in which insurgency is expected to develop. As such, their presence is as crucial to the process of movement emergence as a conducive political environment. Indeed, in the absence of this supportive organizational context, the aggrieved population is likely to be deprived of the capacity for collective action even when confronted with a favorable structure of political opportunities. If one lacks the capacity to act, it hardly matters that one is afforded the chance to do so.

Cognitive liberation

While important, expanding political opportunities and indigenous organizations do not, in any simple sense, produce a social movement. In the absence of one other crucial process these two factors remain necessary, but insufficient, causes of insurgency. Together they only offer insurgents a certain objective "structural potential" for collective political action. Mediating between opportunity and action are people and the subjective meanings they attach to their situations. This crucial attribution process has been ignored by proponents of both the classical and resource mobilization perspectives. As Edelman has pointed out: "our explanations of mass political response have radically undervalued the ability of the human mind . . . to take a complex set of . . . cues into account [and] evolve a mutually acceptable form of response" (1971: 133). This process must occur if an organized protest campaign is to take place. One of the central problematics of insurgency, then, is whether favorable shifts in political opportunities will be defined as such by a large enough group of people to facilitate collective protest. This process, however, is not independent of the two factors discussed previously. Indeed, one effect of improved political conditions and existent organizations is to render this process of "cognitive liberation" more likely. I will explore the relationship between this process and each of these factors separately.

As noted earlier, favorable shifts in political opportunities decrease the power disparity between insurgents and their opponents and, in doing so, increase the cost of repressing the movement. These are objective structural changes. However, such shifts have a subjective referent as well. That is, challengers experience shifting political conditions on a day-to-day basis as a set of "meaningful" events communicating much about their prospects for successful collective action.

[. . .]

To summarize, movement emergence implies a transformation of consciousness within a significant segment of the aggrieved population. Before collective protest can get under way, people must collectively define their situations as unjust and subject to change through group action. The likelihood of this necessary transformation occurring is conditioned, in large measure, by the two facilitating conditions discussed previously.

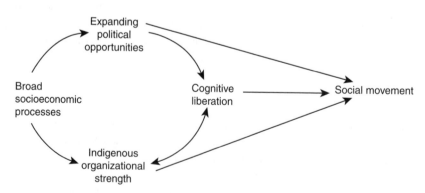

Figure 1 A political process model of movement emergence

Shifting political conditions supply the necessary "cognitive cues" capable of triggering the process of cognitive liberation while existent organizations afford insurgents the stable group-settings within which that process is most likely to occur.

It is now possible to outline in broader fashion the alternative model of movement emergence proposed here. That model is shown in Figure 1. As the figure shows, the generation of insurgency is expected to reflect the favorable confluence of three sets of factors. Expanding political opportunities combine with the indigenous organizations of the minority community to afford insurgents the "structural potential" for successful collective action. That potential is, in turn, transformed into actual insurgency by means of the crucial intervening process of cognitive liberation. All three factors, then, are regarded as necessary, but insufficient, causes of social insurgency.

References

Curtis, R.L. and Zurcher, L.A. 1973. 'Stable Resources of Protest Movement: the Multi-organizational Field'. *Social Forces*, 52: 53–60.

Edelmna, M. 1971. *Politics as Symbolic Action*. Chicago: Markham.

Eisinger, P.K. 1973. 'The Conditions of Protest Behaviour in American Cities'. *American Political Science Review*, 67: 11–28.

Freeman, J. 1973. 'The Origins of the Women's Liberation Movement'. *American Journal of Sociology*, 78: 792–811.

Gamson, W.A. 1975, *The Strategy of Social Protest*. Homewood, Ill.: The Dorsey Press.

Gerlach, L.P. and Hine, V.H. 1970. *People, Power, Change: Movements of Social Transformation*. Indianapolis and New York: Bobbs-Merrill.

Hicks, J.D. 1961. *The Populist Revolt*. Lincoln, Nebr.: University of Nebraska Press.

Katz, I. and Gurin, P. eds. 1969. *Race and the Social Sciences*. New York: Basic Books.

Kornhauser, W. 1959. *The Politics of Mass Society*. Glencoe, Ill: The Free Press.

Lipset, S.M. 1950. *Agrarian Socialism. The Cooperative Commonwealth Federation in Saskatchewan*. Berkeley: University of California Press.

Lipset, S.M. and Wolin, S. 1965. *The Berkeley Student Revolt*. New York: Doubleday Anchor.

Melder, K.E. 1964. 'The Beginnings of the Women's Rights Movement in the United States'. PhD thesis, New Haven: Yale University.

Oberschall, A. 1973. *Social Conflict and Social Movements*. Englewood Cliffs, N.J.: Prentice-Hall.

Olson, M. 1965. *The Logic of Collective Action*. Cambridge, Mass.: Harvard University Press.

Rule, J. and Tilly, C. 1975. 'Political Process in Revolutionary France: 1830-1832'. In Merriman, J.M. ed. *1830 in France*. New York: New Viewpoints.

Chapter 26

Charles Tilly

SOCIAL MOVEMENTS
AND NATIONAL POLITICS

The rise of social movements

THE **REALITY ITSELF** was largely a nineteenth-century creation. People
have to be sure, banded together more or less self-consciously for the pursuit of
common ends since the beginning of history. The nineteenth century, however, saw
the rise of the social movement in the sense of a set of people who voluntarily and
deliberately commit themselves to a shared identity, a unifying belief, a common
program, and a collective struggle to realize that program. The great bulk of the
earlier uprisings and popular fervors to which we are tempted to apply the term were
fundamentally defensive actions by groups which had long existed. During the aggressive seventeenth-century expansion of states, for example, the standard case was the
concerted resistance by the people of long-established communities to the imposition
of new forms of taxation which infringed their rights and jeopardized their survival.
Although plenty of nineteenth-century movements had defensive origins, the remarkable feature of that century was the shift to the deliberate constitution of new groups
for the offensive pursuit of new rights and advantages.

Here we need a distinction. The general phenomenon we are examining is the
organized, sustained, self-conscious challenge to existing authorities. A wide variety
of authorities receive such challenges; not only rulers of states, but also bishops,
bosses, landlords, and college presidents. Let us retain the name *social movement* for
that general sort of challenge to existing authorities. A special, crucial class of social
movements pits challengers against the people who run national states. Let us call
them *national* social movements. These are my claims:

- that the national social movement took shape and spread as a way of doing
  political business in western countries during the nineteenth century

- that the development of national electoral politics and the proliferation of created associations as vehicles for collective action promoted the rise of the national social movement
- that the availability of a model of action at the national level facilitated the formation of social movements at other levels, in the form of challenges to other authorities than the managers of national states
- that the characteristic structures and histories of social movements vary significantly as a function of the kinds of authorities to which they are oriented, and that national social movements therefore differ importantly from other kinds
- that analysts of social movements have ordinarily taken national social movements as their starting points, and have therefore confused a crucial but historically specific form of action with the whole phenomenon

Two things happened in the nineteenth century, then: National social movements crystallized and multiplied, and other social movements became much more common.

The rise of the national social movement belongs to the same complex of changes which included two other profound transformations in the character of popular collective action—the growth of national electoral politics, and the proliferation of created associations as the vehicles of action.

[. . .]

Let me spare you a review of the various ambiguous, and sometimes sloppy uses to which the concept *social movement* has been put. My aim here is neither to castigate other conceptualizers, nor to plead for more precise, adequate, and comprehensive definitions, nor yet to argue that "social movement" is a poor concept because it is historically specific. Far from it. I want to argue that the recognition of the historical specificity of the forms of collective action is the beginning of wisdom. I hope to situate the concept of social movement in its historical setting, and to suggest how its strengths and weaknesses reflect the realities of that historical setting.

To be specific, I want to argue the following points: It is a mistake to conceive of a social movement as a group somehow paralleled to (but also opposed to) a party. Indeed, it is a mistake to think of a social movement as a group of any kind. Instead, the term *social movement* applies most usefully to a sustained *interaction* between a specific set of authorities and various spokespersons for a given challenge to those authorities. The interaction is a coherent, bounded unit in roughly the same sense that a war or a political campaign is a unit. Such interactions have occurred from time to time ever since there were authorities of any kind. The broadest sense of the term *social movement* includes all such challenges. In a narrower sense, however, the national social movement draws its form and meaning from an interaction with the authorities who staff a national state. To improve on Wilkinson, Heberle, and other group oriented theorists, we need a definition on this order:

> A social movement is a sustained series of interactions between power holders and persons successfully claiming to speak on behalf of a constituency lacking formal representation, in the course of which those persons

make publicly visible demands for changes in the distribution or exercise of power, and back those demands with public demonstrations of support.

A *national* social movement, then, pits such challengers against the people who run a national state. Like all such definitions, this one poses practical choices: setting some minimum number of interactions, arriving at tests of the "success" of claims to speak for a constituency, deciding how little formal representation is a lack of it, defining thresholds for the visibility of demands and the demonstrations of support for them, and so on. But the definition excludes a variety of phenomena—religious innovations, crusades, local rebellions, and others—to which the term *social movement* has often been loosely applied. In this narrower sense, both the concept of social movement and the sort of interaction the concept fits best are products of the nineteenth-century growth of popular electoral politics on a national scale. In any case, the definition does not single out groups, but interactions.

No groups? Let me be clear on that point. Groups are crucial to social movements, as armies are crucial to wars and parties to electoral campaigns. At one point or another in the history of every social movement, the organizers of the challenge in question claim to speak for at least one important group which has an interest in the challenge's outcome. (In the French winegrowers movement of 1907, one of the points at issue between Marcellin Albert and Ernest Ferroul was who had the right to speak for the winegrowers as a whole.) The organizers may well recruit participants and supporters from the group whose interest they claim to represent. (Albert's genius was his ability to draw local communities of winegrowers into the common regional effort.) The activists with respect to any particular challenge commonly originate in well-defined groups, and often form new groups in the process of making the challenge. (The creation of the General Federation of Winegrowers marked a major transition in the movement of 1907; the start of sustained negotiations between group and government.) At the very center of the nineteenth-century transformation which made the social movement a standard way of doing political business came a great broadening of the conditions under which new groups could form and mount challenges to the authorities, and old groups could bring challenges into the public arena.

In order to see the nineteenth-century transition more clearly, we should reflect on the specific means that ordinary people use to act together on their interests, and on how those means changed in the nineteenth century. Over the last few hundred years, ordinary people have used a remarkable variety of means to act together. If we run forward in time from the era of the Camisards to our own day, we encounter inter-village fights, mocking, and retaliatory ceremonies such as Riding the Stang and Katzenmusik, attacks on tax collectors, petitions, mutinies, solemn assemblies, and many other forms of action, most of them now long abandoned, in the early period. As we approach our own time we notice electoral rallies, demonstrations, strikes, attempted revolutions, mass meetings, and a great variety of other means, most of them unknown in the time of the Camisards.

Now, there are two important things to notice about these forms of action. First, they are forms: learned, understood, sometimes planned and rehearsed by the participants. They are not the outbursts and "riots dear to authorities and crowd psychologists." Second, at a given point in time a particular group of people who shared an interest had only a few of these means at their disposal. At their disposal?The group knew, more or less, how to execute them, and was capable of identifying some conditions in which it would be both possible and legitimate to use those means. The women of seventeenth-century Narbonne knew how to attack the tax collector, but they also knew how to assemble and deliberate, how to seize the goods of a baker who overcharged for bread, how to conduct a *charivari*. They did not, however, have at their disposal the creation of an association, the launching of a strike, the organization of a demonstration, or any number of other means which are commonplace in our own time.

Let us think of the set of means which is effectively available to a given set of people as their repertoire of collective action. The analogy with the repertoire of theater and music is helpful because it emphasizes the learned character of the performance and the limits to that learning, yet allows for variation and even continuous change from one performance to the next. The repertoire of collective action typically leaves plenty of room for improvisation, innovation, and unexpected endings. Change in our repertoires occurs through three main processes.

1   The invention or adoption of new means, e.g., the deliberate creation of the "sit-in" by American civil rights workers of the 1950s.
2   The evolution and adaptation of means which are already available, e.g., the way London radicals expanded the long-established custom of sending a delegation to accompany a petition into mass marches with thousands of supporters for a petition to Parliament.
3   The abandonment of means which have proved inappropriate, ineffective, impractical, or dangerous, e.g., the Parisian crowd's abandonment of ritual execution, with the display of tailors heads on pikes, after the initial years of the Revolution.

This last example identifies one of the difficulties in the serious study of repertoires: how to distinguish a form of action which is in some sense known and available, but is in fact never used because a likely opportunity for its effective use never comes along. The answer must again draw on the analogy with music and theater. If the performer never performs the piece in public or in private we eventually conclude that the performer has forgotten it, or never knew it. The commonsense rule of thumb has the advantage of confining the study of repertoires to forms of action which real actors have performed, rehearsed, or at least discussed.

Why study repertoires?

The study of repertoires provides a splendid opportunity for joining the general analysis of collective action to the concrete realities of day-to-day contention. For any particular set of people who share an interest, we may undertake to describe the means of action realistically available to them. In the context of their time, what forms of action did the Protestants of the seventeenth-century Cévennes have at their disposal? What forms did they know, and what forms were feasible? What were the likely costs and consequences of the alternatives open to them? Assembling in village councils to petition the intendant, for example, was a standard procedure of the time, but it was a dangerous and ineffectual way to resist a royal policy as vigorously pursued as the drive against Protestantism. The collective appeal to a powerful patron had worked well in an earlier age, but became less and less feasible as the seventeenth-century French state expanded its range and power. And so on.

The inventory of available means of collective action draws us at once into a specification of opportunities, threats, repression, facilitation, power, and—most important—the relative costs and likely benefits of the array of choices actually confronting the group in question. It is not necessary to assume that the Camisards, or any other set of collective actors that concerns us, were cool calculators in their own right. In fact, the Camisards had an extraordinary capacity for hysteria, rage, delusion, and blind devotion. All that is necessary is a logic of the situation which limits the options, entails some likely costs and consequences for each option, and provides us with enough information to begin the reconstruction of the decision rules the participants followed.

If the prevailing repertoire of collective action changes significantly at some point in time, the change is prima facie evidence of a substantial alteration in the structure of power. In France, to take the case I know best, the largest repertoire changes of the last four centuries appear to have occurred around the middle of the seventeenth century and again around the middle of the nineteenth century. The Fronde and the Revolution of 1848 are convenient markers for the shifts in repertoire. At the earlier point, the most visible change was the rapid decline of the classic form of rebellion of some constituted body (a village, a military unit, a trade, or something else) which consisted of assembling, deliberating, stating grievances, formally suspending allegiance to the governing authority, choosing a temporary alternate leader, then setting conditions for a return to obedience. In contemporary English, only the word mutiny comes close to capturing the character of that old form of rebellion.

During the Wars of Religion and the many rebellions of the early seventeenth century, groups of peasants and artisans who rebelled had frequently elected a local noble as their capitaine. That is one reason why, at the end of the seventeenth century, the intendant of Languedoc scanned the Camisards anxiously to see if they had access to Protestant nobles; a link between Protestant countrymen and the regional nobility was much to be feared. By then, however, that link and that form of rebellion had almost disappeared. The defeat of the Fronde and the seventeenth-century co-optation of the nobility, I believe, played a major part in destroying it. The seventeenth-century rise of royal power and expansion of the state was one of the two or three most important alterations in the structure of power over the last four centuries. A major alteration in the repertoire of popular collective action accompanied it.

The nineteenth-century change in the prevailing repertoire collective action is better documented, and no less dramatic. Around the time of the Revolution of 1848 the tax rebellion consisting of an attack on the collector or his premises went into rapid decline. Although protests of high prices and food shortages continued in other forms, the standard bread riot practically disappeared. So did the charivari and a number of other theatrical displays of contempt or moral disapproval. During the same period, the preplanned protest meeting, the electoral rally, the demonstration, the strike, and a number of related forms were crystallizing and becoming frequent. A great alteration in the repertoire was going on.

Was there a concomitant alteration in the structure of power? I believe there was. It included an emphatic nationalization of politics, a greatly increased role of special-purpose associations, a decline in the importance of communities as the loci of shared interests, a growing importance of organized capital and organized labor as participants in power struggles. As a consequence of these massive changes, the available means of acting together on shared interests changed as well. The same sorts of correlated transformations were occurring elsewhere in Western Europe during the nineteenth century: perhaps somewhat earlier in Great Britain, perhaps a bit later in Germany, on varied schedules according to the particular interplay of capitalism and statemaking in one region or another.

Repertoire, social movements, and contemporary collective action

Mapping and explaining the changes in the collective action repertoire is an important task, but it is not the task of this essay. The nineteenth-century changes connect with the previous discussion of social movements in two important ways. First, the nineteenth-century repertoire is still with us today. The strike, the demonstration, the protest meeting, and other forms of action that were novelties then are commonplaces today. As compared with the large alterations in the nineteenth century, the subsequent changes in repertoire have been relatively minor. To be sure, new forms of terrorism have arisen, demonstrations have motorized, mass media have reshaped our perceptions and our tactics. Set against the disappearance of the food riot, the withering away of satirical street theater, or the first flowering of the various forms of action based on special-purpose associations, the twentieth century's innovations nevertheless look small. The nineteenth-century repertoire comprises the basic means of action open to today's participants in national social movements.

Second, and more important, the rise of the concept and of the reality of the social movement were part of the same transformation that brought the new repertoire into being. As parties, unions, and other associations specializing in the struggle for power grew in importance, so did the idea—and the reality—of parallel streams of people, guided by shared interests and beliefs, which overflowed the narrow channels of elections or labor-management negotiations which were being dug at the same time. Those parallel streams were national social movements. Seen from the perspective of national power structures, they are coherent phenomena; they exist so long as they offer a challenge to dominant interests and beliefs. Seen from the bottom up, they are usually much more fragmented and heterogeneous: shifting factions, temporary alliances, diverse interests, a continuous flux of members and hangers-on.

National states, then, played an essential part in the creation of the modern national social movement. They play an essential part in the movement's operation today. No doubt rough equivalents of the national social movement appear any time authorities at *any* level monopolize decisions and resources which are vital to the interests of the rest of the population. The distinctive contribution of the national state was to shift the political advantage to contenders who could mount a challenge on a very large scale, and could do so in a way that demonstrated, or even used, their ability to intervene seriously in regular national politics. In particular, as electoral politics became a more important way of doing national business, the advantage ran increasingly to groups and organizers who threatened to disrupt or control the routine games of candidates and parties. State toleration or promotion of various sorts of electoral association, furthermore, provided an opportunity, a warrant, and a model for the action of associations that were quasi-electoral, semielectoral, or even nonelectoral. Signaling that you had a large number of committed supporters became an increasingly effective way to score political points. The short-run logic of the demonstration paralleled the long-run logic of the national social movement. In both cases organizers sought to display the numbers, commitment, and internal discipline of the people behind a particular set of claims on some powerful body. In both cases, the coalition mounting the action was often fragile and shifting; if from the viewpoint of the powerful the challenge was sustained and coherent, from the viewpoint of the participants it was often a hasty, temporary, and risky alliance in a common cause.

The duality of perspective accounts for the chronic puzzlement and empirical difficulty experienced by sociologists and historians who seek to study social movements systematically. From the top down, the rise and fall of a movement does normally have a sort of natural history. In the contemporary United States a frequent scenario runs like this: small, scattered sets of people begin voicing a grievance or making a demand; more people join them; the separate sets of concerned individuals start to communicate and coordinate; activists, leaders, spokespeople, and formal associations become visible; the activists make claims to speak for larger constituencies (all blacks, all farmers, sometimes all citizens); the groups involved take action to dramatize their programs, demonstrate their strength and determination, enlist new support; power holders respond variously by means of concessions, bargains, co-optation, repression, or alliances; the activists routinize and/or demobilize their action. Many protests stall in the earlier phases of this sequence. But the full sequence is roughly what observers of the contemporary United States mean by the rise and fall of a social movement. Other countries have their own standard sequences—similar, but not identical. In each country participants, power holders, and observers customarily speak of the sequence as the history of a *group*—a fairly determinate set of people sharing a common interest who mobilize and then demobilize around that interest.

The group image is a mystification. In real social movements, involvement ebbs and flows, coalitions form and dissolve, fictitious organizations loom up and fade away, would-be leaders compete for recognition as the representatives of unorganized constituencies, leaders make deals with police and politicians. The parallels with the mounting of demonstrations are impressive. At the extreme (as John McCarthy and Mayer Zald have said) professional social movement organizations manage to keep movements going despite little or no contact with the publics on whose behalf they claim to be acting; they manage by finding elsewhere the resources to sustain a challenge.

What is more, organizers, brokers, some participants, and some authorities commonly know that they are not dealing with a group durably organized around a well-defined interest. Yet they collaborate in maintaining the illusion. Why? Because the group image is essential to a social movement's political logic: the demonstration that committed, determined citizens support an alternative to the existing distribution or exercise of power. The movement leaders threaten implicitly that the committed, determined citizens will withdraw their support from the existing power structure, devote their support to some alternative, or even attack the current system. Within a system of parliamentary representation, such a threat is often an effective way of doing political business outside the routines of parties and elections, precisely because of its possible impact on parties and elections.

Social movements do arise within churches, labor unions, schools, firms, and other settings dominated by authorities who are not managers of the national state. They differ in character from national social movements as a function of the structural peculiarities of the settings in which they develop. For example, challenges to religious authorities commonly require an extensive doctrinal justification, and play themselves out in the form of doctrinal disputes. Social movements within twentieth-century labor unions, in contrast, ordinarily settle for a modicum of doctrine, and a concerted bid to win offices and steer strategy. Yet national social movements occupy a privileged position, shaping other social movements more than other movements shape them. This is not only because the states to which national movements are oriented control more resources than other organizations do, but also because states hold an exceptional power to define actors in any arena as legitimate or illegitimate, hence to support some actors and destroy others. As a result, the sequence of actions which characterizes the national social movement within a given state tends to reappear within other settings.

The national social movement's standard sequence does not result from the internal logic of a group's development. It corresponds to the process by which a national political system shapes, checks, and absorbs the challenges which come to it. In the United States, the character of electoral politics strongly affects the course of any social movement on a national scale which passes the first stage of the standard sequence, whether or not the movement begins by challenging the national state directly. To the extent that the grievances in question promise to become electoral issues and the people concerned with those grievances an electoral bloc, every existing group which has an interest in the next round of elections responds to the movement as a potential source of competition, collaboration, or support. The American system therefore creates three main destinations for any national social movement: (1) dissolution; (2) merging of the organized activists into one of the major political parties; or (3) constitution of a durable pressure group devoted to influencing both the government and the major parties. In countries where single-constituency and single-issue parties loom larger, on the other hand, the third destination is less likely. Either dissolution or the co-optation of the activists by an existing party may well occur in such a country, but a fourth outcome is also a distinct possibility; (4) creation of a new if usually temporary, political party. If characteristic differences in the standard paths of national social movements appear from one country or era to another, then, they are more likely to be due to differences in political contexts than to differences in the character of the people who join social movements. That domination of the paths of social movements by their political context is not easy to see: among other things, the leaders and entrepreneurs of a movement have a strong investment in making it appear to be continuous, coherent, and an outgrowth of its own internal logic.

From the bottom up, however, the coincidence of a particular interest, a particular population, a particular set of beliefs, and a particular program of action which characterizes a social movement turns out to be quite temporary; when the interest, the population, the beliefs, and the program move in different directions—as they inevitably do—the most active participants are generally quite aware of the change. In fact, they seek to control and disguise it at the same time. But in that case, should the student of social movements follow the interest, the population, the beliefs, or the program? So long as we mistakenly think of a social movement as a coherent group rather than as a political product, as a solo performance rather than as an interaction, the problem remains insoluble.

The solution is nevertheless at hand. The solution is (1) to study the collective action of particular groups, and then (2) ask under what conditions, from the perspective of national centers of power, that collective action appears to form part of a social movement. We look for a sustained *interaction* in which mobilized people, acting in the name of a defined interest, make repeated broad demands on powerful others via means which go beyond the current prescriptions of the authorities.

This way of proceeding shakes off the confusion between abstract definition and historically specific phenomenon. It recognizes the historical specificity of the social movement. It ties the national social movement, by definition, to the national state. Like elections and party politics, national social movements are ways of connecting particular interests to the national structure of power. As modes of interaction between citizens and authorities, they grew up with national politics. The implicit attachment of the general concept *social movement* to that historically specific reality clarifies why contemporary sociological models of social movements ring hollow when brought to bear on major conflicts and collective actions outside our own era.

We might, of course, take the opposite tack: instead of narrowing the notion of social movement to the historically specific phenomenon which brought it into being, broaden our models so they break the bounds of time and place. Suppose we think that, in and out of national states, challenges to authorities or actions in pursuit of shared beliefs have important common properties. Those common properties are, in fact, quite elusive. But if they can be shown to exist, then we need a conception of social movements which does *not* rely implicitly on the existence of national states and national politics. In that case, nevertheless, we also need recognition of the distinctive type of social movement which came to prominence in the nineteenth century: the sustained challenge to national authorities in the context of electoral politics. In either case, the renewed models of social movements should break with the old group logic and rebuild around the logic of political processes.

[. . .]

PART FIVE

New social movements

DURING THE COURSE of the 1970s, the emergence of collective action in areas previously (relatively) unaffected by contentious politics triggers new conceptualisations and analyses. Such areas include gender difference, human rights, the environment, peace, self-realisation and, more generally, the quality of life. In brief, social movements appear to be less concerned with the distribution of wealth and resources than with the 'grammar of forms of life'. This phrase, used by Jürgen Habermas in the seminal article we re-propose below (*New Social Movements*, 1981), captures a shift from conflicts over material wellbeing to conflicts over cultural fulfilment. Such conflicts characterise what are described as 'new' social movements, which are understood as resistance against the 'colonisation' of everyday life and as attempts to revitalise buried possibilities of expression and communication. Pursuing post-materialist values, and concerned with spiritual and symbolic aspects of life, new social movements are seen as a collective response to the rationality and bureaucratisation of the dominant society. Habermas distinguishes between old politics, enacted by entrepreneurs and workers in traditional industrial conflicts, and new politics, involving the middle classes and the younger generation, both with higher levels of formal education. New social movements, described as a colourful mixture of groups who inhabit the periphery rather than the core of industrial production, are linked together by a common critical attitude towards growth. In other words, they express an implicit rejection of the conventional objectives pursued by the traditional labour movement, which on the contrary relies on industrial development and economic growth for its own future emancipation. A new social movement such as the 'green movement', for example, focuses on the destruction, pollution and ecological impairment, rather than the emancipatory process, generated by economic growth.

It should be noted that Habermas's interest in social movements stems from, and is consistent with, his concern with modernity and democratic transformation. Against pessimistic views that modern societies are bound to develop into all-pervasive bureaucratic systems, he elaborates the notion of communicative action leading to change. Communication, in his view, is an emancipatory practice, on the one hand, and a consensus-creating process, on the other, and new social movements may themselves contribute to this process when their action fulfils the principles of 'discursive democracy' (Habermas, 1981; 1992).

Concepts such as the 'grammar of forms of life' and the 'colonisation of everyday life' return in a different guise in the work of Claus Offe. In *New Social Movements: Challenging the Boundaries of Institutional Politics* (1985), the author notes the growing fusion of the political and the non-political spheres of life. He argues that the dividing line separating institutional concerns and private issues is becoming increasingly blurred. In response to this tendency, he sees a neoconservative project aiming to restore a distance between the spheres of private life as this manifests itself in civil society, and the institutional sphere as this expresses itself through state authority. Such a project intends to reassert the universal validity of institutions such as the market, the family and scientific truth, as if these had an independent, unchangeable existence, unaffected by political philosophies and practices. New social movements, according to Offe, are engaged in a reverse effort, namely they try to 'politicise' the institutions of civil society, therefore rejecting their universal validity. Paradoxically, by doing so, they share with the neoconservative project the aim of making them autonomous from state control.

The identification of two contrasting political paradigms is crucial for an under-standing of new social movements. The old paradigm, characterising the immediate post-war years, revolved around the issues of economic development, democratic consensus and the welfare state. In a way that echoes Habermas' analysis, Offe remarks that growth was deemed both interminable and satisfactory, supposedly generating wellbeing for all. This model of development entailed a clear separation of private and institutional concerns, whereby citizens, absorbed as they were in their day-to-day life, would decline participation in the political sphere. The new political paradigm, instead, implies that action cannot be categorised as either public or private, and that there is a non-institutional space of political activity that transcends the space of economic development and the welfare state. Offe's analysis proceeds with a discussion of issues, values, modes of action and actors characterising new social movements. It is interesting to note that, when identifying the actors participating in new social movements, he replicates the suggestion of Habermas that these are individuals from the middle classes, but also mentions 'people outside of the labour market', such as the unemployed, students and housewives. In brief, these actors share one common trait: they are all extraneous to the core industrial working class. On the other hand, he remarks that participants in new social movements do not identify themselves with a specific social class, but rather with precise issues, gender, age, locality or the human race as a whole.

Before even dealing with 'new' social movements, Alain Touraine finds it necessary to define what a social movement is. *An Introduction to the Study of Social Movements* (1985) is an effort to classify the different approaches to the subject matter and disentangle social movements from the ideologies and opinions of those who study them. In order to do so, the author lists a series of different forms of social conflicts, including those whose stake is the 'control of the main cultural patterns, that is, of the patterns through which our relationships with the environment are normatively organised'. Touraine's use of the term social movement refers to these specific types of social conflicts, which he describes as evolving according to the changing nature of the societies in which they are active. Social movements, in the past, had precise limits, because the field of their action, namely the capacity of a society to produce itself, was itself limited. With societies capable of producing symbolic goods, codes and information, social movements extend their field of action to all aspects of social and cultural life. Touraine does theorise that some 'new' characteristics can be attributed to some social movements, for example that they are no longer inspired by the image of an ideal future society. New social movements, he argues, are in search of creativity, they are less socio-political and more socio-cultural. These movements show that the distance between civil society and the state is increasing, while 'the separation between private and public life is fading away'. However, he is concerned that, because such movements can no longer be subsumed into official political parties, they lose any capacity to access and modify the state apparatus. On the other hand, he warns that, as it took some time in the nineteenth century to appreciate the effectiveness of the labour movement, it may take just as much time to perceive the capacity of new social movements to produce change. In Touraine's contribution the traces of one of his persistent arguments are found, namely that societies have central, core, conflicts enacted by major antagonistic groups (Touraine, 1981; 1984; 1987). If new social movements are segmented, localised, diverse expressions of conflict; if they represent excluded minorities and victimised cohorts, they will have to transform themselves into actors who join the core conflicts of the society in which they live. And if class is no longer a unifying factor, other variables or loci should be found which make new social movements major, central, antagonistic actors.

The variable class is totally abandoned by Alberto Melucci, one of the major theorists who introduced the term 'new social movements' into sociological literature. Conflicts, in his analysis, are more likely to arise 'in those areas of the system that are most directly involved in the production of information and communicative resources'. The excerpt we propose here is not one of his initial formulations of the nature and characteristics of new social movements, but a defence, ten years on, of his analysis and the concepts underpinning it. The crucial dimensions of daily life, in his view, are constructed 'through the production and processing of information'. *A Strange Kind of Newness: What's 'New' in New Social Movements?* (1994) reiterates the idea that the private sphere is subject to social control and manipulation, but at the same time it is in this very sphere that individuals and groups lay their claim to autonomy. New social movements, therefore, are challenges to the apparatus governing the production of information and their alleged neutrality. They perform collective action that relates to daily life and identity, thus detaching themselves from traditional organised political contention and from the official political system as a whole. Melucci, as we said, abandons the very concepts of class and class relation-ships, which he sees as inseparably linked with capitalist industrial society. Class, he suggests, was a crucial variable for the understanding of conflicts in an era when the central site of the transformation of resources was the traditional industry. The industrial system and the institutional apparatus supporting it had in factory work their own constitutive logic: the problem is whether the system whose constitutive logic is the production of information can generate similar antagonistic conflicts.

While shifting from the economic-industrial system to the cultural sphere, new social movements focus on personal identity, the time and space of life, 'and the motivation and codes of daily life'. Symbolic challenges, movements incorporate traces of past conflicts that they re-elaborate in new fashions, and their action relies on hidden or submerged networks which may at times remain invisible but become operative during periods of mobilisation.

The analysis of Carol Mueller adopts the notion of submerged networks, whose validity she assesses in relation to the women's movement in the US. *Conflict Networks and the Origins of Women's Liberation* (1994) is a theoretical and historical excursus into women's mobilisation, whose inception finds two types of explanation. The first is based on structural theories linking mobilisation with changes in the objective conditions of women. The second explanation is inspired by Melucci's concept of submerged networks and their capacity to re-emerge and generate visible conflict. Mueller reviews the two theories against the background of the history of women's liberation movements, and finds that the rise of feminist consciousness cannot be accounted for with a structural analysis alone. Such analysis faces a severe limitation, in that it views collective action as a mere product of objective conditions, or as a result of subjective beliefs. Between objective conditions and subjective beliefs another layer of explicative tools should be found which grasps the concrete process whereby groups of individuals are compelled to act together. In conclusion, Mueller's study suggests that collective identities are developed in face-to-face interactions within submerged networks of association. Here, structural conditions of injustice turn into shared beliefs activating precise programmes for change. However, her argument is that such programmes receive proper articulation when collective identities created within submerged networks 'achieve an independent existence' and, becoming public, acquire political influence. In this sense, while the concept of submerged networks is helpful for the explanation of how mobilisation is activated, it is insufficient for the explanation of how mobilisation itself becomes politically influential.

New social movement theory, as well as most theories examined so far in this book, seem to be Western creations characteristically stemming from, and exclusively applicable to, advanced countries. Developing countries face totally different conditions, with intermittent economic crisis and endemic political disarray making disadvantaged people overwhelmed with day-to-day tasks of pure survival. And yet, resistance and collective action in these countries are widespread and social theorists interpreting them are both well aware and, at times, critical of the approaches adopted by their counterparts in developed regions. The text we propose below is the opening chapter of a collective book edited by Arturo Escobar and Sonia Alvarez, where the authors engage in a discussion around theories of mobilisation and provide examples thereof occurring in South America. *Theory and Protest in Latin America Today* (1992) sets off with listing an array of forms of collective action performed by squatters, ecologists and feminists. Movements of black and indigenous groups, workers' cooperatives and peasants' struggles are also mentioned, while the emergence is noted of new forms of understanding of resistance and social change. The new forms of collective action, it is suggested, have encouraged a process of theoretical renewal, so that, for example, orthodox Marxist perspectives have slowly been abandoned and new social movement theories cautiously adopted. It is of interest to note that while the challenges of new social movements, due to their anti-authoritarianism and political creativity, are fully appreciated in Latin America, their ability to produce social change is questioned. It is true that new social movement theorists themselves would argue that the impact of such movements is not measurable in political or material terms, but is mainly found in the cultural arena. However, this argument may not suffice in countries where social change is a global necessity, incorporating substantial, inescapable, material aspects. As Escobar and Alvarez remark: 'Social movements in Latin America must be seen as economic, political, *and* cultural struggles'.

References

Habermas, J. (1981), *The Theory of Communicative Action*, Cambridge: Polity Press.
Habermas, J. (1992), *Between Facts and Norms*, Cambridge, Mass.: MIT Press.
Touraine, A. (1981), *The Voice and the Eye: An Analysis of Social Movements*, Cambridge: Cambridge University Press.
Touraine, A. (1984), *Le retour de l'acteur*, Paris: Fayard.
Touraine, A. (1987), *The Workers' Movement*, Cambridge: Cambridge University Press.

Chapter 27

Jürgen Habermas

NEW SOCIAL MOVEMENTS

IN THE LAST TEN TO TWENTY YEARS, conflicts have developed in advanced Western societies that, in many respects, deviate from the welfare-state pattern of institutionalized conflict over distribution. These new conflicts no longer arise in areas of material reproduction; they are no longer channeled through parties and organizations; and they can no longer be alleviated by compensations that conform to the system. Rather, the new conflicts arise in areas of cultural reproduction, social integration, and socialization. They are manifested in sub-institutional, extra-parliamentary forms of protest. The underlying deficits reflect a reification of communicative spheres of action; the media of money and power are not sufficient to circumvent this reification. The question is not one of compensations that the welfare state can provide. Rather, the question is how to defend or reinstate endangered life styles, or how to put reformed life styles into practice. In short, the new conflicts are not sparked by *problems of distribution*, but concern the *grammar of forms of life*.

This new type of conflict is an expression of the "silent revolution" in values and attitudes [. . .] from "old politics," which revolve around questions of economic, social, domestic and military security, to "new politics." This entails problems of quality of life, equality, individual self-realization, participation, and human rights. According to social statistics, the "old politics" are supported by entrepreneurs, workers, and the professional middle class. New politics, on the other hand, find more support in the new middle class, the younger generation, and those groups with higher levels of formal education. These phenomena correspond to the hypothesis of internal colonization.

If we can assume that growth in the economic-administrative complex spurs erosive processes in the life-world, then we can expect old conflicts to be overlapped

Reprinted from *Telos* (1981) 49: 33–37. See http://www.telospress.com

by new ones. A line of conflict arises between, on the one hand, the center composed of strata *directly* involved in the production process and interested in maintaining capital growth as the basis for the compromise of the welfare state and, on the other hand, a colorful mixture of groups on the periphery. Among the latter are those groups that are farther removed from the "productivist core of performance" in late capitalist societies, those who are more sensitive to the self-destructive consequences of the growth in complexity, or who are more seriously affected by them. The bond that unifies these heterogeneous groups is the critique of growth. Neither the bourgeois liberation movements nor the organized workers' movements provide a model for this type of protest. Historical parallels are more often found in the social-romantic movements of early industrialism, led by craftsmen, plebeians, and workers; in the defensive movements of the populist middle class; in the attempts to escape motivated by bourgeois critiques of civilization undertaken by reformers, *Wandervogel*, and so on.

The rapid changes in scenes, groupings, and topics makes it very difficult to classify the current potential for protest and retreat. To the extent that organizational cores form in parties or associations, the members are recruited from the same diffuse reservoir. The following key phrases are currently used to identify various trends in the Federal Republic of Germany; the anti-nuclear and environmental movement; the peace movement (encompassing the North-South conflict); the citizens' action movement; the alternative movement (which comprises urban scenarios with squatters and alternative projects as well as communities in the country); minorities (the elderly, homosexuals, disabled people, etc.); the psychological scene with support groups and youth sects; religious fundamentalism; the tax protest movement; parent associations' school protest; resistance to "modernist reforms"; and finally, the women's movement. Furthermore, independence movements struggling for regional, linguistic, cultural or religious autonomy are also of international significance.

I would like to differentate the emancipatory potential from the potential for resistance and retreat in this spectrum. After the period of the American civil rights movement, which has long since concluded in the particularistic self-affirmation of black sub-cultures, the only movement that follows the tradition of bourgeois-socialist liberation movements is the feminist movement. The struggle against patriarchal oppression and for the realization of a promise that is deeply rooted in the acknowledged universalist foundations of morality and legality lends feminism the impetus of an offensive movement, whereas all other movements are more defensive in character. The movements of resistance and retreat seek to *stem* or block the formal, organized spheres of action in favor of communicative structures; they do not seek to conquer new territory. To be sure, an element of particularism links feminism to these movements: the emancipation of women means more than the merely *formal* attainment of equality and elimination of male prejudices. It means the toppling of concrete life styles determined by male monopolies. The historical legacy of the sexual division of labor, to which women were subjected in the nuclear bourgeois family, also gives them access to virtues, to a set of values that are both in contrast and complementary to the male world and at odds with the one-sided rationalized praxis of everyday life.

Within the resistance movements one can distinguish between the defense of traditional and social property and a defensive which already operates on the basis of a rationalized life-world and tries out new forms of cooperation and community. This criterion allows us to separate the old middle-class protest against the threat which major technical projects posed to neighborhoods, parents' protest against comprehensive schools, the tax protest, and even most independence movements, from the core of the new conflict potential: i.e., from the *youth and alternative movement*, for which a critique of growth based on *environmental and peace concerns* provides the common focus. I would like to support, at least cursorily, the argument that these conflicts can be understood as resistance to tendencies to colonize the life-world.

The objectives, attitudes, and behavior prevalent in youthful protest groups can at first be grasped as reactions to specific *problem situations* perceived with great sensitivity: *"green" problems*. The large industrial intervention in ecological balances, the scarcity of non-renewable natural resources, and the demographic development present industrially developed societies with serious problems. Yet, these challenges are largely abstract and require technical and economic solutions that must, in turn, be planned globally and implemented by administrative means. What sparks the protest, however, is the tangible destruction of the urban environment, the destruction of the countryside by bad residential planning, industrialization and pollution, health impairments due to side effects of civilization-destruction, pharmaceutical practices, and so forth. These are developments that visibly attack the *organic foundations of the life-world* and make one drastically conscious of criteria of livability, of inflexible limits to the deprivation of sensual-aesthetic background needs.

Problems of Over-Complexity: Certainly, there are good reasons to fear the potential for military destruction, nuclear power plants, atomic waste, gene manipulation, storage and central utilization of private data, etc. These real fears, however, combine with the horror of a new category of literally invisible risks that can be grasped only from the vantage point of the system. These risks intrude into the life-world, but at the same time they explode the dimensions of the life-world. The fears function as catalysts for a feeling of being overwhelmed by possible consequences of processes for which moral responsibility can be assumed, inasmuch as we set them in motion both technically and politically, but for which we can in fact not be responsible because of their uncontrollable magnitude. In this case, resistance is directed toward abstractions that are forced upon the life-world. They must be addressed within the life-world, although they supercede the *sensually* focused, spatial, social, and temporal *boundaries of complexity* even of extremely differentiated life-worlds.

Burdens on the Communal Infra-Structure: An obvious component of the psychology movement and renewed religious fundamentalism and a motivating force behind most of the alternative projects and many citizens action groups is the pain of withdrawal symptoms in a culturally impoverished and unilaterally rationalized praxis of everyday life. Thus, ascribed characteristics such as sex, age, skin color, even neighborhood and religion, contribute to the establishment and delimitation of communities, the creation of sub-culturally protected communications groups which further the search for personal and collective identity. High value is placed on the particular, the provincial, small social spaces, decentralized forms of interaction and de-specialized activities, simple interaction and non-differentiated public spheres. This is all intended to promote the revitalization of buried possibilities for expression and communication. Resistance to reformist intervention also belongs here. Such intervention becomes its opposite because the means of its implementation run counter to the declared, social-integrative objectives.

The new conflicts thus arise at the seam between system and life-world. I have already indicated how the exchange between private and public sphere, on the one hand, and economic and administrative system, on the other, takes place via the media of money and power. I have also outlined how this exchange becomes institutionalized in the roles of the employed and the consumer, the client and the citizen (*Staatsbürger*). Precisely these roles are the target of protest. Alternative praxis is opposed to the profit-oriented instrumentalization of professional labor, the market-dependent mobilization of labor, the extension of competitiveness and performance pressure into elementary school. It is also directed against the process whereby services, relations and time become monetary values, against the consumerist redefinition of private life spheres and personal life styles. Furthermore, the clients' relation to public service agencies is intended to be broken and restructured according to the participatory model of self-help organizations. This direction is particularly characteristic for reform models in the area of social and health policy (for example, in the case of psychiatric care). Finally, those forms of protest that range from the undirected explosion of youthful disturbances (Zurich burns) to calculated or surrealistic violations of the rules (such as the American civil rights movement and student protests) to violent provocations and intimidation negate the definitions of the citizens' role as well as the routines of a goal-oriented realization of interests.

The partial dissolution of the social roles of employees and consumers, of clients and citizens, should, according to the *programmatic conceptions* of some theoreticians, clear the path for *counter-institutions* developed from within the life-world in order to limit the particular dynamic of the economic and political-administrative system of action. On the one hand, these institutions are supposed to branch off from the economic system into a second, informal sector that no longer is profit-oriented. On the other hand, these institutions are supposed to counter the party system with new forms of an expressive "politics of the first person" which, at the same time, is supposed to have a democratic base. According to this conception, such institutions would render inactive the abstraction and neutralization process by virtue of which work and political opinion have been linked to media-directed interactions in modern societies. The capitalist firm and the mass party (as an "ideologically neutral organization to attain power") organize their social realms of influence through labor markets and constructed public spheres. They treat their employees and their electors as an abstract labor force or as subjects of decision, and they differentiate and distance those spheres in which alone personal and collective identities could be formed as the *environment* of the system. The counter-institutions, on the other hand, are supposed to re-integrate a section of the formally organized areas of action, save it from the influence of media intervention, and restore these "liberated areas" to the mechanism of understanding which coordinates action.

Regardless of how unrealistic these notions may be, they remain important for the polemical significance of the new resistance and retreat movements which are reacting to the colonization of the life-world. This significance is hidden in the self-image of the participants just as it is in the ideological depiction of the enemy when the rationality of the maintenance of the status quo in economic and administrative systems of action are identified with each other; that is, whenever rationalization of the life-world is not carefully distinguished from the increasing complexity of the social system. This confusion explains the mutually disruptive fronts that obscure political oppositions which are set up between the anti-modernism of the young conservatives and the new-conservative defense of a post-modernism that robs a modernism alienated from itself of its reasonable content and its possibilities for the future.

Chapter 28

Claus Offe

NEW SOCIAL MOVEMENTS: CHALLENGING THE BOUNDARIES OF INSTITUTIONAL POLITICS

AMONG POLITICAL SOCIOLOGISTS and political scientists who analyze the changing structures and dynamics of West European politics, it became commonplace in the seventies to observe the fusion of political and nonpolitical spheres of social life. The continued analytical usefulness of the conventional dichotomy of "state" and "civil society" was questioned. Processes of fusion could be observed not only on the level of global sociopolitical arrangements, but also on the level of citizens as the elementary political actors. The dividing line that delineates "political" concerns and modes of action from "private" (e.g., moral or economic ones) was becoming blurred.

We see the contours of a rather dramatic model of political development of advanced Western societies: as public policies win a more direct and more visible impact upon citizens, citizens in turn try to win a more immediate and more comprehensive control over political elites by means that are seen frequently to be incompatible with the maintenance of the institutional order of the polity. Since the midseventies, a number of mostly conservative analysts have described this cycle as highly vicious and dangerous, one which, in their view, must lead to a cumulative erosion of political authority and even the capacity to govern, unless effective measures are taken that free the economy from overly detailed and ambitious political intervention and that immunize political elites from the pressures, concerns, and actions of citizens. The proposed solution, in other words, is a restrictive redefinition of what can and should be considered "political," and the corresponding elimination from the agenda of governments of all issues, practices, demands, and responsibilities that are defined as being "outside" the proper sphere of politics. This is the neoconservative project of insulating the political from the nonpolitical.

[. . .]

In spite of their obvious political opposition to the content of the neoconservative project, the politics of the new social movements shares an important analytical insight with the proponents of this project. This insight is the following: The conflicts and contradictions of advanced industrial society can no longer be resolved in meaningful and promising ways through etatism, political regulation, and the proliferating inclusion of ever more claims and issues on the agenda of bureaucratic authorities. It is only after this shared analytical premise that neoconservative politics and movement politics diverge in opposite political directions. Whereas the neoconservative project seeks to *restore* the nonpolitical, noncontingent, and uncontestable foundations of civil society (such as property, the market, the work ethic, the family, and scientific truth) in order to safeguard a more restricted—and *therefore* more solid—sphere of state authority and no longer "overloaded" political institutions, the politics of new social movements, by contrast, seeks to politicize the institutions of civil society in ways that are not constrained by the channels of representative-bureaucratic political institutions, and thereby to *reconstitute* a civil society that is no longer dependent upon ever more regulation, control, and intervention. In order to emancipate itself from the state, civil society itself—its institutions of work, production, distribution, family relations, relations with nature, its very standards of rationality and progress—must be politicized through practices that belong to an intermediate sphere between "private" pursuits and concerns, on the one side, and institutional, state-sanctioned modes of politics, on the other.

The "new politics" of the new social movements can be analyzed, as can any other politics, in terms of its social base, its issues, concerns, and values, and its modes of action. In order to do so, I will employ the term "political paradigm."

[. . .]

The old paradigm

The core items on the agenda of West European politics in the period from the immediate postwar years until the early seventies were issues of economic growth, distribution, and security.

[. . .]

The social, economic, and political order that was adopted in the late forties and early fifties was built upon a highly encompassing liberal-democratic welfare-state consensus that remained unchallenged by any significant forces on either the political Right or Left. Not only was this constitutional accord firmly based in a broad "posttotalitarian" consensus, but it was also actively enforced and sanctioned by the international configuration of forces that emerged after World War II.

This is true at least of three central elements of the constitutional postwar accords, all of which were adopted, justified, and defended in terms of their conduciveness to growth and security. First, [. . .] investment decisions were instituted as the space of action of owners and managers acting in free markets and according to criteria of profitability; this freedom of property and investment had been overwhelmingly advocated and justified not in terms of moral philosophy and natural right but in the "functional" terms of a growth and efficiency that no alternative arrangement was thought to be capable of accomplishing to a comparable extent. Second, capitalism as a growth machine was complemented by organized labor as a distribution and social-security machine. It is only the basis of a prevalent concern with growth and real income that both the preparedness of organized *labor* to give up more far-reaching projects of societal change in exchange for a firmly established status in the process of income distribution and the preparedness of *investors* to grant such status to organized labor can be explained. On both sides, the underlying view of society was that of a "positive sum" society in which growth is both continuously possible (so as to make the strong position of unions in distributive conflicts tolerable to capital) and considered generally as satisfying and desirable (so as to make "system-loyal" unions and socialist parties—specializing in the task of channeling growth dividends back to the workers rather than pursuing goals of changing the "mode of production"—acceptable to workers). The third most important element of the constitutional design of the postwar period [. . .] was a form of political democracy that was representative and mediated through party competition. Such an arrangement was well suited to limit the amount of conflicts that were transferred from the sphere of civil society into the arena of public policy.

[. . .]

The implicit sociological assumption underlying the constitutional arrangements of the liberal welfare state was that "privatistic," family-, work-, and consumption-centered patterns of life would absorb the energies and aspirations of most people, and that participation in and conflict over public policy would for that reason be of no more than marginal significance in the lives of most citizens. This constitutional definition of the respective spaces of action of capital and labor, of the state and civil society, was a correlate of the centrality of the values of growth, prosperity, and distribution. The dynamic force of the political-economic system was industrial production and productivity-increasing innovation, and the task that remained for public policy was to create security and thus the conditions under which this dynamic process could continue to operate.

[. . .]

The new paradigm

This brief account of the configuration of values, actors, issues, and institutions of the "old politics" may provide us with a background against which the "new paradigm" can now be compared.

[. . .]

The major part of the social-scientific literature dealing with new concerns and movements simply emphasizes rupture and discontinuity, by using terms like "new protest movements," "new politics," "new populism," "neoromanticism," "antipolitics," "unorthodox political behavior" and "disorderly politics," or it describes the means by which conflict is typically carried out within the politics of the new paradigm as "unconventional." The most encompassing, though still less than all-inclusive label by which activists of these movements themselves refer to the "new politics" is the term "alternative movements," which is equally void of positive content, as is the case with the related terms "counter-economy," "counter-institutions," and "counter-public".

The new movements politicize themes which cannot easily be "coded" within the binary code of the universe of social action that underlies liberal political theory. That is to say, where liberal theory assumes that all action can be categorized as either "private" or "public" (and, in the latter case, rightfully "political"), the new movements locate themselves in a third, intermediate category.

[. . .]

The space of action of the new movements is a space of *noninstitutional politics* which is not provided for in the doctrines and practices of liberal democracy and the welfare state.

This raises a conceptual problem: What do we mean by noninstitutional *politics*, in contrast to "private" modes of action? Precision in this respect appears particularly relevant as the term "new social movements" is often used in a way which would also include private concerns of, for instance, religious or economic kinds. A minimum requirement for using the word "political" for some mode of action is that the actor makes some explicit claim that the *means* of action can be recognized as legitimate *and* the *ends* of action can become binding for the wider community. Only those social movements that share these two characteristics have a political quality and will therefore interest us here.

[. . .]

Throughout, the following discussion, I will focus on four of these movements which appear to be the most important ones as measured by their qualitative mobilization success as well as their manifest political impact. These are the ecology or environmental movements, including concerns having to do not only with the natural but also with the built (urban) environment; human rights movements, most importantly the feminist movement, fighting for the protection of the identity and dignity and for equitable treatment of those defined by gender, age, race, language, and region; pacifism and peace movements; and movements advocating or engaging in "alternative" or "communal" modes of the production and distribution of goods and services. Let us first explore some ideal-typical common characteristics of these movements; these characteristics are evident in the movements' *issues, values, modes of action*, and *actors*.

Dominant *issues* of new social movements consist in the concern with a (physical) territory, space of action, or "life-world," such as the body, health, and sexual identity; the neighborhood, city, and the physical environment; the cultural, ethnic, national, and linguistic heritage and identity; the physical conditions of life, and survival for humankind in general.

Diverse and incoherent as these issues and concerns appear to be, they have a common root in certain values which, as I will argue later, are not in themselves "new" but are given a different emphasis and urgency within the new social movements. Most prominent among these *values* are autonomy and identity (with their organizational correlates such as decentralization, self-government, and self-help) and opposition to manipulation, control, dependence, bureaucratization, regulation, etc.

A third element of the new paradigm is the *mode of action* of new social movements. This typically involves two aspects: the mode by which individuals act together in order to constitute a collectivity ("internal mode of action") and the methods by which they confront the external world and their political opponents ("external mode of action"). The first is already referred to by the term social movements; the mode by which multitudes of individuals become collective actors is highly informal, ad hoc, discontinuous, context-sensitive, and egalitarian. In other words, while there are at best rudimentary membership roles, programs, platforms, representatives, officials, staffs, and membership dues, the new social movements consist of participants, campaigns, spokespeople, networks, voluntary helpers, and donations. Typically, in their internal mode of action, new social movements do not rely, in contrast to traditional forms of political organization, on the organizational principle of differentiation, whether in the horizontal (insider vs. outsider) or in the vertical dimension (leaders vs. rank and file members). To the contrary, there seems to be a strong reliance upon de-differentiation, that is, the fusion of public and private roles, instrumental and expressive behavior, community and organization, and in particular a poor and at best transient demarcation between the roles of "members" and formal "leaders." Concerning the external mode of action, we find demonstration tactics and other forms of action making use of the physical presence of (large numbers of) people. These protest tactics are intended to mobilize public attention by (mostly) legal though "unconventional" means. They are paralleled by protest demands whose positive aspects are articulated mostly in negative logical and grammatical forms, as indicated by key words such as "never," "nowhere," "end," "stop," "freeze," "ban," etc. Protest tactics and protest demands indicate that the (actually or potentially) mobilized group of actors conceives of itself as an ad-hoc and often single-issue veto alliance (rather than an organizationally or even ideologically integrated group) which leaves ample room for a wide variety of legitimations and beliefs among the protesters. This mode of action also emphasizes the principled and nonnegotiable nature of concerns, which can be seen as a virtue as well as something necessitated by the relatively primitive organizational structures involved.

Social movements relate to other political actors and opponents not in terms of negotiations, compromise, reform, improvement, or gradual progress to be brought about by organized pressures and tactics but, rather, in terms of sharp antinomies such as yes/no, them/us, the desirable and the intolerable, victory and defeat, now or never, etc. Such a logic of thresholds, obviously, hardly allows for practices of political exchange or gradualist tactics.

Movements are *incapable* of negotiating because they do not have anything to offer in return for any concessions made to their demands. They cannot promise, for instance, lower levels of energy consumption in return for the discontinuation of nuclear energy projects in the way trade unions can promise (or at least practice) wage restraint in return for employment guarantees. This is due to the movements' lack of some of the properties of formal organizations, most importantly the internal bindingness of representative decisions by virtue of which formal organizations can make sure to some extent that the terms of a political deal will be honored. They also typically lack a coherent set of ideological principles and interpretations of the world from which an image of a desirable arrangement of society could be derived and the steps toward transformation could be deduced. Only if such a theory about the world—and its own role in changing the world—were available to the movements, a practice of exchanging long-term gains for short-term losses, a practice of tactical rationality and alliance formation could be expected from these political actors. Movements are also *unwilling* to negotiate because they often consider their central concern of such high and universal priority that no part of it can be meaningfully sacrificed (e.g., in issues linked to the values of "survival" or "identity") without negating the concern itself.

Finally, concerning the *actors* of the new social movements, the most striking aspect is that they do *not* rely for their self-identification on either the established political codes (left/right, liberal/conservative, etc.) nor on the partly corresponding socioeconomic codes (such as working class/middle class, poor/wealthy, rural/urban population, etc.). The universe of political conflict is rather coded in categories taken from the movements' issues, such as gender, age, locality, etc., or, in the case of environmental and pacifist movements, the human race as a whole. To be sure, the insistence upon the irrelevance of socioeconomic codes (such as class) and political codes (ideologies) that we find on the level of self-identification of new social movements (and often of their opponents), and which is part of their very "newness" (and distinguishes them from "old" social movements), by no means implies that the social base and political practice of these movements *is in fact* as amorphous and heterogeneous in class and ideological terms. As far as their social base is concerned, it consists, of three rather sharply circumscribed segments of the social structure, namely (1) the new middle class, especially those elements of it which work in the human service professions and/or the public sector, (2) elements of the old middle class, and (3) a category of the population consisting of people outside the labor market or in a peripheral position to it (such as unemployed workers, students, housewives, retired persons, etc.).

The new paradigm divides the universe of action into three spheres (private vs. noninstitutional political vs. institutional political) and claims the sphere of "political action within civil society" as its space, from which it challenges both private *and* institutional-political practices and institutions.

[. . .]

Chapter 29

Alain Touraine

AN INTRODUCTION TO THE STUDY OF SOCIAL MOVEMENTS

Types of social conflicts

THERE IS AN ALMOST GENERAL AGREEMENT that social movements should be conceived as a special type of social conflict. Many types of collective behavior are not social conflicts: panics, crazes, fashions, currents of opinion, cultural innovations are not conflicts, even if they define in a precise way what they react to. A conflict presupposes a clear definition of opponents or competing actors and of the resources they are fighting for or negotiating to take control of. Such an elementary definition leaves the way open to many different approaches, but it already draws two limits which should not be trespassed. A social conflict cannot be analyzed entirely as a feature of a social system. If a "society" feels threatened or even no longer wants to survive, the manifestation of this societal crisis cannot be analyzed as a social conflict. The agents of this conflict must be identified as specific social categories. On the other side, if a collective actor cannot define its goals in social terms—if for example a group wants its specificity to be recognized—its struggle for freedom or identity cannot by itself create a social conflict. Even when the conflict is very far from being a zero-sum game, it must be defined by a "field," that is, by "stakes" which are valued and desired by two or more opponents. So all kinds of social conflicts have in common a reference to "real"—that is, organized—actors and to ends which are valued by all competitors or adversaries. Within this broad definition, it is necessary to separate various kinds of social conflicts.

(1) A first and easily perceived category of social conflict is the competitive *pursuit of collective interests*. In its most extreme form, it opposes individuals or groups who want to maximize their advantages on a market.

[. . .]

(2) Both similar and opposed to the first type is the *reconstruction of a social, cultural, or political identity*. Here the opponent is defined more as a foreigner or invader than as an upper class, a power elite, or management. The actor defines himself as a community whose values are threatened by invasion or destruction.

[. . .]

(3) *A political force* aims at changing the rules of the game, not just the distribution of relative advantages in a given organization. In this case, the definition of the actors and of the stakes of their conflict seems easy, because either the conflict is strongly organized or it has a great capacity for mobilization. In both cases, each camp clearly defines itself, its opponent, and the aspect of the decision-making process or of the rules of the game which should be changed or maintained. Most studies of industrial relations refer themselves, often explicitly, to such an image of social conflict.

[. . .]

(4) In the same way, as the defense of an identity is the opposite side, the negative equivalent, of the collective pursuit of interest, *the defense of a status or privileges* is the negative equivalent of a political pressure.

[. . .]

(5) Above this political, institutional level of analysis, exists a different type of social conflict, whose stake is *the social control of the main cultural patterns*, that is, of the patterns through which our relationships with the environment are normatively organized. These cultural patterns are of three main kinds: a model of knowledge, a type of investment, and ethical principles. These representations of truth, production, and morality depend on the capacity of achievement, of self-production.

[. . .]

(6) *Creation of a new order* is the opposite of the conflict-loaded self-production of society. The most extreme form of such a "critical action" is *revolution*, which always aims at recreating a community, establishing a new social order, more rational or more national, but defined by its integration and its capacity to eliminate conflicts.

[. . .]

(7) It is appropriate to give a very concrete name to the positive historical conflicts at their highest level: they are *national conflicts*, because the identity and continuity of a changing, developing country cannot be based on social actors and social relations which are precisely transformed, destroyed, or created by the process of historical change— for example, of industrialization. State and nation are the only actors which can maintain their identity and proclaim their continuity throughout a process of change. In all countries, conflicts about the control of change are conflicts about the State.

[. . .]

(8) The negative equivalent of national conflict is *neocommunitarianism*, the effort to reject a historical transformation which comes from abroad and destroys traditional values and forms of social organization. It could be called an antirevolution, and it is as important at the end of the twentieth century as the revolutionary movements were a century ago.

[. . .]

To make my hypothesis quite clear, I will use the concept "social movements" *only* to refer to conflicts around the social control of the main cultural patterns, that is, type 5.

New social movements?

The most serious critique of the notion of social movement is that it corresponds, like all macrosociological concepts, to a specific type of society. We cannot analyze our societies with the concepts of caste or *Stand* and less and less of class. In the same way, is not social movement an abstract name for labor movement, a generalization of a given type of industrial society? Some introduce a more positive critique: let's substitute in our vocabulary "minorities" for social movements, let's abandon all references to a new society and recognize that, in our mass society protest movements do not pretend to become a majority and to get legitimate power but define themselves as minorities. They do not pretend to transform society; they are liberal or libertarian, and try to lower the level of social control and integration. They fight for a society defined by its diversity, adding ethnic or moral pluralism to political pluralism and free enterprise. The most extreme form of these critiques asserts that all models of collective life should be respected and the only paramount value is individualism: the only possible movement should be antisocial, pushing back the invasion of collective controls and organizations, destroying statuses and roles to free the individual, his desires, dreams, and imagination.

All these critiques, excessive as they sometimes are, help us to free ourselves from social and political models which were inherited from a declining type of society. I have already indicated some deep differences between industrial social movements and present-day conflicts. We must now deepen our analysis.

All social movements in the past were limited, because the field of their action— that is, the capacity of a society to produce itself—was limited, even in the most achievement-oriented societies. What I call *historicity*, the capacity to produce an historical experience through cultural patterns, that is, a new definition of nature and man, was limited by what I call "metasocial guarantees of social order." Men thought they lived in a microcosm included in a macrocosm whose laws imposed a definition of human nature and legitimated social norms. All social movements, at the same time as they were defining stakes and enemies, were referring to a metasocial principle which was called order of things, divine rule, natural law, or historical evolution (the idea of modernity is one of the last metasocial principles). In our times, we feel that our capacity of self-production, self-transformation, and self-destruction is boundless. Industrial societies were able to transform "means of production" to invent mechanical devices and systems of organization, but our society invents technologies to produce symbolic goods, languages, information. It produces not only means but ends of production, demands, and representations. It is already able to transform our body, our sexuality, our mental life. The result is that the field of social movements extends itself to all aspects of social and cultural life. This conclusion is the opposite of the structural Marxist idea according to which social life is controlled by a central agency. The public space strictly limited in a bourgeois society was extended to labor problems in an industrial society and now spreads over all fields of experience: private life becomes public and social scientists who announced some years ago that, after a long period of public life, we were withdrawing into private life, did not see that the main political problems today deal directly with private life—fecundation and birth, reproduction and sexuality, illness and death, and, in a different way, with home-consumed mass media.

This extraordinary transformation, which makes all principles and rules problematic, creates two main obstacles to the formation of social movements. The first one is the disappearance of metasocial limits which provided collective action with a principle of unity which was both negative and positive. Marcuse and others raised the question: when gods are dead, when guilt and redemption lose their meaning, what can we oppose to utilitarianism or hedonism? The Western experience can be considered as a short and dramatic period of secularization, which corresponds to the economic takeoff but rapidly ends up in a utilitarian consumer society. Big Brother is not a dangerous enemy for social movements in democratic societies; egotism is. But here is exactly the point where new social movements enter the scene. Past social movements were linked to metasocial principles, but they opposed themselves to the domination of tradition and natural principles; new social movements are threatened by utilitarianism, but they defend the self and its creativity against interest and pleasure. Domination can no longer be challenged by a call to metasocial principles; only a direct call to personal and collective freedom and responsibility can foster protest movements. In a parallel way, ruling groups are no longer motivated by a Protestant ethic or its equivalent; only self-realization and creativity can motivate them as entrepreneurs. Social movements are no longer spurred by the images of an ideal society but by the search of creativity. The utilitarian tradition is the main limit and obstacle to social movements today as religion was in more traditional cultures.

New social movements are less sociopolitical and more sociocultural. The distance between civil society and State is increasing while the separation between private and public life is fading away. The continuity from social movement to political party is disappearing; political life tends to be a depressed area between a stronger State in a changing international environment and, on the other side, sociocultural movements. The main risk is no longer to see social movements absorbed by political parties, as in Communist regimes, but a complete separation between social movements and State. In such a situation, social movements can easily become segmented, transform themselves into defense of minorities or search for identity, while public life becomes dominated by pro- or anti-State movements. That is what is happening today, especially in Germany and the United States, with peace movements. It is possible that through such "historical" movements, new social movements will eventually achieve a high capacity of political action, progressing from *Bürgeriniziativen* to a Green party and inventing new forms of political life; but a different evolution is equally possible: the crystallization of an anti-State movement, more and more distinct from scattered sociocultural movements. This situation corresponds to the beginning of many industrial societies when anarchist, communist, and Christian groups were challenging State and church while, far from them, weak unions, wildcat strikes, and riots expressed a confused mixture of workers' grievances and of decline of preindustrial crafts and cities.

The main condition for social movements to take shape is the consciousness that we are entering a new type of social life. During the sixties and early seventies, the crisis of industrial values prevailed over the notion of postindustrial society. The first new social movements were so closely linked with the counterculture that they collapsed when rising expectations were replaced by shrinking prospects. Thus, during the late seventies and even, in Europe, the early eighties, our historical experience has been dominated by the idea of crisis. Individual and national life seemed to be determined by unforeseeable events, like changes in the dollar or the price of oil, Japanese competition or Soviet military pressure. I criticized, as early as in 1969, the notion of postindustrial society, as it had been conceived by D. Bell, that is, as a hyperindustrial society. Fifteen years later, after a short period of enthusiasm for the "third wave," few observers, especially in business circles, are ready to speak of a postindustrial revolution. A new industrial revolution or a new leap forward in industrial productivity seems to be a more adequate expression. Americans in general have been very cautious in their judgments, while more voluntaristic countries like Japan and France are still speaking of an electronic revolution, in the first case because it is identified with the pride of a Japan made number one, in the second because French government agencies are filled with anguish as they consider the advance of the United States and Japan in many high-tech industries.

Postindustrial society must be defined in a more global and radical way today, as a new culture and a field for new social conflicts and movements. A broad occupational definition of an information society is misleading and cannot justify the idea that a different society is taking shape. On the contrary, postindustrial society must be defined more strictly by the technological production of symbolic goods which shape or transform our representation of human nature and of the external world. For these reasons, research and development, information processing, biomedical science and techniques, and mass media are the four main components of postindustrial society, while bureaucratic activities or production of electrical and electronic equipment are just growing sectors of an industrial society defined by production of goods more than by new channels of communications and the creation of artificial languages.

Only the organization of new social movements and the development of different cultural values can justify the idea of a new society that I prefer to call a *programmed* more than just a postindustrial society. The comparison with the history of industrial society is once more useful: in the Western World, crises of old values and new economic challenges come first before new social actors and conflicts take shape; new forms of political life and new ideologies appear even later. This is a practical reason why sociology today must give a central importance to the concept of social movement—not only to separate itself from an old definition of its object as the *study of society*, which should be replaced by the *study of social action*, but, more concretely, because the construction of a new image of social life requires, right now, the concept of social movement as a bridge between the observation of new technologies and the idea of new forms of political life. This concept could not play a central role in previous forms of social thought; for the first time, it can become the keystone of sociological analysis.

The danger here is to be lured by voluntaristic assumptions. The concept of social movement is useful when it helps one to rediscover social actors where they have been buried beneath either structural Marxist or rationalist theories of strategies and decisions. During the seventies, the "dominant ideology" was that ethnic minorities, like all dominated groups, school students, hospital inmates, and others had to be defined by the exclusion, labeling, and stigmatization they suffered, in other words, as victims. Only an analysis based on the idea of social movement can challenge directly and efficiently such a view and help rediscover that these alienated and excluded categories are nevertheless actors and are often more able than the "silent majority" to analyze their situation, define projects, and organize conflicts which can transform themselves into an active social movement. In the same way, how many Jews today would accept to be defined without any reference to Jewish culture or to Israel? A similar use of the concept "social movement" can aid in the criticism of an image of the school system which emphasizes the impact of social inequality on academic results and future occupational achievements. Instead of considering teachers and pupils as determined by social and cultural inequalities beyond their reach, the emphasis must be put on the autonomy of the school system, on its capacity to increase or decrease inequality of opportunities, so that education can be conceived as a field of debates and projects which can probably not be interpreted as direct social movements but, in a more limited and indirect way, as manifestations of a tension between education as socialization and as "individuation," opposition which expresses a more general conflict. In situations which are generally interpreted in terms of participation or exclusion, of conformity and deviance, the idea of social movement introduces a different approach because it tries to evaluate the capacity of various categories to transform themselves into actors of their own situation and of its transformation.

But we should distrust too simple images of social movements as "conscious and organized" actions. Especially in our times: today, as at the beginning of the Industrial Revolution, it is easier to describe masses, "dangerous classes," riots, or the formation of a new elite than social movements which are not yet organized. Cultural orientations and political conflicts are more visible than social problems, and these are too easily analyzed in term of marginality and exclusion. It took some time in the nineteenth century to discover the "political capacity of the laboring classes"; we are only approaching an analogous stage of evolution of the new social movements.

Let's consider three more examples of the complex nature of new social conflicts. The actions against the industrial use of nuclear energy have revealed a new kind of protest, against decision makers who have the power to shape national life for a long period of time in a "technocratic" way. This action tries to foster a grass-roots democracy. But at the same time, they are oriented by a defensive and communitarian counterculture often loaded with irrationalism. This duality can be compared with the first stages of the labor movement when anticapitalist protest was mixed with the defense of semi-independent craftsmen displaced by industry.

The women's movement, beyond its equalitarian goals, has destroyed traditional images of the "feminine nature," but it has often been linked with an ideology which was inherited from the labor movement and which imposed upon it categories of analysis and protest which did not correspond to the motivations of militant women.

In a more general way, from the seventies until today, the displacement of protest from the economic to the cultural field has been linked with an opposite tendency, the privatization of social problems, an anxious search for identity and a new interest for the body, demands which can lead to the definition of new social norms or, in an opposite way, to an individualism which excludes collective action. It takes few pages to define and defend the concept of social movement, but it should take many years for sociologists to disentangle various components of complex social and cultural actions, and to identify the presence of social movements in collective behavior which has many more components.

[. . .]

Chapter 30

Alberto Melucci

A STRANGE KIND OF NEWNESS: WHAT'S "NEW" IN NEW SOCIAL MOVEMENTS?

IN SYSTEMS OF HIGH INFORMATION DENSITY, individuals and groups must possess a certain degree of autonomy and formal capacities for learning and acting that enable them to function as reliable, self-regulating units. Simultaneously, highly differentiated systems exert strong pressure for integration. They shift social control from the content of action to its languages, from the external regulation of behavior to interference in the cognitive and motivational preconditions for it. Conflicts tend to arise in those areas of the system that are most directly involved in the production of information and communicative resources but at the same time subjected to intense pressures for integration. Today, the crucial dimensions of daily life (time and space, interpersonal relations, birth and death), the satisfying of individual needs within welfare systems, and the shaping of personal and social identity in educational systems are constructed through the production and processing of information.

Individuals and groups are allocated increasing amounts of information resources with which to define themselves and to construct their life spaces. At the same time, however, these same processes are regulated by a diffuse social control that passes beyond the public sphere to invade the very domain where the sense of individual action takes shape. Dimensions that were traditionally regarded as private (the body, sexuality, affective relations), or subjective (cognitive and emotional processes, motives, desires), or even biological (the structure of the brain, the genetic code, reproductive capacity) now undergo social control and manipulation. The techno-scientific apparatus, the agencies of information and communication, and the decision-making centers that determine policies wield their power over these domains. Yet, these are precisely the areas where individuals and groups lay claim to their autonomy, where they conduct their search for identity by transforming them into a space where they reappropriate, self-realize, and construct the meaning of what they are and what they do.

Conflicts are carried forward by temporary actors who bring to light the crucial dilemmas of a society. The conflicts I describe here, which do not exhaust the range of social conflicts, concern the production and the appropriation of resources that are crucial for a global society based on information. These same processes generate both new forms of power and new forms of opposition: Conflict only emerges insofar as actors fight for control and the allocation of socially produced potential for action. This potential is no longer exclusively based on material resources or on forms of social organization; to an increasing extent, it is based on the ability to produce information.

Conflicts do not chiefly express themselves through action designed to achieve outcomes in the political system. Rather, they raise a challenge that recasts the language and cultural codes that organize information. The ceaseless flow of messages only acquires meaning through the codes that order the flux and allow its meanings to be read. The forms of power now emerging in contemporary societies are grounded in an ability to "inform" that is, to "give form." The action of movements occupies the same terrain and is in itself a message broadcast to society conveying symbolic forms and relational patterns that cast light on "the dark side of the moon"—a system of meanings that runs counter to the sense that the apparatuses seek to impose on individual and collective events. This type of action affects institutions because it selects new elites, it modernizes organizational forms, and it creates new goals and new languages.

At the same time, however, this action challenges the apparatuses that govern the production of information, and it prevents the channels of representation and decision making in pluralist societies from adopting instrumental rationality as the only logic with which to govern complexity. Such rationality applies solely to procedures, and it imposes the criterion of efficiency and effectiveness as the only measure of sense. The action of movements reveals that the neutral rationality of means masks interests and forms of power; it makes clear that it is impossible to confront the massive challenge of living together on a planet, by now become a global society, without openly discussing the ends and values that make such cohabitation possible. Movements highlight the insuperable dilemmas facing complex societies, and by doing so force them openly to assume responsibility for their choices, their conflicts, and their limitations.

By drawing on forms of action that relate to daily life and individual identity, contemporary movements detach themselves from the traditional model of political organization, and they increasingly distance themselves from political systems. They move in to occupy an intermediate space of social life where individual needs and the pressures of political innovation mesh. Because of the particular features of movements, social conflicts can become effective only through the mediation of political actors, even though they will never restrict themselves to only this. The innovative thrust of movements, therefore, does not exhaust itself in changes to the political system brought about by institutional actors. Nevertheless, the ability of collective demands to expand and to find expression depends on the way in which political actors are able to translate them into democratic guarantees.

As my thinking in this area has developed, I have gradually abandoned the concept of class relationships. This concept is inseparably linked with capitalist industrial society, but I used it as an analytical tool to define a system of conflictual relationships within which social resources are produced and appropriated. The notion of class relationships has been a tool with which to analyze systemic conflicts and forms of domination in complex societies. It is a traditional category that I employed to focus on the relational and conflictual dimension of the production of the basic orientations of a society. In systems like contemporary ones, where classes as real social groups are withering away, more appropriate concepts are required. This must be accomplished without ignoring the theoretical problem that the category of class relationships has left behind as its legacy. That problem can be defined as knowing what relations and what conflicts are involved in the production of the crucial resources of a particular system. Addressing this question is essential to an understanding of the dual articulation of autonomy and dependence that characterizes the political system and the relationship between movements and processes of representation and decision making.

The theoretical problem is therefore whether there are forms of conflict that engage the constitutive logic of a system. The notion of mode of production is too closely associated with economic reductionism. Production cannot be restricted solely to the economic-material sphere; it embraces the entirety of social relationships and cultural orientations. The problem is thus whether one can still talk of antagonist conflicts, that is, conflicts that involve the social relationships that produce the constitutive resource of complex systems: information. Analysis of exchanges internal to the political market, or the knowledge we have acquired concerning strategic behavior in organizations and political systems, shows that many contemporary conflicts, sometimes even violent ones, are the expression of social categories or groups claiming access to representation. A demand for inclusion in an institutional system of benefits may even be radical, but it implies not so much antagonism toward the logic of the system as pressure for redistribution.

[. . .]

New movements?

This analytical framework helps to clarify a recurrent issue in the debate of the last ten years which concerns the "newness" of contemporary conflicts. What is new about the new social movements? As one of those who introduced the term "new social movements" into sociological literature, I have watched with dismay as the category has been progressively reified. Newness is by definition a relative concept, which here has the temporary function of signaling a number of comparative differences between the historical forms of class conflict and today's emergent forms of collective action. If analysis and research fail to specify the distinctive features of the new movements, we are trapped in arid debate between the supporters and critics of newness. On one hand, there are those who claim that many aspects of contemporary forms of action can be found in previous phenomena of history and that their alleged newness derives only from the myopia of the present from which so many sociologists suffer, especially when they are emotionally involved with their subject of study. On the other hand, the defenders of the newness of contemporary movements endeavor to show that these similarities are only formal and that phenomena change their meanings when set in different systems.

Both the critics of the newness of new movements and the proponents of the paradigm commit the same epistemological mistake: They consider contemporary phenomena to constitute a unitary empirical object, and on this basis either seek to define their newness or deny or dispute it. When faced with the women's movement rather than the peace movement, one side in the debate tries to mark out differences with respect to the past, the other stresses continuity and comparability with previous events.

The controversy strikes me as futile. Contemporary phenomena, in their empirical unity, are made up of a variety of components, and if these elements are not separated out, comparison between forms of action belonging to mutually distinct historical periods is based on an epistemological misunderstanding. It is not a question of deciding whether the empirical data observed are equivalent or comparable, instead, the question is whether their meaning and the place they occupy in the system of social relations can be considered to be the same. Thus, it becomes extremely difficult to decide, for example, how far the modern women's movement, as a global empirical phenomenon, is new compared with the first feminist movements of the nineteenth century.

[. . .]

Information societies

Where, then, can we locate the action of contemporary movements? Through an ever-growing interlacement of economic structures, complex societies produce apparatuses of political regulation and cultural agencies. Material goods are produced by information systems and symbolic universes controlled by huge organizations. They incorporate information and become signs circulating through markets of worldwide proportions. Conflicts move from the economic-industrial system to the cultural sphere. They focus on personal identity, the time and space of life, and the motivation and codes of daily behavior. Conflicts lay bare the logic now gaining its sway over highly differentiated systems. These systems allocate increasing amounts of resources to individuals, who use them to become autonomous loci of action; but the systems also exact increasing integration. In order to maintain themselves, they must extend their control by regulating the deep-lying sources of action and by interfering with the construction of its meaning. Contemporary conflicts reveal the contradictions in this process and bring to the fore actors and forms of action that cannot be fitted into the conventional categories of industrial conflict or competition among interest groups. The production and reappropriation of meaning seem to lie at the core of contemporary conflicts; this understanding requires a careful redefinition of what a social movement is and what forms of action display its presence.

In the course of history, societies have run through the gamut of the resources that drive every living system (matter, energy, information). There have been societies structured on material resources and societies that have depended on energy for their growth (steam and electricity as the engines of industrialization). Now, societies exist that rely on information for their survival, control of the environment, expansion into space, and the delicate equilibrium that preserves them from total war.

[. . .]

In a system whose most advanced sectors employ over 50 percent of the population in activities involving the production, processing, and circulation of information, this basic resource structures social life. Information is a symbolic and therefore reflexive resource. It is not a thing; it is a good which to be produced and exchanged presupposes a capacity for symbolization and decodification. It is a resource that becomes such for the society as a whole only when other needs have been satisfied and when the capacity for symbolic production has been sufficiently freed from the constraints of reproduction. The notion of "post-material society" captures, at least in part, these transformations in progress. Systems that increasingly rely on information resources presume the acquisition of a material base and the ability to build symbolic universes endowed with autonomy (which, in turn, become conditions for the reproduction or the broadening of the material base itself).

[. . .]

Power cannot be exercised, therefore, solely over the content of communications and over the manifest expressions of action. To be effective, power must shift its basis and take control of codes. Codes become formal rules, the organizers of knowledge, the new foundation of power.

[. . .]

Simultaneously, the potentially limitless extension of information increases the margins of uncertainty for the entire system. Uncertainty derives first from the difficulty of establishing nexuses in the enormous mass of information that we transmit and receive. This difficulty derives from the fact that the passage from information to knowledge is not guaranteed; indeed, sometimes the deluge of information actually impedes knowledge. Uncertainty affects the meaning of individual action because the disproportionate growth of information increases the options but also makes the decision difficult. The individual answer to the question, Who am I? becomes problematic.

As a result, complex systems are required to produce decisions in order to reduce uncertainty. An information system expands its decision-making capacity to keep pace with this requirement to cope with uncertainty. It assumes the features of a decisional, contractual system: decisional because reducing uncertainty means assuming the risk of the decision; contractual because, in order to decide, agreement must be reached over the rules of the game.

[. . .]

Individually and socially produced identity must constantly cope with the uncertainty created by the ceaseless flow of information, by the fact that individuals belong simultaneously to a plurality of systems, by the variety of their spatiotemporal frames of reference. Identity must be forever reestablished and renegotiated. The search for identity becomes a remedy against the opacity of the system, against the uncertainty that constantly constrains action. Producing identity means stepping up the flow of information from the system and making it more stable and coherent.

Symbolic challenges

Contemporary movements have passed from sequence to coexistence. Slices of experience, past history, and memory coexist within the same empirical phenomena. They become working components in the single action system of the movement. The traces of the past that persist in contemporary phenomena are not simply legacies of history or residues on which new accretions build themselves; they help to shape patterns of collective action in which historical and cultural elements coexist or blend. In what has been called the ecological movement, for example, we find traditional forms of resistance to the impact of modernization coexisting with a religious fundamentalism that draws its renewed energy from the appeal to Nature, pressures for a new ethical code regulating humanity's relationship with Nature, and political demands for the democratic control of energy policies. All these elements are blended together, perhaps temporarily, in that concrete actor of mobilization that we call a movement.

[. . .]

Second, movements are not occasional emergencies in social life located on the margins of the great institutions; nor are they residual elements of the social order. In complex societies, movements are a permanent reality. They may be more or less visible and they may emerge as political mobilization in cyclical form but their existence and their effects on social relationships are neither sporadic nor transitory.

In contemporary societies, a specific sector or subsystem for collective action is becoming a differentiated and stable component in the working of the system. Movements acquire a certain independence from both the daily life of individuals and from political action by creating a specific space for their actions. The differentiation of complex systems is so extensive that collective action can acquire autonomous status. Noninstitutionalized, collective action separates from those other forms of action with which it was formerly confused (political action, in particular). In the industrial age, social conflicts were incorporated into struggles for citizenship, just as in the history of the workers' movement anticapitalistic social struggle and the fight against the bourgeois state coincided. When these two levels separate, as they do in contemporary societies, movements lose their character as personages engaged in a confrontation–clash with a state for citizenship rights. Instead, they form themselves into social networks, where a collective identity is negotiated and given shape.

Two features of these networks can be identified. First, a movement network is a field of social relationships where, through negotiation among various groups, a collective identity is structured. In this social field, the orientations and constraints of action are defined and redefined within the solidarity networks that link individuals together in their daily lives. Second, a movement network is a terrain in which identity is recomposed and unified. Networks within the movement insure a certain degree of continuity and stability in the identities of individuals and groups in a social system where this identity is constantly fragmented or destructured. The movement provides individuals and groups with a relatively stable point of reference from which to rebuild identities split among the various memberships, roles, and time scales of social experience.

[. . .]

Contemporary movements display a two-pole pattern of functioning. The normal situation is a network of small groups submerged in daily life that require personal involvement in the creation and experimentation of cultural models. These networks only come into the open over specific problems, for example, mobilizations for peace. Although the hidden network is composed of small, separate groups, it is a circuit of exchanges. Individuals and information circulate through the network, and there are specific agencies (the professionalized nuclei) that insure a certain amount of unity. The hidden network allows multiple membership; is part-time with respect to both the life course and to the amount of time it absorbs; and requires the personal commitment and affective solidarity of those who belong to it.

The bipolar model shows clearly that latency and visibility have different functions and that they are reciprocally linked. Latency makes the direct experience of new cultural models possible, and it encourages change by constructing meanings and producing codes. Its cultural output often challenges dominant social pressures. Latency is a sort of underground laboratory for antagonism and innovation. When the small groups come out into the open, they do so in order to confront political authority on specific grounds. Mobilization has a multilayered symbolic function. It proclaims opposition against the logic that guides decision making with regard to a specific public policy. At the same time, it acts as a medium that reveals to the rest of society the connection between a specific problem and the logic dominating the system. Third, it proclaims that alternative cultural models are possible, specifically those that its collective action already practices and displays. The mobilization unifies the thrust of cultural innovation, antagonistic demands, and other levels that comprise the movement's action.

These two poles are reciprocally linked to each other. Latency makes visible action possible because it provides the solidarity resources it needs and builds the cultural framework within which mobilization takes place. Visible action strengthens the hidden networks, boosts solidarity, creates further groups, and recruits new militants who, attracted by the movement's public action, join its hidden networks. Mobilization also encourages the institutionalization of certain fringe elements in the movement and of new elites that have formed in the area.

For this model to persist and to operate effectively, certain conditions have to be fulfilled. These include:

1   A high degree of variability in the environment that prevents the groups in the hidden network from closing in on themselves.

2   High elasticity in the political system, which does not obstruct the delicate phases of passage from one pole to the other.

3   Area agencies and umbrella organizations, or temporary organizations, able to insure internal communications (during latency, mainly the former) and external communications (during mobilization, mainly the latter). These forms of leadership are compatible with a multifaceted structuring of groups and does not impede the typical structuring of the area.

The two-poles model seems to indicate that public mobilization is the moment of direct contact with political systems. In latency phases, only the professionalized nuclei maintain chiefly instrumental contacts with some sector of the political system. If the goal of the movement is mainly symbolic in nature, why should it engage in exchange relations with the political system, which are always part of a logic of representation? The main reason seems to be that collective actors must preserve areas of autonomy from the system, areas in which they can undertake change. This is the laboratory where formal models are created and which the movement fills with content addressed to specific goals. Thus, a relationship with the political system, in the form of some kind of exchange, is a condition for the safeguarding or the extension of this autonomy.

A relationship of this kind can only come about by establishing a pact; this pact is not the basis of the exchange but only a condition for its furtherance. This logic is first delineated in the action of umbrella organizations and agencies as the mobilization proceeds. The pact—a circumscribed and reversible exchange with the institutions—simultaneously makes power visible. Power that is usually neutralized by procedures comes out into the open to take responsibility, that is, to exercise authority, in a pact. Thus, it becomes possible for movements to measure the distance that separates them from power, as well as to accept, disenchanted, the confrontation. Through these means it becomes possible for society to openly address the dilemmas that social movements have uncovered through their action, as well as to create or adapt the political institutions best suited to cope with those dilemmas.

Chapter 31

Carol Mueller

CONFLICT NETWORKS AND THE ORIGINS OF WOMEN'S LIBERATION

The origins of the women's movement

WHILE THE ORIGINS of women's mobilization in the United States are well documented, two different explanations have been proposed to account for the beginning of the movement. The first explanation corresponds to the structural theories of the European new social movements literature that attempt to link changes in the objective condition of the mobilized group with changes in consciousness. Survey research is the tool usually employed with the goal of correlating clusters of attitudes reflecting a new collective consciousness with the subgroup defined by the objective condition.

[. . .]

The second explanation corresponds in many ways to Melucci's emphasis on the generative role of submerged networks. A review of these theories suggests both the strengths and the weaknesses of Melucci's conceptions of submerged networks and collective identities in an understanding of the origins of the U.S. women's movement. To make these theories accessible to a European audience, I characterize them as the structural and the submerged network theories.

Structural theories

Explanations based on changes in technology and the division of labor argue that "the decline in fertility and the shift of productive work from home to factory in the past two centuries has upset the equilibrium of sex stratification in industrial societies," thus paving the way for a shift of consciousness and the mobilization of women (Huber 1976, 372). Based on a historic analysis of women's work and child-care responsibilities, Huber documents that, after 1940, the female work force was increasingly composed of married women with children. She argues that the double burden of paid work and domestic work was so onerous that women were compelled to see that they were treated unjustly by society. From Huber's perspective, the contemporary women's movement is the "unplanned result" of the technological changes that transformed women's work and child-care responsibilities. She predicts that the movement will continue as long as women bear this double burden.

Although Huber describes objective conditions that might logically lead women to develop an "injustice frame," she does not demonstrate empirically that the women experiencing these changes were, in fact, developing a new consciousness (or collective identity). For this kind of data, it is necessary to turn to Klein (1984) who has made this connection between structural position and changed consciousness. Looking at three different dimensions of women's traditional roles—domestic employment, motherhood, and marriage—she, like Huber, describes changes brought about through mature industrialization. She links these objective, structural changes to shifts over time in public opinion toward greater tolerance for women's work outside the home, for reduced fertility and family size, and for the social acceptability of either single status or divorce. Despite the momentous changes occurring in women's lives throughout the century, she notes, it was not until the 1960s that public opinion polls indicated large numbers of women were endorsing a nontraditional role.

Klein's (1984) analysis is based on the overtime data from the National Election Studies, which have been gathered since the 1950s by the Survey Research Center at the University of Michigan. They indicate that, by the end of the 1960s, the majority of women were in favor of nontraditional roles for women based on social equality, and an increasing number felt that women faced discrimination. Klein characterizes this cluster of attitudes as a "feminist consciousness." Her data indicated that, by 1972, women who were psychologically more likely to support nontraditional roles for women were themselves found in structural positions where they were more likely to work outside the home, to have a job with high occupational status, to achieve more than a high school education, to be single, divorced, or separated, to live in a large metropolitan area, to have a mother who had worked, to be politically liberal, and to be little involved in organized religion. The more of these characteristics a woman possessed, the more likely she was to have a highly developed feminist consciousness.

Klein's data reveal a paradoxical finding, however. Despite the sharp increase in feminist consciousness among women, it was even higher among men. By 1972, men were even more likely than women to believe that society rather than nature or biology was responsible for women's roles; to support an equal role for women in business and industry; and to endorse equal employment treatment. Yet, needless to say, men did not create the women's movement nor did they encourage women's mass mobilization. This anomalous finding points to the limitations of the structural explanation of the origins of the women's movement. Despite Klein's careful connection of structural changes in women's roles to changes in public consciousness, to some extent, changes in social structure affected the consciousness of men and women similarly.

The structural theories and Klein's careful documentation of the rise of a feminist consciousness help to account for the large public support for the women's movement during the 1970s and, also, its considerable political influence after the period of mass mobilization beginning in 1970, but it cannot explain the origins of the movement for two simple reasons: (1) a new consciousness that is shared equally by men and women cannot explain why women rather than men formed a movement; and (2) widespread support among women for greater equality does not explain why some few specific individuals of the millions of American women affected by structural changes did, in fact, create a movement. To try to explain the origins of the movement with a structural analysis alone faces the same limitations that Melucci has identified in some of the European literature on new social movements: "Approaches based on the *structure/motivation* dualism ... view collective action either as a product of the logic of the system or as a result of personal beliefs" (1989, 21). The basic problem is that "both the macrostructural factors and the individual variables imply an unbridgeable gap between the level of explanation proposed and the concrete process that allows a certain number of individuals to act together" (1988, 332).

Melucci's proposed solution is an intermediate level of analysis in which submerged networks are studied as the source of new collective identities that encompass the definition of specific possibilities and limits of action. At the same time, relationships are activated within localized, submerged networks and particular individuals make commitments to act together in pursuit of specific goals. Applied to the origins of women's liberation, a generally diffuse feminist consciousness, while perhaps necessary, is not enough. To explain origins, specific individuals must be identified who have formed emotional bonds from their interaction, negotiated a sense of group membership, and made a plan for change (or series of plans), however tentative, with goals, means, and a consideration of environmental constraints: a collective identity.

The submerged networks

Previous scholarship on the women's movement has provided many of the pieces necessary for the kind of analysis that Melucci proposes.

[. . .]

[T]he movement originated simultaneously in two different social locations in the mid to late 1960s from their respective sources among, first, the "older branch" of women active in national politics who were involved in the new State Commissions on the Status of Women, and a, second, "younger branch" of women who had been participants in the civil rights movement and the New Left. The origins of the movement in these two branches can be explained by the availability of compatible communications networks, a series of "crises" that focused each branch of women on feminist issues, and experienced organizers in the younger branch who could weld together local groups into a national movement. It was the older branch that created the National Organization for Women (NOW), which eventually became the major social movement organization for the movement. The younger branch developed the small groups, consciousness-raising, and the less conventional tactics of the movement.

[. . .]

[Y]ounger women were radicalized by the humiliations they experienced from their male colleagues in the social movements of the 1960s.

[. . .]

[C]onflict and struggle played a role in developing collective identities in the submerged networks of both branches of the movement. It was in part the struggle over the notion of the emerging collective identity that led to cultural innovation, organizational segmentation, and the spread of movement groups in the five years preceding the Women's Strike. This event, in August 1970, marked the symbolic beginning, the public "coming out," of the movement.

The processes of negotiation and identity construction in the two branches reflected the very different political cultures of electoral and movement politics in the mid 1960s. The older branch, or what came to be called "equal rights feminism," was based in the policy debates, organized interests, and campaign obligations of political actors in state and federal governments. The conflicts that led to changes in women's consciousness arose from policy debates regarding women's rights. In this context, the collective identity that developed followed the model of the civil rights movement in emphasizing the source of women's problems in systematic patterns of discrimination that could be eliminated or mitigated primarily through appropriate legislation, regulations, litigation, and enforcements but not excluding marches and demonstrations. Through conflict with Commission members, congressional representatives, officials, and the media over the Equal Rights Amendment, the interpretation of Title VII of the Civil Rights Act, employment policy, the enforcement practices of the Equal Employment Opportunities Commission, and a host of other policies, a relatively small network of politically well-connected women developed a conception of gender equality or collective identity that was thoroughly radical in its implications.

[. . .]

The conflict that occurred over the formulation of this identity among equal rights women led to a proliferation of organizations devoted to efforts on behalf of specific constituencies, issues, or policies. In 1967, for instance, women from the United Auto Workers were forced to withdraw from NOW because their union opposed inclusion of the Equal Rights Amendment in the NOW Bill of Rights (they formed the Congress of Labor Union Women). Further segmentation occurred with inclusion of abortion in the NOW Bill of Rights, which led women more concerned with issues of economic discrimination to leave and form the Women's Equity Action League (WEAL). Further division occurred when younger women from the New York NOW chapter charged the national organization with an elitist decision making structure and formed the October 17 Movement (later known as The Feminists).

In 1968, two of NOW's lawyers walked out in disgust over the inefficiency of the organization, taking two of its most important cases. They then formed other social movement organizations—first, Human Rights for Women and, later, the Legal Defense Fund—to support sex discrimination cases. The proliferation of equal rights organizations reflected not only important differences of emphasis among women searching for political solutions to multiple sources of discrimination, but also the pursuit of an area of action where individual women could create a highly personal interpretation of their collective identity. Unfortunately, for present purposes, accounts of these conflicts are devoted almost exclusively to the policy provisions involved in the debates and tell us little about the face-to-face process of collective identity construction as it occurred.

In contrast, there is a rich literature on the evolution of collective identity in the submerged networks of younger women who came to constitute the women's liberation branch of the movement. Whereas the older branch identified what they came to understand as the "overt" discrimination against women that appeared in employment, politics, credit, and educational opportunities, the younger branch turned to the personal politics associated with women's status as a minority. The collective identity that emerged had no precursor in the liberal politics of the early civil rights movement. It came to be identified as "women's liberation."

Prior to 1970, women's liberation had been a "movement of friends" in the submerged networks of civil rights and the New Left. Several detailed historical accounts indicate the intensity of the social interactions and the high level of emotional investment of the young people who were experimenting with the creation of new social forms of living as well as the means of achieving political goals. From 1964 to 1967, isolated pairs or small groups of activist women began to voice a sense of uneasiness to each other about what they perceived as a different and unequal role for women in the actual day-to-day activities of these movements. Attempts to articulate this uneasiness about women's assignment to the mundane and routine activities of kitchen work, mimeographing, typing, and cleaning evoked reactions of scorn and fury from the male radicals—first in the Student Nonviolent Coordinating Committee (SNCC), the major youth organization of the civil rights movement, and soon after in Students for a Democratic Society (SDS), the leading student organization of the New Left in the United States throughout the 1960s. The younger women were rebuffed time after time as they tried to discuss their concerns regarding gender differences within the limits of debate prescribed by the leaders of the civil rights and New Left movements. Conflict, ridicule, and exclusion greeted their attempts to extend the emotional bonds forged during the early 1960s to the sense of injustice and grievances arising from women's personal experiences within the movements.

As they continued to receive rebukes and scorn from the male radicals [. . .] women's confusion and search for a new identity turned to rage and alienation. The submerged networks of women that had developed within the New Left organizations moved outside to begin an autonomous existence in major cities in the East Coast and the Midwest.

[. . .]

The collective identity that came to be associated with "women's liberation" in the early 1970s developed out of this process of conflict and negotiation.

[. . .]

Through the processes associated with identity construction, the movement experienced extraordinary growth between 1969 and 1970. By mid 1970, *Notes from the Second Year*, a feminist journal of 126 pages, sold over forty thousand copies. The number of movement periodicals increased from two in 1968 to sixty-one in 1972. Small groups proliferated throughout the country, and regional conferences to coordinate their activities had become commonplace by 1970. By August 1970, the highly diverse submerged networks of equal rights feminists and women's liberation were ready to emerge as womanhood united, the historic actor.

[. . .]

Conclusion

This case study focuses on two moments in the life of the contemporary women's movement—the first mass mobilization of U.S. women in the Women's Equality Day Strike of August 1970, and the five-year period preceding the Strike—when the two branches of contemporary U.S. feminism were constructing a new identity through a process of internal conflict and organizational segmentation. These two stages in the development of the movement point to both the strengths and the weaknesses of Melucci's intermediate level of analysis for a comprehensive theory of social construction.

Melucci's theory is most telling when it calls attention to that level of face-to-face interaction where collective identities are developed in submerged networks through a process of social negotiation. It is at this point that structural sources of personal injury—such as the contradiction that younger branch women felt between their high levels of education and the low status they experienced in the personal politics of the 1960s movements—are translated into a shared sense of injustice focused on grievances that are articulated as part of a program for change. The case study also demonstrates, however, that the creative tensions that fuel these negotiations spring as much from internal competition and conflict within movement networks as from the inadequacy of means for realizing goals. Although the new collective identity of women continued to change in the submerged networks of the movement and to be challenged by countermovements such as those that arose in the mid 1970s to oppose early feminist victories in abortion rights and the Equal Rights Amendment, the collective identity soon took on a life of its own.

The independent existence or "thingness" of the identity of "women" that existed in the early 1970s suggests that a comprehensive theory of social movement construction cannot restrict its attention to the intermediate level of submerged networks if it is concerned with the political influence and cultural changes achieved by the movement. The collective identities created within submerged networks achieve an independent existence once they become public through the movement's explanatory apparatus of manifestos, programs, press conferences, banners, slogans, insignia, costumes, and guerrilla theater that attempt to account for the movement and its collective actions. Through these devices, a collective identity becomes public that has a potential for political influence. It is then subject to attempts at distortion and marginalization of state, media, and countermovements.

[. . .]

At this public stage of movement development, when the collective identity becomes a historic actor, it would be an empirical as well as a theoretical mistake to equate the public persona of this collective identity [. . .] with the collective identity of Melucci's submerged networks.

[. . .]

The distinction between these two levels of analysis is important not only for our appreciation of Melucci's strengths and weaknesses but also for locating his contribution within the developing work on the social movement of social movements. As this work has proliferated, it has become increasingly important to identify theoretical contributions in terms of appropriate levels of analysis.

The most comprehensive attempt to specify these levels is Klandermans's (1992) essay in which he distinguishes three levels of social construction: (1) public discourse and the formation and transformation of collective identities; (2) persuasive communication during mobilization campaigns by movement organizations, their opponents, and countermovement organizations; and (3) what he terms "consciousness raising" during episodes of collective behavior.

[. . .]

While Klandermans's typological distinctions are extremely useful in ordering this growing field of research, our lengthy consideration of Melucci's theory of collective identity suggests several modifications. After Melucci has so carefully indicated that the submerged networks are part of the latency phase of social movements, an "invisible process" out of the public eye, it is inappropriate that this process should be considered a part of public discourse. In fact, as Melucci argues, it is partly the freedom from public scrutiny that permits people to interact in small groups where experimentation and negotiation of identities can result in the development of new social codes and goals for action. Thus, when selecting groups for study in Milan, Melucci deliberately chose the most grass-roots level of participation because, he noted, leaders were more likely to present, what was to him, a falsely unified version of the collective identity if they had to interact frequently with public actors such as media representatives or officials. It was only at the grass-roots level, he felt, that such false presentations (which should properly be considered part of public discourse) could be avoided and maximum heterogeneity in experimentation and negotiation be observed.

On the other hand, our case study of the public phase, or "coming out," of the women's movement at the Women's Strike for Equality Day indicates that collective identities do become a part of public discourse and, potentially, historic actors if the movement attempts to bring about social or political change. At this public level of analysis, a different set of social and political actors, particularly the representatives of formal organizations, will attempt to influence the nature of the collective identity and fit it to their own interests and systems of meaning.

These observations suggest the utility of four rather than three levels of analysis: public discourse, persuasive communication initiated by movement organizations, "consciousness raising" from participation in episodes of collective action, and the creation of collective identities in submerged networks. To the extent that the four levels of analysis have a natural sequencing in a cycle of protest, it seems likely that social movements based on a major reconstruction of collective identities will require either a lengthy or an intensive period for the gestation of the new identity. An ideal typical sequence would progress from least to most public awareness (and, undoubtedly, back again). Groups of individuals in submerged networks would experiment with new collective identities and action proposals, increasingly taking their new social constructions into conflict with targets of change or potential converts outside their own small circle just as the New York radical feminists crowned a sheep "Miss America." As a collective identity takes shape, potential activists may come together and create a social movement organization with a public declaration announcing their new collective identity like the women from the State Commissions on the Status of Women who formed the National Organization for Women and drew up a Bill of Rights for women in the mid 1960s. Collective actions such as those associated with women's Strike for Equality Day offer opportunities for direct experience of action and perceptual change based on the newly revealed collective identity. Finally, the national media may be attracted by the newsworthiness of the confrontation or the importance of the values at stake, and the social reconstruction represented by the new collective identity may become a part of public discourse.

[. . .]

Over the course of any social movement, these processes of social construction will cycle back and forth between levels in increasingly complex patterns depending on the degree to which all sectors of society become involved and how quickly the movement is controlled.

Yet, the search for stages is somewhat premature in a field that is only now beginning to distinguish one level of analysis from another.

[. . .]

Melucci's contribution lies in highlighting an intermediate level of analysis in a latency phase that may precede the creation of formal organizations. His work suggests the importance of the opening skirmishes between members of submerged networks and symbolic representations of the dominant cultural code through collective actions that begin a more public phase of the movement.

[. . .]

To understand how several hundred women throughout the United States constructed the new identity of women as historic actor that became an influential political force for change in the status of women, it is necessary to understand the origins of the women's movement in the preceding decade. It is here that Melucci's theory is most convincing.

References

Huber, Joan. 1976. "Toward a Socio-Technological Theory of the Women's Movement." *Social Problems* 23:371–88.

Klandermans, Bert. 1992. "The Social Construction of Protest and Multiorganizational Fields." In *Frontiers in Social Movement Theory*, edited by Aldon D. Morris and Carol McClurg Mueller. New Haven: Yale University Press.

Klein, Ethel. 1984. *Gender Politics: From Consciousness to Mass Politics*. Cambridge: Harvard University Press.

Melucci, Alberto. 1988. "Getting Involved: Identity and Mobilization in Social Movements." In *From Structure to Action: Comparing Social Movement Research across Cultures*, edited by Bert Klandermans, Hanspeter Kriesi, and Sidney Tarrow, pp. 329–48. Vol. 1 of *International Social Movement Research*. Greenwich, Conn.: JAI Press.

Melucci, Alberto. 1989. *Nomads of the Present: Social Movements and Individual Needs in Contemporary Society*. Philadelphia: Temple University Press.

Chapter 32

Arturo Escobar and Sonia E. Alvarez

THEORY AND PROTEST
IN LATIN AMERICA TODAY

SINCE THE EARLY 1980s, Latin America has seen, in the minds of many, its worst crisis of the century. In 1982, Mexico's announcement that it could not meet its debt payment obligations unleashed the infamous "debt crisis." What followed is well known by now: repeated attempts at economic stabilization and adjustment; "austerity" measures that quickly translated into rapidly declining living standards for popular and middle classes; industrial decline in the wake of the adoption of strong neoliberal and free market economic policies, even negative growth rates in some countries—in sum, a "reversal of development." And the social and political implications of these changes were no less onerous and menacing. Social exclusion and violence of all kinds significantly increased. "Transitions to democracy" begun during the first half of the decade became more and more difficult to achieve and increasingly limited in scope as the decade progressed. Even nature seemed to have taken issue with the region, as tornados, volcanos, earthquakes, and, more recently, the resurgence of cholera brought on the region more than its usual share of nature-related but socially aggravated hardships.

In the midst of all this, one might be surprised to find any significant degree of struggle and organizing on the people's part. On the contrary, one might expect the population to be so overwhelmed by the tasks of daily survival and so fragmented and downtrodden by the intensified exclusion, exploitation, and, in many cases, repression that it would be practically impossible for people to find the time or energy to mobilize and fight for a better life. At best, one would expect to find spontaneous manifestations of popular rage and frustration, such as the so-called International Monetary Fund (IMF) riots witnessed in Santo Domingo or Caracas, among other places.

But even this would seem to corroborate the fact that people were more or less quiescent in their daily lives, exploding only when they could not take it anymore. After all, the 1960s, the decade when both development and revolution had reached their height, had been left well behind. The 1980s was another story altogether, clearly inimical to people's efforts at organizing for change. Yet despite all this, what one found in practically every country of the region was an impassioned experience of resistance and collective struggle on many fronts, even if less visible than in former decades and, at times, submerged.

It was the richness, novelty, and variety of this experience that motivated us to write this book. Popular mobilization by no means disappeared during the 1980s, and it is unlikely that it will in the 1990s. Indeed, the mosaic of forms of collective action is so diverse that one even doubts whether a single label can encompass them all. From squatters to ecologists, from popular kitchens in poor urban neighborhoods to Socialist feminist groups, from human rights and defense of life mobilizations to gay and lesbian coalitions, the spectrum of Latin American collective action covers a broad range. It includes, as well, the movements of black and indigenous peoples; new modalities of workers' cooperatives and peasant struggles; middle- and lower-middle-class civic movements; the defense of the rain forest; and even cultural manifestations embodied, for instance, in Afro-Caribbean musical forms (such as salsa and reggae) and incipient antinuclear protest in some countries.

[. . .]

[T]he 1980s witnessed the appearance of new forms of understanding and discussion on resistance and social change that marked a significant discontinuity with past forms of analysis. These new forms of theoretical awareness have been fostered by equally significant changes in historical conditions and, more specifically, by changes in the popular practices of resistance and collective action themselves. Critical reflection in the region has recognized the questionable and limited character of the approaches widely accepted until the 1960s and 1970s—namely, functionalism and Marxism. But, more importantly, it has embarked on a systematic effort at renewing our understanding of the complex processes that account for the evolution of Latin American societies today.

This process of theoretical renewal has centered around the nature of social movements to such an extent that a veritable explosion of writings on this topic has occurred, particularly since the early 1980s. And the character of these writings has been continuously changing. During the first years of the past decade, many collective forms of protest, especially in urban areas, were characterized in an undifferentiated manner as "new social movements" (NSMs). NSMs were believed to give expression to "new popular interests," to practice "new ways of doing politics," and even to embody the possibility of creating a "new hegemony by the masses." Highly optimistic assessments of these movements and their actual or potential contributions to radical social change appeared in increasing numbers in social science journals and alternative newspapers throughout much of the region. In most analyses, the catchall concept of NSMs lumped ecclesiastical base communities and urban protest of various kinds together with ethnic movements and primarily middle-class ecology, feminist, and gay liberation movements. All of these movements, some theorists insisted, challenged the state's economic and political models and called into question authoritarian and hierarchical ways of doing politics.

This optimism was tempered in the second half of the decade as some of the movements declined, even in the context of democratic consolidation, as in Southern Cone countries. Some studies in these countries painted a sobering picture, suggesting that NSMs were unable to move from the confrontational tactics of the transition period to the strategies of negotiation and compromise necessitated by the new democratic status quo. A certain pessimism thus set in. More recent studies, however, have systematically investigated what has happened to social movements beyond the transition period or, more generally, how they have fared in relation to the economic, social, and political crisis of the 1980s. These studies have opened up new questions [. . .].

Also in the second, half of the 1980s, continuities between old and new practices and structural determinants began to be recognized as a step toward reassessing the "newness" of the movements. At the same time, the use of European theories was more thoroughly examined and empirical studies were more systematically conducted and evaluated. Although these developments did not result in a clearly defined "paradigm" or research program, they did advance and transform significantly the state of the field, making it possible to launch a new wave of research and theorizing for the 1990s.

The most recent literature on social movements takes for granted the fact that a significant transformation has occurred in both reality and its forms of analysis. The "old" is characterized by analysis couched in terms of modernization and dependency; by definitions of politics anchored in traditional actors who struggled for the control of the state, particularly the working class and revolutionary vanguards; and by a view of society as an entity composed of more or less immutable structures and class relations that only great changes (large-scale development schemes or revolutionary upheavals) could significantly alter. In contrast, the new theories see contemporary social movements as bringing about a fundamental transformation in the nature of political practice and theorizing itself. According to these theorists, an era that was characterized by the division of the political space into two clearly demarcated camps (the bourgeoisie and the proletariat) is being left behind. In the new situation, a multiplicity of social actors establish their presence and spheres of autonomy in a fragmented social and political space. Society itself is largely shaped by the plurality of these struggles and the vision of those involved in the new social movements.

Whatever one might think of these claims, the clearest indication of the need for continued research on social movements is the persistence of multiple forms of collective mobilization in the continent. These manifestations indicate great complexity not only at the level of the actors but [. . .] also in terms of modes of organization and action, causes and goals of the struggle, magnitude and composition of the forces, relation to political parties and the state, and so forth.

[. . .]

What is important to emphasize at present is that these collective manifestations are found in all countries of the region—in varying political regimes, "levels of development," cultural contexts, and traditions of protest.

If a point of origin for the current wave of protest forms and styles were to be assigned, we would have to say that they emerged out of the historical conjuncture that started to coalesce in the late 1960s and has since branched out in a number of directions. The two factors most commonly cited in this regard are (1) the crisis of development in most of the region [. . .] and (2) the crisis of political parties and mechanisms of representation on all sides of the spectrum, from traditional parties in most countries to leftist parties and 1960s style guerrilla groups.

[. . .]

To refer to social movements in terms of "collective identities" represents a new trend and a new way of thinking. Social action is understood as the product of complex social processes in which structure and agency interact in manifold ways and in which actors produce meanings, negotiate, and make decisions.

[. . .]

In terms of strategy, it is important to convey the range of tactics, strategic initiatives, and forms of political organization developed by collective actors in their struggles, especially those that deviate from conventional ways of doing politics. The range of these forms, once again, is vast, from those practiced by small women's organizations to those adopted by movement-inspired political party coalitions.

[. . .]

In some cases, strategies have shifted from resistance to protest and from protest to proposal, without implying any linear movement from one to another of these forms but rather suggesting their coexistence and mutual feedback. The question of strategy, of course, is intimately linked to how social actors construct a collective identity for themselves, often out of conflictual roles and positions. This is our final axis of analysts.

Trends in Latin American social movements theory and research

Research and theorizing on social movements have become central issues in the Latin American social sciences landscape.

[. . .]

[The] distinction regarding social movements theories—differentiating those concerned with strategy and those centered on the notion of identity—is already well established. Resource mobilization theories, which make up the first group, dominate in the Anglo-Saxon world and highlight questions of strategy, participation, organization, rationality, expectations, interests, and the like. The identity-centered theories, dominant in continental Europe and Latin America, emphasize the processes by which social actors constitute collective identities as a means to create democratic spaces for more autonomous action. Referred to by some as the "new social movements approach," this school can be situated generally within poststructuralist and post-Marxist trends of growing importance since the 1970s. Some are also influenced by theories of postmodernism.

[. . .]

Latin American researchers' neglect of the concerns addressed by resource mobilization approaches has been costly in terms of understanding the concrete practices, constraints, and possibilities of the movements. Not only have "new identities" been celebrated prematurely, the presence of old features within them has also been overlooked. A sort of "cross-pollination" of research—between identity-centered and resource mobilization approaches, quantitive and qualitative methods, endogenous and external theories—is deemed necessary.

[. . .]

One issue that should be addressed [. . .] is that of determining what constitutes a "social movement." This is by no means a simple question. Alain Touraine, whose work has been among the most influential in Latin America, showed the complexity at hand when he asserted that "most of all, the empiricist illusion must be clearly rejected. It is impossible to define an object of study called 'social movements' without first selecting a general mode of analysis of social life on the basis of which a category of facts called social movements can be constituted" (1992: 63).

What all this means is that the definition of what counts as a "social movement" involves a complex epistemological process. It is therefore not surprising that few scholars have actually ventured a definition, some even believe that the whole idea of a "social movement" as a description of collective action should be abandoned because it traps our language in conceptual traditions that have to be discarded.

[. . .]

Related to the question of what constitutes a social movement is the issue of their newness, in other words, what is *new* about new social movements? This question is usually raised as a criticism of NSMs theorists. As some put it, the "new" is really in the theorists' minds. "Out there," some would say, the practices have always been the same, multiple and heterogeneous; it is only that theorists, burdened by paradigms, were unable to see them. In dismantling this "epistemological misunder-standing," Alberto Melucci made the important observation that both critics and adherents of the "newness" paradigm share "the same epistemological limitation. Both sides regard the contemporary phenomena as a unitary empirical object. Starting from this unity, the supporters seek to qualify its novelty, the critics deny or question it" (1989: 336). Underlying this limitation is a conception of social movements as "personages" moving on the historical stage like characters of an epic drama endowed with an unchanging essence. In other words, researchers assume the existence of unitary, coherent collective social agents moving along the historical flow. This assumption, Melucci insisted, hides the changing character of collective action at the level of orientations, meanings, levels and historical systems. If one takes into consideration these aspects, many of the debates around this question, he concluded, would vanish.

To deny, on the other hand, that there is anything new in today's collective action—in relation, say, to the earlier part of the century—is to negate the changing character of the world and its history. Of course, some things remain the same, and it is important to acknowledge the continuity of forms and practices. But as historical contexts change, so do peoples' ways of seeing and acting in the world, as well as the theories that seek to explain both actions and their contexts. Despite important continuities, Latin America in the 1980s is certainly very different from Latin America in the 1920s, 1930s, and even 1950s. Women, for instance, do not organize in the same way today as they did in the 1920s, nor do women's struggles have the same ideological and symbolic content that they had then. Social conflict has moved to previously untouched terrains, and at least some new practices have been developed. Even "classical" social actors such as workers and peasants have models of action that are very different from those of earlier movements. Similarly, not all the actors of today were present fifty years earlier, nor were people subjected to the same economic, social, and political forces. For example, there was not much of a gay or an ecology movement in previous decades, nor did the cities see so many varied forms of protest.

[. . .]

One of the key features associated with new social movements, in the minds of many of their proponents, is the emphasis on their autonomy vis-à-vis more conventional political arenas, such as political parties and the state. In some cases, this insistence on autonomy has not been sufficiently critical but stems, instead, from the analysts' desires, particularly in Latin America where the analysts are often external to the movement and tend to romanticize the movement's spontaneity and autonomy. As the experiences of countries such as Italy, Mexico, and Brazil show, the relationship between social movements and political parties is a dialectical one in which both movements and parties potentially stand to win a good deal.

Another important feature of contemporary social movements is the role of cultural factors in their constitution and actions. Yet, especially in the Latin American case, these aspects have received little theoretical attention and are not well understood, partly because of the dominance of economic and political forms of analysis. [S]ocial movements in Latin America must be seen as economic, political, *and* cultural struggles. This view has important consequences in terms of how researchers are to approach the movements. A prerequisite for this task is a critical reinterpretation of the nature of development and modernity in ways that stress their fundamental cultural nature.

[. . .]

References

Melucci, A. (1989), *Nomads of the present*, London: Hutchinson.
Touraine, A. (1992), 'Beyond Social Movements', *Theory, Culture and Society*, 9:125–45.

PART SIX

New directions

THE EXPANSION OF THE FIELD of study of social movements has been accompanied by a multiplication of approaches and perspectives. According to Della Porta and Diani (1999: 14), the intensification in contacts between scholars worldwide has given opportunities 'to compare the merits and limitations of the various paradigms'. While attempts have been made to combine different theoretical perspectives into a new synthesis, analysts have followed a variety of new directions, and if it would be too optimistic to claim that an integrated theory of social movements is taking shape, surely the complexity brought by new contributions has substantially enriched the debate (Ruggiero, 2000). We start this section of the book with Bert Klandermans, who makes a fresh case for social-psychological analysis of social movements. This type of analysis, he notes, has been abandoned by resource mobilisation theorists because, traditionally, social-psychological perspectives depicted social movements as unconventional, irrational, forms of collective behaviour. By emphasising the importance of structural factors, resource mobilisation theorists distanced themselves from analyses focused on participation in social movements as the result of predisposing psychological traits. They, rather, saw participation as the consequence of rational decisions, of the weighing of costs and benefits offered by the availability of material and organisational resources. In *Mobilization and Participation: Social-Psychological Expansions of Resource Mobilization Theory* (1984), Klandermans attempts to overcome the weaknesses of traditional psycho-sociological approaches, focusing on the interactions between individuals generating mobilisation. The author uses 'expectancy-value theory' to measure the willingness of individuals to participate in social movements. This theory relates action to the perceived attractiveness of prospective consequences, but in applying it to social movements Klandermans proposes to modify the theory in some crucial aspects. The goal of social movements, he reminds us, is the acquisition of 'collective goods', therefore participation is not merely based on individual decisions. Expectations, in other words, are not only related to the possible outcome of action, but also to the choice of others to participate and share such expectations. Klandermans' paper, based on the study of a mobilisation campaign by industrial workers in the Netherlands, tries to unveil the interactive dynamics among participants in social movements using social psychology as a tool to lead resource mobilisation theory towards a new direction.

It is certainly a new direction the one drawn by David Snow and colleagues, who are concerned with the issue of support for, and participation in, social movement organisations. *Frame Alignment, Micromobilization and Movement Participation* (1986) looks at the processes whereby individual orientations, values and beliefs become congruent (or align) with activities, goals and ideologies of social movement organisations. Inspired by Goffman's (1974) 'frame analysis', this paper sets off with the notion that individuals forge their own 'schemata of interpretation' which allow them to make sense of the world surrounding them. Frames render events meaningful and interpretations possible, functioning as guiding philosophies for action. For individuals to participate in social movements, therefore, their interpretive frameworks must coincide with those possessed by the movement they join: frame alignment processes conjoin participants' expectations and organisation objectives. The authors distinguish between different types of frame alignment processes. The first they term 'frame bridging', and is referred to the linkage of two or more ideologically congruent but structurally unconnected frames. 'Bridging' occurs when potential participants are provided with the organisational tools to express their grievances. By 'frame amplification' the authors mean the clarification and strengthening of an interpretive frame, whereas with 'frame extension' they refer to the efforts made by a social movement organisation to encompass previously overlooked values and beliefs of potential adherents. In doing so, social movements enlarge their participants pool by making their interpretive framework more comprehensive. Finally, 'frame transformation' is required when support and participation are weak, new values have to be nurtured and old meanings reframed. In brief, Snow and colleagues attempt to provide a conceptual bridge that links social psychological interpretations with considerations of the structural and organisational aspects of social movement participation.

Ron Eyerman and Andrew Jamison are drawn by a similar desire to find new concepts and theoretical pointers that lead towards an understanding of social movements in a comprehensive way. Their *Social Movements: A Cognitive Praxis* (1991) is an analysis of movements as collective processes producing knowledge. The roots of their approach can be found in Max Scheler's programme for the sociology of knowledge formulated in the early 1920s. According to Scheler, this specific branch of sociology should not confine its attention to official, established, forms of knowledge, but should also encompass moral, religious and symbolic knowledge. This suggestion was well received by anthropologists, who studied and compared cultural world views and belief systems in informal groups and communities. Eyerman and Jamison, in the same vein, study the way in which social movements produce knowledge, positing therefore that their action amounts to cognitive praxis. For example, action by environmental movements tends to develop knowledge within the spheres of the natural and technological sciences and ecology. On the other hand, movements for civil rights will tend to produce knowledge and new sensitivities in the realm of spiritual and moral values. The cognitive approach, according to these authors, brings the debate on social movements beyond the impasse allegedly caused by 'particular-ist' and resource mobilisation theorists. The former are seen as exclusively focused on the actors involved and on their self-definition. The latter are imputed with over-emphasising the operational aspects of social movements, the effectiveness of their organisations and their mobilising strength. A cognitive approach, it is stressed, shows that movements may translate scientific ideas into social and political beliefs, and that their action and critique may bring renovation.

As we have remarked above, if the contributions included in this section point to new directions for the study of social movements, at the same time they belie an attempt to identify an integrated approach that may combine the diverse schools of thought. The aim of Mario Diani, even before attempting to merge different theories into a comprehensive perspective, is to provide an analytical definition of social movements based on a systematic comparison of existing conceptualisations. Concepts, he warns, cannot be identified with theories, but they may be regarded as cornerstones of theorising. Efforts aimed at unifying different approaches and theories, therefore, are incongruent if a precise definition of the subject matter is unavailable. With this in mind, the author moves on to trace some common analytical elements found in a variety of diverse theoretical traditions. His proposal for a syn-thesis, therefore, is addressed to the definitional aspects of social movements rather than to the schools of thought theorising on them. In *The Concept of Social Movement* (1992), Diani proceeds in a cumulative fashion, that is he singles out some elemen-tary factors which are commonly shared by definitions of social movements and then adds up more nuanced elements with a view to reaching a comprehensive definition. Initially, he finds that in the specialist literature the presence of informal interactions involving individuals, groups and organisations is widely acknowledged. He therefore suggests that a basic characteristic of a social movement should be: 'a network of informal interactions between a plurality of individuals, groups and/or organisations'. Drawing in more detail on other contributions, he then adds that social movement participants are engaged in conflict aimed at promoting or opposing social change. In a final addition of factors, the notion of identity is highlighted, therefore specifying that social movements are networks of informal interactions between a plurality of individuals, groups and/or organisations, engaged in a political or cultural conflict, on the basis of a shared collective identity. According to Diani, such definition is precise enough to avoid the evocative nature of many social movement conceptualisations and to make the subject matter a specific focus for research and analysis. The definition, in his view, may also contribute to the integration of different theoretical perspec-tives, while the emphasis on networks, conflict and identity may challenge 'some conventional wisdom inherited from' these perspectives.

It is hard to establish the degree of consensus encountered by Diani's painstaking construction of a concept of social movement. The constitutive elements he identifies may be central, but they appear to be mingled with other factors identified by alter-native conceptualisations. McAdam, McCarthy and Zald, for example, are equally aware that the different theoretical traditions, when analysing social movements, may have to identify similar sets of factors, but such factors they group as follows: the structure of political opportunities and constraints faced by social movements, the forms of organisations available, and the collective processes of interpretation that mediate between opportunity and action. In *Comparative Perspectives on Social*

Movements (1996), the authors avoid adopting a precise concept of social movements, their concerns being, rather, addressed to the way in which movements emerge and develop. In a shorthand designation of the three sets of factors they identify, they refer to political opportunities, mobilising structures and framing processes, thus alluding to three different schools of thought whose contribution they critically assess. After discussing each of these separately, they attempt to link them together by examining the question of movement emergence. The factor 'opportunity' is closely linked with the factor 'mobilising structures', so that the effects of both is said to be interactive rather than independent. Opportunities, in their turn, may set in motion framing processes that undermine the legitimacy of the system and encourage the establishment of yet more mobilisation structures. A similar argument is put forward when the issue of movement development is addressed, so that the authors outline the possibilities of a sustained dialogue between scholars working in a variety of national contexts and from a variety of perspectives. Their comparative focus is made more explicit in the final part of their contribution, where the authors again take up their three concepts or factors, suggesting that 'each can be used to illuminate cross-national differences and similarities in movement dynamics'.

We have mentioned above the case made by Klandermans for a novel psycho-sociological approach to the study of social movements. In previous parts of this book we have also presented an analysis of 'the crowd' and the 'politics of mass society', by Le Bon and Kornhauser respectively. Both authors belong to a tradition which associates collective behaviour to emotionally charged, irrational public conduct (Klandermans, 1997). This tradition links passionate action with 'traditional conflict', in which primitive behavioural elements predominate. One has to think of the 'mob', a mobile and unpredictable aggregation of individuals where participants are affected by the presence of others and where the crowd itself acts as a spur to irrationality. Collective aggregations are seen as dangerous or even terrifying, as participants are rendered immature, susceptible to the calls of unscrupulous leaders and compelled by their 'inner demons' (Goodwin, Jasper and Polletta, 2001). We have shown how this perception of social movements was later subjected to severe criticism, with scholars shifting attention from the psychological dynamics of collective behaviour to the mechanisms of collective action. Structural, rationalistic, organisational or symbolic factors were introduced in the analysis of social movements. Emotions and passions were carefully shunned, perhaps due to the pejorative tone displayed against these variables in previous accounts. The final contribution included in this section examines collective action by rethinking the role of emotions. Craig Calhoun advocates a sociological study of emotions, not as autonomously psychological phenomena, but as shaped by social interaction and cultural understanding. In *Putting Emotions in Their Place* (2001), the author remarks that passionate feelings are central to movement participation as they are to the shaping of collective action. He suggests that the opposition between 'irrational' and 'rationalistic' should be superseded, as acts led by passions may be meaningful responses to a situation and may help apprehend and make sense of the world (Crossley, 2002). Passions, we are reminded, occupied a central position along with 'interest' in utilitarian analysis: think of the role played by 'happiness' in arguments around preferable social practices and systems. Feeling and thinking were both necessary for the establishment of a civil society and the achievement of common understanding and solidarity

(Smith, 1984 [1759]). Calhoun links emotions to moral norms and injunctions, while stressing that feelings and cognition cannot be fully separated. Such separation, he observes, is due to the excessive dualism with which Western cultures construct their variable: for example, thinking vs. feeling, mind vs. body, public vs. private, conscious vs. unconscious, and so on. He then introduces a third category, namely 'perception', and blending his variables together he remarks that social movements build new normative structures for emotions, and through collective perceptions of the surrounding world, they indeed produce emotions, rather than simply reflecting the emotional orientations of participants.

References

Crossley, N. (2002), *Making Sense of Social Movements*, Buckingham: Open University Press.

della Porta, A. and Diani, M. (1999), *Social Movements: An Introduction*, Oxford: Oxford University Press.

Goffman, E. (1974), *Frame Analysis*, Cambridge: Harvard University Press.

Goodwin, J., Jasper, J.M. and Polletta, F. (eds) (2001), *Passionate Politics: Emotions and Social Movements*, Chicago: University of Chicago Press.

Klandermans, B. (1997), *The Social Psychology of Protest*, Oxford: Blackwell.

Ruggiero, V. (2000), 'New Social Movements and the "centri sociali" in Milan', *The Sociological Review*, 48(2): 167—185.

Smith, A. (1984 [1759]), *Theory of Moral Sentiments*, Indianapolis: Liberty Classics.

Chapter 33

Bert Klandermans

MOBILIZATION AND PARTICIPATION: SOCIAL-PSYCHOLOGICAL EXPANSIONS OF RESOURCE MOBILIZATION THEORY

RESOURCE MOBILIZATION THEORY was a reaction to traditional social-psychological theories of social movements. Those theories focused on what attracted people to participation in social movements. Amongst the explanations were: personality traits, marginality and alienation, grievances and ideology. These explanations tended to be based on the assumption that participation in a social movement, like other forms of collective behavior, is an unconventional, irrational type of behavior. Thanks to resource mobilization theorists themselves, these approaches became increasingly questionable. Attempts to show that movement participants have characteristic personality traits were not very successful. Marginality and alienation, for example, were not the typical background of participants in such divergent movements as fascism in Germany, the student movement, the civil rights movement, the union movement, political protest movements, the environmental, antiabortion, and antinuclear movements, and the unemployed movement. The importance of grievances and ideology as determinants of participation in a social movement has been ambiguous.

In contrast to traditional social-psychological interpretations, resource mobilization theory emphasizes the importance of structural factors, such as the availability of resources to a collectivity and the position of individuals in social networks, and stresses the rationality of participation in social movements. Participation in a social movement is seen not as the consequence of predisposing psychological traits or states, but as the result of rational decision processes whereby people weigh the costs and benefits of participation.

Resource mobilization theory went too far in nearly abandoning the social-psychological analyses of social movements. In this paper a fresh case is made for a social-psychological analysis of mobilization and participation in a social movement. By combining new insights in psychology with resource mobilization theory, the weaknesses of earlier social-psychological approaches in the field can be overcome.

Social psychology and resource mobilization theory

Social psychology can expand resource mobilization theory in an important way by revealing processes of social-movement participation on the individual level. To resource mobilization theorists, participation results from "weighing" costs against benefits. However, little attention is given to weighing these at the individual level. Nor is much attention given to the interaction between individuals that generates mobilization.

Identifying the interaction between individuals as the appropriate level of analysis has significant theoretical consequences. It takes into account the psychological truism that people behave in a perceived reality. Individual decisions to participate in a social movement are based on perceived costs and benefits of participation. That perceived reality is capable of being influenced, and both social-movement leaders and adversaries try to do so. Persuasion is an important element in every mobilization campaign. The efficacy of a mobilization campaign in persuading the individual is a key determinant of participation.

Movement participation denotes activities ranging from signing a petition to sabotage, and from part-time or one-time to full-time activity. The perceived costs and benefits for different activities can vary greatly. Moreover, there can be substantial differences in perceived costs and benefits between individuals, across regions, and during the life cycle of the movement. This has important implications for mobilization campaigns. By timing, and by their choice of strategy and arena, social-movement organizations can profoundly influence the costs and benefits of participation.

A general criticism of resource mobilization theory has been that it underestimates the significance of grievances and ideology as determinants of participation in a social movement. This shortcoming results from confusing the individual and societal levels of analysis. The fact that grievances and ideology cannot explain the rise of social movements does not mean that they do not play a role in the decisions of individuals to participate in a social movement. One of the aspirations of this social-psychological expansion of resource mobilization theory is to find a more satisfying theoretical solution for the problem of grievances and ideology as determinants of participation in a social movement.

Persuasion and activation: a social-psychological theory of mobilization and participation

Participation in a social movement fluctuates. Alternatingly, a movement has its rank and file in action and then it falls back on its cadre. Mobilization plays an important part in these fluctuations. The remainder of this article will focus on participation in a social movement and on the way it changes as a result of mobilization attempts.

The willingness to participate

A person will participate in a social movement if s/he knows the opportunities to participate, if s/he is capable of using one or more of these opportunities, and if s/he is willing to do so. This paper elaborates the third condition by applying expectancy-value theory to movement participation. In general this theory attempts to relate action to the perceived attractiveness or aversiveness of expected consequences. The key elements of the theory are expected outcomes (expectations) and the value of these outcomes. Theoretically, values and expectations combine in a multiplicative way. Even if the value of an outcome is very high it will not motivate individuals as long as they do not believe that the outcome can be produced by their efforts. Usually different outcomes (material and nonmaterial) are distinguished. For each outcome a value-expectancy product can be calculated. Motivation is defined as the sum of these different value-expectancy products.

A rational-choice framework does not imply that feelings, emotions or sentiments are unimportant in relation to movement participation. Nor does it argue that potential participants are consciously multiplying and adding values and expectations. The usefulness of the framework is that it provides a device for the systematic analysis of the variety of beliefs, expectations and attitudes that are related to participation in a social movement.

However, before this general theoretical framework can be applied to movement participation, it has to be modified in an important way. The goals of social movements are "collective goods." Obtaining a collective good is not directly contingent on the decision of an individual to participate. Rational individuals will not participate in the production of a collective good unless selective incentives motivate them to do so. Though Olson's argument has been criticized, it clarified the distinction between collective benefits and selective benefits. If one finds it untenable that only the latter motivates movement participation, one must acknowledge that the relationship between participation and collective benefits is different from the relationship between participation and selective benefits.

Collective benefits and participation. Both Gamson (1975) and Schwartz (1976) argue that people participate in activities to produce a collective goal precisely because they are aware that the good would never be produced if everyone sat back and waited for someone else to do something. Oberschall (1980) remarked that this was especially true for people who are strongly in favor of the collective good. Fireman and Gamson (1979) and Fleishman (1980) stressed the importance of feelings of responsibility and solidarity in this connection. Schwartz and Oberschall added the probability of success as very important. In their analysis the probability of success is related to the number of participants. Oberschall pointed out that the important question for the individual is what his/her participation will contribute to the probability of success. From a hypothesized relationship between the number of participants and the probability of success, the individual contribution as a function of the number of participants can be derived.

These arguments do not touch the fundamental issue, namely, *that persons have to decide to participate at a point when they do not know whether others will participate.* There is a social-psychological solution to this problem. Although people do not know what others will do, they have *expectations*. Based on their expectations about the behavior of others, people assess the probability of success and their own contribution to it. The expectation that participation helps to produce the collective good can therefore be categorized as follows:

a   expectations about the number of participants;
b   expectations about one's own contribution to the probability of success;
c   expectations about the probability of success if many people participate.

These expectations combine in a multiplicative way with the value of the collective good to produce the expected collective benefits of participation.

Applying expectancy theory yields the hypothesis that the value of a collective good is a function of its instrumentality for social changes which the movement hopes to achieve and of the value of changes. To form an opinion about this instrumentality, an individual must have knowledge about the collective good and its implications.

Participation and selective costs and benefits. Selective costs and benefits are by definition contingent on participation. Expectations about, and values of, these incentives directly influence the willingness to participate. In the literature there are different classifications of selective costs and benefits. An important distinction is that between expected reactions of significant others and expected material costs and benefits like money, time, injury, entertainment.

Motives. The willingness to participate in a social movement can be defined as a function of the perceived attractiveness or aversiveness of the expected consequences of participation. This signifies that willingness to participate is function of:

(a) the expectation that participation will help to produce the collective good and the value of the collective good—the *collective motive*; (b) the expected selective costs and benefits and the value of these costs and benefits. As distinguished in the reactions of significant others, these comprise the *social motive*. As they relate to nonsocial costs and benefits, they comprise the *reward motive*.

Expectations or instrumentalities and values combine in a multiplicative way and the three motives in an additive way. The value of a collective good will be zero if it is not believed to be instrumental for valued societal changes, or if the changes it is said to be instrumental for are not valued. The value of a collective good will be negative if it is believed to hinder valued societal changes, or if changes are valued negatively.

If the value of the collective good is zero, the collective motive will be zero. If this value is negative the motive will be negative, unless the expectation component is zero.

The collective motive will also be zero if the expectation that participation will help to produce the collective good is zero: persons will not be motivated by the collective good if they do not feel that their participation contributes to the probability of success, or do not believe that enough other people will participate, or do not feel there is any chance of success even if many people participate.

Since the different motives combine in an additive way, they can compensate one another. If the collective motive is weak, zero or negative, the other motives can be so strong that a person is willing to participate. If the collective motive is strong, the social motives and/or reward motives can be negative without making a person unwilling to participate. Of course there are also situations in which the collective motive does not outweigh negative social and/or reward motives, either because the collective motive is too weak, or because the social and reward motives are too negative.

[. . .]

Mobilization

Mobilization attempts by a movement organization have the aim of winning participants, that is, persuading people to support the movement organization by material and non-material means. Mobilization attempts always contain two components. These are called consensus mobilization and action mobilization.

Consensus mobilization is a process through which a social movement tries to obtain support for its viewpoints. It involves (a) a collective good, (b) a movement strategy, (c) confrontation with the opponent, (d) results achieved. Neither collective goods nor types of action are fixed quantities. They change, and this requires renewed consensus mobilization. Consensus mobilization does not take place in a vacuum. Collective goods and actions are controversial. Opponents, counter-movements, rival organizations counter the arguments of a social movement. A social movement will have to go into these arguments. In short, a "paper war" is waged to promote or to discourage the mobilization of consensus. The degree of success with which consensus is mobilized around the collective goods can be measured by the extent to which these goods are known and valued. Whether people value a collective good depends on the extent to which consensus mobilization succeeded in making them believe that this good is instrumental for valued social changes.

Action mobilization is the process by which an organization in a social movement calls up people to participate. Consensus mobilization does not necessarily go together with action mobilization, but action mobilization cannot do without consensus mobilization. Action mobilization involves motivating people to participate. Ideally, social movement organization will take a variety of approaches, appealing both to collective and to social and reward motives. They have every reason to do so. Participation because of collective motives means that both the collective good and the type of participation are attractive. But it will seldom be the case that each and every member of a collectivity is won over to the collective good and the form of participation in the time available. Particularly if nearly unanimous participation is demanded, there is always a certain percentage who, lacking complete consensus, will have to be mobilized using social and/or reward motives. Another factor to be contended with is the occurrence of free-rider behavior. Since free riders take a positive stand on the collective good but do not believe that its production depends on their participation, it is not of much use to appeal to collective motives. What remains is to try to mobilize them using social and/or reward motives. Here, again, the chance that a social movement decides to do this will be greater if a higher degree of participation is required.

A mobilizing organization will try to make the benefits of participation and the costs of nonparticipation as high as possible, and the costs of participation and the benefits of nonparticipation as low as possible. Apart from influencing the three motives directly, a movement also has indirect means of controlling the costs and benefits of participation. Two important ones are (a) the choice of the type of action and (b) the choice of the scene. A movement can choose among several types of action, from moderate to militant. With its choice of the type of action, a movement can determine to a large extent the costs and benefits of participation. A movement can fight where it is strongest, that is, in sectors of society with strong movement networks where it can organize many people. Resource mobilization literature has shown that people are more easily mobilized in such sectors. The premise here is that this is probably because a more favorable cost-benefit ratio can be created in such sectors.

Psychologically speaking, there will be an element of projection in estimates of the number of participants in a movement. A person who does not wish to participate will make a lower estimate of the number of participants than a person who does wish to take part. In a collectivity this has all the look of a self-fulfilling prophecy: if many people think that few people will participate, many people will have doubts about the efficacy of their own participation. Thus a downward spiral ensues which is fatal to the willingness to participate. Mobilization efforts attempt to reinforce the view that "many people will participate." If this is not successful, the prophecy fulfills itself.

Method

The theory of mobilization and participation has been applied in research on mobilization campaigns of the union movement, the women's movement and the peace movement. This paper presents data from a study of the effects of a mobilization campaign by the Industrial Workers' Union of the Dutch Union Federation, the largest union of industrial workers in the Netherlands.

[. . .]

Research design

Mobilization campaigns often last several months. In this case the campaign started in August 1978, and the negotiations were not completed until June 1979. In such a situation, longitudinal research is to be preferred. From the end of November 1978 through July 1979 we interviewed a group of union members about once a month. We chose the timing so that the interviews fell shortly before or after an important event. Although a total of seven waves were held, for methodological reasons a design was developed which ensured that no respondent would be interviewed more than three times. Seven groups of members were selected and interviewed.

[. . .]

When the similarity of the seven groups was controlled on a number of variables, the differences found were so few that the groups can be used for comparison with no difficulty. In addition, this design has many advantages. We can get a picture of the course of the campaign by comparing the outcomes of the successive interviews.

We can also study the effect of a single event by comparing the outcomes of the interviews before and after that event while controlling for repeated measurement.

[. . .]

Discussion

The theory formulated in this paper aims at a break with both the traditional social-psychological approaches to social movements and the neglect of social-psychological analyses by resource mobilization theory. Contrary to the traditional social-psychological approach, participation in a social movement is assumed to be rational. The emphasis is not on personality characteristics or psychological states, but on the psychological process of weighing costs and benefits. One of the objections to the traditional approach is that it defines participation as tension release, and thus it does not matter in which movement a person participates. In the theory presented in this article it does. Participation is seen as a rational choice in the situation as the person perceives it, and as a way to obtain desired outcomes. In the eyes of the participant, participation is a means of reaching valued goals.

These goals and their relation to factors such as relative deprivation and frustration have been the subject of much discussion in social-movement literature. Resource mobilization has ruled this discussion out without solving the problem. The theory developed in this article attempts to reconcile the social psychological and resource mobilization approaches in this respect. Feelings of relative deprivation or frustration do not necessarily evoke agreement with the goals of a movement which pretends to remedy these feelings: goals have to be perceived as instrumental to the elimination of these feelings. The research results support the validity of this argument. Theoretical emphasis must therefore shift from relative deprivation to the perceived instrumentality of the collective good for the elimination of relative deprivation. Such perceptions do not originate spontaneously. Consensus mobilization is needed for this. Campaigns are needed which explain the situation and make clear why the collective good will bring relief. Agreement with the goals of the movement does not necessarily lead to participation: a person may doubt whether participation will help to achieve the goals, social and/or reward motives may be too negative.

Theories that stress the rationality of participation in a social movement have to solve the problem of the dilemma of collective behavior. As Olson (1977) stated it, rational persons will not participate in a social movement unless selective incentives motivate them to do so. Resource mobilization theory does not really solve that problem. Concepts like ideological incentives, feelings of solidarity or responsibility, the perceived indispensability of an individual's contribution, differences between action forms in vulnerability to free riding, different production functions, or thresholds, do not really touch the heart of the matter, which is that persons have to decide at a point when they do not know whether others will participate. This article argues that the problem can be solved on a social-psychological level. Since people have expectations about others' behavior, they can formulate their "own" production functions. As the evidence presented demonstrates, this production function heavily influences the willingness to participate. On a collective level, the expectation that others will participate works as a self-fulfilling prophecy. Counter to Olson's argument, a collective good *can* motivate persons to participate in a social movement if they expect that others will also participate.

Moreover, if the expectancy component is a little larger than zero, a collective motive to participate can exist if the collective good is valued highly. If a person comes from a supportive social background (positive social motive) then there can be quite a few nonsocial costs of participation (negative reward motive) before the balance turns to the negative.

The evidence presented makes it clear that expectations, in combination with selective costs and benefits, are of great importance for the choice a person makes among alternative forms of action. For instance, in the eyes of some respondents the goal could be reached by moderate action. Why should they take the higher risks of militant action? For those who did not believe moderate action to be effective, it did not make much sense to accept the costs of such action. They preferred to participate in militant action, even though the perceived costs were higher.

People's expectations are based on past experiences. In a mobilization campaign a movement organization tries to influence these expectations. Resource mobilization theory is used the mobilization concept in a rather specific way. By making the distinction between consensus and action mobilization we generated the processes of convincing and acting. The research results on the spread of knowledge and the beliefs about the instrumentality of shorter working time showed the instance of consensus mobilization as a separate process. Schwartz (1976) made a similar distinction between "ignorance reduction" and "organizational disciplinization." The importance of such distinctions is that they [see] "convincing" and "activating" as two different processes [...]

References

Fireman, Bruce and William A. Gamson 1979 "Utilitarian logic in the resource mobilization perspective." Pp. 8–45 in Mayer N. Zald and John D. McCarthy (eds.), *The Dynamics of Social Movements*. Cambridge, MA: Winthrop.

Fleishman, John A. 1980 "Collective action as helping behavior: effects of responsibility diffusion on contributions to a public good." *Journal of Personality and Social Psychology* 38:629–37.

Gamson, William A. 1975 *The Strategy of Social Protest*. Homewood, IL: Dorsey.

Oberschall, Anthony. 1980 "Loosely structured collective conflict: a theory and an application." Pp. 45–68 in Louis Kriesbery (ed.), *Research in Social Movements, Conflict and Change*, Volume 3. Greenwich, CT: JAI.

Olson, Mancur. 1977 *The Logic of Collective Action, Public Goods and the Theory of Groups*. Cambridge, MA: Harvard University Press.

Schwartz, Michael. 1976 *Radical Protest and Social Structure*. New York: Academic Press.

Chapter 34

David A. Snow, E. Burke Rochford, Jr., Steven K. Worden and Robert D. Benford

FRAME ALIGNMENT PROCESSES, MICROMOBILIZATION, AND MOVEMENT PARTICIPATION

A LONG STANDING and still central problem in the field of social movements concerns the issue of support for and participation in social movement organizations (SMOs) and their activities and campaigns. There is growing recognition that a thoroughgoing understanding of this issue requires consideration of both social psychological and structural/organizational factors.

[. . .]

Our aim in this paper is to move forward along this line, both conceptually and empirically, by elaborating what we refer to as frame alignment processes and by enumerating correspondent micromobilization tasks and processes. By *frame alignment*, we refer to the linkage of individual and SMO interpretive orientations, such that some set of individual interests, values and beliefs and SMO activities, goals, and ideology are congruent and complementary. The term "*frame*" (and framework) is borrowed from Goffman (1974:21) to denote "schemata of interpretation" that enable individuals "to locate, perceive, identify, and label" occurrences within their life space and the world at large. By rendering events or occurrences meaningful, frames function to organize experience and guide action, whether individual or collective. So conceptualized, it follows that frame alignment is a necessary condition for movement participation, whatever its nature or intensity. Since we have identified more than one such alignment process, we use the phrase *frame alignment process* as the cover term for these linkages. By *micromobilization*, we refer simply to the various interactive and communicative processes that affect frame alignment.

We illustrate these processes with data derived primarily from our studies of the Nichiren Shoshu Buddhist movement, of Hare Krishna, of the peace movement, and of urban neighborhood movements. Drawing upon these empirical-materials, on Goffman's frame analytic perspective (1974), which we extend and refine for our purposes, and on a range of literature pertinent to the issue of movement participation, we discuss and illustrate the frame alignment processes we have identified, and elaborate related micromobilization tasks and processes.

[. . .]

Types of frame alignment processes

Earlier we defined frame alignment as the linkage or conjunction of individual and SMO interpretive frameworks. We now propose and elaborate four types of frame alignment processes that are suggested by our research observations, and which attend to the blind spots and questions discussed above. The four processes include: (a) frame bridging, (b) frame amplification, (c) frame extension, and (d) frame transformation. For each variant of alignment we indicate correspondent micromobilization tasks and processes. The underlying premise is that frame alignment, of one variety or another, is a necessary condition for movement participation, whatever its nature or intensity, and that it is typically an interactional accomplishment.

Frame bridging

By frame bridging we refer to the linkage of two or more ideologically congruent but structurally unconnected frames regarding a particular issue or problem. Such bridging can occur at the organizational level, as between two SMOs within the same movement industry, or at the individual level, which is the focal concern of this paper. At this level of analysis, frame bridging involves the linkage of an SMO with what McCarthy (1986) has referred to as unmobilized sentiment pools or public opinion preference clusters. These sentiment pools refer to aggregates of individuals who share common grievances and attributional orientations, but who lack the organizational base for expressing their discontents and for acting in pursuit of their interests. For these sentiment pools, collective action is not preceded by consciousness or frame transformation, but by being structurally connected with an ideologically isomorphic SMO.

This bridging is effected primarily by organizational outreach and information diffusion through interpersonal or intergroup networks, the mass media, the telephone, and direct mail. In recent years, opportunities and prospects for frame bridging have been facilitated by the advent of "new technologies," namely the computerization of lists of contributors or subscribers to various causes and literature (McCarthy, 1986). The micromobilization task is first, to cull lists of names in order to produce a probable adherent pool, and second, to bring these individuals within the SMO's infrastructure by working one or more of the peviously mentioned information channels.

[. . .]

The appropriateness of viewing micromobilization as largely a bridging problem has been suggested by a number of recent studies demonstrating the salience of both interpersonal and group networks in relation to the emergence and diffusion of social movements and their SMOs. Yet, to focus solely on networks as the key to understanding participation patterns can easily yield a misguided and overly mechanistic analysis. Networks frequently function to structure movement recruitment and growth, but they do not tell us what transpires when constituents and bystanders or adherents get together. Since a good portion of the time devoted to many SMO activities is spent in small encounters, an examination of the nature of those encounters and the interactional processes involved would tell us much about how SMOs and their constituents go about the business of persuading others, effecting switches in frame, and so on. McCarthy and Zald alluded to such concerns when they suggested that sometimes "grievances and discontent may be defined, created, and manipulated by issue entrepreneurs and organizations" (1977: 1215), but this provocative proposition has neither been examined empirically nor integrated into a more general understanding of constituent mobilization. Our elaboration of the other variants of frame alignment addresses these considerations, thus moving us beyond the frame bridging process.

Frame amplification

By frame amplification, we refer to the clarification and invigoration of an interpretive frame that bears on a particular issue, problem or set of events. Because the meaning of events and their connection to one's immediate life situation are often shrouded by indifference, deception or fabriction by others, and by ambiguity or uncertainty (Goffman, 1974), support for and participation in movement activities is frequently contingent on the clarification and reinvigoration of an interpretive frame. Our research experiences and inspection of the literature suggest two varieties of frame amplification: value amplification and belief amplification.

Value Amplification. Values can be construed as modes of conduct or states of existence that are thought to be worthy of protection and promotion. Because individuals subscribe to a range of values that vary in the degree to which they are compatible and attainable, values are normally arrayed in a hierarchy such that some have greater salience than others. Value amplification refers to the identification, idealization, and elevation of one or more values presumed basic to prospective constituents but which have not inspired collective action for any number of reasons. They may have atrophied, fallen into disuse, or have been suppressed because of the lack of an opportunity for expression due to a repressive authority structure (Tilly, 1978) or the absence of an organizational outlet (McCarthy, 1986); they may have become taken for granted or cliched; they may not have been sufficiently challenged or threatened; or their relevance to a particular event or issue may be ambiguous. If one or more of these impediments to value articulation and expression is operative, then the recruitment and mobilization of prospective constituents will require the focusing, elevation, and reinvigoration of values relevant to the issue or event being promoted or resisted.

Examples of value amplification were readily apparent among several of the SMOs we studied. Particularly striking was the ongoing value amplification in which local neighborhood activists and SMOs engaged in order to generate mobilizable sentiment pools. In following the careers of five local SMOs associated with three different campaigns through 1985, values associated with family, ethnicity, property, and neighborhood integrity were continuously highlighted and idealized.

[. . .]

The use of value amplification as a springboard for mobilizing support was also evident in the peace movement. Fundamental values such as justice, cooperation, perseverance, and the sanctity of human life were repeatedly embellished. The movement's most frequently idealized values, however, were those associated with democracy, particularly the values of equality and liberty. Peace activists amplified such values by asserting their "constitutional right" to speak out on the nuclear arms race, national security, and foreign policy.

[. . .]

Belief Amplification. Broadly conceived, beliefs refer to presumed relationships "between two things or between some thing and a characteristic of it" (Bem, 1970: 4), as exemplified by such presumptions as God is dead, the Second Coming is imminent, capitalists are exploiters, and black is beautiful.

[. . .]

Frame extension

We have noted how SMOs frequently promote programs or causes in terms of values and beliefs that may not be especially salient or readily apparent to potential constituents and supporters, thus necessitating the amplification of these ideational elements in order to clarify the linkage between personal or group interests and support for the SMO. On other occasions more may be involved in securing and activating participants than overcoming ambiguity and uncertainty or indifference and lethargy. The programs and values that some SMOs promote may not be rooted in existing sentiment or adherent pools, or may appear to have little if any bearing on the life situations and interests of potential adherents. When such is the case, an SMO may have to extend the boundaries of its primary framework so as to encompass interests or points of view that are incidental to its primary objectives but of considerable salience to potential adherents. In effect, the movement is attempting to enlarge its adherent pool by portraying its objectives or activities as attending to or being congruent with the values or interests of potential adherents. The micromobilization task in such cases is the identification of and the alignment of them with participation in movement activities.

Evidence of this variety of frame alignment was readily discernible in the movements we studied. In the case of the peace movement, frame extension is commonplace. Movement leaders frequently elaborate goals and activities so as to encompass auxiliary interests not obviously associated with the movement in hopes of enlarging its adherent base. The employment of rock-and-roll and punk bands to attract otherwise uninterested individuals to disarmament rallies, and the dissemination of literature explicating the services sacrificed by a community as a result of an escalating defense budget are illustrative of this practice.

[. . .]

Frame extension was also operative in both the Nichiren Shoshu and Hare Krishna movements, but at a more interpersonal level. In the case of Nichiren Shoshu, the operation of this process was particularly evident at the point of initial contact between prospective recruits and movement members. The primary aim of these initial recruitment encounters was not to sell the movement or to get individuals to join, but simply to persuade the prospect to attend a movement meeting or activity. Toward that end, members attempted to align the prospect's interests with movement activities, practices, or goals. They did this by first trying to discover something of interest to the prospect, and then emphasized that this interest could be realized, Hare Krishna devotees strategically attempted to assess the interests of persons contacted in various public places in an effort to relate the movement's religious philosophy to individual interests and concerns.

[. . .]

Frame transformation

Thus far we have noted how the alignment of individuals and SMOs may be effected through the bridging, amplification, and grafting or incorporation of existing interpretive frames and their attendent values and beliefs. The programs, causes, and values that some SMOs promote, however, may not resonate with, and on occasion may even appear antithetical to, conventional lifestyles or rituals and extant interpretive frames. When such is the case, new values may have to be planted and nurtured, old meanings or understandings jettisoned, and erroneous beliefs or "misframings" reframed (Goffman, 1974: 308) in order to garner support and secure participants. What may be required, in short, is a transformation of frame.

According to Goffman (1974: 43–44), such a transformation, which he refers to as a "keying," redefines activities, events, and biographies that are already meaningful from the standpoint of some primary framework, in terms of another framework, such that they are now "seen by the participants to be something quite else." What is involved is "a systematic alteration" that radically reconstitutes what it is for participants that is going on (Goffman, 1974: 45).

We have identified two such transformation processes that are pertinent to movement recruitment and participation: transformations of domain-specific and global interpretive frames. We shall first consider the similarities between these two alignment processes, and then turn to their differences.

The obvious similarity is that both involve a reframing of some set of conditions, be they biographic or social, past, present, or future. The objective contours of the situation do not change so much as the way the situation is defined and thus experienced. Two analytically distinct aspects comprise this interpretive change. First, there is a change in the perceived seriousness of the condition such that what was previously seen as an unfortunate but tolerable situation is now defined as inexcusable, unjust, or immoral, thus connoting the adoption of an injustice frame or variation thereof (Gamson et al., 1982).

But the development and adoption of an injustice frame is not sufficient to account for the direction of action. A life of impoverishment may be defined as an injustice, but its relationship to action is partly dependent, as attribution theorists would argue, on whether blame or responsibility is internalized or externalized. Thus, the emergence of an injustice frame must be accompanied by a corresponding shift in attributional orientation.

Evidence of such a shift manifested itself repeatedly in research on conversion to the Nichiren Shoshu Buddhist movement, as illustrated by the words of a 20-year-old convert:

> Before joining Nichiren Shoshu I blamed any problems I had on other people or on the environment. It was always my parents, or school, or society. But through chanting I discovered the real source of my difficulties: myself. Chanting has helped me to realize that rather than running around blaming others, I am the one who needs to change.

Since Nichiren Shoshu is a religious movement that emphasizes personal transformation as the key to social change, it might be argued that this feature of alignment is pertinent only to participation in religious, personal growth, and self-help movements. But this clearly is not the case; for a shift in attributional orientation is also frequently a constituent element of mobilization for and participation in movements that seek change by directly altering sociopolitical structures. In the case of participation in such movements, however, the shift involves a change from fatalism or self-blaming to structural-blaming, from victim-blaming to system-blaming.

[. . .]

We have thus far suggested that transformations of both domain-specific and global interpretive frames are contingent on the development and adoption of injustice frames and correspondent shifts in attributional orientation, but we have yet to distinguish between the two types of transformations. We now turn to that consideration by examining how they differ in terms of scope.

Transformation of Domain-specific Interpretive Frames. By transformation of domain-specific interpretive frames, we refer to fairly self-contained but substantial changes in the way a particular domain of life is framed, such that a domain previously taken for granted is reframed as problematic and in need of repair, or a domain seen as normative or acceptable is reframed as an injustice that warrants change. We construe "domain" broadly to include an almost infinite variety of aspects of life, such as dietary habits, consumption patterns, leisure activities, social relationships, social statuses, and self-perception. While each of these as well as other domains of life can be and frequently are interconnected, they can also be bracketed or perceptually bounded (Goffman, 1974: 247–300), as often occurs in the case of single-issue movements. The interpretive transformation that occurs with respect to one domain may affect behavior in other domains, but the change of frame is not automatically generalized to them.

Domain-specific transformations frequently appear to be a necessary condition for participation in movements that seek dramatic changes in the status, treatment, or activity of a category of people. Concrete examples include movements that seek to alter the status of a category of people such as women, children, the aged, handicapped, and prisoners, or that seek to change the relationship between two or more categories, as in the case of many ethnic and racial movements. In each case, a status, pattern of relationships, or a social practice is reframed as inexcusable, immoral, or unjust.

[. . .]

Support for and participation in some SMOs is thus partly contingent in the reframing of some domain-specific status, relationship, practice, or environmental feature or condition. Yet there are still other movements for which a far more sweeping transformation is frequently required in order to secure more than nominal participation.

Transformations of Global Interpretive Frames. In this final frame alignment process, the scope of change is broadened considerably as a new primary framework gains ascendance over others and comes to function as a kind of master frame that interprets events and experiences in a new key. What is involved, in essence, is a kind of thoroughgoing conversion that has been depicted as a change in one's "sense of ultimate grounding" (Heirich, 1977) that is rooted in the "displacement of one universe of discourse by another and its attendant rules and grammar for putting things together" (Snow and Machalek, 1983: 265–66). Domain-specific experiences, both past and present, that were formerly bracketed and interpreted in one or more ways are now given new meaning and rearranged, frequently in ways that previously were inconceivable, in accordance with the new master frame.

[. . .]

One of the major consequences of this more sweeping variety of frame transformation is that it reduces ambiguity and uncertainty and decreases the prospect of "misframings" or interpretive "errors" and "frame disputes" (Goffman, 1974: 301–38). In short, everything is seen with greater clarity and certainty.

[. . .]

Summary and implications

We have attempted to clarify understanding of adherent and constituent mobilization by proposing and analyzing frame alignment as a conceptual bridge that links social psychological and structural/organizational considerations on movement participation. We have pursued this task by addressing three deficiencies in research on movement participation—neglect of grievance interpretation, neglect of the processual and dynamic nature of participation, and overgeneralization of participation-related processes, and by identifying and elaborating six concrete points. First, participation in SMO activities is contingent in part on alignment of individual and SMO interpretive frames.

Second, this process can be decomposed into four related but not identical processes: frame bridging, frame amplification, frame extension, and frame transformation. Third, initial frame alignment cannot be assumed, given the existence of either grievances or SMOs. Fourth, frame alignment, once achieved, cannot be taken for granted because it is temporally variable and subject to reassessment and renegotiation. As we have noted, the reasons that prompt participation in one set of activities at one point in time may be irrelevant or insufficient to prompt subsequent participation. Fifth, frame alignment, in one form or another, is therefore a crucial aspect of adherent and constituent mobilization. And sixth, each frame alignment process requires somewhat different micromobilization tasks.

Taken together, these observations suggest several sets of questions and propositions that subsequent research ought to address. A first set of questions concerns the relationship between types of frame alignment and types of movements. Is each of the frame alignment processes identified more likely to be associated with some kinds of movements rather than others? Frame bridging, for example, appears to be the modal type of alignment associated with low demand, professional social movements that often are difficult to distinguish from conventional interest groups. Similarly, value amplification might be hypothesized as the modal type of alignment associated with two sets of movements: those that are reactive in the sense that they defend the status quo, such as many conservative movements; and those that arise among people who are segmentally organized in relation to dominant power structures [. . .] and who have constituted, as a result, long-standing subcultures of resistance and contention, such as Catholics in Northern Ireland, Palestinians in the Middle East, Rastafarians in Jamaica, the Basque in Spain, and Blacks in South Africa. In a similar vein, we suspect that frame transformation of the global variety, given its extensive scope and radical nature, is most likely to be associated with participation in movements that share two characteristics: they have "world-transforming" goals or aspirations in the sense that they seek total change of society across all institutions.

[. . .]

While each of the frame alignment processes may be operative in varying degrees at some point in the life history of most movements, what we are hypothesizing is that there is a kind of elective affinity between forms of alignment and movement goals and perspectives, such that we can speak of modal types of alignment for particular types of movements. Investigation of this hypothesized relationship becomes especially important when we consider that the differential success of participant mobilization efforts may be due in part to variation in the capacity of SMOs to skillfully effect and then sustain a particular type of alignment.

A second issue concerns the relationship between types of frame alignment and what Tarrow (1983a, 1983b) has referred to as "cycles of protest." Cycles of protest are characterized by, among other things, "the appearance of new technologies of protest" that "spread from their point of origin to other areas and to other sectors of social protest" (Tarrow, 1983a:39), thus adding to what Tilly (1978) refers to as the "repertoire" of protest activity. *But* cycles of protest do not function only as crucibles out of which new technologies of social protest are fashioned; they also generate interpretive frames that not only inspire and justify collective action, but also give meaning to and legitimate the tactics that evolve. Just as some forms of innovative collective action become part of the evolving repertoire for subsequent SMOs and protesters within the cycle, so it seems reasonable to hypothesize that some movements function early in the cycle as progenitors of master frames that provide the ideational and interpretive anchoring for subsequent movements later on in the cycle.

[. . .]

Perhaps the occurrence, intensity, and duration of protest cycles are not just a function of opportunity structures, regime responses, and the like, but are also due to the presence or absence of a potent innovative master frame and/or the differential ability of SMOs to successfully exploit and elaborate the anchoring frame to its fullest. Hypothetically, the absence of innovative master frames may account in part for the failure of mass mobilization when the structural conditions seem otherwise ripe; or a decline in movement protest activity when the structural conditions remain fertile may be partly due to the failure of SMOs to exploit and amplify the anchoring frame in imaginative and inspiring ways. In either case, latent structural potential fails to manifest itself fully.

A third set of issues implied by the foregoing considerations concerns the factors that account for variation in the relative success or failure of framing processes in mobilizing potential constituents. In arguing that one or more varieties of frame alignment is a necessary condition for movement participation, we have proceeded as if all framing efforts are successful. But clearly that is not the case. Potential constituents are sometimes galvanized and mobilized; on other occasions framing efforts fall on deaf ears and may even be counter-productive. This obdurate fact thus begs the question of why framing processes succeed in some cases but not in others. There are at least two sets of factors at work here.

One involves the content or substance of preferred framings and their degree of resonance with the current life situation and experience of the potential constituents. Does the framing suggest answers and solutions to troublesome situations and dilemmas that resonate with the way in which they are experienced? Does the framing build on and elaborate existing dilemmas and grievances in ways that are believable and compelling? Or is the framing too abstract and even contradictory? In short, is there some degree of what might be conceptualized as frame resonance? We propose that one of the key determinants of the differential success of framing efforts is variation in the degree of frame resonance, such that the higher the degree of frame resonance, the greater the probability that the framing effort will be relatively successful, all else being equal. Many framings may be plausible, but we suspect that relatively few strike a responsive chord and are thus characterized by a high degree of frame resonance. Consideration of this issue calls for closer inspection than heretofore of not only the nature of the interpretive work and resources of SMOs, but also of the degree of fit between the resultant framings or products of that work and the life situation and ideology of potential constituents.

The second set of factors that we think bears directly on the relative success or failure of framing efforts concerns the configuration of framing hazards or "vulnerabilities" (Goffman, 1974: 439–95) that confront SMOs as they go about the business of constructing and sustaining particular frame alignments. The excessive use of frame bridging techniques by SMOs, for example, may lead to an oversaturated market. Consequently, a movement may find itself vulnerable to discounting, particularly when potential adherents and conscience constituents are inundated by a barrage of similar impersonal appeals from a variety of competing SMOs.

Frame amplification, too, has its own vulnerabilities, as when a movement fails to consistently protect or uphold those core values or beliefs being highlighted. If, on the other hand, a value becomes discredited or loses its saliency, or a belief is popularly refuted, it may drag associated frames down along with it.

Similar hazards may be associated with the frame extension process. If, for instance, an SMO fails to deliver the promised auxiliary and incidental benefits, suspicion of the construction of an exploitative fabrication may arise. Moreover, the very use of such inducements that are not central to the movement's stated goals may result in the trivialization of the sincerity of its claims and objectives, and perhaps of even the movement itself. Social movement organizations and coalitions further run the risk of clouding a frame when they extend their primary frame to encompass goals and issues beyond the scope of their original platform. Adherents and conscience constituents may not embrace the extended frame as enthusiastically as they would a relatively clear, domain-specific frame. Indeed, popular support may be withdrawn following a frame extension strategy.

[. . .]

Frame transformation is not immune to its own vulnerabilities. Domain specific conversion, for example, though resistent to small changes in opinion climate, is often so narrowly based that either a sudden failure or an unexpected success may test the organization's adaptive abilities. Another risk associated with this form of frame alignment is the occasional fostering of an excessive and unbridled enthusiasm that threatens to spill over into domains extraneous to the movement's frame, thereby undermining its integrity and the movement's mode of operation. Movements involved in global transformation, on the other hand, are less likely to find such generalized enthusiasm problematic, but may find themselves devoting a greater proportion of their resources to internal frame maintenance or "ideological work" to ward off external symbolic threats in the form of ridicule or the downkeyings of "deprogrammers" and other opponents.

The foregoing observations suffice to illustrate that the frame alignment process is an uneasy one that is fraught with hazards or vulnerabilities throughout a movement's life history, and particularly at certain critical junctures, as when SMOs seek to establish coalitions or when they are attacked by countermovements. The ways in which SMOs manage and control these frame vulnerabilities, as well as interpretative resources in general, thus seem as crucial to the temporal viability and success of an SMO as the acquisition and deployment of more tangible resources, which to date have received the lion's share of attention by research informed by the resource mobilization frame.

[. . .]

One might ask, of course, what difference it makes whether we can specify empirically how and in what contexts frame alignment of one variety or another is effected. Is it not enough to know that frame alignment is produced and constituents are mobilized? The answer is *no* for several reasons. As Tilly (1978) and his associates have shown, collective actors come and go. Some show up when not anticipated. Others fail to mobilize and press their claims, even when they appear to have a kind of natural constituency. And those that do show up vary considerably in terms of how successful they are. The argument here is that the reasons why some show up and others do not, why some stay in contention longer than others, and why some achieve greater and more enduring success, have to do not only with changes in opportunities and the expansion and appropriation of societal resources, but also with whether frame alignment has been successfully effected and sustained.

References

Bem, Daryl J. 1970. *Beliefs, Attitudes, and Human Affairs*. Belmont, CA: Brooks/Cole Publishing.

Gamson, William A., Bruce Fireman, and Steven Rytina. 1982. *Encounters with Unjust Authority*. Homewood, IL: Dorsey.

Goffman, Erving. 1974. *Frame Analysis*, Cambridge: Harvard University Press.

Heirich, Max. 1977. "Change of Heart: A Test of Some Widely Held Theories about Religious Conversion." *American Journal of Sociology* 83:653–80.

Klandermans, Bert. 1984. "Mobilization and Participation: Social-Psychological Expansions of Resource Mobilization Theory." *American Sociological Review* 49:583–600.

McCarthy, John D. 1986. "Prolife and Prochoice Movement Mobilization: Infrastructure Deficits and New Technologies." In *Social Movements and Resource Mobilization in Organizational Society: Collected Essays*, edited by Mayer N. Zald and John D. McCarthy. New Brunswick, NJ: Transaction Books.

McCarthy, John D. and Mayer N. Zald. 1977. "Resource Mobilization and Social Movements: A Partial Theory." *American Journal of Sociology* 82:1212–41.

Snow, David A. and Richard Machalek. 1983. "The Convert as a Social Type." Pp. 259–89 in *Sociological Theory*, edited by Randall Collins. San Francisco: Jossey-Bass.

Snow, David A. and Richard Machalek. 1984. "The Sociology of Conversion." *Annual Review of Sociology* 10:167–80.

Tarrow, Sidney. 1983a. *Struggling to Reform: Social Movements and Policy Change During Cycles of Protest*. Ithaca, NY: Cornell University.

Tarrow, Sidney. 1983b. "Resource Mobilization and Cycles of Protest: Theoretical Reflections and Comparative Illustrations." Paper presented at the meetings of the American Sociological Association, Detroit.

Tilly, Charles. 1978. *From Mobilization to Revolution*. Reading, MA: Addison-Wesley Publishing Co.

Chapter 35

Mario Diani

THE CONCEPT OF SOCIAL MOVEMENT

Introduction

SOCIAL MOVEMENT STUDIES have grown impressively in recent years. At the same time, efforts to merge originally distant approaches into a more comprehensive one have been made. Quite surprisingly, these attempts have largely passed over any discussion of the concept of 'social movement'. While several scholars have provided analytical definitions of it, we still lack, to my knowledge, a systematic comparison of these conceptualisations. This article aims to fill this gap, discussing the concept of social movement as it has been formulated by some influential contributors to the field since the 1960s.

Focusing on the conceptual level seems important to me, for a number of reasons. I share the view that, while concepts cannot be identified with theories, they are nevertheless the cornerstone of any theorising. Therefore, any effort to synthesise different approaches risks to be flawed, if little or no attention is paid to concept definition. This holds even more true for social movements studies. There, even an implicit, 'empirical' agreement about the use of the term is largely missing. In fact, social and political phenomena as heterogeneous as revolutions, religious sects, political organisations, single-issue campaigns are all, on occasion, defined as social movements. This terminological ambiguity entails, however, a loss of specificity and theoretical clarity. This is reflected in that many valuable analyses of social movements pay hardly any attention to the concept itself. They rather move immediately to more substantive questions, such as the factors which account for mobilization processes or the difference between old and new movements. This is perfectly legitimate, of course. Yet, one may sometimes feel that the same topics might be as successfully treated without mentioning 'social movements' at all, adopting rather concepts such as 'collective action', 'social change', 'social conflict' and the like. The question therefore rises, what does 'social movements' specifically refer to.

The absence of discussion concerning the concept of social movement has been usually attributed to the heterogeneity and incompatibility of the different approaches, which would make any synthesis impossible. In contrast to this view, I argue that a common thread exists between the analyses of social movements, produced within otherwise very diverse intellectual traditions. My goal here is to highlight this linkage and to identify the elements, that are common to the different 'schools'. These elements connote social movements as a specific social dynamic which is logically related to, yet distinct from, the ones mentioned above. It consists in a process whereby several different actors, be they individuals, informal groups and/or organisations, come to elaborate, through either joint action and/or communication, a shared definition of themselves as being part of the same side in a social conflict. By doing so, they provide meaning to otherwise unconnected protest events or symbolic antagonistic practices, and make explicit the emergence of specific conflicts and issues. This dynamic is reflected in the definition of social movements as consisting in networks of informal interaction between a plurality of individuals, groups and/or organisations, engaged in a political and/or cultural conflict, on the basis of a shared collective identity.

[. . .]

A proposal for synthesis

The definitions [available] emphasise at least four aspects of social movement dynamics: a) networks of informal interaction; b) shared beliefs and solidarity; c) collective action on conflictual issues; d) action which displays largely outside the institutional sphere and the routine procedures of social life.

Networks of informal interaction

The presence of informal interactions involving individuals, groups and organisations is widely acknowledged. Even Touraine [. . .] adopts a very peculiar definition, stresses the view of social movements as collective actors where organisations, individuals and groups all play a role. Even where the emphasis is put on a 'set of opinions and beliefs' [. . .] the transformation of these ideas into action requires the interaction between specific SMOs, constituents, adherents and bystander publics. Interaction is further stressed in notions such as 'social movement sector' (SMS) or 'micro mobilisation context'.

[. . .]

Defined as any small group setting in which processes of collective attribution are combined with rudimentary forms of organisation to produce mobilisation for collective action, this concept greatly modifies the basically hierarchical conception of relationships between constituents and SMOs, proposed by the RM theorists in their earlier formulations, forming a perspective more consistent with such notions as Melucci's 'social movement area'.

The characteristics of these networks may range from the very loose and dispersed links [. . .] to the tightly clustered networks which facilitate adhesion to terrorist organizations. Such networks promote the circulation of essential resources for action (information, expertise, material resources) as well as of broader systems of meaning. Thus, networks contribute both to creating the preconditions for mobilisation (which is what RMT has mostly emphasised) and to providing the proper setting for the elaboration of specific world-views and life-styles (as described by Melucci).

In spite of their different emphasis, these definitions agree in recognising the plurality of actors involved in social movements and the informality of the ties which link them to each other. A synthetic definition of this aspect of the concept of social movements therefore may run as follows:

'A social movement is a network of informal interactions between a plurality of individuals, groups and/or organisations'.

Shared beliefs and solidarity

To be considered a social movement, an interacting collectivity requires a shared set of beliefs and a sense of belongingness. Respective authors refer to 'a set of opinions and beliefs' (McCarthy and Zald); 'solidarity' (Melucci); 'identity' (Touraine, Melucci, Tilly). [Others] emphasise the continuity of social movements, which relies upon 'group identity' and 'ideologies'. Identity and ideology are defined here in the broad sense of the term, which makes them very close to sets of beliefs.

[. . .]

Collective identity and solidarity can be considered synonymous in this context, in so far as it is hard to conceive of the former without the latter, i.e. of a sense of belongingness without sympathetic feelings, associated with the perception of a common fate to share. The case is different for the definition proposed by McCarthy and Zald. Their notion of social movements as 'sets of opinions and beliefs' does not necessarily imply the presence of shared feelings of belongingness. However, their more recent work, and in particular the emphasis on the role of 'micro-mobilization contexts' and 'frame alignment processes' testify to their growing concern for the interactive processes of symbolic mediation which support individuals' commitment.

Collective identity is both a matter of self- and external definition. Actors must define themselves as part of a broader movement and, at the same time, be perceived as such, by those within the same movement, and by opponents and/or external observers. In this sense, collective identity plays an essential role in defining the boundaries of a social movement. Only those actors, sharing the same beliefs and sense of belongingness, can be considered to be part of a social movement. However, 'collective identity' does not imply homogeneity of ideas and orientations within social movement networks. A wide spectrum of different conceptions may be present, and factional conflicts may arise at any time. Therefore, the construction and preservation of a movement's identity implies a continuous process of 'realignment' and 'negotiation' between movement actors.

The presence of shared beliefs and solidarities allows both actors and observers to assign a common meaning to specific collective events which otherwise could not be identified as part of a common process. It is through this 'framing process' that the presence of a distinct social actor becomes evident, as well as that of related issues. Indeed, social movements condition and help constitute new orientations on existing issues and also the rise of new public issues.

[. . .]

The process of identity formation cannot be separated from the process of symbolic redefinition of what is both real and possible. Moreover, such collective identity may persist even when public activities, demonstrations and the like are not taking place, thus providing for some continuity to the movement over time.

Taking these qualifications into account, we can define the second component of the concept of social movement as follows:

> 'The boundaries of a social movement network are defined by the specific collective identity shared by the actors involved in the interaction'.

Collective action on conflictual issues

Some of the views reviewed here put a specific emphasis on conflict as a core component of the concept of social movement (Touraine, Melucci, Tilly). Others emphasise that social movements define themselves with respect to processes of social change (Turner and Killian, McCarthy and Zald). Even these latter, however, acknowledge that as promoters or opponents of social change social movements become involved in conflictual relations with other actors (institutions, countermovements, etc.). If there is at least broad agreement concerning the fact that conflict is a distinctive feature of a social movement, the notion of conflict is understood in very different ways by different scholars. Touraine claims that the term 'social movements' applies only to conflicts about historicity, while others use the term in a looser and more inclusive way. Melucci considers typical of social movements only those actions which challenge the mechanism of systemic domination, while American scholars tend to subsume under that heading any protest event, including those referring to negotiable issues. Finally, some authors consider as social movements networks of collective action which are exclusively or primarily oriented towards cultural and personal change (Melucci and Turner and Killian), while others focus on actors in the political sphere (Tilly, McCarthy and Zald).

On a closer look, however, many of these inconsistencies prove to be more apparent than real. [W]hen analysing other types of conflicts than those concerning historicity, Touraine attaches different qualifications (e.g. nationalist, communitarian, cultural) to the label 'movement'. Along similar lines, Melucci differentiates between social movements which operate at the systemic level and other types of collective action. He speaks for instance of 'conflictual action', meaning a kind of behaviour which implies collective identity and the presence of a conflict, yet which does not break the limits of compatibility of the system. In other words, both Touraine and Melucci use the term 'social movement' to identify a specific category of phenomena within a broader category of 'movements', whereas other scholars use the term to mean movements of any kind.

Another presumed source of inconsistency consists in conceptions which focus on political movements and those emphasising that social movements are also, and often mainly involved in cultural conflicts. Several authors maintain that the true bulk of social movement experience has to be found in the cultural sphere: what is challenged is not only the uneven distribution of power and/or economic goods, but socially shared meanings as well, that is the ways of defining and interpreting reality. Social movements tend to focus more and more on self-transformation. Conflicts arise in areas previously considered typical of the private sphere, involving problems of self-definition and challenges to the dominant life-styles, for example. The difference with those who insist on the political side of movements like McCarthy and Zald and Tilly is undeniable. Yet, this is a difference in emphasis rather than one concerning incompatible notions of what a social movement is. Indeed, the existence of cultural movements has never been denied either by Resource Mobilization theorists nor by proponents of the 'political process' perspective.

The opportunity to include both cultural and political movements within the broader category of social movements bring us to the third component of the concept:

> 'Social movement actors are engaged in political and/or cultural conflicts, meant to promote or oppose social change either at the systemic or non-systemic level'.

Action which primarily occurs outside the institutional sphere and the routine procedures of social life

Until the early 1970s debates on social movements were dominated by structural functionalists [. . .] who put a great emphasis on the non-institutionalised nature of their behaviour. Today, social movement scholars are more cautious on this point. The aspects of 'collective effervescence' and 'nascent state' which had been emphasised [. . .] as a distinctive feature of social movements are now more closely associated with the phase of their emergence. From very different perspectives, it has been demonstrated that social movements continue even when collective effervescence is over, and that this is not immediatley followed by institutionalisation. There is actually a more complex pattern of interaction between non-institutional aspects and institutional ones, wherein social movements may either be an agent of change at the level of symbolic codes or create new opportunities for interest intermediation. Moreover, movements may also develop without going through a phase of 'collective effervescence'. In other words, collective identities may arise that are strong enough to foster sustained collective action, yet that do not imply a 'nascent state'.

If the relationship between non-institutional behaviour and social movements is not strong enough to identify the former as a fundamental component of the latter, the same holds true for the idea that social movements may be distinguished from other political actors because of their adoption of 'unusual' patterns of political behaviour. Several scholars maintain that the fundamental distinction between movements and other social political actors is to be found in the contrast between conventional styles of political participation (such as voting or lobbying political representatives) and public protest. However, while the recourse to public protest is undoubtedly a qualifying element of political movements, it plays only a marginal role in movements oriented to personal and cultural change. If one accepts, as I do, that even the latter may be subsumed under the concept of social movements, then there is no reason to introduce this specification in the definition of the concept.

Another widely shared assumption, at least in the more conventional version of the idea of social movements as 'unusual' phenomena, is that organisations involved in social movements are basically loosely structured. While informality and looseness are essential properties of the system of interaction, the same is not necessarily true for the single units of the system. Even though many loosely structured organisations are actually part, possibly the dominant one, of social movement networks, they are by no means their only component. Indeed, the spectrum of SMOs is so wide and differentiated as to prevent any clear restriction of its boundaries; a key role in social movements may be played by such heterogeneous organisations as churches [. . .]; local branches of trade unions [and] neighbourhood solidarity organisations. Moreover, the choice between a grassroots organisation or a bureaucratic lobby appears more and more frequently dependent upon tactical calculations by social movement actors. Even collective behaviour theorists agree that a proper understanding of social movements requires principles from both collective and organisational behaviour.

This discussion suggests that features such as the extra-institutional nature of social movements, the prevalence of violent or disruptive political protest and the loose structure of social movement organisations cannot really be taken as fundamental characteristics of a social movement. These may however be extremely useful in differentiating between types of movements, or between different phases in the life of a specific movement. Thus, the following synthetic definition of the concept of social movement can be put forward:

'A social movement is a network of informal interactions between a plurality of individuals, groups and/or organisations, engaged in a political or cultural conflict, on the basis of a shared collective identity'.

[. . .]

Conclusions

I would argue that this definition of social movements may constitute the bulk of a programme of research and theorising that adopt 'social movements' as an analytical, rather than a merely evocative, concept. It may also contribute to the integration of different theoretical perspectives. During the 1970s, the resurgence of scholarly interest for social movements had focused either on the structural determinants of new conflicts (mostly in Europe) or on mobilisation processes (mostly in the USA). Emphasising the interplay between networks, identity and conflicts challenges some conventional wisdom inherited from these traditions. On the one hand, it challenges the idea that the study of social movements may be equated to the study of new social conflicts. While there is an obvious strong correlation between movements and conflicts, the concept proposed here accepts that, in principle, conflicts can arise even in the absence of social movements. How single, isolated conflicts may become a movement is a central matter for investigation. To this purpose, attention must necessarily be paid to social networks and processes of meaning construction. On the other hand, stressing the importance of social networks prevents one from confusing the analysis of 'social movements' with the analysis of 'social movement organisations' or 'mobilisation processes'. This also bears substantial implications in terms of research strategy.

[. . .]

I do not pretend that the view proposed here is absolutely original. I would rather argue that it reflects — and partially expands on — recent efforts towards theoretical integration in the field.

Chapter 36

Ron Eyerman and Andrew Jamison

SOCIAL MOVEMENTS: A COGNITIVE APPROACH

B y studying social movements as cognitive praxis we mean that they are producers of knowledge and that knowledge creation itself should be seen as a collective process. The dimensions of cognitive praxis have come to take on a number of different meanings as we have worked with them in our studies of environmentalism.

[. . .]

It was Max Scheler who most ambitiously defined a program for the sociology of knowledge in the early 1920s (Scheler 1980). He said that the sociology of knowledge had been limited up to then by confining attention to certain more established forms of knowledge. If ways of knowing were to be compared across cultures, however, it was necessary to broaden the framework and to include not just organized or institutionalized knowledge, but also moral, religious, metaphysical, even mystical types of knowledge under the purview of the sociology of knowledge. This insight, and the program accompanying it, were largely lost to sociologists of knowledge as most of them have come to confine their interest to one type, usually one or another established scientific field. As the sociology of knowledge has been transformed into a sociology of science, on the one hand, and a sociology of social thought on the other, the broader ambitions that Scheler articulated have faded, only to be rediscovered by anthropologists seeking to explain differences in cultural worldviews and belief systems.

Our cognitive approach is rooted in this rediscovery, and attempts to grasp both formalized and informal modes of knowledge production within social movements. We want to argue that social movements are actually constituted by the cognitive praxis that is entailed in the articulation of their historical projects. The actual types of knowledge that a social movement articulates or is interested in obviously varies from movement to movement. Thus, while environmental movements tend toward the more formalized natural and technical sciences, and have contributed to both theoretical and empirical fields in ecology and technology, the cognitive praxis of the American civil rights movement was almost entirely informal, what Scheler would have called religious, moral, and spiritual. Civil rights activists articulated moral principles and spirituality. Their cognitive praxis was thus rooted in a vastly different intellectual space and tradition than that of environmentalism.

[. . .]

Cognitive praxis is the most basic of our concepts. It provides what we have called in our earlier work the core identity of a social movement. It is a kind of deep structure that allows us to draw certain boundaries around a movement as it develops over time, as well as to evaluate the current status and potential of actual movements.

There is something fundamental missing from the sociology of social movements, something that falls between the categories of the various schools and is left out of their various conceptualizations. That something is what we mean by cognitive praxis. It is not that sociologists of social movements are not aware of a certain cognitive dimension in the activities of the movements they study, but it is something that they are unable to theorize in that it remains marginal to their main concerns. As it is for most social movement activists themselves, the cognitive interests and activities of the movements being studied by sociologists are largely taken for granted. They are the unreflected assumptions of analysis rather than the objects of investigation.

The problem begins in the very act of defining a social movement. For the particularists and for most resource mobilization sociologists, a social movement is defined empirically. Indeed it is seldom defined at all, but rather it is studied as an empirical phenomenon. For the particularists, a movement is seen from the vantage point of the actor and thus definition is made by those being studied: self-definition. For the resource mobilization school of thought, a movement is defined in operational terms: organizations are distinguished from sectors, or industries, and the movement dissolves into the particular mechanisms of mobilization and recruitment that are being analyzed.

[. . .]

Much of the recent sociolological discussion about social movements has been concerned with the relationship between the new and the old movements of the nineteenth century. Some contend that the new movements are to be distinguished from the old because of their specificity, and even more for their classlessness. This means that the new social movements of our time are not so much struggling for power as for autonomy, not seeking political results as much as "cultural" or sociocultural change. There is, many claim, a fundamental difference between the new social movements with their partial goals and the old social movements of the working class.

An opposing school of thought seeks to understand the new movements in terms of the old, either in class terms or in terms of some kind of cyclical theory of history. The new social movements are thereby seen as signalling the emergence of new class actors – a professional class, a middle class, a managerial class, or a combination thereof.

Environmental activism has been depicted by many sociologists and by many representatives of the "old" social movements as a kind of middle-class activism, as have many forms of feminism and peace activism. The point here is not that the new social movements are similar to the old; rather, the new movements are seen as antagonistic to the old, the implicit or explicit class enemies of the working class. Of course, the more sophisticated analysts look for points of possible alliance or convergence between the new and the old, but most class-oriented analyses tend to downplay the historical importance of the new movements, since they do not represent a class that has become embroiled in what Alain Touraine calls the "struggle for historicity" (Touraine 1981).

The cyclical explanations draw a somewhat different set of distinctions between the old and the new social movements. In this perspective, social movements are seen as being linked to particular historical cycles: business cycles, generational cycles, "long waves" of economic development, etc. Movements are themselves seen as cyclical, having their own lifecycles and their own internal dynamics, related to, but not necessarily identical with, the larger historical cycles of the political or economic spheres. The new movements are thus similar to the old in that they are both responses to "crisis" or critical, declining conjunctures in a business or political cycle. The movements of our time and the movements of the nineteenth century can be seen as fundamentally similar kinds of social phenomena, that is, responses to crisis.

From there, the various explanations differ as to just what social movements stand for. Most functionalists see movements as symptoms of crisis, or of systemic disfunction, which fade away as the crisis is resolved. Others see movements as initiators of change, by identifying problems that need to be dealt with and even taking part in the problem solution process. For our purposes, cyclical theories are important for indicating continuities between the new social movements and the old ones of the nineteenth century. What is crucial is that social movements are seen as processes, and not as things-in-themselves, as historical moments rather than ahistorical organizations. It is in that spirit that we want to examine some of the cognitive similarities between the old and the new social movements.

[. . .]

Let us return to our own research on environmental movements. Our original intention had been to study environmentalism on its own, and compare organizational conglomerations in three countries. But as the study developed, we realized that a common historical framework was essential if we were to compare developments in three countries. This is not the place to present that scheme, which we have described in detail elsewhere; the point to be made here is that in making a historical scheme we found it impossible to separate environmentalism from other new social movements or from its roots in the 1960s. Reading social movements historically means also identifying their relations to other movements.

Environmentalism was a product of the 1960s. For developing countries, the situation is more complicated, as environmentalism was also a product of "knowledge transfer," that is an import from the West as well as something homegrown. For industrialized countries, however, environmentalism was one of the unintended results of the 1960s, even though its development into a social movement differed from country to country.

What all industrial countries seem to have gone through is a period of revolt in the 1960s. It was primarily a student movement, and the main focus was on the war in Vietnam, although the "imagination" of the new left [. . .] was certainly more all-encompassing. The new left had its roots in the enormous expansion of the tertiary sector, and within it the system of higher education, in the two decades following the end of the Second World War. The postwar techno-economic paradigm was excessively science-based; this was the age of Big Science, epitomized by nuclear energy, industrial automation, and petrochemical products. And the science-based firms required highly skilled workers with college education. Universities were thus transformed into teaching factories, and the knowledge that was transmitted and produced was itself transformed into marketable commodities. As a capsule characterization, the student movement of the 1960s can be seen as an international revolt against these developments, a massive cry of outrage against the modern scientific-technological state.

The student movement was first and foremost a defense of freedom: freedom of speech, freedom of research, freedom of expression, freedom of personal career choice. It was a "great refusal" to participate in the use of science and technology – and all knowledge – in the corporate system, and, more precisely, in the "military-industrial complex" (Marcuse 1969). The movement experimented with new forms of relevant education, inventing the teach-in, the counter course, the free school, the concerned professional academic. The student movement practiced its cognition more than articulating it; it was in what we would call its organizational dimension that the student movement defined its movement place. In the 1960s, the new processes of social learning that have become so central to the new social movements first emerged. The affinity group, the national network, the underground of alternative media, and the creative use of electronic media are all products of the student movement.

In our terms, the 1960s represented the first phase of the new social movements, a period of awakening after the big sleep of postwar prosperity. Out of apathy arose a new generation of social actors, who created a new movement; more than anything else, the 1960s stood for a recognition of direct democracy. Students organized themselves for a "democratic society" in the US and Germany, and their actions sought to rediscover what democratic behavior was all about. Industrial society had become in the eyes of many students a bureaucratic, mass society without ideology or any coherent value system. Like the beat generation before them, the students sought escape, color, adventure; but they also sought meaning and expressed solidarity with their own racially oppressed countrymen and peoples of the third world. Out of apathy arose a generation that took to the streets in the name of a vague, all-encompassing liberation. In the words of Todd Gitlin, the movement in the US was a "fusion of collective will and moral style. The movement didn't simply demand, it did. By taking action, not just a position, it affirmed the right to do so; by refusing to defer, it deprived the authorities of authority itself" (Gitlin 1980: 84).

The cosmology of the student movements was given many names, from self-management to people's power to direct action, but what all had in common was a general quest for "liberation" and a general opposition to what Herbert Marcuse in 1964 called "one-dimensional thought." What eventually came to be called the new left stood, like the "old" left before it, for opposition to forces of reaction, but its leftism was new in the sense that it embodied new tactics, new models of social organization, and new sources of inspiration. Particularly important was the influence of the existential philosophy of Camus and Sartre, the humanist psychology of Fromm and Laing, and the third world prophets – Che Guevara, Mao Tse-tung, Franz Fanon, Ho Chi Minh. The student movement translated these influences, and many others, into a kind of liberation cosmology, articulated not so much in any one theory as in massive displays of collective ceremony, from the cultural revolution in China to the Woodstock rock festival in the US. Political and cultural at the same time, the student movement of the 1960s rapidly fragmented into a number of separate movements; in our terms, the student movement of the 1960s was not a social movement in its own right, but was rather a phase in a period of social movement.

Environmental problems were one of the concerns of the 1960s movement, but while the war in Vietnam continued, environmental protest was of secondary importance. Already in the early 1960s, in *Our Synthetic Environment*, Murray Bookchin had combined an ecological critique with a social one, and many antiwar teach-ins included lectures on the ecological damage caused by the American military in Vietnam. But environmentalism, like feminism, remained secondary, even marginal, increasingly dubious to the leaders of the student movement as they grew increasingly infatuated with Marxism and Leninist strategies. By the time the first Earth Day was held in 1970 and new environmental protest groups started to establish themselves throughout the industrialized countries, the student movement had split apart into the range of issue-specific new social movements that still form such a conspicuous part of our collective political culture.

For us, environmentalism and feminism represent a specialization of the all-encompassing new left, a part of a niche-seeking strategy that has continued to characterize the new social movements. The ecological cosmology was one of a number of "limited" liberation cosmologies; and together with feminism epitomized the second, more constructive, phase of social movement which, depending on the country, lasted from the late 1960s on through the 1970s. The new social movements provided specification, a kind of specialization to the rather overextended cosmological ambitions of the 1960s.

Both feminism and environmentalism are inconceivable without the student movement of the 1960s. Their reconceptualizations of nature and gender, and of social relations more generally, were impossible without the articulation of a more fundamental belief in liberation. The 1960s opened the space for the later movements to fill with specific meanings. It provided a number of organizational innovations as well, from the rural commune to the massive demonstration, the rock festival to the encounter group. These were, of course, developed further in the later phases of social movement, but they were created in the 1960s as political phenomena.

From our perspective, distinguishing new social movements from each other is rather arbitrary. They are, in many respects, component parts of the same social movement, a period of historical creation that emerged in the 1960s and that had by the end of the 1980s, largely been incorporated into established politics, in the guise of green parties, mainstream public interest organizations, women's studies departments, environmental bureaucracies, etc. Like the old social movements of the nineteenth century, the movement space that was, for a time, so vital and experimental, has come to be occupied by other social forces, and the cognitive praxis of the new social movements has been "transferred" into more established forums: the mass media, the academy, the marketplace, and, of course, the various national and international agencies that have been established or reformed in response to the concerns of the movements. It is not necessary to bemoan the demise of the movement in order to accept its historical significance; indeed, it would be our contention that it is only by seeing the movement historically and dynamically – and by accepting its passing as a social movement – that its real achievements can be appreciated. The movement, in a sense, has come and gone, and it ain't left nothing unaffected.

Our purpose [. . .] has been to develop the concept of cognitive praxis through exemplification. We have focused on the dimensions of cognitive praxis, rather than the individual articulators of that praxis, the movement intellectuals. [I]t might be useful to pause and point to what we have learned thus far: what has the identification of cognitive praxis told us about social processes of knowledge production?

On the one hand, we have shown the active role that social movements play in translating scientific ideas into social and political beliefs. In the nineteenth century, as well as in the recent past, social movements have provided an audience for new scientific paradigms, but even more so, a politicizing dialogue partner for scientists presenting new ideas about nature and society. New concepts have been popularized by social movements and they have been given new, more human, meanings and connotations. The ideas of evolution and of ecology, as well as the very concepts of sociology and economics, have found in social movements a space to develop, to grow, to take on new, more substantial meaning.

Secondly, our approach has pointed to the historical function of social movements as social laboratories. Again in the nineteenth century as well as in the recent past, social movements have experimented with new ways of producing knowledge, new organizational forms and principles. Experimentation in this regard is also a kind of translation process; social movements have transferred activities that have been applied to natural processes, to social or societal processes. Cooperative research, alternative technology, participatory policy-making, technology assessment, have all grown out of the cognitive praxis of social movements.

Third, social movements have provided societal, or cultural, critiques of dominant techno-economic paradigms, and in their critiques new paradigms have found sources of inspiration. The critique of mechanization, like the contemporary critique of reductionism and mass production, have made it possible for the radical innovators to formulate their radical new ideas. Obviously, we have only scratched the surface of what is a crucially important mechanism of social and economic transformation, but its contours are at least clear: out of critique grows renovation. The process is not perhaps as direct or systematic as might be hoped, but history does not seem to work very systematically. Indeed, our attempt to make social movements visible by identifying the dimensions of their cognitive praxis might make some small contribution to a "systematization" of technological change, but then the policy makers and the technocrats would have to leave their comfortable habitat and enter into the messy world of social movement.

References

Gitlin, T. (1980), *The Whole World is Watching: Mass Media in the Making and Unmaking of the New Left*, Berkeley: University of California Press.

Marcuse, H. (1969), *An Essay on Liberation*, Boston: Beacon.

Scheler, M. (1980), *Problems of a Sociology of Knowledge*, London: Routledge and Kegan Paul.

Touraine, A. (1981), *The Voice and the Eye: An Analysis of Social Movements*, Cambridge: Cambridge University Press.

Chapter 37

Doug McAdam, John D. McCarthy, and Mayer N. Zald

COMPARATIVE PERSPECTIVES ON SOCIAL MOVEMENTS

INCREASINGLY ONE FINDS movement scholars from various countries and nominally representing different theoretical traditions emphasizing the importance of the same three broad sets of factors in analyzing the emergence and development of social movements/revolutions. These three factors are (1) the structure of political opportunities and constraints confronting the movement; (2) the forms of organization (informal as well as formal), available to insurgents; and (3) the collective processes of interpretation, attribution, and social construction that mediate between opportunity and action. Or perhaps it will be easier to refer to these three factors by the conventional shorthand designations of *political opportunities*, *mobilizing structures*, and *framing processes*.

The emerging consensus among movement scholars regarding the importance of these three factors belies the very different and oftentimes antagonistic perspectives in which they developed. We begin by discussing each factor separately, with an eye to acknowledging the divergent intellectual streams that have influenced work on each.

Political opportunities

While it is now common for movement scholars to assert the importance of the broader political system in structuring the opportunities for collective action and the extent and form of same, the theoretical influences underpinning the insight are actually fairly recent. In the United States it was the work of *political process* theorists that firmly established the link between institutionalized politics and social movements/revolutions. Drawing on this work, a number of European scholars schooled in the *new social movements* tradition brought a comparative dimension to the study of *political opportunity structures.*

[. . .]

Though the work of all of these scholars betrays a common focus on the interaction of movement and institutionalized politics, this shared focus has nonetheless been motivated by a desire to answer two different research questions. Most of the early work by American scholars sought to explain the *emergence* of a particular social movement on the basis of *changes in the institutional structure or informal power relations of a given national political system.* More recently, European scholars have sought to account for *cross-national differences in the structure, extent, and success of comparable movements* on the basis of *differences in the political characteristics of the nation states in which they are embedded.* The first approach has tended to produce detailed historical case studies of single movements or protest cycles, while the second has inspired more cross-national research based on contemporaneous descriptions of the same movement in a number of different national contexts. In both cases, however, the researcher is guided by the same underlying conviction: that social movements and revolutions are shaped by the broader set of political constraints and opportunities unique to the national context in which they are embedded.

Mobilizing structures

If institutionalized political systems shape the prospects for collective action and the forms movements take, their influence is not independent of the various kinds of *mobilizing structures* through which groups seek to organize. By mobilizing structures we mean *those collective vehicles, informal as well as formal, through which people mobilize and engage in collective action.* This focus on the meso-level groups, organizations, and informal networks that comprise the collective building blocks of social movements and revolutions constitutes the second conceptual element in our synthesis of recent work in the field.

As was the case with the work on political opportunities, the recent spate of research and theorizing on the organizational dynamics of collective action has drawn its inspiration largely from two distinct theoretical perspectives. The most important of these has been resource mobilization theory. As formulated by its initial proponents, resource mobilization sought to break with grievance-based conceptions of social movements and to focus instead on *mobilization processes* and the formal organizational manifestations of these processes.

[. . .]

The second theoretical tradition to encourage work on the organizational dynamics of collective action has been the political process model. Indeed, one of the characteristics by which scholars in this tradition are known is their common dissent from the resource mobilization equation of social movements with formal organization.

[. . .]

While some proponents of these approaches initially treated the two models of movement organization as mutually exclusive, over time the profusion of empirical work inspired by both has led to a growing awareness among movement scholars of the diversity of collective settings in which movements develop and organizational forms to which they give rise. So instead of debating the relative merits of these "opposing" characterizations, movement scholars have increasingly turned their attention to other research agendas concerning the organizational dynamics of social movements. Among the more interesting of these agendas are (1) comparison of the "organizational infrastructures" of countries both to understand historic patterns of mobilization better and to predict where future movements are likely to arise, (2) specification of the relationship between organizational form and type of movement, and (3) assessment of the effect of both state structures and national "organizational cultures" on the form that movements take in a given country.

Framing processes

If the combination of political opportunities and mobilizing structures affords groups a certain structural potential for action, they remain, in the absence of one other factor, insufficient to account for collective action. Mediating between opportunity, organization, and action are the shared meanings and definitions that people bring to their situation. At a minimum people need to feel both aggrieved about some aspect of their lives and optimistic that, acting collectively, they can redress the problem. Lacking either one or both of these perceptions, it is highly unlikely that people will mobilize even when afforded the opportunity to do so. Conditioning the presence or absence of these perceptions is that complex of social psychological dynamics – collective attribution, social construction – that [. . .] have [been] referred to as *framing processes*. Indeed, not only did Snow et al. coin, or more accurately, modify and apply Erving Goffman's term, to the study of social movements, but in doing so helped to crystallize and articulate a growing discontent among movement scholars over how little significance proponents of the resource mobilization perspective attached to ideas and sentiments. In reasserting their importance, Snow and his colleagues drew not only on Goffman's work, but ironically on the collective behavior tradition which resource mobilization had sought to supplant as the dominant paradigm in the field.

[. . .]

But Snow was not alone in asserting the importance of the more cognitive, or ideational dimensions of collective action. Two other streams of recent work have also called for further attention to the role of ideas or culture more generally in the emergence and development of social movements and revolutions. For many of the new social movement scholars it was the centrality of their cultural elements that marked the new social movements as discontinuous with the past. Small wonder then that the work of many of the most influential new social movements theorists focused primarily on the sources and functions of meaning and identity within social movements.

[. . .]

In undertaking this volume, we were guided by four aims. First, we wanted to abstract from the voluminous literature on social movements those three concepts that have emerged as the central analytic foci of most scholarship in the area. Second, by taking their theoretical measure we hoped to refine and sharpen our understanding of each of these concepts.

[. . .]

The third goal is to advance our understanding of the dynamic *relations* among opportunities, mobilizing structures, and framing processes. Whereas most scholarship has focused on one or another of these factors, we use this volume to sketch a broader analytic framework on social movements/revolutions that combines the insights gained from the study of all three factors. Finally, we wanted to explore the comparative uses of this emerging framework by discussing the concepts of political opportunities, mobilizing structures, and framing processes in cross-national perspective.

[. . .]

Linking opportunities, mobilizing structures, and framing processes

[. . .]

The problem is there exist many relationships between our three factors. Which ones become relevant depends upon the research question of interest. We emphasize two such questions here. The first concerns the origins of social movements and revolutions; the second, the extent and form of the movement over time. In each case we are interested in understanding the factors and processes that shape the movement: its emergence on the one hand, and its ongoing development on the other.

The question of movement emergence

Understanding the mix of factors that give rise to a movement is the oldest, and arguably the most important, question in the field. Moreover, virtually all "theories" in the field are, first and foremost, theories of movement emergence. That includes the various perspectives touched on earlier. Proponents of collective behavior see strain, variably conceived, and the shared ideas it gives rise to, as the root cause of social movements. Though there is great diversity among those working in the new social movements tradition, most proponents of the perspective betray adherence to at least a broadly similar account of the movement emergence. That account highlights the role of the distinctive material and ideological contradictions in postmaterial society in helping to mobilize new political constituencies around either nonmaterial or previously private issues. Resource-mobilization theorists focus on the critical role of resources and formal organization in the rise of movements. The political process model stresses the crucial importance of expanding political opportunities as the ultimate spur to collective action.

In our view all of these theories have something to recommend them. [. . .] We share with proponents of the political process perspective the conviction that most political movements and revolutions are set in motion by social changes that render the established political order more vulnerable or receptive to challenge. But these "political opportunities" are but a necessary prerequisite to action. In the absence of sufficient organization – whether formal or informal – such opportunities are not likely to be seized. Finally, mediating between the structural requirements of opportunity and organization are the emergent meanings and definitions – or frames – shared by the adherents of the burgeoning movement. As both collective behavior and new social movements theorists have long argued, the impetus to action is as much a cultural construction as it is a function of structural vulnerability.

Having stressed the significance of all three of our factors, it is important to add that their effects are interactive rather than independent. No matter how momentous a change appears in retrospect, it only becomes an "opportunity" when defined as such by a *group* of actors sufficiently well organized to act on this shared definition of the situation. Implicit in this description of the beginnings of collective action are two critically important interactive relationships. The first concerns the relationship between framing processes and the kinds of "objective" political changes thought to facilitate movement emergence. The point is, such changes encourage mobilization not only through the "objective" effects they have on power relations, but by setting in motion framing processes that further undermine the legitimacy of the system or its perceived mutability.

[. . .]

Expanding political opportunities, then, derive their causal force from the interaction of those structural and perceptual changes they set in motion.

A similar reciprocal dynamic defines the relationship between organization and framing processes. Framing processes clearly encourage mobilization, as people seek to organize and act on their growing awareness of the system's illegitimacy and vulnerability. At the same time, the potential for the kind of system critical framing processes [. . .] is, we believe, conditioned by the population's access to various mobilizing structures.

[. . .]

Besides defining the broad parameters of a model of movement emergence, our three factors can also be used to shed light on a second question concerning the beginnings of collective action. This is the critically important, yet woefully neglected, question of movement form. That is, under what conditions can we expect a given type of movement (e.g., grassroots reform movement, public interest lobby, revolution) to emerge? The important implication of the question is that the various types of movements are simply different forms of collective action rather than qualitatively different phenomena requiring distinct explanatory theories. This is most germane to the study of revolutions, a form of collective action that has, in recent years, come to be studied as a phenomenon distinct from other categories of movements. We demur. Rather than assuming difference, we need to treat movement type as a variable and seek to account for variation in type on the basis of particular combinations of opportunities, mobilizing structures, and collective action frames.

[. . .]

Thus, type of opportunity may dictate the broad category of movement, but the formal and ideological properties of the movement are apt to be more directly influenced by the organizational forms and ideological templates available to insurgents. And these, in turn, are largely a product of the mobilizing structures in which insurgents are embedded on the eve of the movement.

The question of movement development and outcomes

Having used our three factors to analyze the timing and form of movement emergence, we turn our attention to the later stages of collective action. What can a perspective stressing the role of opportunities, mobilizing structures, and framing processes tell us about the dynamics of movement development? A great deal, we think. Indeed, we see a lot of continuity between the processes shaping movement emergence and those influencing the ongoing development and eventual decline of collective action. The similarities and differences between these two phases of collective action should become clearer as we discuss each of the three factors.

Political opportunities. Little needs to be added to our earlier discussion of this factor. Suffice it to say, the broad political environment in which the movement is embedded will continue to constitute a powerful set of constraints/opportunities affecting the latter's development. So, for example, cross-national differences in the more stable, institutional features of political systems should have significant effects on the trajectories of particular movements.

[. . .]

Besides helping to account for cross-national differences in the development of comparable movements, a focus on *changes* in the structure of political opportunities can contribute to our understanding of the shifting fortunes of a single movement.

[. . .]

So the structure of political opportunities, as defined by both the enduring and volatile features of a given political system, can be expected to continue to play a major role in shaping the ongoing fortunes of the movement. What is different from the emergent phase is the fact that, after the onset of protest activity, the broader set of environmental opportunities and constraints are no longer independent of the actions of movement groups. The structure of political opportunities is now more a product of the interaction of the movement with its environment than a simple reflection of changes occurring elsewhere. Thus to understand fully the impact of the environment on the developing movement we will need to look much more closely at the movement itself and specifically those of its features which appear to account for much of its capacity to reshape the broader political landscape.

The organizational structure of the movement

The relevant organizational question in regard to movement emergence is whether insurgents have available to them "mobilizing structures" of sufficient strength to get the movement off the ground. However, once collective action is underway, the nature of the organizational challenge confronting the movement changes significantly. It is no longer the simple availability of mobilizing structures, but the organizational profile of those groups purporting to represent the movement that becomes important. The nature of these groups is apt to change a great deal as well. While movements often develop within established institutions or informal associational networks, it is rare that they remain embedded in these *nonmovement* settings. For the movement to survive, insurgents must be able to create a more enduring organizational structure to sustain collective action. Efforts to do so usually entail the creation of the kinds of formal social movement organizations (SMOs) stressed as important by resource-mobilization theorists. Following the emergent phase of the movement, then, it is these SMOs and their efforts to shape the broader political environment which influence the overall pace and outcome of the struggle.

[. . .]

Framing processes

As with political opportunities, framing processes remain just as important to the fate of the ongoing movement as they were in shaping the emergence of collective action. Movements are no less dependent on the shared understandings of their adherents during the later stages of insurgency than they were early on. The difference is that, in the mature movement, framing processes are far more likely (1) to be shaped by conscious, strategic decisions on the part of SMOs, and (2) to be the subject of intense contestation between collective actors representing the movement, the state, and any existing countermovements. We take up each of these issues in turn.

Framing is no less a collective process during the early days of the movement than it is later on. But the collective settings within which framing takes place and the nature of the framing process are apt to be very different at the two points in time. We can expect the initial framing processes to be less consciously strategic than later efforts. In fact, at the outset, participants may not even be fully aware that they are engaged in an interpretive process of any real significance. This is certainly not the case later on as various factions and figures within the movement struggle endlessly to determine the most compelling and effective way to bring the movement's "message" to the "people."

In the absence of such a strong strategic self-consciousness, the initial framing process also has a more emergent, inchoate quality to it than do later framing efforts. Accordingly, the outcome of the process is less predictable than it is later on, when insurgents are typically acting to reaffirm or, at most, extend an existing ideological consensus. That is, later framing efforts tend to be heavily constrained by the ideas, collective identities, and worldviews adopted previously.

Finally, and most important, later framing processes tend, far more than the earlier efforts, to be the exclusive "property" of formal SMOs. Established organizations or institutions may serve as the *settings* within which initial framings get fashioned, but typically they are not produced by the recognized leadership as a part of normal organizational procedures. This tends to change during the later periods of movement development. So just as the structure of political opportunities comes, in part, to be responsive to SMO actions, so do later framing efforts come to be the product of formal organizational processes.

Besides these changes in the *internal* character of movement framing processes, the broader *environmental* context in which framing takes place differs dramatically between the early and later stages of collective action. While the political establishment is apt to be either unaware or amused and unconcerned by initial framing efforts, their reaction is expected to change if and when the movement is able to establish itself as a serious force for social change. Assuming this happens, later framing efforts can be expected to devolve into intense "framing contests" between actors representing the movement, the state, and any countermovements that may have developed. To complicate matters further, these contests will not be waged directly but, rather, will be filtered through various news media. Thus the outcome of later framing efforts will turn, not only on the substantive merits of the competing frames, but on the independence, procedures, and sympathies of the media.

Using the perspective comparatively

Unlike earlier theoretical approaches to the study of social movements, the perspective outlined has emerged out of a sustained dialogue between scholars working in a wide variety of national contexts. As a result the perspective has always had an implicit comparative focus. However, we aim to make this implicit focus more explicit. To do so we will again take up each of our three central concepts, suggesting how each can be used to illuminate cross-national differences and similarities in movement dynamics.

Political opportunities

As was noted earlier, most research on political opportunities has sought to show how *changes* in some aspect of a political system created new possibilities for collective action by a given challenger or set of challengers. Thus, the concept has typically been employed in case study fashion to help explain the emergence of a particular movement or "cycle of protest." Recently, however, the concept has informed a very different, and explicitly comparative, research agenda. Instead of focusing on the role of expanding political opportunities in facilitating the emergence of a single movement, scholars have begun to compare movements cross-nationally, seeking to explain variation in their size, form of organization, and degree of success by reference to cross-national differences in the formal structures of political power.

[. . .]

Mobilizing structures

A similar comparative turn can be discerned in recent work by movement scholars on the origins and effects of various mobilizing structures.

[. . .]

The variety of these efforts suggests the rich potential for comparative work in this area. [R]esearchers have sought to understand cross-national variation in (1) the likely institutional locations of mobilization, (2) the role of the political system in structuring the organizational profile of the movement, and (3) the effect of the organizational structure in facilitating or constraining movement survival.

Framing processes

Reflecting the recency of the framing concept and the somewhat underdeveloped nature of theory in this area, it is perhaps not surprising that our third concept has yet to yield much in the way of comparative research. We are convinced, however, that the potential for such research is as great with this concept as with the other two.

In the essay introducing the section on framing processes, we seek to refine our conceptual understanding of the concept by distinguishing between five related, but clearly distinct, topics. These are (1) the *cultural tool kits* available to would-be insurgents; (2) the *strategic framing efforts* of movement groups; (3) the *frame contests* between the movement and other collective actors – principally the state, and countermovement groups; (4) the *structure and role of the media* in mediating such contests; and (5) the *cultural impact* of the movement in modifying the available tool kit.

Besides sharpening our understanding of the basic framing concept, the preceding list is useful for the clear comparative lines of research it suggests. Indeed, all five topics lend themselves easily to cross-national research on framing dynamics. For example, as regards the first topic, one could imagine a comparative mapping of ideas and attitudes.

[. . .]

That is, instead of comparing countries in terms of their "infrastructural deficits and assets," one could seek to discern which ideational themes were especially resonant in which national contexts.

Our second topic suggests a narrower research agenda focusing on the similarities and differences in the framing strategies employed by movement groups in specified countries. Or by seeking to include as objects of study the framing efforts of the state and countermovement groups as well as the movement the researcher could well expand the empirical focus to address our third topic as well.

[. . .]

Our fourth topic, the role of the media in shaping public and policymaker perception of the movement, would make for an interesting and important comparative study. To better understand the role of the media in movement dynamics one could study cross-national variation in media characteristics – for example, degree of autonomy from the state, operating procedures, editorial orientation, and so forth – and seek to link these differences to variation in movement outcomes.

[. . .]

Finally, one could also make our fifth topic the object of systematic comparative research. The goal would be to assess the extent to which a given movement has managed, in a number of countries, to reshape the terms of public discourse. So, for example, one could imagine a comparative study of "the feminization of public discourse," designed to gauge the ideational impact of the women's movement in all Western industrial democracies. Or to take a much debated historical case, one could seek to determine whether "American exceptionalism" in its relative lack of class consciousness was as much the effect as the cause of a weak labor movement. That is, by assessing the shifting ideational content of public discourse throughout the West one might be able to determine whether America was always "exceptional" in its antagonism to labor, or whether class movements in other countries went more successful in encoding labor's interests into public discourse.

Conclusion

Reflecting the ambitious aims of this book, we have covered a lot of ground in this introductory essay. Specifically, we have tried to do four things here. First, we sought to sketch a broad analytic perspective on social movement that we see as having emerged among movement scholars over the past decade or so. This perspective stresses the determinant and interactive effect of *political opportunities, mobilizing structures*, and *framing processes* on movement dynamics. Second, we tried to identify the various intellectual influences that have contributed to our understanding of each of these three concepts. Third, we sought to infuse the perspective with a sense of dynamism by addressing two questions of long-standing interest to movement scholars and identifying the *relationships* between our three factors that we see as especially critical in shaping (1) the emergence or (2) the development or decline of collective action. Finally, we sketched what we see as the inherent comparative nature and empirical promise of the perspective.

It should be obvious how seriously we take the comparative agenda. Much of the richness of the perspective sketched here is owed to the cross-national discourse that informs it. This book is an attempt not only to synthesize the fruits of that discourse but to encourage and contribute to it as well. For only by abandoning the limits of the nationally specific case study approach to the study of social movements can we ever hope to advance our understanding of collective action.

Chapter 38

Craig Calhoun

PUTTING EMOTIONS IN THEIR PLACE

THERE SEEMS LITTLE DOUBT about the importance of emotions to movement participation and to the shaping of collective action and specific events. Alas, there is equally little doubt about the minimal place accorded emotions in the leading theories within the field. Emotions were banished from the study of social movements, to a very large extent, in reaction against a tradition of collective behavior analysis that ran from Le Bon through Turner and Killian and Neil Smelser. This older tradition approached collective behavior mainly from the outside, as something that irrational others engaged in. When attention turned to movements (not merely episodes) and to struggles with which analysts had sympathy (and in which they might engage themselves), the perspective changed. The argument that we should think in terms of collective action (not just behavior) marked that shift of perspective, opening up an internal analysis of something that "people like us" might do. It was seen as rational in the sense of reasonable, self-aware product of choice as well as (more narrowly) strategic, interest-based, calculated in terms of efficient means to an end. The new framing of the problem also suggested a redefinition of the range of appropriate objects of study. Under the label "collective action," social scientists grouped protests together with trade struggles, the insurgencies of labor together with the attempts of capitalists to control prices. Even more, the study of social movements—enduring, concerted action, often carefully planned and supported by substantial formal organization—encouraged an opposition to explanations of specific events of collective behavior as explicable by socio-psychological processes. With the bathwater of some very serious biases, the baby of emotions was commonly thrown out. It is hard to get emotions back into the field partly because they were not merely neutrally absent from it but expelled in an intellectual rebellion that helped to give the field its definition.

At the same time, I would like us to recall how old an issue in social science we are addressing. Certainly, as I suggested above, we cannot understand this issue [. . .] without seeing how it builds on problematic foundations, such as mind/body dualism. Already basic for Plato, this dualism takes a distinctively influential form in Epictetus's teachings that we must treat our bodies as external in much the same way we treat other people, farm animals, and volcanoes. What is internal is clearly mind. Augustine opened up the space of this interior to the self, but continued the emphasis on control over body—and emotions. On top of this come distinctions like rational/irrational, motive/action, individual/social. The point is simply that we cannot start into the effort to think emotions better without grappling with the heritage that has produced the very idea of emotions—and the distinction of these from reason. The tradition of reasoning which we inherit, in other words, has been built in part by putting emotions in a specific and contained place. This has been resisted, by Romantics, Freudians, mystics, and postmodernists. But it has not been escaped. It thus structures how we approach our more specific problem of providing a place for emotions in the study of social movements.

Most contributors to this volume have tacitly situated their attempts to bring emotions back in as either a challenge or an amendment to the reigning conventional wisdoms of political process theory, resource mobilization, and rational choice. Of course, approaches are not identical, but what they share in common is a more or less instrumental approach to questions of collective action. Instrumental thinking is dominant in the field because of the specific post-1960s struggles that have defined it, but it exists and has the intellectual power it has because of a much longer history linking reason to control (including control over emotions).

Some [. . .] have simply wished to amend such an instrumental approach by suggesting that among the things movement organizers need to manage, among the tactics for mobilization they may employ, among the strategies they may use against their enemies, emotions and their manipulation ought to figure more prominently. Others have seen attention to emotions as more of a challenge to instrumental approaches. At least tacitly, they have suggested that emotions alert us to different ways in which movement participants are motivated, achieve solidarity with each other, and shape their actions.

Bedeviling this discussion is a tendency to see emotions as somehow "irrational," either explicitly or simply implicitly because of the opposition to "rationalistic" analytic approaches. We would do well to remember that passions figured quite strongly alongside interests in the founding of modern utilitarianism and instrumental political analysis. [F]or Machiavelli, Hobbes, and even Bentham, passions remained directly and in their own right a focus of attention. They saw human action as shaped fundamentally by passions, they saw a need to tame and organize passions, they saw passions shaping the otherwise inexplicable source of differences in what people found pleasurable and painful without which a utilitarian calculus could not be put in motion.

It is helpful also to remember Adam Smith's (1984 [1759]) devotion to a "theory of moral sentiments" and in general the extent to which the Scottish moralists were concerned with historical, cultural, and social structural variations in the ways in which emotional bonds and lines of conflict were institutionalized. Alongside their development of a notion of civil society they brought forward a notion of common sense, by which they meant not simply a lowest common denominator of reason but a capacity to achieve common understanding shaped by feeling as well as thinking.

A key distinction between emotions and interests in this discourse concerns relations to morality. Arguments from interests have commonly suggested that morality is a matter of "mere ought" with no material force. One of the advantages to taking emotions seriously is to see better how moral norms and injunctions come to have force. This helps us thus to distinguish the compelling from the good—in either the sense of interests and their many goods, or of morality as only an abstract ideal. This is not to say that mere strength of emotions constitutes a basis for moral judgment. Rather, as Charles Taylor (1989) has suggested, we come to know the higher goods that define us as persons and bring order to our moral judgments by reflecting on our strongest responses.

With this in mind, we would do well to ask more clearly, "emotions in relation to what else"? The answer may not be interests. Attachment to money or power or the other sort of resources that some movement analysts treat as objective interests is as much a matter of emotion—as the classical utilitarians saw—as attachment to one's nation or one's children. The question for them in each case was the extent to which one pursued the ends thus given with means provided by reason.

An alternative but closely related distinction would contrast emotions to cognition. This has the advantage of removing the implication that thinking always results in some normatively understood achievement of "rationality." Here, however, I would raise two other concerns: (1) How fully can we separate cognition and emotion? (2) Don't we need a third category to complement them, that of perception?

It seems to me a good case could be made that much of what we are seeking to do is to bring the relationship among cognition, emotion, and perception to the forefront of our attention. If this is right, we are also presumably challenging not one but two of sociology's long-standing resistances: to cultural and psychological analysis. Any serious sociology of emotions must be more than an ad hoc call to look at the additional variable of "emotionality." It requires frameworks for bringing intrapsychic and cultural dimensions of meaning and action into clear relationship with social organization.

I suspect that few who have read this far are likely to question the virtue of paying serious attention to culture in the production of meaning and identity. Intrapsychic factors are another matter. It is interesting how many psychoanalytic concepts are imported into the sociology of emotions with how little attention to a psychoanalytic framework of analysis.

[. . .]

Psychoanalysis suggests a complex view of intrapsychic relations, in which the challenges of balancing and organizing relations among drives and emotions, inhibitions and repressions, indeed, pleasures and pains, are assigned to a distinct faculty of selfhood—the ego. I do not want to argue a case here for ego-analysis as opposed to other psychoanalytic schools.

[. . .]

Indeed, my point is not to argue for psychoanalysis as such, but for the idea that if we are to be serious about emotions, we should think about them with the aid of models of intrapsychic processes that do justice to their complexity. While we may have good reason analytically to distinguish emotions from cognition and perception, we also have good reason to see each influencing the other.

It is worth asking why emotions so automatically *seem* opposed to cognition and interests? I suggest the answer lies in one of Western culture's pervasive dualistic constructions. Think of the analogies among these paired oppositions:

1	thinking	feeling
2	mind	body
3	public	private
4	male	female
5	pride	shame
6	controlled	uncontrolled
7	conscious	unconscious
8	higher	lower
9	outer	inner
10	individuating	general (or shared)

Predominant usage has placed the positive valance on the first in each pair, but of course this can be reversed—as it has been by Rousseau, Romantics, and many of us since the 1960s:

1	inauthentic	authentic
2	artificial	natural
3	repressive	expressive

The short but difficult moral to this story is that in order to do a really good job studying the place of emotions in social movements (as of movements in social life), we need to try to transcend, not reproduce, the pervasive dualism. Indeed, it is partly because emotions appear usually on the embarrassing side of the dichotomy that they have been understudied by those who would take movements seriously rather than treat them only as instances of deviant collective behavior.

[. . .]

At the same time, we need to understand how the dualism itself affects the ways in which people deploy notions of both reason and emotion. In seeking to transcend it in our own work, we should not fail to attend to its efficacy in structuring the movements we study.

So far, [. . .] I have been speaking of emotions more or less as a group. This is a problem, however, since one of the first answers to the question I asked a few moments ago— "emotions in relation to what else?"—ought to be, "other emotions." We need to differentiate and specify emotions, and see that it is every bit as much of a challenge to relate them to each other as to cognition or perception.

I do not propose to try to list all the emotions from anger to fear, shame to hate, joy to love, thrill to pride. I do want to add a couple of suggestions: (1) These work differently from each other. (2) There are patterns and challenges in relating these to each other, and these may be very important for movement analyses. Some emotions may get in the way of others; some may specifically call forth others.

[. . .]

[W]e need to see the ways in which people not only have emotions but have many emotions with dynamic relations among them. It seems to me that movement activity is often shaped not just by a single pervasive emotional source but by participants' shifting emotional orientations—as they express hatred, for example, and feel needs to balance it with more solidaristic emotions.

This is one place where the idea of an "emotional habitus," which Anne Kane introduced with a lineage from Elias, Bourdieu, and de Sousa, may be helpful. People do not simply display characteristic emotions, but have characteristic ways of relating emotions to each other, and of relating emotions to cognition and perception. These involve a sense of how to act, how to play the game, that is never altogether conscious or purely reducible to rules—even when it seems strategic. Moreover, I think we should probably follow Bourdieu in seeing the habitus as a result of the individual's inscription into social relationships, not as something altogether portable and interior to the individual.

One of the problems with the pervasive dualism in Western thinking about emotions is that it keeps locating emotions inside individuals. It leads us to look for their roots in biographical experience or perhaps in biochemical reactions in their brains. Sociology should remind us to look also at social relations. As the concept of habitus suggests, emotions are produced and organized—played out—in interpersonal relations. These are both immediate, and emotions are particularly important in directly interpersonal dynamics, but also indirect. We maintain emotional relationships to large-scale organizations and whole fields of relationships—from our kin to business worlds and social movements.

This is not just a matter of noting that organizations call on us to perform emotional labor, though this is true. It is also a matter of the way in which we invest ourselves in and achieve our identities through emotional relationships to other people and complex organizations.

We are in danger of a sort of "sampling on the dependent variable" in studies of emotions. We see emotions as contrary to cognition, disruptions in organizational processes, challenges to stable institutions. I would suggest, however, that institutions, and organizations, and relationships all gain their relative stability in part from people's emotional investments in them. In other words, we have huge emotional investments in the everyday status quo. It may look like we are relatively unemotional as we go about our tasks, but disrupt the social structure in which we work, and our emotional investments in it will become evident.

[. . .]

What this means for us as students of social movements is that we need to be careful not to ascribe emotions to movements as though everyday maintenance of social structures were not equally a matter of emotions. In addition, this point focuses attention on a range of emotions—or at least patterns in emotions—which have to do with the nature of social relationships as such. A sociology of emotions ought to help us to understand commitment, trust, security, and investment as well as anger, shame, and joy. If we see emotions only in connection with disruptions to social life, we shall exaggerate the importance of certain emotional dynamics and miss others.

Relatedly, this should focus our attention on the link between a sociology of emotions and the politics of identity. The latter is not simply a matter of pointing to multicultural variations, but of seeing the centrality of problems of recognition. Any structure of social relations extends to those who live within it some degree of occasion for recognizing themselves through their social relationships. But this is variable; social movements arise with recognition as one of their goals precisely for this reason. But this is not because those who are not recognized become emotional, while those who are recognized remain reasonable. The emotions are bound up in the whole field and organization of relations from the beginning.

Here we should also consider a range of other problematic oppositions which we sometimes treat as ontologically given, and therefore as automatically useful in analysis rather than in need of continual critical examination: individual/collective, nation/individual, and structure/culture, among others.

Paying attention to emotional investments in everyday social structures should help us understand (among other things) why predictability reduces fear.

[. . .]

Having suggested that we should watch out for seeing emotions only in relation to social disruptions, I want to return in closing to some specific points about social movements.

Because they involve steps outside ordinary structural routines, social movements do indeed make emotions prominent. This is one of the points to Victor Turner's (1969) idea of liminality. It would be a mistake to view this as simply a matter of "breakdown" theories of collective action, however. In the first place, the claim is not that collective action arises because of a breakdown in normative order, but that nonroutine action removes some of the everyday social relationships in which emotions are invested stably and gives occasion for the workings of other emotions or other patterns in the appearance of emotions. Secondly, as Turner emphasizes, emotions may be organized through ritual. They do not simply arise and run amok when conventional repressions are lifted. What are expressed in ritualized occasions for liminality are often reversals of conventional norms. This may be emotionally cathartic, but that is precisely because emotions were already invested in the existing norms (and the usual patterns of repression).

Social movements differ greatly, however, in the extent to which they involve steps outside established routines and normative organizations of emotions. We must make more of this. It is touched on under the rubric of "high-risk mobilizations," but this is only one issue. To a considerable extent in the modern world, social movements have become normal, everyday routines. We need more clearly to distinguish those that are not. One problem in this is the investment many movement analysts (especially those broadly sympathetic to the movements of the 1960s) made in seeing movement activity as rational and reasonable rather than deviant, as many collective behavior analysts had presented it.

Social movements also differ in the extent to which and manner in which they build new normative structures for emotions.

[. . .]

Movements produce emotions; they do not simply reflect emotional orientations brought to them by members. This goes beyond evoking emotions to attract members to recurrently reproducing them in order to secure commitment, maintain shared meanings, and indeed, offer the "high" of emotional release as a "selective incentive" to their participants. Recurrent occasions for "peak" emotional engagement may be more or less ritualized and more or less consciously managed by movement leaders. There may be a pattern of escalation in the kinds of emotional engagements required to keep movement participation exciting. Just as crowds may have to get bigger to keep attracting news media, emotional catharses may be escalated to keep attracting participation—and this is potentially dangerous, as it often propels movements towards climactic confrontations.

The issue is not just extent of emotional engagement, though, but the kind of balancing involved, as for example fear-inducing confrontations with police call for solidarity-affirming communal experiences. We should not forget the extent to which the emotional dynamics of movements are driven by fatigue as well as excitement. This may be easy for a reader to recognize, and a sign to an author to stop writing.

References

Smith, A. (1984 [1759]), *Theory of Moral Sentiments,* Indianapolis: Liberty Classics.
Taylor, C. (1989), *Sources of the Self,* Cambridge: Harvard University Press.
Turner, V. (1969), *The Ritual Process,* Chicago: Aldine.

PART SEVEN

Globalisation and social movements

THIS PART OF THE BOOK will examine the transnationalisation of collective action with a particular focus on what has been termed 'Global Justice Movement' (GJM) in the Anglo-Saxon world, 'mouvements altermondialistes' (movements for an alternative world) in France, 'globalisierungskritische Bewegungen' (movements critical of globalisation) in Germany, or 'movement of movements' in other definitions (Klein, 2001). In the last few decades, particularly since the nineties, social movements have widened their space of action and adopted a more global perspective (Ruggiero, 2002). They have started to target supranational economic and political institutions implying that the nation-state, either as a political or geographical entity, is no longer the only locus of conflict. On the one hand, global movements contest the current neoliberal globalisation, which is seen as exclusively market oriented. Protests erupted at international meetings, such Washington, Seattle, Genoa, and more recently in Rostock, but also the gatherings such as the World Social Forum in Porto Alegre, Mumbai and elsewhere suggest that social movements are expressions of collective identity resulting from, and challenging, globalisation itself. On the other hand, social movements express a form of 'globalisation from below' through the construction of global networks and protest campaigns, and promote what Appadurai in his contribution calls the 'utopian face of globalisation'.

The contributions presented in this part address various aspects of the transnationalisation of collective protest. First, the argument is made that changes in the environment, namely globalisation processes, transnationalisation of politics and technological innovations have created a context which is favourable to the emergence of transnational social movements. Second, transnational collective action is possible because it relies on pre-existing movement organisations operating either at a local or transnational level. Third, these contributions show that the local and the global dimensions, in terms of issues and organisations, are often linked and frequently overlap.

This section opens with Arjun Appadurai, who emphasises the role of 'progressive movements', as he terms those movements which aim to build a third space of circulation independent from state and market. Such movements are seen as promoters of *Grassroots Globalisation*. This is the utopian face of globalisation concerned with issues such as human rights, poverty, gender equality, peace, the environment and other humanist goals. Analysing the Indian organisation Shack/Slum-Dwellers International (SDI), Appadurai points out a number of innovative features that characterise it and its links with the movement for global justice. In particular, his emphasis is on what he calls 'deep democracy', a modality and a set of principles promoting self-governance by poor people.

In this way Appadurai deals with two familiar issues raised in the debate among and on social movements. First, through the analysis of SDI he shows that movement organisations and NGOs can practice specific means of urban governance without becoming tools of state and market interests. Second, he shows that contemporary social movements, including the GJM and its local nodes, are no longer utopian in traditional terms, nor are they engaged in the construction of what they believe will be a future perfect society (see Ruggiero's contribution in this part). In developing democratic practices and projects from below, grassroots movements are more interested in changing social, political and economic relations in the current society and building their future 'here and now'.

The contribution by Marjorie Mayo also focuses on local organisations with transnational links. Here, some of characteristics of the GJM come to light: the role of political opportunities in facilitating the development of social movement organisations, the connection between local and global dimension either in terms of issues or mobilisation, the movement multi-issue approach to globalisation, and the contribution of globalisation processes of knowledge to social movements. In her essay, *Globalisation and Gender: New Threats, New Strategies,* Marjorie Mayo examines the case of Development Alternatives for Women for a New Era (DAWN), a network of women that brings together activists, scholars, researchers and policy makers from the South. DAWN began in 1984, on the eve of a UN international meeting in which a ten-year action plan for the advancement of women was drawn. In contrast to other feminist agendas, DAWN aims to challenge the structural causes and symptoms of female oppression and to formulate a vision of an alternative future. DAWN's goal is not to integrate women into the current economic development, but to question and change the very principles of economic development that reproduce inequality and various forms of oppression.

DAWN possesses many of the traits characterising the global justice movement and transnational protest. According to Mayo, its approach is holistic, in the sense that it addresses the social, political, and cultural arenas simultaneously. It challenges economic as well as cultural male–female power relations. Also, it combines the local with the global, showing the continuity between the two in the international context. Finally, DAWN's analysis and strategy have been developed by academics and researchers, but have also been shaped by experience achieved on the ground.

There is a turning point in the transnationalisation of collective action: the battle of Seattle. Jackie Smith (*Globalizing Resistance: The Battle of Seattle and the Future of Social Movements*) focuses on this battle, arguing that protests at the Third Ministerial Meeting of the World Trade Organization in November 1999 relied on pre-existing networks of local, national, and transnational groups which had already been involved in previous struggles for global economic justice. These networks included formal social movement organisations such as unions, consumer groups, and environmental organisations; but also extra-movement organisations such as churches, community organisations and informal friendship networks. In this contribution we learn that the degree of transnationalism can vary enormously. Transnational ties can be informal, diffused, routinised or formalised. These ties and networks play an important role in setting up protest agendas, shaping collective identities, and mobilising protesters. They also provide activists with knowledge of other groups operating in different areas of the world, other international organisations, and other contentious issues relating to globalisation. As Smith argues, groups with formalised transnational connections are more likely to increase awareness and criticism of the global trading system.

After Seattle, the debate around the global nature of contemporary movements has continued. Smith and other authors observe that protests in Seattle displayed a wide geographical range of participation. While many protesters were activists from the US and Canada, many others had travelled from other parts of the world and yet others came from the world South, where they were already participants in transnational organisations or networks.

According to Smith, global political processes determine changes in movement tactics: 'As political authority moves towards global institutions, we should expect similar changes in social movement repertoires'. Some older forms of protest may still be adapted to the new political context, though addressed to global, rather than national, institutions. In Seattle, for example, traditional disruptive protests, such as blockades and demonstrations, shifted their targets and were used to prevent international meetings from taking place. However, innovative tactics were also deployed, such as information exchange through the use of the Internet, the setting up of Independent Media Centres based on new technologies, and more disruptive technological forms of protests such as e-mail and fax jamming.

The growing importance of transnational social movements and international nongovernmental organisations is also emphasised by Khagram, Riker and Sikkink (*From Santiago to Seattle: Transnational Advocacy Groups Restructuring World Politics*). In their contribution various forms of transnational contentious action are examined, and the authors argue that transnational coalitions can develop only after the emergence of communication networks and after sustained mobilisations involving groups in at least three countries. 'It is difficult to imagine a movement emerging without prior network or coalition activity'. In the last thirty years or so, non-state collective action has affected international norms and contributed to the re-shaping of world politics. For this reason, Khagram, Riker and Sikkink call for a dialogue between two different fields of political studies: international relations and social movement studies. There are in fact some similarities between contentious politics theorists and students of international relations, and the dialogue could be beneficial for both. Khagram, Riker and Sikkink focus on the dual process whereby social movements construct meanings, or *frames*, and authorities construct norms in the international arena. Norms can inspire collective action and shape political opportunities, from which social movements may develop their collective beliefs. In the same way, collective movements can attempt to turn their beliefs into international norms.

In Donatella Della Porta's and Sidney Tarrow's contribution (*Transnational Protest and Global Activism*), the growth of transnational activism is related to changes in institutional and cultural environments and to social movement reacting to these changes. The authors focus on three different processes of transnationalisation. Diffusion is the spread of ideas, repertoires and organisational forms from one country to another. This process does not imply the existence of networks or organisational links between activists. A notable example of transnational diffusion was the spread of American student movement's frames and practices to West Germany through students who had studied in the US in the sixties. The second process is termed domestication, and consists of the internalisation of conflicts over decisions that have originated elsewhere. Protests against IMF decisions in several Latin American countries in the eighties are examples of internalisation. Externalisation, the third process, describes the request to supranational institutions to intervene in domestic problems, for example movement organisations addressing the EU so that pressure is put on domestic governments. According to Della Porta and Tarrow the shift of collective action from a national to a transnational dimension was facilitated by environmental, cognitive and relational changes. By environmental changes they refer to a mix of political, technological and economic transformations. Although important changes in global environment can encourage the transnationalisation of collective action, they are not sufficient to produce it. As the authors put it 'Cognitive change within and relational change between actors must be the active forces for such a fundamental change'. Cognitive change refers to a new perspective of non-state actors framing and adapting their tactics to new targets. Relational change refers to the growing international links among movement actors.

The idea that the 'Battle of Seattle' and the Global Justice Movement represent a turning point in the recent history of social movements returns in the work of Nicola Montagna. In his contribution, the author identifies three main constituents of the movement for global justice: informal networks organised at a transcontinental level; campaigns and protest repertoires targeting economic and political supranational institutions; and a common identity based on *framing processes* that define neo-liberal globalisation as the main cause of poverty, social injustice, and environmental disaster. Montagna shows that the GJM engaged in the 'Battle of Seattle' was the result of transnational ties among groups, civil society organisations and individuals that developed throughout the nineties (Pianta, 2001). These transnational mobilising structures grew tremendously over the years, providing the background for the expansion of contentious action across borders and making globalisation the main arena of conflict. The movement for global justice, it is argued, also emerged as a consequence of unprecedented developments in communication technologies, increasing density in the relations among state and non-state actors, and the establishment of a supranational public sphere.

In his essay *Dichotomies and Contemporary Social Movements* Vincenzo Ruggiero identifies a number of features that distinguish global movements, here labelled as Contemporary Social Movements (CSM). He explores some dichotomies characterising such movements, for example: movements as producers of identity versus movements as pursuers of resources, movements as expressions of the local versus movements as the result of the global, movements as expression of rationality versus movements as the outcome of passion. According to Ruggiero, due to their transnational nature, contemporary social movements are potentially able to link struggles which are rooted in local conditions with campaigns expressing global concerns. They are also better equipped than their predecessors to supersede the dichotomies mentioned above, for example, unify the establishment of identity with the pursuit of resources. It is, ultimately, in the organisational model adopted that Ruggiero sees the 'newness' of contemporary social movements, namely in their acting as members of a 'free city', a city whose strength derives less from the effectiveness of leaders than from the collective motivation of citizens. These movements, in his view, draw their strength from the participatory intensity of their members. Non-delegated action shapes and consolidates their choices, values and lifestyles. Participants' identities are not pre-set, but rather shaped through action. Liberation is simultaneous with action: to change the world and to change oneself are coexisting aims.

References

Klein, N. (2001), 'Reclaiming the Commons', New Left Review, 9: 81–89.
Pianta, M. (2001), La globalizzazione dal basso, Rome: Manifestolibri.
Ruggiero, V. (2002), 'Attac: A Global Social Movement?', Social Justice, 29 (1–2): 48–60.

Chapter 39

Arjun Appadurai

GRASSROOTS GLOBALIZATION

CELLULAR GLOBALIZATION does indeed have a more utopian face. The happier face is what has sometimes been called international civil society, those networks of activists concerned with human rights, poverty, indigenous rights, emergency aid, ecological justice, gender equity, and other fundamentally humanist goals who form nonstate networks and interest groups across national boundaries. From Greenpeace to Doctors Without Borders, from the Narmada Bachao Andolan to the Public Eye on Davos, the variety of these movements is vast and their numbers seem to be growing all the time.

Social scientists have begun to notice that there is a complex convergence between what used to be seen in isolation as civil society institutions, transnational organizations, and popular social movements. In some loose way they can all be treated as NGOs or as transnational NGOs. But this is a huge category, ranging from churches and large philanthropic organizations to multilateral bodies and scientific societies. I am speaking here more narrowly of what Keck and Sikkink have called transnational activist networks (1997). Such networks now are active in virtually every area of human equity and welfare ranging from health and environment to human rights, housing, gender, and indigenous people's rights. They are sometimes relatively local and regional in scope and sometimes truly global in their reach and impact. At the upper ends they are vast, well-funded, and widely known networks that have become mega-organizations. At the other end, they are small and fluid, bare networks, working quietly, often invisibly but also across national and other lines. The study of these networks has grown increasingly lively, especially among political scientists concerned with new forms of international bargaining, with expanding the study of social movements, and with the third space outside of market and state.

Many of these transnational activist networks are explicitly involved in the major debates about globalization, and some of them were made highly visible in the loudly publicized street protests of Seattle, Milan, Prague, Washington, D.C., Davos, and elsewhere in Europe and the United States in recent years. But the vast majority of these movements are engaged in much less publicized and much more targeted forms of advocacy and coordination in pursuit of specific policy changes at the local, national, and global levels. They have often succeeded in slowing down major official moves to set global policies on trade, environment, debt, and the like, usually by forcing transparency, by putting pressure on specific states, and by circulating information about forthcoming policy decisions rapidly across state boundaries by electronic means so as to mobilize protest.

Yet protest is not the key word with many of these movements, who also frequently explore partnerships with multilateral agencies, with their own home states, with major global funders, and with other forces in local and international civil society. These partnerships have not been explored very much by social scientists, and they constitute a crucial part of the David and Goliath leverage through which such networks have become effective.

I myself am engaged in a long-term study of one such important movement, the Shack/Slumdwellers International (SDI) and especially of its Indian node, which is an alliance of three different activist bodies: Society for the Promotion of Area Resource Centres, an NGO; Mahila Milan, an organization of poor urban women, with roots in Mumbai and devoted principally to small-scale savings and housing issues; and the National Slum Dwellers Federation, a remarkable older organization of male slum dwellers active in more than thirty cities in India. This troika of organizations, itself an unusual formation, has been functioning as an Alliance in India since the mid-1980s and has been a key member of SDI for about a decade. SDI is active in about twenty countries in Asia and Africa and has already made some major dents on such issues as establishing methods for leveraging people's savings movements to obtain bridge finance from major funders for pro-poor projects; in setting standards through which secure tenure in land and housing can be obtained for urban shack and pavement dwellers; and in contributing to the worldwide movement, notably led by countries like China, in making access to sanitary facilities a central goal of state policy. In working on these goals, what SDI (Appadurai 2000) has done is to find new ways of organizing poor people in cities in the practices of what I have elsewhere called "deep democracy" (2002), in order to move away from existing models of agitational politics, or of simple downstreaming of charitable funds, or of simple outsourcing of traditional state functions, all paths that continue to be followed by many NGOS. Rather, SDI has focused on building the capacity of poor people in cities to explore and practice specific means of urban governance with an eye to building their own capacity to set goals, achieve expertise, share knowledge, and generate commitment. In this, they have made remarkable uses of such practices as daily savings, not to establish an entre-preneurial habit for the purpose of turning the urban poor into microcapitalists, but to establish certain protocols and principles for genuine self-governance. In effect, the urban poor that the Alliance has been able to "federate," their own key political term, have developed elements of a shadow urban government in many cities, notably in Mumbai, where they have established their own credible facilities to provide themselves with basic infrastructure and also with basic access to legal and political security.

What is most interesting about this exercise in capacity building (also organized through transnational exchanges between federations across countries for more than a decade) is that it has involved exploring and building new partnerships with members of local, state, and central governments in India, South Africa, Thailand, and Cambodia and more recently in Nepal, Zimbabwe, Kenya, and elsewhere. Ways have also been found to establish grounds for partnership with the United Nations system, notably with the United Nations Centre for Human Settlements, and even with the World Bank and other major state or quasi-state development bureaucracies in Europe, Africa, and Asia.

In this process, the Alliance has made remarkable strides in the substantial problems of urban poverty in many cities in India and beyond. Their global links, networks, exchanges, and perspectives have been key assets for them in strengthening the work and morale of their local federations. They have not only scaled up their ability to make material interventions, for example, in the matter of relocating slum dwellers, building toilets, and creating savings-based housing co-operatives among the urban poor in many cities. They have also found new ways to channel these global exercises into building the capabilities of the poorest of the urban poor to be direct architects of their local political worlds. And, so far, amazingly, they have done so without becoming mere tools of state organizations, multilateral funders, political parties, or other major vested interests. This is cellular democratization at work.

The case of SDI and of other transnational housing movements, is of course, not unique. There are many such cellular formations in action, some more highly developed than others. Some are more visible, since they are involved in dramatic global issues such as the future of large dams. Others, working on humbler issues like housing and savings, are less visible. But they are all commonly involved in shaping a third space, in which markets and states are not only forced to recognize their importance but are in the process of having to concede genuine political space to these voices and actors when global decisions about key issues are made.

This is a not a fairy tale, nor is it at an end. It is a major struggle, filled with risks, hazards, contradictions, disappointments, and obstacles. But such movements are, in their aspirations, democratic both in form and in telos. And increasingly they are constructing the global not through the general language of universal problems, rights, or norms but by tackling one issue, one alliance, one victory at a time. The great progressive movements of the past few centuries, notably the working class movements which have characterized the nineteenth and twentieth centuries, always worked with universalist principles of solidarity, identity, and interest, for aims and against opponents, also conceived in universalist and generic terms. The new transnational activisms have more room for building solidarity from smaller convergences of interest, and though they may also invoke big categories, such as "the urban poor," to build their politics, they build their actual solidarities in a more ad hoc, inductive, and context-sensitive manner. They are thus developing a new dynamics in which global networking is put at the service of local imaginings of power.

Much else could be said about these movements, their form, function, and significance. But I need to return to the key themes of this essay. I point to such transnational and transurban activist movements because in their transnational character, they too work through the cellular principle, coordinating without massive centralization, reproducing without a clear-cut central mandate, working occasionally in the larger public eye but often outside it, leveraging resources from state and market to their own ends, and pursuing visions of equity and access that do not fit many twentieth century models either of development or of democracy. We need to watch them, for the coming crisis of the nation-state may lie not in the dark cellularities of terror but in the utopian cellularities of these other new transnational organizational forms. Here lies a vital resource that could counter the worldwide trend to ethnocide and ideocide and here too lies the answer, however incipient, obscure, and tentative, to the strained relationship between peace and equity in the world we inhabit. At any rate, let us hope that this utopian form of cellularity will be the theater of our struggles. Otherwise, let us say goodbye both to civilians and to civility.

References

Appadurai, A. 2000. 'Spectral Housing and Urban Cleansing'. *Public Culture*, 12: 627–51.
Appadurai, A. 2002. 'Deep Democracy'. *Public Culture*, 14: 21–47.
Keck, M.E. and Sinkkink, K. 1997. *Activists Beyond Borders*, Ithaca: Cornell University Press.

Chapter 40

Marjorie Mayo

GLOBALIZATION AND GENDER: NEW THREATS, NEW STRATEGIES

Women, development and globalization: differing approaches

GLOBALIZATION and the accompanying spatial reorganization of economic activities have created new gender hierarchies, it has been argued, hierarchies 'which are intensified through class, ethnic and national membership' (Young 2001: 33). Women have been identified among the most exploited labour of the sweatshops of the global factories, prime victims of the processes of capitalist globalization. And neoliberal economic policies have been held responsible for transforming the public policy environment in ways detrimental to women (Elson 2002).

On the other hand, capitalist globalization has opened opportunities for paid labour (however poorly paid). Although employment cannot simply be equated with empowerment, these opportunities have, in some contexts, increased the scope for women to challenge patriarchal social relations (Pearson and Jackson 1998: 11). The processes of capitalist globalization have not been entirely negative or beyond contestation. It is not theoretically helpful, nor does it promote political action by or for women, it has been argued, 'to turn into frightened rabbits when confronting the "snake" of globalization' (Young 2001: 46). Far from remaining passive victims, women have been actively developing strategies to defend their interests both as women and as workers and to challenge their oppression, globally as well as locally.

The nature of this oppression has been the subject of varying interpretations, however. The facts might seem relatively clear. As the *Human Development Report* of the United Nations Development Programme pointed out in 1999, no country treated its women as well as its men, according to measures of factors such as life expectancy, wealth and education (UNDP 1999). As Nussbaum has summarized women's position: 'women in much of the world lack support for fundamental functions of a human life. They are less well nourished than men, less healthy, more vulnerable to physical violence and sexual abuse. They are much less likely than men to be literate, and still less likely to have pre-professional or technical education' let alone enjoy full and effectively enforceable legal and political rights (Nussbaum 2002: 45).

[. . .]

From 'Women in Development' to 'Gender and Development'

In summary, the resurgence of second-wave feminism in the North began to impact upon development debates in the 1970s. There was pressure on particular governments (including the USA) and there was increasing pressure on the United Nations system, including pressure from Scandinavian NGOs. It was in response to these pressures that the UN designated 1975 as the International Year of Women, with a Women's Conference on the themes of Equality, Development and Peace, followed by the UN Decade for Women, from 1976 to 1985 (Young 1993). While much of the impetus was to rest with national governments, to set up structures to address women's issues, this was to be within the broad framework of international support and the growth of a number of international women's NGOs and networks. As Young concluded, even if the development industry was not significantly changed, 'the UN's promotion of the issue gave a considerable fillip to the women involved' (ibid.: 29).

Then as now, feminists had varying perspectives, and differing priorities for policy agendas. There was a predominant emphasis at this period, however: that of Women in Development (Young 1993). Women in Development has been described as an 'add-on' to mainstream policy and planning practice. The broad aim was to 'bring' or 'integrate' women into the planning process. Planners and policy-makers had been affected by gender blindness, it was argued, failing to understand that women had key roles as farmers as well as wives and mothers, or failing to recognize that development projects that involved women's input could actually increase the burdens on already overworked women.

Women in both North and South engaged in research and publications, as well as lobbying to challenge these gender-blind assumptions and to provide the evidence to argue for more positive policy responses. But these responses tended to be limited to 'add-on' initiatives such as support for small-scale income-generating activities, with a particular focus on projects to help poor women to provide more effectively for their families, as part of the wider focus on tackling poverty. Although women were raising demands for gender-equity as well as gender-awareness and meeting basic needs most donors and more traditional NGOs preferred not to engage directly with more challenging aspects of women's oppression, unequal relations between women and men and the ways in which these relationships were being affected by structural processes of change, internationally as well as locally. Many Third World governments were similarly uninterested in addressing these more challenging aspects, believing that Western-exported feminism was ethnocentric and irrelevant if not actually divisive, labelling Third World socialists and feminists as 'bourgeois imperialist sympathizers' (Moser 1993: 67).

Mainstream Women in Development has been categorized as lying 'squarely within the framework of what has been called liberal feminist theory' (Young 1993: 129). The underlying premise was that women are rational individuals seeking to maximize their interests – but are disadvantaged in doing so as a result of their restricted access to economic, social and political life. The policy implications of liberal feminism have been characterized as focusing on the removal of such legal and institutional barriers for women, making the economic and social system more 'user-friendly' for women. Meanwhile, liberal feminists hoped that economic development and modernization would widen opportunities and dissolve some of the grosser forms of patriarchal belief systems more generally.

Critics of Women in Development have pointed to its failure to challenge the underlying processes of development in a more fundamental way, or indeed to challenge gender relations more fundamentally either. In contrast, Gender and Development was developed as an approach that questioned the view that the basic problem was how to integrate women into existing structures. On the contrary, it was precisely these structures and processes that were giving rise to women's disadvantage – and so were in need of fundamental change.

Gender and Development attempted to be holistic, addressing social, political and cultural dimensions as well as exploring the ways in which the development of a (global) market economy was impacting upon women of different classes, colours and creeds. While recognizing the contribution of socialist development theories, as an approach, Gender and Development was critical of what was seen as the lack of value given to reproductive work in socialist approaches and the absence of structures allowing for challenge and dissent (ibid.).

In terms of their policy implications, Women in Development and Gender and Development have shared many objectives. Both have emphasized the importance of breaking down the barriers that prevent women from gaining an adequate income, for example, and both have emphasized the importance of challenging institutional arrangements and attitudes that disadvantage women. But Gender and Development has differed from Women in Development in its emphasis upon empowering women to challenge the structural causes of their oppression, including the structures of unequal gender relationships. Whether or not this has made Gender and Development less acceptable to mainstream development in practice has been more questionable, perhaps.

[. . .]

Development Alternatives with Women for a New Era (DAWN): critical feminist perspectives from the South

DAWN has been credited with having made the best articulation of the empowerment approach (Moser 1993). This network of women from the South – actively engaged in feminist research and working for equitable, gender-just and sustainable development – was launched at the United Nations Third World Conference of Women in Nairobi in 1985 (Bunch et al. 2001). This was a timely intervention, and one that attracted enormous interest – some 2,000 women attended the DAWN workshops in Nairobi (Stienstra 2000). This was a period in which there were increasing criticisms of the approaches that had been predominant in the previous decade, focusing as these did upon integrating women into existing structures and processes of development. By 1984, when the DAWN network was forming and planning its input to the Nairobi conference, the inadequacies of such approaches had become increasingly apparent.

'We are now more aware of the need to question in a more fundamental way the underlying processes of development into which we have been attempting to integrate women,' they argued (Sen and Grown 1987, quoted in Young 1993: 133).

> Throughout the Decade (The UN Decade for Women) it has been implicit that women's main problem in the Third World has been insufficient participation in an otherwise benevolent process of growth and development. Increasing women's participation and improving their shares in resources, land, employment and income relative to men were seen as both necessary and sufficient to effect dramatic changes in their economic and social position. Our experiences now lead us to challenge this belief. (ibid.)

DAWN set out to analyse the conditions of the world's women and to formulate a vision of an alternative future, a world where inequality based on class, gender and race is absent from every country and from relationships among countries.

> We want a world where basic needs become basic rights and where poverty and all forms of violence are eliminated. Each person will have the opportunity to develop her or his full potential and creativity, and women's values of nurturance and solidarity will characterize human relationships. In such a world women's reproductive role will be redefined: childcare will be shared by men, women and society as a whole. (DAWN 1985, quoted in Moser 1993: 75)

This was a vision of an alternative future informed by political economy, drawing upon socialist approaches as well as feminist concerns.

Although DAWN was independent of any particular political party or parties, the collapse of the former USSR and Eastern and Central European socialist states at the turn of the 1990s presented challenges. Implicitly, if not explicitly, socialism had been seen to represent an alternative development future (providing that previous inadequacies, especially inadequacies in relation to feminist agendas, could be remedied). The 'new world order' of the post-1989 situation required some rethinking.

The outcome of DAWN's analysis of this 'new world order' was to focus upon the international economic system, globalization and the impact of the neoliberal strategies that were now being presented as the only way forward, globally. DAWN decided to tackle the predominance of neoliberal agendas head on. The strategy that DAWN developed from the 1990s centred upon contributing to key international events such as the International Conference on Population and Development in Cairo, in 1994, the World Summit on Social Development in Copenhagen in 1995 (including the recall conference in Geneva in 2000) and the Fourth World Women's Conference in Beijing in 1995. DAWN focused on researching and critically analysing capitalist globalization as neoliberal strategies have been impacting upon women in different countries – and relating this analysis to the specific policy concerns of the international event in question. DAWN has researched the impact of the debt crisis on women, for example, as well as focusing on environmental sustainability, militarism, reproductive health and rights (including HIV/AIDS) and political restructuring in the context of the increasing marketization of governance.

DAWN does plan ahead, taking account of key events coming up internationally and preparing evidence to put to these. But the approach is also flexible and organic. If an important unexpected event comes up, then DAWN will respond, if it can, even if this was not previously in the work schedule.

Although DAWN's analysis has been developed by academics and researchers, this has been rooted in the experiences of poor women in the South. By introducing this analysis that 'related the daily experiences of women to colonial relations between countries and the macroeconomic policy framework', it has been argued, 'DAWN gave women a new way of viewing global processes and development issues' (Bunch et al. 2001: 224). DAWN has specifically focused upon linking the micro and the macro, holistically, highlighting the connections between women's daily lives and the wider economic, social, cultural and political framework. This approach, it has been suggested, has transformed debates on Women in Development, and helped to mobilize women worldwide into a political constituency (ibid.).

DAWN has developed this global role from relatively small beginnings, organizationally. Following the successful launch in Nairobi, DAWN's founders organized a meeting in Rio to launch an ongoing programme of research and advocacy. A steering committee was established with a secretariat based first in Bangalore, India, then in Rio de Janeiro, Brazil, next at the University of the West Indies and more recently, from 1998, at the University of the South Pacific in Fiji. This rotation of the secretariat's base has been explained as having been set up to ensure that 'different regions of the South will benefit from its analysis and advocacy work and that DAWN will eventually earn a profile in each of these regions' (ibid.: 226).

The steering committee has members from the different regions of the South and regional co-ordinators have responsibility for ensuring that there is a strong and effective regional dimension to DAWN's work – a particular feature of DAWN's work programme at the beginning of the twenty-first century. As DAWN's 2001 publicity brochure has explained, 'DAWN is emphasising work at the regional level in an effort to extend its reach and influence, connect more closely with the priorities of women's civil society organisations in each region, and help strengthen capacity to deal with issues arising from the impacts of globalisation'.

[. . .]

In addition, research co-ordinators facilitate research and analysis and advocacy work on the key themes of the environment, reproductive rights and population and alternative economic frameworks in the context of globalization (Bunch et al. 2001).

Activists attend regional meetings so that the analysis is informed by and linked to advocacy and campaigning. These connections between consistent analysis and effective organizing have been central to DAWN's approach – although members of DAWN themselves have also reflected on the difficulties of developing and sustaining these links between researchers and women working at the grass-roots (DAWN 1990; Stienstra 2000).

Since the mid-1990s, in addition to strengthening its own regional links, DAWN has also strengthened its links with other progressive networks. From 1996, for instance, DAWN worked with the Structural Adjustment Program Review Initiative, an NGO initiative involving a wide range of civil society groups in evaluating World Bank structural adjustment programmes (Bunch et al. 2001). DAWN has been credited with playing a key role here, 'at the forefront of signalling the harmful effects of structural adjustment on women', alerting women in the North that 'this was not simply a Southern's women's problem, but one that would also reshape the lives of women in the North' (Stienstra 2000: 79).

[. . .]

In developing [a] range of networks, regionally and internationally, DAWN has been strategic. There have been issues on which it has been possible to work with Northern governments, for example, just as there have been issues on which it has been possible to work with Southern governments. But DAWN has been mindful of the need to hold on to its own progressive feminist agenda. So, for example, while DAWN has been extremely critical of neoliberal global agendas, DAWN's research also drew attention to the fact that 'everywhere in the South, anti-feminist reactionaries draw strength from the opposition to neoliberalism. If the anti-globalisation movement fails to recognise the twin dangers of neoliberalism on the one side and fundamentalism on the other,' the DAWN website DAWNInforms continued, 'it will not address the concerns of half of humanity. If the choice were between the Republican Party in the U.S.', this article continued, 'and Afghanistan's Taliban, as a woman, I would take my chances with the Republicans' (DAWN 2002). (DAWN has, of course, also been concerned to critique Christian fundamentalism – as DAWNInforms explained, one of the highlights of the World Social Forum meeting in Porto Alegre in 2001 was the surprise demonstration against the conservative Republican Bush administration's then expected attack on abortion rights which would also impact upon overseas reproductive health programmes.)

DAWN has been similarly strategic in building alliances with feminists and working with anti-global campaigners in the North as well as in the South. At the World Social Summit in Copenhagen, for instance, DAWN organized a hugely successful and massively well-attended event, with a panel that included poor women from the North. Some men from Southern delegations were overheard expressing some surprise when they heard about this. What could women from the North possibly know about poverty and why on earth were they being given a platform? Also overheard were the most lucid explanations from Southern women who had actually attended the event, explaining the common underlying causes, rooted in the processes of globalization, dominated as these were by neoliberal policy agendas.

DAWN has been clear about maintaining feminist perspectives within campaigns around globalization. For example, while DAWN was actively involved in the Women's Caucus, and there were public events running all day, during the 'Battle of Seattle', the daily newspaper that was produced by a group of NGOs failed to provide adequate cover. So DAWN's webpage included some critical reflections on the ways in which North/South women's activities were generally marginalized by the male-commanded NGO and social movement resistance in Seattle.

Commenting on the paradoxes of working for gender justice with social movements, more generally, DAWN's Southeast Asia co-ordinator reflected: 'Post-Beijing, DAWN has been active in inter-linking with social movements and male-led NGOs in what we refer to as negotiating gender in the male-stream.' DAWN was involved in a range of global groupings and networks including the International Council of the World Social Forum. There were increasing intersections, it was argued, both of analysis and collaboration among the movements for economic justice, people-centred social development, and recently for peace, civil liberties and democracy. But DAWN was also clear that 'we are at the same time opposing the marking and disciplining of women's bodies and agencies by fundamentalist communitarian ideologies and resistance struggles that, just like the state, turn women into motherhood idols and icons' (DAWNInforms 2002).

[. . .]

DAWN's particular contribution

DAWN has been considered unusual, if not unique, in being a progressive feminist network which is so effective in international arenas – without being dominated by groups of white women from the North, who have often been seen as tending to play leading roles at this level (Stienstra 2000). DAWN's research has benefited from the particular expertise of academics who have been committed to promoting processes of dialogue, rooting their analyses in the experiences of women in a wide range of different situations in the South. These specialists have brought their professional skills as academics and researchers, together with their skills and contacts in policy arenas, nationally and internationally. DAWN has been highly proficient in operating at this global level, preparing policy papers, collecting evidence from different contexts to support their arguments and then presenting these at preparatory commission meetings and full international gatherings.

DAWN has clearly been recognized as making strategic impacts, including impacts at global events such as Cairo, Vienna, Rio, Copenhagen, Geneva and Beijing. *Marketisation of Governance* went on to provide a critical analysis of the ways in which the very processes of globalization themselves have been pressing in alternative directions. In addition to providing this research and analysis, DAWN has also worked to strengthen progressive feminist movements and social movements more generally.

The author was personally involved in one specific example that illustrates DAWN's contributions to international solidarity. This was when DAWN effectively acted as informal mentor to another international NGO – an NGO concerned with community development, preparing for the recall Social Summit in Geneva in 2000.

DAWN shared a platform at a joint event – providing a briefing beforehand about how to assemble the case to be put, involving the organization's membership by gathering examples from member organizations in different member-states. This enabled the NGO's case to be put effectively, supported with the evidence, locally, nationally and regionally, to demonstrate achievements and shortcomings, where governments had so far failed to live up to previous commitments on the issues in question. DAWN also shared contacts and specific knowledge and skills about the practicalities of organizing such events internationally.

Operating at the global level poses particular challenges. As if the challenges of taking on global institutions were not enough, there are also formidable logistical problems to be addressed. The spread of e-mail has been recognized as a key factor which has been of assistance to DAWN in overcoming these logistical problems, facilitating the exchange of information and views on the drafting of papers, for instance. But DAWN has also benefited from its expertise in attracting funding to support face-to-face meetings and attendance at international events.

Operating at the global level poses challenges, too, in relation to issues of representation and democratic accountability. After the success of DAWN's first interventions at Nairobi, there were expressions of interest from others who wanted to join the group. After careful reflection, however, DAWN decided not to become a membership organization. Setting up a formal organization would have been a huge task in itself, with its own organizational logic and requirements. Even if they had decided to pursue this option, having a formal organization would not, of itself, have resolved the dilemmas inherent in ensuring democratic representation internationally. On balance, then, DAWN opted to focus on providing research and analysis as a think tank of progressive feminist lobbyists from the South, albeit closely informed by the experiences of women at the grass-roots.

[. . .]

Bibliography

Bunch, C., P. Antrobus, S. Frost and N. Reilly (2001) 'International Networking for Women's Human Rights', in M. Edwards and J. Gaventa (eds), *Global Citizen Action* (London: Earthscan), pp. 217–29.

DAWN (1985) *Development Crisis and Alternative Visions: Third World Women's Perspective* (Delhi: DAWN).

—— (1990) *Interregional Meeting and General Report* (Rio de Janeiro: DAWN).

—— (2002) DAWNInforms <www.dawn.org.fj/publications/DAWNInforms>.

Elson, D. (2002) 'Gender Justice, Human Rights, and Neo-liberal Economic Policies', in M. Molyneux and S. Razavi (eds), *Gender Justice, Development and Human Rights* (Oxford: Oxford University Press), pp. 78–114.

Moser, C. (1993), *Gender, Planning and Development,* London: Routledge.

Nussbaum, M. (2002) 'Women's Capabilities and Social Justice', in M. Molyneux and S. Razavi (eds), *Gender Justice, Development and Rights* (Oxford: Oxford University Press), pp. 45–77.

Pearson, R. and C. Jackson (eds) (1998) *Feminist Visions of Development* (London: Routledge).

Sen, G. and C. Grown (1987) *Development, Crises, and Alternative Visions* (New York: Monthly Review Press).

Stienstra, D (2000) 'Making Global Connections Among Women' in R. Cohen and S. Rai (eds), *Global Social Movements* (London: Athlone), pp. 62–82.

Taylor, V. (2000) *Marketisation of Governance* (Cape Town: SADEP, University of Cape Town).

UNDP (1999) *Human Development Report* (New York: UNDP).

Young, B. (2001) 'Globalization and Gender: A European Perspective', in R. Kelly, J. Bayes, M. Hawkesworth and B. Young (eds) *Gender, Globalization and Democratization* (Oxford: Bowman and Littlefield), pp. 27–48.

Young, K. (1993) *Planning Development with Women* (London: Macmillan).

Youngman, F. (1986) *Adult Education and Socialist Pedagogy* (London: Croom Helm).

Chapter 41

Jackie Smith

GLOBALIZING RESISTANCE: THE BATTLE OF SEATTLE AND THE FUTURE OF SOCIAL MOVEMENTS

Background: the Seattle ministerial

THE ORIGINAL 1994 WTO [World Trade Organization] agreement committed member states to a Millennium Round of talks that would expand trade liberalization policies under the WTO. The United States and other Western nations were strong advocates of WTO expansion, and they extensively tried to advance these goals before the Seattle meeting. For many states in the global South, however, the WTO was a disappointment. Although initially attracted by the promise of greater access to Western markets and greater influence in the IMF and World Bank, Southern governments found themselves left out of important WTO decisions. Key deliberations were held in closed-door, "Green Room" meetings organized at the behest of the United States, Canada, European Union, and Japan (referred to as "the Quad"). Secret agreements were then presented to Southern members who were most vulnerable to pressure from the powerful Quad states (Vidal 1999; Zoll 1999). Southern governments also realized fewer economic rewards from expanded trade under the WTO than they had expected. Their agenda in Seattle was therefore to review existing agreements and to make them more equitable rather than to support a Millennium Round that would expand the WTO regime under rules they saw as highly skewed toward Western and corporate interests. This division among states was an important cause of the ultimate breakdown of talks in Seattle. In addition to this North-South split, there were divisions between European and U.S. interests over food safety standards and agricultural issues. In short, governments faced difficult prospects for staging a successful meeting in Seattle. All hope of bridging the North-South gap was effectively lost when President Clinton succumbed to pressure from protesters and called for labor protections within the WTO.

Social movement forces allied against the WTO expansion also contributed to these difficulties. Strong European resistance to genetically modified foods made it difficult for European governments to liberalize regulations on agricultural imports. Farmers' movements, which are strong in many European countries, also fought against cuts to subsidies and other agricultural supports. Southern governments benefited from analyses of researchers who were intellectual leaders of the anti-WTO movement. Certainly, Southern challenges to Quad dominance in the WTO were bolstered by massive protests of Quad states' own citizens. It would be hard to argue that the Seattle Ministerial would have failed as miserably as it did without tens of thousands of protesters surrounding the meeting site.

The major protest slogan was "No WTO" (or "Hell no, WTO" if you were a steel worker or Teamster), but there was no clear consensus among protest groups about whether the WTO itself should be abolished or reformed. What was clear was that virtually all protesters in the streets of Seattle sought to democratize and incorporate values other than profit making into global economic institutions.

These goals could not be promoted effectively in national contexts for a number of reasons. First, for citizens of countries with small markets and little economic power, attempting to influence domestic policies is useless because these governments carry little weight in international negotiations. Second, in countries like the United States (as well as in global economic institutions), economic policies are considered technical, not political, decisions. They are formulated by bureaucrats in the U.S. Treasury Department and in the Trade Representative's Office, and they are not open to democratic scrutiny for reasons of trade-secret protection and competitiveness. Most citizens know very little about these offices and are deterred by the technical language. Third, the WTO agreement has removed key decisions from national policy debates. WTO limits on citizens' ability to affect even national policies have made the WTO agreement itself a target. Even in the United States, which wields the strongest influence in the WTO, citizens cannot simply work within domestic contexts to affect changes. They may seek to influence WTO policies domestically, but they gain more leverage as collective actors at the multilateral level where they can exploit differences among states.

Movement origins: structures and identities

The Seattle resistance grew from earlier local, national, and transnational mobilizations against trade liberalization agreements, World Bank and IMF policies, and failures to protect human rights and the environment. The Seattle protests were novel because of substantial participation by citizens from the United Slates and other advanced industrialized countries against an international organization. They also involved a web of transnational associations and movement networks that developed out of activist streams of the 1980s and 1990s. This web facilitated cooperation and exchange across national boundaries.

The organizations most prominent in Seattle had previously mobilized against global trade and multilateral financial policies. Labor organizations, consumer groups (most notably Nader's Public Citizen), and major North American environmental organizations began focusing on trade liberalization especially during negotiations around the Canada–U.S. Free Trade Agreement and subsequent North American Free Trade Agreement (see, e.g., Audley 1997; Aaronson 2001; Ayres 1998; Shoch 2000; Naim 2000). Seattle's neoliberal trade opposition had even earlier roots. Perhaps the earliest resistance began in the global South with resistance to IMF-imposed structural adjustment policies (Walton and Seddon 1994). Environmental and human rights campaigners increasingly tried to curb World Bank lending for projects that threatened peoples and ecosystems in the global South (Fox and Brown 1998; Keck and Sikkink 1998; Rich 1994). These efforts drew the attention of Northern peace activists in the 1980s. Many of the older activists in Seattle, particularly those mobilized around "Jubilee 2000" or affiliated with peace movement organizations like the Women's International League for Peace and Freedom, traced their opposition back to the 1980s mobilizations around Third World debt and its relationship to conflict and economic justice in Central America and other developing regions (see, e.g., Smith 1994; Marullo, Pagnucco, and Smith 1996). Partly as a result of these struggles, the annual World Bank/IMF meetings became sites of protest rallies in the late 1980s (Scholte 2000; Gerhards and Rucht 1992). An international "Fifty Years Is Enough" campaign emerged in the mid-1990s to mobilize against the 1995 "celebration" of the fiftieth anniversary of the Bretton Woods conference and the founding of the World Bank and IMF (Foster 1999:143–153; Cleary 1996; 88–89).

Research on social movements has shown that formal social movement organizations play important roles in framing movement agendas, cultivating collective identities, and mobilizing collective actions. At the same time, churches, community organizations, friendship networks, and professional associations provide resources for movements and often engage in similar kinds of protest-oriented activities, even though these are not their principal purpose. Because these "extra-movement" groups have routine contacts with broad segments of society, they promote wider social movement participation and legitimacy (McCarthy 1996; C. Smith 1996). The anti-WTO protests included many of these "extra-movement" organizations and informal networks as important participants. For instance, many churches and unions with standing committees on social justice or solidarity issues had at least some regular contact with social movements. Many U.S. labor unions provided logistical and financial support so that their members could participate in an entire week of protest and educational activity. Also, churches played an important role by disseminating information about the protests and by providing meeting spaces, legitimacy, and other resources. Jubilee 2000 was based largely in churches and faith-based social justice organizations, and the event drew many protesters to Seattle. School groups, in particular those opposing sweatshop labor, also helped raise awareness of protests and mobilize participation. In addition, protest organizers worked consciously to cultivate ties with community groups and with an active social movement sector in the Pacific Northwest.

✱ But the Seattle protests also were built upon transnational mobilizing structures that shaped leadership and strategies. For instance, the rapid expansion of transnational social movement organizations (TSMOs) during the past fifty years provided many activists with substantive knowledge of the political views of groups from different parts of the world, opportunities to gain skills and experience in international organizing work, expertise in international law, and familiarity with multilateral negotiations (Sikkink and Smith 2002). TSMO growth promoted transnational dialogue and helped organizers to coordinate interests and propose policies that accounted for the needs of people in both the global North and the global South. By facilitating flows of information across national boundaries, organizations with transnational ties helped cultivate movement identities, transcend nationally defined interests, and build solidary identities with a global emphasis (cf. Gamson 1991). These identities are crucial for long-term mobilization and alliances across national boundaries where routine face-to-face contact is rare. They require deliberate efforts to define "who *we* are" in order to sustain activists commitment.

TSMOs must demonstrate wide geographic representation if they are to be effective in multilateral political arenas. Engaging participants from many different countries lends credibility to an organization's agenda and, until recently, it was a central criterion for official UN accreditation. It also provides an organization with first-hand information on conditions in a variety of countries, facilitating efforts to link local examples to global policy debates. To cultivate a diverse membership these organizations must create spaces for transnational dialogue on common goals and strategies (Smith, Pagnucco, and Chatfield 1997). While most protesters in Seattle were from the United States and Canada, there were many from other parts of the world, particularly among the speakers at protest rallies and teach-ins. Southern activists and scholars comprised 30 to 40 percent of the panelists at the largest protest rallies and the People's Assembly. Many of the activists from poor countries traveled to Seattle as a consequence of their participation in transnational associations. Data on TSMOs show a trend toward greater participation of global South countries. The Ministerial's location in Seattle meant underrepresentation of Southern activists, but when UN conferences are held in the South they draw many Southern representatives (Clark, Hochstetler, and Friedman 1998; Smith, Pagnucco, and Lopez 1998)

In the process of building coalitions and joint strategies, activists learn each other's positions and, where conditions favor it, build relationships and trust that are crucial for ongoing cooperation (Rose 2000). For instance, while Western environmental and labor activists might accept a policy or promoting environmental and labor protections through existing WTO mechanisms, dialogues with their counterparts in developing countries led to a position opposing the extension of WTO authority into other areas. As a result, the common statement endorsed by nearly 1,500 citizens' organizations from eighty-nine countries called on governments to adopt "a moratorium on any new issues or further negotiations that expand the scope and power of the WTO." It also called for review of existing agreements to address their negative effects on human and labor rights, health, women's rights, and the environment. While it is difficult to determine the effects of these kinds of joint statements, the process of preparing them and, for many groups, the decisions about whether or not to sign them, can involve extensive group deliberations about shared interests and identities.

Table 1 maps the major organizational participants in the Seattle anti-WTO actions. We hope to learn whether the participants are principally national or transnational organizations, and whether transnational groups differ from the others in their mobilization roles. Prevalent TSMO roles suggest that globalization processes, like consolidation processes of the modern nation-state, affect how people associate for political purposes.

Table 1 Mobilizing Structures behind the "Battle of Seattle" and "N30"

Type of Transnational Tie	Movement[a]	Extra-Movement
No formal TN ties	Local chapters of national SMOs (e.g., NOW) Neighborhood no-WTO Committees United for a Fair Economy	School groups Friendship networks
Diffuse TN ties	Direct Action Network Reclaim the Streets Ruckus Society Coalition for Campus Organizing	Union Locals Some churches
Routine TN ties	Public Citizen Global Exchange Reinforest Action Network United Students against Sweatshops Council of Canadians Sierra Club	AFL-CIO United Steel Workers of America International Longshore and Warehouse Union Some churches
Formal transnational organization[b]	Greenpeace Friends of the Earth International Forum on Globalization Third World Network Peoples Global Action 50 Years Is Enough Network Women's Environment and Development Organization	International Confederation of Free Trade Unions European Farmers Union

[a] This list is illustrative, not comprehensive. The organizing scheme draws from McCarthy's (1996) distinction between social movement structures, which are explicitly designed to promote social change goals, and "non movement" (here extra-movement) mobilizing structures. The latter group is important for social movements but their basic organizational mandates encompass goals beyond those of social movements.

[b] Organizations may vary in formalization and hierarchy: Friends of the Earth and Greenpeace have defined organizational structures and institutional presence; groups like People's Global Action resist forming an organizational headquarters and Reclaim the Streets sustains a loose, network-like structure relying heavily on electronic communication and affinity groups.

While the table is not an exhaustive list of organizations protesting in Seattle, it does include those most directly involved. The table clarifies an important division of labor between groups with formalized transnational ties and those with diffuse ties. Groups with no ties or with diffuse transnational ties and groups with informal and decentralized organizations were principally involved in mobilizing and education, as well as in efforts to "shut down" the meetings.

Groups with formalized transnational connections were also involved in education and mobilization, but they played more important roles in framing and informing protester critiques of the global trading system. They also lobbied government delegations and relayed information from official meetings to protest groups that lacked official accreditation. They supported other groups' mobilization efforts by developing educational materials, speaking at rallies and teach-ins, and bringing in speakers from the global South. These groups were the international specialists that had ready access to detailed information about WTO processes and regulations. They could produce examples of the effects of global economic policies, and frequently they had privileged access to official documents and delegations. As in national contexts where the different foci of local versus national groups create rifts in group identities and perceptions, there is some evidence of conflict across this division of labor, although it does not appear to have seriously detracted from protest efforts.

Groups without formal transnational ties are principally local chapters of national groups and local groups formed around the anti-WTO mobilization. United for a Fair Economy, for instance, is a national group focusing on inequalities in the U.S. economy. These groups were important in local participant mobilization in Seattle, and they often worked with or were mobilized because of groups like Direct Action Network, Public Citizen, or others with more extensive transnational ties. Groups with diffuse ties include regional organizations whose memberships cross the U.S.-Canada border and/or groups with other transnational ties that grow out of their organizing efforts. For instance, the Berkeley-based Ruckus Society (whose leaders include former Students for a Democratic Society organizers) primarily brings together Canadians and Americans for nonviolence training. The Coalition for Campus Organizing does progressive organizing on college campuses, and recently it has focused on sweatshops and educational issues, including issues raised by the WTO General Agreement on Trade in Services (GATS). Its international work has led to cooperation with student organizations in Canada.

Organizations listed as having "routine" transnational ties typically are national organizations which have staff devoted to international organizing or solidarity building, have standing committees to work on international issues (e.g., Sierra Club, AFL-CIO, Public Citizen), or have sustained cooperation with activists from other countries (e.g., Global Exchange, USAS). In practice, these organizations' transnational interpersonal and inter-organizational contacts can substantially affect their agendas and frames.

Organizations with formal transnational structures incorporate transnational cooperation into their operational structures. Groups like Greenpeace and Friends of the Earth have a federated structure with national-level branches that disseminate information on global campaigns but often tailor it to national needs. Their headquarters facilitate research and information exchange and, in the some cases, conduct global-level direct action protests and lobbying. The International Forum on Globalization (IFG) is a cadre organization made up of international experts on globalization. Founded in 1994, it produces educational materials and organizes teach-ins about global financial integration. IFG leaders have been called "paradigm warriors" because they advance public debate about globalization. Third World Network has a similar structure, although it consists entirely of scholars and experts from the global South. People's Global Action (PGA) is a loose coalition of mostly grassroots organizations with a website, but no headquarters. PGA includes many groups from India and other parts of the global South that came together after

Zapatista organizers issued an electronic call for an international meeting (PGA 2000). It has convened several international meetings on globalization since the mid-1990s and supported protests at earlier meetings of the WTO and G-7 countries. The 50 Years Is Enough Network is one example of what may be an increasingly common coalitional form. Rather than having national branches, groups sharing the network's views join as partners to participate in joint statements and actions. This maintains local groups' autonomy while keeping them informed about global issues and offering flexibility about campaign participation. The important point is that these organizations have formal mechanisms for sustained transnational communication and cooperation.

Extra-movement mobilizing structures for the Seattle protests also demonstrate transnational linkages. The International Confederation of Free Trade Unions (ICFTU) held its annual conference in Seattle just prior to the WTO gathering, attracting labor leaders from over 100 countries. These international exchanges promote labor solidarity and force U.S. labor leaders to confront their isolationist and nationalist positions. Churches also often promote transnational exchanges and solidarity (C. Smith 1996), such as missions, solidarity work in support of affiliated churches, and fact-finding visits. Because they help link global identities and interests with routine social activities, both religious and labor alliances can advance transnational mobilization to a general audience.

This overview demonstrates that globalization processes affect how social movements mobilize and organize. Substantial transnational ties among key organizations lie behind the Seattle protests, suggesting a transnational-national (or local) division of labor. Transnational ties can be diffuse, growing out of shared purposes, or formal. In between, we find numerous innovative mechanisms for transnational cooperation. Groups with routinized transnational structures seem to be more involved in lobbying and information gathering than national and local groups, which disseminate information and mobilize protesters. Although this chapter is only a snapshot of a single protest episode, the data show that social movements have developed formalized, integrated, and sustained organizational mechanisms for transnational cooperation around global social-change goals. This development is reinforced by the political demands of the global policy process, political socialization, and globally oriented identity construction.

Global political processes and movement tactics

Innovative repertoires

Although many tactics used in Seattle are adaptations of earlier repertoires, others are innovative in the sense that they target multilateral arenas and that they often involve TSMOs. Transnational associations are not new, but the last half-century has seen an explosion in their numbers. Their tactics often rely on new technologies, ironically the same ones that have fueled the global economic expansion the protesters resist.

Organization and Mobilization. One of the most basic innovations is the creation of transnational associations. Others include the creation of transnationally oriented movement media, such as the NGO newspapers at intergovernmental conferences. These papers present counterhegemonic interpretations of negotiations and highlight the proposals and activities raised by challenger groups. Such newspapers have proved important in pressing governments to take up concerns of challenger groups and in providing alternatives to great-power dominated conference frames. They have been used at many inter-governmental conferences, including those on nuclear disarmament, Law of the Sea, human rights, and women's and environmental issues (Atwood 1997; Clark, Friedman, and Hochstetler 1998; Levering 1997; Willetts 1996).

Borrowing Official Templates. Activists in Seattle and other multilateral contexts structure their collective action around official templates. For example, one of the Seattle coalitions organized a "Peoples' Assembly" to parallel official deliberations. Daily panels centered on a different agenda item such as environment and health, women, human rights, labor, and agriculture.

Another way that challengers borrow official forms is by getting sympathetic experts or even movement activists onto national delegations to international meetings. Because international negotiations are highly technical, governments look beyond their diplomatic corps to fill their delegations. In some fields, such as human rights, environment, and women's issues, some of the most widely respected experts are social movement activists. Their expertise and familiarity with the international negotiation processes make them a rich resource for governments seeking to influence negotiations. While they are obviously not likely to appear on delegations of countries opposing their views, activist experts may sit on delegations of sympathetic countries. Or they may force their way onto a delegation by using national laws such as the U.S. Federal Advisory Council Act that requires government advisory panels at international meetings to represent a fair balance of viewpoints. When movement sympathizers serve on delegations, they are often conduits of information between official and popular forums.

Another form of official template borrowing involves dramaturgy in the application of international legal principles. In Seattle, the Program on Corporations, Law, and Democracy and the National Lawyers Guild Committee staged a "Global People's tribunal on Corporate Crimes against Humanity." Its purpose was to dramatically "bring to trial" corporate practices around the world. "Witnesses" included a former sweatshop worker from the Philippines who had worked for a Gap subcontractor until she was fired for promoting union activities, a farmers' organization representative from India discussing the effects of Monsanto's seed marketing practices on Indian farmers, and an Indian medical doctor who treated victims of Union Carbide's 1984 chemical disaster in Bhopal. The lawyer-activists facilitating the event educated the audience and "jury" on the relevant international law and tribunal procedures, and the Tribunal issued an "indictment" for crimes against humanity of the governments under whose laws the guilty corporations were established. The appeal to international law against state and corporate practices serves to emphasize the legitimacy or worthiness of the protesters' cause even in the authorities' own terms.

Electronic Activism. Perhaps the most significant innovations result from the same technological innovations that have advanced economic globalization, namely, electronic communications and exchange. These were likely introduced simultaneously to both national and transnational protest repertoires as technologies facilitating inexpensive transnational communications became widely available. Both national and transnational social movement groups make extensive use of Internet sites and electronic list serves to expand communication with dispersed constituencies and audiences. These communication networks allow organizers to almost instantaneously transmit alternative media accounts and images of protests to contrast those of mainstream, corporate-owned media outlets. Alternative electronic media networks also rapidly disseminate information about resistance against economic globalization in the global South, such as the Mexican student strikers. This conflict escalated shortly after Seattle as students rallied in solidarity with jailed Seattle protesters. New technologies also allowed transmission of police radio communications during the protests that undermined authorities' legitimacy.

Rather than rely solely on the mainstream media to convey the images of the protests to the general public, activists organized an "Independent Media Center" (IMC) in Seattle, issuing press badges to volunteer photographers, video recorders, and reporters (no formal credentials necessary) wanting to cover the protests. IMC volunteers had access to a press office and could post their reports, pictures and video (some for direct cable broadcast) onto a website linked to other movement sites.

Electronic civil disobedience also becomes possible as commerce and other essential activities are linked to the flow of electronic information. Anti-WTO protesters who could not get to Seattle could satisfy their desire to join in the protests by engaging in electronic "sit-ins" at the WTO Internet site to block other information-seekers' access to the site. At least one hacker developed a "mirror" site that drew in unwitting information seekers who thought they were viewing the official WTO web page. The site was subtly different from the official one, and carried criticisms of the WTO (*Seattle Post Intelligencer*, November 29, 1999, A1) More confrontational "e-protest" fakes the form of e-mail and fax jamming, where large faxes (e.g. protest letters written one word per page) and e-mail messages are sent to disrupt routine flows of information to targets.

Reviewing the tactics employed in Seattle, we find a protest repertoire that both adapts forms that have been typical of national social movement repertoires and expands the repertoire to address multilateral institutional arenas. This protest repertoire can be attributed to the global-level reorganization of political and economic relations in which challengers themselves play a role. Events in Seattle should be examined as part of a more continuous process of evolving forms of contentious politics that began late in the nineteenth century, but gathered momentum especially during the latter half of the twentieth century, through which challengers have increasingly sought to influence international policy and processes (see, e.g., Chatfield 1997; Keck and Sikkink 1998). The Battle of Seattle, then, was not the first, nor likely the last, in the contest to shape global economic, political, and societal integration. It is part of an interactive process of contention between elites and popular challengers that will have implications for the course of future conflicts and institutional changes.

References

Aaronson, Susan Ariel. 2001. *Taking Trade to the Streets: The Lost History of Public Efforts to Shape Globalization*. Ann Arbor: University of Michigan Press.
Atwood, David. 1997. "Mobilizing Around the United Nations Special Session on Disarmament." Pp. 141–158 in *Transnational Social Movements and Global Politics: Solidarity beyond the*

State, edited by J. Smith, C. Chatfield, and R. Pagnucco. Syracuse, N.Y.: Syracuse University Press.

Audley, John J. 1997. *Green Politics and Global Trade: NAFTA and the Future of Environmental Politics*. Washington D.C.: Georgetown University Press.

Ayres, Jeffrey M. 1998. *Defying Conventional Wisdom: Political Movements and Popular Contention against North American Free Trade*. Toronto: University of Toronto Press.

Chatfield, Charles. 1997. "Intergovernmental and Nongovernmental Associations to 1945." Pp 19-41 in *Transnational Social Movements and World Politics: Solidarity beyond the State*, edited by J. Smith, C. Chatfield, and R. Pagnucco. Syracuse, N.Y.: Syracuse University Press.

Clark, Ann Marie, Elisabeth J. Friedman, and Kathryn Hochstetler. 1998. "The Sovereign Limits of Global Civil Society: A Comparison of NGO Participation in UN World Conferences on the Environment, Human Rights, and Women." *World Politics* 51:1–35.

Cleary, Seamus. 1996. "The World Bank and NGOs." Pp. 63–97 in *The Conscience of the World: The Influence of Non-governmental Organisations in the UN System*, edited by P. Willetts, Washington. D.C.: Brookings Institution.

Foster, John. 1999. "Civil Society and Multilateral Theatres." Pp. 129–195 in *Whose World Is It Anyway? Civil Society, the United Nations, and the Multilateral Future*, edited by J. W. Foster and A. Anand. Ottawa: United Nations Association of Canada.

Fox, Jonathan, and L. David Brown. 1998. *The Struggle for Accountability: The World Bank, NGOs, and Grassroots Movements*. Cambridge, Mass.: MIT Press.

Gamson, William A. 1991. "Commitment and Agency in Social Movements." *Sociological Forum* 6:27–50.

Gerhards, Jürgen, and Dieter Rucht. 1992. "Mesomobilization: Organizing and Framing in Two Protest Campaigns in West Germany. *American Journal of Sociology* 98:555–595.

Keck, Margaret, and Kathryn Sikkink. 1998. *Activists beyond Borders*." Ithaca, N.Y.: Cornell University Press.

Levering, Ralph A. 1997. "Brokering the Law of the Sea Treaty: The Neptune Group." Pp. 225–242 in *Transnational Social Movements and Global Politics: Solidarity beyond the State*, edited by J. Smith, C. Chatfield, and R. Pagnucco. Syracuse, N.Y.: Syracuse University Press.

Marullo, Sam, Ron Pagnucco, and Jackie Smith, 1996. "Frame Changes and Social Movement Contraction: U.S. Peace Movement Framing after the Cold War." *Sociological Inquiry* 66:1–28.

McCarthy, John D. 1996. "Mobilizing Structures: Constraints and Opportunities: Adopting, Adapting and Inventing." Pp. 141–151 in *Political Opportunities, Mobilizing Structures and Framing: Social Movement Dynamics in Cross-National Perspective.*, edited by D. McAdam, J. McCarthy, and M. Zald. New York: Cambridge University Press.

Naim, Moisés. 2000. "Foreign Policy Interview: Lori's War." *Foreign Policy* 118:28–55.

PGA. 2000. "The Accelerating History of PGA" *Worldwide Resistance Roundup Inspired by Peoples Global Action* Bulletin 5, February (UK Edition).

Rich, Bruch. 1994. *Mortgaging the Earth: The World Bank, Environmental Impoverishment and the Crisis of Development*. Boston: Beacon Press.

Rose, Fred. 2000. *Coalitions across the Class Divide: Lessons from the Labor, Peace, and Environmental Movements*. Ithaca, N.Y.: Cornell University Press.

Scholte, Jan Aart. 2000. "Cautionary Reflections on Seattle" *Millennium: Journal of International Studies* 29:115–121.

Shoch, James. 2000. "Contesting Globalization: Organized Labor, NAFTA, and the 1997 and 1998 Fast-Track Fights." *Politics and Society* 28:119–150.

Sikkink, Kathryn, and Jackie Smith. 2002. "Infrastructures for Change: Transnational Organizations, 1953–1993." In *Restructuring World Politics: The Power of Transnational Agency and Norms*, edited by S. Khagram, J. Riker, and K. Sikkink. Minneapolis: University of Minnesota Press.

Smith, Christian. 1994. *Resisting Reagan*. Chicago: University of Chicago Press.

———. 1996 "Correcting a Curious Neglect, or Bringing Religion Back In." Pp. 1–25 in *Disruptive Religion: The Force of Faith in Social Movement Activism*, edited by C. Smith. New York: Routledge.

Smith, Jackie, and Timothy Patrick Moran. 2000. "WTO 101: Myths about the World Trading System" *Dissent* (spring): 66–70.

Smith, Jackie, Ron Pagnucco, and Charles Chatfield. 1997. "Transnational Social Movements and Global Politics: A Theoretical Framework." Pp, 59–77 in *Transnational Social Movements and Global Politics: Solidarity beyond the State*, edited by J. Smith, C. Chatfield, and R. Pagnucco. Syracuse, N.Y.: Syracuse University Press.

Smith, Jackie, Ron Pagnucco, and George Lopez, 1998. "Globalizing Human Rights: Report on a Survey of Transnational Human Rights NGOs," *Human Rights Quarterly* 20:379–412.

Vidal, John. 1999. "The Trade Talks Collapse: Real Battle for Seattle." *The Observer* (London), December 5, 20.

Walton, John, and David Seddon. 1994. *Free Markets and Food Riots: The Politics of Global Adjustment*. Cambridge, Mass.: Blackwell.

Willetts, Peter. 1996. *The Conscience of the World: The Influence of NGOs in the United Nations System*. London: C. Hurst.

Zoll, Dan. 1999. "Developing Nations Complain of Being Shut Out of Ministerial Planning Process." Pp. 1, 8 in *World Trade Observer*, www.worldtradeobserver.org.

Chapter 42

Sanjeev Khagram, James V. Riker and Kathryn Sikkink

FROM SANTIAGO TO SEATTLE: TRANSNATIONAL ADVOCACY GROUPS RESTRUCTURING WORLD POLITICS

AT THE CLOSE OF THE TWENTIETH CENTURY, transnational advocacy groups gave a visible and startling manifestation of their power in the massive demonstrations against the World Trade Organization (WTO) meetings in Seattle, Washington, where they contributed to shutting down global negotiations and captured world attention for their cause. The protest in Seattle was not an isolated, spontaneous event but rather a conscious tactic of an increasingly coordinated and powerful movement against globalization that often targets international organizations such as the WTO, the World Bank (WB), and the International Monetary Fund (IMF).

[. . .]

We join other scholars and policymakers who now assert that international nongovernmental organizations and transnational social movements are emerging as a powerful new force in international politics and are transforming global norms and practices (see, for example, Risse-Kappen 1995; Smith, Chatfield, and Pagnucco 1997; Lipschutz 1992; Keck and Sikkink 1998; Boli and Thomas 1999; Stiles 1998; Risse, Ropp, and Sikkink 1999; Peterson 1992; Florini 2000). Others see these nonstate actors as sources of resistance "from below" to globalization that challenge the authority and practices of states and international institutions that shape the parameters for global governance (Falk 1997; Waterman, Fairbrother, and Elger 1998; Mittelman 2000; Naim 2000; O'Brien et al. 2000). Indeed the networks, coalitions, and movements we study [. . .] become active participants in "de facto global governance" (Shaw 2000). Some analysts even herald the emergence of a global civil society and its corresponding notion of global citizenship (Dorsey 1993; Wapner 1995; Lipschutz 1992; Falk 1993, 1998; Commission on Global Governance 1995, 1999; Naidoo 2000; Reinicke and Deng 2000). Many different terms are now used to describe these new forms of global governance— "complex multilateralism," "heterarchic governance," "multi-level structures of transnational governance," or "networked minimalism" (O'Brien et al. 2000; Knight 2000; Smith 2000; Nye and Donahue 2000). All stress a similar phenomena—the increase in new nonstate actors, new arenas for action, and the blurring of distinctions between domestic and global levels of politics.

[. . .]

The social movements literature has developed intermediate theoretical propositions about when social movements emerge, what forms they take, the roles they play in social life, the types of impacts they have, and (to a lesser extent) the conditions under which they can be effective. Because this literature has always focused directly on nonstate actors, its emerging synthesis of theoretical concepts and propositions provides a potentially rich source of insights for the international relations student of transnational collective action (for example, McAdam, McCarthy, and Zald 1996; Tarrow 1998). There is an emerging subfield of social movement theory devoted to theorizing transnational collective action and as this type of study develops, it could benefit from insights from international relations (IR) theory.

But if social movement scholars have been "myopically domestic," IR scholars have been equally myopically state-centric, so each can benefit from the insights of the other. The (neo-)realist and (liberal-)institutionalist paradigms that have dominated the study of IR until very recently focused exclusively, and in a self-conscious way, on the pre-dominant role of states in world politics (Krasner 1985; Keohane 1989; Katzenstein, Keohane, and Krasner 1998). Even the recent challenge from many self-described "constructivist" scholars of IR has been primarily focused on ideas and norms and not so much on the role of nonstate actors in shaping those ideas and norms.

We believe strongly that dialogue between the two sets of scholars is potentially fruitful: First, the debates about norms and ideas in international relations could benefit from engagement with older debates over framing and collective beliefs in the social movements literature. Second, the political opportunity structure debates in social movement theory could be usefully informed by IR literatures that explore the dynamic interaction of domestic politics and the international system. After describing the main forms and dimensions of transnational collective action [. . .] we will turn to these two potential theoretical dialogues.

Forms of transnational collective action

We argue that the essential types or forms of transnational collective action or contentious politics are *international nongovernmental organizations (or transnational nongovernmental organizations), transnational advocacy networks, transnational coalitions, and transnational social movements*. As a starting point we present a typology of these forms of transnational collective action because we believe that the form that transnational collective action takes may influence its goals and effectiveness.

[. . .]

Nongovernmental organizations (NGOs) are private, voluntary, nonprofit groups whose primary aim is to influence publicly some form of social change. Generally, NGOs are more formal and professional than domestic social movements, with legal status and paid personnel. *Domestic nongovernmental organizations* draw membership from one country, though the focus of their efforts may be directed internationally. *International nongovernmental organizations (INGOs)* have a decision-making structure with voting members from at least three countries, and their aims are cross-national and/or international in scope.

Domestic and international NGOs are primary actors that constitute transnational collective action.

[. . .]

We will discuss three types of configurations—transnational networks, transnational coalitions, and transnational movements (and associated transnational movement organizations)—involving different degrees of connection and mobilization.

Transnational advocacy networks are the most informal configuration of nonstate actors. Networks are sets of actors linked across country boundaries, bound together by shared values, dense exchanges of information and services, and common discourses (Keck and Sikkink 1995, 1998). While some networks are formalized, most are based on informal contacts. The essence of network activity is the exchange and use of information. Networks do not involve either sustained coordination of tactics, as with coalitions, or mobilizing large numbers of people in the kind of activity we associate with social movements.

[. . .]

A *transnational coalition* involves a greater level of transnational coordination than that present in a transnational network. Transnational coalitions are sets of actors linked across country boundaries who coordinate shared strategies or sets of tactics to publicly influence social change. The shared strategies or sets of tactics are identified as *transnational campaigns*, which are often the unit of analysis used when researching and analyzing transnational collective action. Such coordination of tactics requires a more formal level of contact than a network because groups usually need to meet to identify and agree upon these shared tactics, to strategize about how to implement the campaign, and to report regularly to each other on campaign progress. The coordinated strategy or tactic can be "noninstitutional," such as a boycott, but transnational coalitions, like domestic social movements, frequently blend institutional and noninstitutional tactics (Tarrow 1998; Meyer and Tarrow 1998).

[. . .]

Transnational social movements are sets of actors with common purposes and solidarities linked across country boundaries that have the capacity to generate coordinated and sustained social mobilization in more than one country to publicly influence social change. In contrast to transnational networks and coalitions, transnational social movements mobilize their (transnational) constituencies for collective action, often through the use of protest or disruptive action. This definition of transnational social movements fits with definitions of domestic social movements that stress mobilization and/or disruption as a defining characteristic of movements (Tarrow 1998; Rucht 1996; Kriesi 1996). Social movement theorists argue that a movement's effectiveness in bringing about social change is linked to its ability to disrupt or threaten a social order (McAdam 1982; Tarrow 1998). We would, then, expect transnational social movements, with their capacity for mobilization and disruption, to be more effective than other forms of transnational collective action. We would also expect transnational movements to have a higher level of transnational collective identity.

But transnational social movements are also the most difficult and rare form of transnational collective action. In order to speak of a truly transnational social movement, we suggest that groups in at least three countries must exercise their capacity to engage in joint and sustained mobilization. What often occurs in practice is that members of transnational networks or coalitions are linked to domestic movements in different countries but the domestic social movements themselves are not directly linked to each other. Other times, a cross-national diffusion of ideas occurs between domestic social movements in similar issue areas without efforts at coordinated mobilization.

These three forms can be viewed as ascending levels of transnational collective action. Often, a transnational coalition will emerge only after a network of communication has first developed, and a transnational movement will add the mobilizational element to an existing transnational coalition. Conversely, a sustained transnational network may be initiated from a shorter-term campaign of transnational coalition. It is difficult to imagine a movement emerging without prior network or coalition activity.

[. . .]

While the definitions of transnational networks, coalitions, and movements are not necessarily comprehensive or mutually exclusive, they do highlight the dominant modality of each type of transnational collective action:

Form	Dominant Modality
transnational network	information exchange
transnational coalition (campaign)	coordinated tactics
transnational movement	joint mobilization

[. . .]

Makers and managers of meaning: norms and framing in transnational collective action

The emergent transnationalist research program is intrinsically linked to concerns with the influence of ideas and norms on world politics (see Katzenstein 1996; Finnemore and Sikkink 1998; see also Kratochwil 1989; Lumsdaine 1993; Klotz 1995;Thomson 1990; Finnemore 1993). Because most transnational nongovernmental actors are relatively weak, their ability to influence international politics is often based on the use of information, persuasion, and moral pressure to contribute to change in international institutions and governments.

[. . .]

The nongovernmental sector is an increasingly important and distinctive actor in this international society. As an ideal type, it represents a third sector distinct from but interacting with government and business, in which the characteristic form of relation is neither authority or hierarchy (as in government and bureaucracy), nor the market, but rather the informal and horizontal network. If the business sector has been characterized by the drive for profit and the government sector by the use of authority, the third sector, or nongovernmental sector, could be characterized by the search for meaning. The individuals and groups in this sector are primarily motivated to shape the world according to their principled beliefs. Of course, many government and business activities are also involved in managing meanings, but for NGOs and movements it is their raison d'être, rather than an ancillary motivation for action.

International arenas such as intergovernmental organizations are key meeting places where governments and businesses interact with transnational nongovernmental actors. These interactions are often far from harmonious, as they represent a clash, not only of forms of organization, as vertical hierarchy encounters horizontal network, but also a clash of purposes, as the purposes of states encounter and conflict with (or converge with) those of businesses and nongovernmental organizations. While most accounts of international organizations succeed in conveying the conflicts of interest, few have captured the role of these organizations as arenas for "consensus mobilization" or the "battle of justifications," nor have they understood the unique role of the nongovernmental sector in these struggles.

Analyzing the third sector has been so difficult exactly because of the intractability of sorting out these kinds of struggles over meaning. Yet we cannot understand transnational networks or coalitions unless we grasp that a significant amount of their activity is directed at changing understandings and interpretations of actors or, in other words, the creation, institutionalization, and monitoring of norms. International relations theorists have tried to conceptualize these processes by thinking about persuasion, legitimacy, socialization, and communicative action (Finnemore 1996; Risse 2000; Risse and Sikkink 1999). Social movement theory can be quite useful in this regard, because scholars from this tradition have been working for decades on these issues, although usually within the bounds of a single state.

Social movement theorists have long been preoccupied with the process of meaning creation, and in the 1990s "the social construction of meaning has become a central part of social movement theory" (Klandermans 1997, 204). Movements help to create and recreate meanings through "framing" or the strategic efforts by groups of people to fashion shared understandings of the world and of themselves that legitimate and motivate collective action. According to Sidney Tarrow, frames are not ideas, but ways of packaging and presenting ideas. Movements then use these frames to attempt the "mobilization of consensus," that is, persuasive communication aimed at convincing others to take their side.

The notion of "framing" from the study of social movements is similar to the process called "strategic social construction" recently identified in IR (Klandermans 1997). Social movements and NGOs often take new ideas and turn them into frames that define issues at stake and the appropriate strategies for action. Carrying this task out transnationally is far more daunting than doing so domestically, but where successful, such activity can have far-reaching effects. Framing occurs not only through what movements say, but also through what they do—through their choices of tactics and the connections between their actions and their rhetoric (McAdam 1996).

[. . .]

Social movement scholarship suggests that if will be particularly difficult to form transnational social movements. In particular, social movement theories suggest that the conditions contributing to the emergence and effectiveness of social movements will be difficult to find and sustain transnationally (Tarrow 1999). For example, they argue that the framing processes critical to social movements will happen among "homogenous people who are in intense regular contact with each other" (McAdam, McCarthy, and Zald 1996, 9). But transnational social movements usually start with participants who are not homogenous. How do we explain why and how non-homogeneous people sometimes engage in transnational collective action?

Likewise, few examples exist of truly transnational collective identities. Social movement theory suggests that social movements emerge from "mobilizing structures" in communities—families, friendship networks, and the "informal structures of everyday life," including schools and churches (McAdam 1988; McCarthy 1996). Yet such mobilizing structures and interpersonal networks are largely absent from the transnational arena. In one sense, these arguments are consistent with out finding, and that of others, that there are very few examples of true transnational social movements. But we still need to explain the emergence of the many international NGOs, transnational networks, and transnational coalitions we discuss in this book. Can certain aspects of social movement theory be modified to help explain the emergence and effectiveness of these other forms of transnational collective action?

One of the main ways these efforts at transnational collective action work is by creating and enforcing international norms. Norms in the IR literature are defined as shared expectations held by a community of actors about appropriate behavior for actors with a given identity (Katzenstein 1996; Finnemore 1996). They are standards for how different actors "ought" to behave. Three aspects of this definition merit attention when specifying norms: (1) What are the shared expectations about appropriate behavior, or how do we know a norm when we see one? (2) Who are the actors that hold these expectations? (3) To which actor identities do these norms apply?

The IR literature also distinguishes between ideas (beliefs held by individuals) and norms (intersubjective beliefs about proper behavior) and makes the useful distinction between causal and principled ideas: causal ideas are ideas about cause and effect, while principled ideas are about right and wrong. Causal ideas are supported by evidence, often scientific evidence; principled ideas may be related to causal ideas, but cannot easily be resolved by appeals to evidence (Goldstein and Keohane 1993). When principled ideas are accepted by a broad range of actors, they become "norms," which are intrinsically intersubjective and held by communities. Like social movement theorists, norms scholars are very interested in the processes through which beliefs held by individuals are transformed into collective beliefs and norms.

[. . .]

Most often states work together to make norms in the context of international organizations. Other transnational actors that promote or accept international norms may be international epistemic communities, multinational corporations, transnational professional groups, and so forth.

Many international norms serve the needs of states for coordination and stability of expectations. But there is a subset of international norms that are not easily explained. They do not promote economic and political coordination and the stability of states. They do not necessarily serve the interests of private firms in maximizing profits. It is this subset of somewhat puzzling norms that is the topic of this book. Why would public authorities adopt norms that limit their own ability to treat individuals, groups, or their physical environment the way they please? Why would public authorities (or for that matter private firms) alter their practices?

We argue that you cannot understand the emergence and effectiveness of this subset of international norms without paying attention to the crucial role of transnational networks, coalitions, and movements. A critical mass of actors must accept the standards of behavior before they can be considered as norms. Because we are concerned about international norms, a certain number of states must accept principles before we can refer to them as norms.

[. . .]

Where international relations theorists talk of norms, social movement theorists tend to talk of collective or shared beliefs (Klandermans 1997). We distinguish between international norms (standards of appropriate behavior held by a critical mass of states) and collective beliefs (or transnational norms) held by transnational networks, coalitions, and movements. This distinction allows us to inquire about the relationship between the collective beliefs of linked NGOs and movements, and international norms. Groups must first work to develop "collective beliefs" or collective action frames for the movement.

In the transnational arena, transnational networks, coalitions, and movements share some collective beliefs or collective action frames. In this process international norms can form part of the "resources" and "political opportunities" from which actors draw to develop their collective beliefs. Other times transnational networks, coalitions, and movements may attempt to transform their collective beliefs into international norms.

[. . .]

Domestic and international opportunity structures and transnational collective action

[. . .]

Many social movement theorists examine social and political opportunity structures in liberal democracies. Thus, the phrases "open" or "closed" opportunity structures generally refer to a continuum within liberal democracies, depending on how porous they are to social organizations (Kitschelt 1986). These studies thus overlook the "really closed" opportunity structure of the authoritarian or semiauthoritarian regime, as compared to the "relatively open" structures of most democratic regimes. The ultimate "closed" domestic political opportunity structure is the repressive authoritarian or totalitarian regime. Not only is the regime "not porous" to societal influences, but it may be actively engaged in physically eliminating its opponents, or actively undermining their capacity to organize.

[. . .]

However, it is not enough to think about the effectiveness of transnational collective action only in terms of domestic opportunity structures. In addition, we need to think systematically about transnational political opportunity structures—that is, what are the consistent dimensions of the international or transnational political environment that provide incentives or constraints for collective action? Social movement theorists are increasingly aware that social movements operate in both a domestic and an international environment: they speak of "multilayered" opportunity structure, including a "supranational" layer or a "multilevel polity," or they highlight how international pressures influence domestic opportunity structures (Oberschall 1996; Klandermans 1997; Marks and McAdam 1996; McAdam 1996; Tarrow 1998, 1999).

We argue that international institutions indeed present clear political opportunity structures for transnational advocacy (see also Tarrow 1999). An international opportunity structure will not displace a domestic political opportunity structure, but will rather interact with it. To understand the effectiveness of transnational collective action, we must understand the dynamic interaction between an international opportunity structure and the domestic structure. This dynamic interaction may be similar to the logic of two-level games spelled out by Robert Putnam, but without the chief negotiator sitting as the linchpin in the center of negotiations (1988).

There appear to be characteristic patterns in this interaction of domestic and international opportunity structures. The "boomerang" pattern and the "spiral model" could both be thought of as models of the interaction between domestic opportunity structures and international opportunity structures (Keck and Sikkink 1998; Risse and Sikkink 1999). Both models suggest that it is blockage in the domestic society that sends domestic social movement actors into the transnational arena. This blockage is often due to repression, authoritarianism, or both. The combination of a closed domestic opportunity structure and an open international opportunity structure initiates the boomerang and the spiral. The interaction in the "spiral model" is more complex. Closed domestic polities generate transnational linkages as domestic activists are "pushed" outward, often to protect their existence. But one of the main goals of the move to the international arena is to liberalize and open domestic regimes. So the spiral model generates sustained change only when it is able to help create a more open domestic opportunity structure—usually through regime change (Risse and Sikkink 1999).

Thus, a two-level interacting political opportunity structure produces outcomes that would be counterintuitive for those only looking at domestic political opportunity structure. For example, it is generally assumed that the state's capacity or propensity for repression will diminish domestic social movement activity (Tarrow 1995; McAdam 1996). But the boomerang model suggests that repression may simultaneously move actors into international arenas to pursue their activities. Repression is the most obvious form of blockage, but a lack of responsiveness may also compel groups to work internationally. For example, feminist groups and groups of indigenous peoples have often found the international arena to be more receptive to their demands than domestic political institutions are.

The perceived degree of openness of international opportunity structures is not absolute, but is rather relative to the openness of domestic structures. For a Chilean human rights activist, the international arena was permissive and open compared to harsh repression at home. But activists in countries with very open domestic opportunity structures may perceive a move to an international institution as one that provides less room for influence. This is the basic argument about the democratic deficit in the European Union.

[. . .]

Some activists charge that governments prefer to move policy decisions to some multilateral institutions exactly because those institutions are less open to societal influence. In many cases transnational activists have developed strategies to try to influence these more closed international institutions, but they see this action as a necessary defensive response, rather than as a desirable strategic move. Where domestic groups have open domestic opportunity structures and responsive national governments, they will not seek out international institutional access, even though the source of their problems is transnational in nature. Rather they will pressure their own governments to represent their interests in international arenas (Tarrow 1995).

The possibilities for dynamic interactions among domestic and political opportunity structures are far reaching. For example, one basic aspect of the domestic opportunity structure is the presence of elite allies and support groups. By considering international opportunities, the universe of potential allies and support groups is dramatically expanded. At the same time, however, these allies may be more difficult to mobilize in transnational space because of distance, language, and cultural differences. Just as potential allies multiply, so too do potentially antagonistic sectors. In other words, the "multiorganizational fields" within which the transnational networks, coalitions, and social movements operate are more complex than those of their domestic counterparts (Klandermans 1997).

Bibliography

Boli, John, and George M. Thomas. 1999. Introduction to *Constructing World Culture: International Nongovernmental Organizations since 1875*. Stanford: Stanford University Press.

Commission on Global Governance. 1995. *Our Global Neighborhood* New York: Oxford University Press.

———. 1999. "The Millennium Year and the Reform Process." Geneva: Commission on Global Governance, November. Available at www.ogg.ch/millennium.htm.

Dorsey, Ellen. 1993. "Expanding the Foreign Policy Discourse: Transnational Social Movements and the Globalization of Citizenship." In *The Limits of State Autonomy: Societal Groups and Foreign Policy Formulation*, edited by David Skidmore and Valerie Hudson, Boulder, Colo.: Westview Press.

Falk, Richard. 1993. "The Making of Global Citizenship." In *Global Visions: Beyond the New World Order*, edited by J. Brecher, J. B. Childs, and J. Cutler. Boston: South End Press.

———. 1997. "Resisting 'Globalization-from-above' through 'Globalization-from-below.'" *New Political Economy* 2: 17–24.

———. 1998. "Global Civil Society: Perspectives, Initiatives, Movements." *Oxford Development Studies* 26, no. 1: 99–110.

Finnemore, Martha. 1993. "International Organizations as Teachers of Norms: The United Nations Educational, Scientific, and Cultural Organization and Science Policy." *International Organization* 47, no. 4: 565–98.

———. 1996. *National Interests in International Society*. Ithaca: Cornell University Press.

Finnemore, Martha, and Kathryn Sikkink. 1998. "International Norm Dynamics and Political Change." *International Organization* 52, no. 4: 887–917.

Florini, Ann, ed. 2000. *The Third Force: The Rise of Transnational Civil Society*. Washington, D.C.: Carnegie Endowment for International Peace and Japan Center for International Exchange.

Goldstein, Judith, and Robert O. Keohane. 1993. "Ideas and Foreign Policy: An Analytical Framework." In *Ideas and Foreign Policy: Beliefs, Institutions and Political Change*. Ithaca, N.Y.: Cornell University Press.

Katzenstein, Peter J., ed. 1996. *The Culture of National Security: Norms and Identity in World Politics*. New York: Columbia University Press.

Katzenstein, Peter, Robert Keohane, and Stephen Krasner. 1998. "International Organization and the Study of World Politics." *International Organization* 52, no. 4: 645–85.

Keck, Margaret, and Kathryn Sikkink. 1995. "Transnational Issue Networks in International Politics." Paper presented at the ninety-first annual meeting of the American Political Science Association, Chicago, Ill., August 31–September 3.

———. 1998. *Activists beyond Borders: Advocacy Networks in International Politics*. Ithaca: Cornell University Press.

Keohane, Robert O. 1989. *International Institutions and State Power*. Boulder, Colo.: Westview Press.

Kitschelt, Herbert. 1986. "Political Opportunity Structures and Political Protest: Anti-Nuclear Movements in Four Democracies." *British Journal of Political Science* 16: 57–85.

Klandermans, Bert. 1997. *The Social Psychology of Protest*. Oxford: Blackwell Publishers.

Klotz, Audie. 1995. *Norms in International Relations: The Struggle against Apartheid*. Ithaca: Cornell University Press.

Knight, W. Andy. 2000. "Sovereignty and NGOs." In *Global Institutions and Local Empowerment: Competing Theoretical Perspectives*, edited by Kendall Stiles. New York: St. Martin's Press.

Krasner, Stephen D. 1985. *Structural Conflict: The Third World against Global Liberalism*. Berkeley and Los Angeles: University of California Press.

Kratochwil, Friedrich. 1989. *Rules, Norms, and Decisions: On the Conditions of Practical Legal Reasoning in International Relations and Domestic Affairs*. Cambridge: Cambridge University Press.

Kriesi, Hanspeter. 1996. "The Organizational Structure of New Social Movements in a Political Context." *Comparative Perspectives on Social Movements*, edited by Doug McAdam, John D. McCarthy, and Mayer N. Zald. New York: Cambridge University Press.

Lipschutz, Ronnie. 1992. "Reconstructing World Politics: The Emergence of Global Civil Society." *Millennium* 21: 389–420.

Lumsdaine, David H. 1993. *Moral Vision in International Politics: The Foreign Aid Regime, 1949–1989*. Princeton: Princeton University Press.

Marks, Gary, and Doug McAdam. 1996. "Social Movements and the Changing Structure of Political Opportunity in the European Union." *West European Politics* 19, no. 2: 249–78.

McAdam, Doug. 1982. *The Political Process and the Development of Black Insurgency*. Chicago: University of Chicago Press.

———. 1988. *Freedom Summer*. New York: Oxford University Press.

———. 1996. "Conceptual Origins, Current Problems, Future Direction." In *Comparative Perspectives on Social Movements: Political Opportunities, Mobilizing Structures, and Cultural Framings,* edited by Doug McAdam, John McCarthy, and Mayer Zald. New York: Cambridge University Press.

McAdam, Doug, John McCarthy, and Mayer Zald. 1996. *Comparative Perspectives on Social Movements: Political Opportunities, Mobilizing Structures, and Cultural Framings,* New York: Cambridge University Press.

McCarthy, John. 1996. "Constraints and Opportunities in Adoption, Adaption and Inventing." In *Comparative Perspectives on Social Movements: Political Opportunities, Mobilizing Structures, and Cultural Framings*. New York: Cambridge University Press.

Meyer, David, and Sidney Tarrow. 1998. *The Social Movement Society: Contentious Politics for a New Century*. Lanham, Md.: Rowman and Littlefield Publishers.

Mittelman, James H. 2000. *The Globalization Syndrome: Transformation and Resistance*. Princeton: Princeton University Press.

Naidoo, Kumi. 2000. "The New Civic Globalism." *The Nation* 270, no. 18 (8 May): 34–36.

Naim, Noises. 2000. "Lori's War: The FP Interview." *Foreign Policy* 118 (spring): 28–55.

Nye, Joseph S., and John D. Donahue, eds. 2000. *Governance in a Globalizing World*. Washington, D.C.: Brookings Institution.

Oberschall, Anthony. 1996. "Opportunities and Framing in the Eastern European Revolts of 1989." In *Comparative Perspectives on Social Movements: Political Opportunities, Mobilizing Structures, and Cultural Framings*. New York: Cambridge University Press.

O'Brien, Robert, Marc Williams, Anne Marie Goetz, and Jan Aart Scholte. 2000. *Contesting Global Governance: Multilateral Economic Institutions and Global Social Movements*. New York: Cambridge University Press.

Peterson, M. J. 1992. "Transnational Activity, International Society and World Politics." *Millennium* 21, no. 3.

Putnam, Robert. 1988. "Diplomacy and Domestic Politics: The Logic of Two-Level Games." *International Organization* 42, no. 3: 427–60.

Reinicke, Wolfgang H., and Francis Deng. 2000. *Critical Choices: The United Nations, Networks, and the Future of Global Governance.* Ottawa: IDRC Books.

Risse, Thomas. 2000. "Let's Argue! Communicative Action in World Politics." *International Organization* 54, no. 1.

Risse, Thomas, and Kathryn Sikkink. 1999. "The Socialization of International Human Rights Norms into Domestic Practices: Introduction." In *The Power of Human Rights.* Cambridge: Cambridge University Press.

Risse, Thomas, Stephen C. Ropp, and Kathryn Sikkink, eds. 1999. *The Power of Human Rights: International Norms and Domestic Change.* Cambridge: Cambridge University Press.

Risse-Kappen, Thomas. 1995. "Bringing Transnational Relations Back In: An Introduction." In *Bringing Transnational Relations Back In: Non-State Actors, Domestic Structures, and International Institutions,* edited by Thomas Risse-Kappen. Cambridge: Cambridge University Press.

Rucht, Dieter. 1996. "The Impact of National Contexts on Social Movement Structures: A Cross-Movement and Cross-National Comparison." In *Comparative Perspectives on Social Movements,* edited by Doug McAdam, John McCarthy, and Mayer Zald. New York: Cambridge University Press.

Shaw, Timothy M. 2000. "Overview—Global/Local: States, Companies and Civil Societies at the End of the Twentieth Century." In *Global Institutions and Local Empowerment: Competing Theoretical Perspectives,* edited by Kendall Stiles. New York: St. Martin's Press.

Smith, Jackie. 2000. "Social Movement, International Institutions and Local Empowerment." In *Global Institutions and Local Empowerment: Competing Theoretical Perspectives,* edited by Kendall Stiles. New York: St. Martin's Press.

Smith, Jackie, Charles Chatfield, and Ron Pagnucco, eds. 1997. *Transnational Social Movements and Global Politics: Solidarity Beyond the State.* Syracuse: Syracuse University Press.

Stiles, Kendall W. 1998. "Civil Society Empowerment and Multilateral Donors: International Institutions and New International Norms." *Global Governance* 4, no. 2: 199–216.

Tarrow, Sidney. 1995. "The Europeanisation of Conflict: Reflections from a Social Movement Perspective." *West European Politics* 18, no. 2: 223–51.

———. 1998. *Power in Movement: Social Movements and Contentious Politics.* 2d ed. Cambridge: Cambridge University Press.

———. 1999, "International Institutions and Contentious Politics: Does Internationalization Make Agents Freer—or Weaker?" Paper prepared for the Convenor Group on "Beyond Center-Periphery of the Unbundling of Territoriality." University of California at Berkeley, April 16–17.

Thomson, Janice E. 1990. "State Practices, International Norms, and the Decline of Mercenarism." *International Studies Quarterly* 34, no. 1: 23–47.

Wapner, Paul. 1995. "Politics beyond the State: Environmental Activism and World Civic Politics." *World Politics* 47, no. 3: 311–40.

———. 1996. *Environmental Activism and World Civic Politics.* Albany: State University of New York Press.

Waterman, Peter, Peter Fairbrother, and Tony Elger, eds. 1998. *Globalization, Social Movements and the New Internationalisms.* Washington, D.C.: Mansell Publishing, Limited.

Chapter 43

Donatella della Porta and Sidney Tarrow

TRANSNATIONAL PROTEST AND GLOBAL ACTIVISM

MODERN SOCIAL MOVEMENTS developed with the creation of the nation-state, and the nation-state has for many years been the main target for protest. Although social movements have often pushed for a conception of "direct" democracy, the institutions and actors of representative democracy have long structured movements' political opportunities and constraints within the boundaries of institutional politics. In fact, for most of the history of the modern national state, political parties were the main actors in democratic representation, linking the formation of collective identities with representative institutions. But at the turn of the millennium, nation-states face a host of new challenges:

- From without, there is the contemporary challenge of terrorism and the rejection of pluralistic and secular government on the part of broad sectors of the world's population;
- from within, there is both widespread disaffection from conventional forms of politics and disillusionment with the active state;
- linking these internal and external challenges are the uncertainties of new forms of internationalization and globalization that connect citizens to a global market but reduce their control over their own fates.

Although the power of the nation-state has by no means disappeared, since the 1960s, social, cultural, and geopolitical changes have begun to transform social movements' institutional and cultural environments. In particular, there has been a shift in the locus of political power—a shift symbolized by the growing use of concepts like "multilevel governance," "the world polity," and "global civil society," which point to the following internal and external developments. *Internally*, there has been a continuing shift in power from parliaments to the executive, and, within the executive, to the bureaucracy and to quasi-independent agencies. Power has moved from mass-parties to parties that have been variously defined as "catchall," "professional-electoral," or "cartel" parties (for a review, see della Porta, 2001), and therefore from party activists to the "new party professionals." *Externally*, there has been a shift in the locus of institutional power from the national to both the supranational and the regional levels, with the increasing power of international institutions, especially economic ones (World Bank, International Monetary Fund [IMF], World Trade Organization [WTO]), and some regional ones (in Europe, the European Union [EU]; in the Western hemisphere, the North American Free Trade Agreement [NAFTA]).

Meanwhile, informal networks have spread across borders (such as international agreements on standards; nongovernmental organization [NGO] coalitions in the areas of human rights, the environment, and peace; and, in a darker vein, drug and human trafficking networks). Many see a shift in the axis of power from politics to the market, with neoliberal economic policies increasing the power of multinational corporations and reducing the capacity of traditional state structures to control them. Taken together, these changes have led to the development of a system of "complex internationalism," which provides both threats and opportunities to ordinary people, to organized nonstate actors, and to weaker states, as we shall argue in our conclusions.

How are social movements reacting to these power shifts in terms of their organizational structures, their collective action frames and identities, and their repertoires of action? At first, scholars assumed that international movements would be similar to those that had developed within the nation-state. More recently, a growing stream of research on social movements has identified three important processes of transnationalization: diffusion, domestication, and externalization. By *diffusion*, we mean the spread of movement ideas, practices, and frames from one country to another; by *domestication*, we mean the playing out on domestic territory of conflicts that have their origin externally; and by *externalization*, we mean the challenge to supranational institutions to intervene in domestic problems or conflicts.

These processes are all important and appear to be widespread. However, the recent evolution of movements focusing on "global justice," peace and war, or both, suggests some additional processes. The most important of these, [. . .] is what we call "transnational collective action"—that is, *coordinated international campaigns on the part of networks of activists against international actors, other states, or international institutions*.

Diffusion, domestication, and externalization

Three broad processes link transnational politics today to the traditions of social movement studies in the past and lay the groundwork for the major changes that we see occurring in the contemporary world.

Diffusion

Diffusion is the most familiar and the oldest form of transnational contention. It need not involve connections across borders, but only that challengers in one country or region adopt or adapt the organizational forms, collective action frames, or targets of those in other countries or regions. Thus, the "shantytown" protests that were used to demand American universities' divestiture from South Africa were a domestic example of diffusion (Soule, 1999), while the spread of the "sit-in" from the American civil rights movement to Western Europe was a transnational one (Tarrow, 1989). Research on protest in Belgium, France, and Germany has also indicated the existence of important cross-national diffusion effects (Reising, 1999:333).

A variant on diffusion is what Tarrow and McAdam call "brokerage," through which groups or individuals deliberately connect actors from different sites of contention. This process was evident as early as the spread of the antislavery movement from England to the European continent in the late eighteenth century (Drescher, 1987) and, in more recent history, in the transfer of the American student movement's themes and practices to West Germany, through students who had studied in the United States in the 1960s (McAdam and Rucht, 1993).

[. . .]

One of the factors that characterizes the new international system is the greater ease with which particular practices or frames can be transferred from one country to another through cheap international travel, the knowledge of common languages, and access to the Internet (Bennett, 2003). But underlying these advantages lies a disadvantage. Every new form of communication both heightens ties between those who already know one another, and raises the walls of exclusion for those lacking access to the new medium of communication (Tilly, 2004). Not only that: although it is undoubtedly easier and faster for information about protest to be communicated across national lines today than it was fifty years ago, the Internet also creates the risk of diffuseness, as those with Internet skills learn to mount their own websites and set themselves up as movement entrepreneurs. In general, research indicates that sustained diffusion processes both require and help to produce transnational networks and identities, to which we will turn in the next section.

Internalization

By internalization, we mean the playing out on domestic territory of conflicts that have their origin externally. Previous research on protest events, collected mainly from newspaper sources from Western Europe, stressed the small number of protests that target international institutions directly. A good part of this research focused on the EU. Using Reuters World News Service and the Reuters Textline, Doug Imig and Sidney Tarrow (2001; also see 1999) found a limited (but growing) number of such protests. Similarly, in Germany, Dieter Rucht (2002) observed a low (and declining) proportion of protests aimed at the international level (with the high point coming in 1960–1964) or at EU institutions. Meanwhile, Marco Giugni and Florence Passy (2002) noted how rarely protests on migrant rights targeted the EU, notwithstanding the increasing Europeanization of legal competences regarding border control. Even environmental action was rarely turned on Brussels: protests with EU targets ranged from 0.8 percent in Italy to 4.6 percent in Germany in the last decade, with no discernible increasing trend (Rootes, 2002). Similarly, few protest events have addressed international organizations other than the EU.

Protest events analysis, however, indicated that protest often addressed national governments regarding decisions that originated or were implemented at a supranational level. In their analysis of protest in Europe, Doug Imig and Sidney Tarrow (2001) found that most EU related events (406 out of 490) were in fact cases of domestication—that is, conflict about EU decisions, but mounted at the national level. And processes of domestication in fact characterized many mobilizations of European farmers (Bush and Simi, 2001). Outside of Europe, as well, many important mobilizations against international institutions followed a similar dynamic. The anti-IMF "austerity protests" of the 1980s took a largely domesticated form (Walton, 2001). Recent Argentine protests were similarly triggered by the pressure of international financial institutions but directed against domestic institutions (Auyero, 2003).

The low level of protest targeting the supranational level might be explained by the political opportunities available to collective actors at other territorial levels of government. In addition, the undeniable "democratic deficit" of international institutions—lacking both electoral responsiveness and accountability in the public sphere (Eder, 2000)—plays an important role. Such mobilizations might in fact be seen as proof of the continued dominance of the nation-state. However, a more careful look shows the emergence, in the course of these campaigns, of innovations both in the organizational structure and in the frames of the protest (della Porta, 2003), as we will see below.

Externalization

A third area in which researchers have observed the emergence of clear transnational trends is in studies focusing on movement organizations that become active supranationally. Within this approach, scholars of international relations have analyzed informational and lobbying campaigns in which national and international NGOs attempt to stimulate international alliances with nationally weak social movements (Keck and Sikkink, 1998). These researchers stress that organized interests and social movements look to international institutions for the mobilization of resources that can be used at the national level. A variant is the construction of transnational coalitions of international NGOs, which reach into these institutions to find allies on behalf of the claims of weak domestic actors in countries of the South (Fox and Brown, 1998).

The strategy of externalization (Chabanet, 2002) has often characterized the mobilization of national groups targeting the EU in attempts to put pressure on their own governments for material or symbolic resources. For instance, British environmental organizations paid increasing attention to the EU (even playing a leading role vis-à-vis other environmental groups) when political opportunities at home were poor (Rootes, 2002). To give another example, with their Euro-strike in 1997, Spanish, French, and Belgian Renault workers protested at the EU level against the closing of the Renault factory of Vilvorde in Belgium (Lefébure and Lagneau, 2002).

[. . .]

In their dealings with international institutions, some movement organizations receive material and symbolic resources, such as the financing of particular projects, or recognition of their legitimacy. On their side, international institutions benefit from low-cost work from voluntary associations; from the information they can provide; from access to local populations; and, of course, from legitimization (for instance, Mazey and Richardson, 1997:10). For the institutionally weak European Parliament, alliances with NGOs provide resources for legitimization vis-à-vis the more powerful European Commission and the European Council. Similarly for the United Nations, NGOs active on human rights help a weak bureaucracy to acquire specialized, and, in general, reliable knowledge, while development NGOs offer high-quality, low-cost human resources (for a summary, see della Porta and Kriesi, 1999).

Externalization processes have, however, some limits. First of all, "boomerangs" and "insider/outsider coalitions" are more likely to emerge when "(1) channels between domestic groups and their governments are blocked or hampered or where such channels are ineffective for resolving a conflict, setting into motion a 'boomerang' pattern ... (2) advocates believe that networking will further their missions and campaigns, and actively promote networks; and (3) conferences and other forms of international contact create arenas for forming and strengthening networks" (Keck and Sikkink, 1998:12). Moreover, they are potentially more effective for movements focusing on internationally established norms (such as human rights) than for those struggling against internationally hegemonic discourse (such as the liberalization of markets for goods and services).

To summarize: these three forms of transnational relations represent an important part of what some scholars have been calling "global social movements" and what others, more modestly, call "transnational politics." They are extremely important, and may be increasing in scope and scale, but they do not represent the most dramatic change we see in the world of contentious politics. This is what we call "transnational collective action," to which we turn in the following section.

Transnational collective action

Transnational collective action is the term we use to indicate coordinated international campaigns on the part of networks of activists against international actors, other states, or international institutions. Both in Western Europe, where it takes a more institutionalized form, and outside Europe, where more vigorous forms have developed in recent years, we see it developing out of the more traditional forms that we have outlined above. We can vividly illustrate this development of new forms from old with the example of anthropologist Hilary Cunningham, who has studied activism on the U.S./Mexican border for over ten years. She began in the early 1990s by studying the "border crossing" of a group of activists linked to the U.S. Sanctuary movement, who offered safe havens to Central American refugees. She compares this experience to more recent activism to reduce the negative effects of the NAFTA agreement (2001:372–79). Between these two episodes, both occurring on the same border and involving the same populations, Cunningham observed a shift from a state-centric movement to a transnational coalition (379–83). In fact, as the movement developed, the role of the state was transformed for its activists. This transformation developed out of environmental, cognitive, and relational changes. We can use these categories to examine the forces behind the development of transnational collective action.

Environmental change

Since the late 1980s, three kinds of changes in the international environment have helped to produce a transnationalization of collective action. First, the collapse of the Soviet bloc encouraged the development of forms of nonstate action that had previously been blocked by Cold War divisions. This produced a wave of Western governmental support for NGO activity in both East-Central Europe and the former Soviet Union as well as the development of homegrown non-state groups that might otherwise have been branded as "pro-communist" in the days of the Cold War. At the same time, the explosion of secessionist movements, border wars, and warlordism that followed the breakup of the Soviet bloc fed an increase of humanitarian aid movements around the world.

Second, the development of electronic communications and the spread of inexpensive international travel have made it easier for formerly isolated movement actors to communicate and collaborate with one another across borders. Related to this, there has been a massive increase in migration flows across borders, which has stimulated both benign forms of immigrant activism (Guarnizo, Portes, and Landolt, 2003) and the more transgressive forms of diasporic nationalism that have exacerbated ethnic and linguistic conflicts (Anderson, 1998).

Finally, the importance of the international environment has been highlighted by the growing power of transnational corporations and international institutions, treaties regulating the international economy, and international events like the global summits of the World Bank, the Group of Eight, and especially the World Trade Organization. These are of course framed by activists as threats, which they indeed are for broad sectors of the world's population; but it is the internationalization of the global environment that produces opportunities for activists from both North and South to engage in concerted collective action. Together, these changes combine into what we call "complex internationalism".

While some analysts appear to think that globalization is sufficient to produce global social movements, changes in the global environment are not sufficient to produce a transnationalization of collective action. Cognitive change within and relational changes between actors must be the active forces for such a fundamental change. The former can best be seen in the changing perspective of nonstate actors active on the international scene, while the latter can be observed in the formation of sustained networks of transnational activists.

Cognitive change

Since social movements are "reflective" actors, their international experiences have been critically analyzed. Tactics and frames that appear to succeed in more than one venue have been institutionalized—for example, in the spread of the practice of demonstrating on the occasion of the periodic meetings of the great international institutions, first within Western Europe in the 1990s and then globally, against the World Bank, the IMF, and the WTO. The formation of the "World Social Forum," created to highlight the distortions of the annual Davos World Economic Forum, eventually produced regional social fora such as the European one that took place in Florence in 2002. Moreover, the tactical adaptation of governmental and police strategies to movement challenges at a transnational level demanded the common elaboration of plans for collective action on the part of activists.

With respect to domestication, although still mainly addressing national governments, many groups of protesters have learned from people like themselves in other countries. This was the case, for instance, for Italian farmers, during the struggle against the implementation of EU quotas on milk production (della Porta, 2003). Similarly, the local movements of the unemployed have learned to pay greater attention to their transnational connections (Chabanet, 2002; Baglioni, 2003). Though it was "domestic," the wave of attacks on McDonald's in France gave rise to a spontaneous wave of similar attacks in other countries and to the popularity of the theme of the "Americanization" of mass culture and commerce.

As for externalization, the "vertical" experience of individual national movements operating internationally has placed many actors in contact with others like themselves and thus encouraged them to develop a more globalized framing of their messages and their domestic appeals. We can see this in the indigenous peoples' movements throughout Latin America, which have adopted many of the same cognitive frames in countries with little else in common (Yashar, 2005).

Relational changes

The most striking developments of the last decade have operated through the relational mechanisms that are bringing together national actors in transnational coalitions. The existence of international institutions as common "vertical" targets has helped to produce the "horizontal" formation of transnational coalitions through the networks of activists that form around them. For example, at the European level, networks of organizations of regionalist movements (Hooghe, 2002), women's organizations (Mazey, 2002), and labor unions (Martin and Ross, 2001) gained some success in the EU. In the same way, indigenous people and human rights organizations have coordinated their efforts and gained access to the United Nations (for a summary, see della Porta and Kriesi, 1999). In parallel, although more slowly, women's concerns and ecological issues advanced in the United Nations, as well as in the World Bank. National women's organizations that participated in the UN NGO conferences for women, especially in Beijing in 1995, encountered others like themselves and forged long-lasting transnational coalitions. The same is true of the "counter-summits" organized around the economic summits at Davos and elsewhere. According to a survey of NGOs, a major perceived advantage of the counter-summit is the consolidation of transnational and trans-thematic linkages between transnational movement organizations (Pianta, 2001).

Relations between movements and governments are a major source of change. Social movements do not act in a vacuum, and, in fact, the strongest influences on their behavior and tactics are the behavior and tactics of the governments they challenge. The last decade has shown that governments also imitate one another, therefore leading to increasing similarities in the contexts in which movement campaigns and protests take place. Increasing interaction facilitates the growth of common identity, and therefore reduces national particularism. One of the major changes in the last half decade has been the adoption of new and more violent tactics on the part of the forces of order against international protesters. This came to a head in Genoa in 2001, but it has been evident since the 1999 protests in Seattle that police forces are following similar strategies in protecting international institutions and conferences.

In summary, reflecting on the successes, but also on the failures of transnational collective action, as well as the experience of working together on temporary campaigns, has led to the creation of transnational organizational structures and the framing of transnational identities. Certainly, social movements have retained their national character, remaining tied to the types of political opportunities present in individual states; but they have also increasingly interacted transnationally. As has been noted, if social movements are to work with success in supranational arenas, they must develop a base of cross-national resources and global strategies that will be significantly different from those deployed in national arenas (Smith, Pagnucco, and Romeril, 1994:126). These arenas offer activists of different world regions the opportunity to meet, form organizational networks, coordinate activity, and construct global frames and programs (Passy, 1999; Smith, 1999).

References

Anderson, Benedict. 1998. *The Spectre of Comparisons: Nationalism, Southeast Asia and the World*. London: Verso

Auyero, Javier. 2003. "The Gray Zone: The Practice and Memory of Collective Violence in Argentina." Unpublished paper presented to the Columbia Workshop on Contentious Politics, September.

Baglioni, Simone. 2003. "Bridging Local and Global: Experiences from the Organizations of the Unemployed Movement in Italy." Paper presented at the conference on Transnational Process and Social Movements, Bellagio, Italy, July 22–26.

Bennett, W. Lance. 2003. "Communicating Global Activism: Strengths and Vulnerabilities of Networked Politics." *Information, Communication & Society*. 6(2):143–68.

Bush, Evelyn, and Pete Simi. 2001. "European Farmers and Their Protests." In *Contentious Europeans: Protest and Politics in an Emerging Polity*, ed. Doug Imig and Sidney Tarrow. Lanham, Md.: Rowman & Littlefield, pp. 97–121.

Chabanet, Didier. 2002. "Les marches européennes contre le chomage, la précarité et les exclusions." In *L'action collective en Europe*, ed. Richard Balme, Didier Chabanet, and Vincent Wright. Paris: Presses de Sciences Po, pp. 461–94.

Cunningham, Hilary, 2001. "Transnational Politics at the Edges of Sovereignty: Social Movements, Crossings and the State at the US–Mexico Border." *Global Networks* 1:369–87.

della Porta, Donatella. 2001. *I partiti politici*. Bologna, Italy: Il Mulino.

———. 2003. "Ambientalismo e movimenti sociali globali." Paper presented at the conference "I conflitti ambientali nella globalizzazione," Florence, Forum per in problemi della pace e della guerra, May 9–10.

della Porta, Donatella, and Hanspeter Kriesi. 1999. "Social Movements in a Globalizing World: An Introduction." In *Social Movements in a Globalizing World*, ed. Donatella della Porta, Hanspeter Kriesi, and Dieter Rucht. New York: Macmillan, pp. 3–23.

Drescher, Seymour. 1987. *Capitalism and Antislavery: British Mobilization in Comparative Perspective*. New York: Oxford University Press.

Eder, Klaus. 2000. "Zur Transformation nationalstaatlicher Oeffentlichkeit in Europa." *Berliner Journal fuer Soziologie* 2:167–84.

Fox, Jonathan, and L. David Brown, eds. 1998. *The Struggle for Accountability: The World Bank, NGOs and Grassroots Movements*. Cambridge, Mass.: MIT Press.

Giugni, Marco, and Florence Passy. 2002. "Le champ politique de l'immigration en Europe: Opportunités, mobilisations et héritage de l'Etat national." In *L'action collective en Europe*, ed. Richard Balme, Didier Chabanet, and Vincent Wright. Paris: Presses de Sciences Po, pp. 433–60.

Guarnizo, Luis E., Alejandro Portes, and Patricia Landolt. 2003. "Assimilation and Transnationalism: Determinants of Transnational Political Action among Contemporary Migrants." *American Journal of Sociology* 108:1211–48.

Hooghe, Liesbet. 2002. "The Mobilization of Territorial Interests and Multilevel Governance." In *L'action collective en Europe*, ed. Richard Balme, Didier Chabanet, and Vincent Wright. Paris: Presses de Sciences Po, pp. 347–74.

Imig, Doug, and Sidney Tarrow. 1999. "The Europeanization of Movements? Contentious Politics and the European Union. October 1983–March 1995." In *Social Movements in a Globalizing World*, ed. Donatella della Porta, Hanspeter Kriesi, and Dieter Rucht. New York: Macmillan, pp. 112–33.

———.2001. "Mapping the Europeanization of Contention." In *Contentious Europeans: Protest and Politics in an Emerging Polity*, ed. D. Imig and S. Tarrow. Lanham, Md.: Rowman & Littlefield, pp. 27–49.

Keck, Margaret, and Kathryn Sikkink 1998. *Activists beyond Borders: Advocacy Networks in International Politics*. Ithaca, N.Y.: Cornell University Press.

Lefébure, Pierre, and Eric Lagneau. 2002. "Le moment Vilvorde: Action protestataire et espace publique européen." In *L'action collective en Europe*, ed. Richard Balme, Didier Chabanet, and Vincent Wright. Paris: Presses de Sciences Po, pp. 495–529.

Martin, Andrew, and George Ross. 2001. "Trade Union Organizing at the European Level: The Dilemma of Borrowed Resources." In *Contentious Europeans: Protest and Politics in an Emerging Polity*, ed. Doug Imig and Sidney Tarrow. Lanham, Md.: Rowman & Littlefield.

Mazey, Sonia. 2002. "L'Union Européenne et les droits des femmes: De l'européanisation des agendas nationaux à la nationalisation d'un agenda européen?" In *L'action collective en Europe*, ed. Richard Balme, Didier Chabanet, and Vincent Wright. Paris: Presses de Sciences Po, pp. 405–32.

Mazey, Sonia, and Jeremy Richardson. 1997. "The Commission and the Lobbying." In *The European Commission*, ed. G. Edwards and G. Spence. London: Cartermill.

McAdam, Doug, and Dieter Rucht. 1993. "The Cross-national Diffusion of Movement Ideas." *Annals of the American Academy of Political and Social Science* 528:56–74.

Mendelson, Sarah E., and John K. Glenn. 2002. *The Power and Limits of NGOs*. New York: Columbia University Press.

Passy, Florence. 1999. "Supranational Political Opportunities as a Channel of Globalization of Political Conflicts: The Case of the Rights of Indigenous People." In *Social Movements in a Globalizing World*, ed. Donatella della Porta, Hanspeter Kriesi, and Dieter Rucht. New York: Macmillan, pp. 148–69.

Pianta, Mario. 2001. *La globalizzazione dal basso*. Rome: Manifestolibri.

Reising, Uwe. 1999. "United in Opposition? A Cross-National Time-Series of European Protest in Three Selected Countries, 1980–1995." *Journal of Conflict Resolution* 43:317–42.

Rootes, Christopher. 2002. "The Europeanization of Environmentalism." In *L'action collective en Europe*, ed. Richard Balme, Didier Chabanet, and Vincent Wright. Paris: Presses de Sciences Po, pp. 377–404.

Rucht, Dieter. 2002. "The EU as a Target of Political Mobilization: Is There a Europeanization of Conflict?" In *L'action collective en Europe*, ed. Richard Balme, Didier Chabanet, and Vincent Wright. Paris: Presses de Sciences Po, pp. 163–94.

Smith, Jackie. 1999. "Global Politics and Transnational Campaign against International Trade in Toxic Waste." In *Social Movements in a Globalizing World*, ed. Donatella della Porta, Hanspeter Kriesi, and Dieter Rucht. New York: Macmillan, pp. 170–88.

Smith, Jackie, Ron Pagnucco, and Winnie Romeril. 1994. "Transnational Social Movement Organisations in the Global Political Arena." *Voluntas* 5:121–54.

Soule, Sarah A. 1999. "The Diffusion of an Unsuccessful Tactic: The Case of the Shantytown Protest Tactic." *The Annals of the American Academy of Political and Social Science* 566 (November):120–31.

Tarrow, Sidney. 1989. *Democracy and Disorder: Protest and Politics in Italy 1965–1975*. Oxford: Clarendon Press.

Tilly, Charles. 2004. *Social Movements, 1768–2004*. Boulder, Colo.: Paradigm.

Walton, John. 2001. "Debt, Protest and the State in Latin America." In *Power and Popular Protest: Latin American Social Movements*, ed. Susan Eckstein. Berkeley: University of California Press, chap. 10.

Yashar, Deborah J. 2005. *Contesting Citizenship: Indigenous Movements, the State, and the Postliberal Challenge in Latin America*. New York: Cambridge University Press.

Chapter 44

Nicola Montagna

SOCIAL MOVEMENTS AND GLOBAL MOBILISATIONS

THE TRANS-NATIONALISATION of social action has accompanied, although in different fashions, the development of social movements since their inception in the eighteenth and nineteenth centuries (Tilly, 2004). In what sense, then, does the contemporary movement for global justice differ from the social movements of the past? In order to answer this question we have to refer to three characteristics of contemporary collective action:

- the existence of national and international networks of individuals, groups, associations, campaigns and movements which span across continents and are informally organised, leaving to participants a high degree of autonomy;
- the organisation of trans-continental protest campaigns focused on neoliberal globalisation;
- the elaboration of global frames, namely of an understanding of global problems and their causes, and the identification of international governmental and economic institutions against which to direct protest.

The presence and combination of these elements make the movement for social justice a specific and original collective actor (della Porta et al, 2006; Tarrow, 2001).

Network organisations

Social movements are not spontaneous events springing from the void. With respect to the movement for global justice, it could be remarked that this movement is the result of networks, movement organisations and individuals operating in civil society who, during the course of the 1990s, have intensified contacts and action (Murphy, 2004; Pianta and Silva, 2003; Smith, 2001).

Because the network structure encourages horizontal relationships among actors, such structure is not a mere reflection of the organisation of society and production (Castells, 1997); it is, rather, the expression of equalitarian and anti-hierarchical identities developed during the twentieth century in opposition to conventional political parties. The network structure is seen by participants as a model for a just society. Networks lend themselves to democratic participation and allow participants to express their opinions and to be heard. Moreover, they promote reciprocity and coordinated action while acknowledging the cultural and political differences among those involved (Montagna, 2007). The movement for global justice is also a 'network of networks', in the sense that actors operating locally interact and communicate with one another with a view to challenging multinational organisations (Brecher and Costello, 1998). This organisational structure allows the movement to attract diverse actors and to adapt mobilisation to a variety of contexts.

The mobilisation of the movement for global justice has been possible thanks to the growth of organisations within civil society, the intensification of contacts between them and their extension across the globe. This movement, therefore, is the result of communication and joint action of thousands of groups acting locally, nationally and trans-nationally. The number of groups whose membership is located in at least three different countries has grown from 178 in 1909 to 4,620 in 1991 (Feld, Jordan and Hurwitz, 1994; Rucht, 1999; Keane, 2003). If we consider the specific category of trans-national movement organisations, their growth rate has been 100% between the 1970s and the 1990s, and 50% between 1993 and 2000 (Smith, 2005). As I have already observed, a section of these organisations have provided the infrastructure to the movement for global justice.

The growth of trans-national movement organisations has been accompanied by their geographical expansion. Although the majority of such organisations' head-quarters are based in developed countries, particularly in key cities which host inter-governmental agencies such as New York and Geneva, between 1973 and 2000 movement organisations based in the South of the world have grown from 13% to 20% (Sikkink and Smith, 2002).

A global frame

In order to explain how such diverse groups of activists have managed to mount joint mobilisation, it may be useful to refer to the concepts of frame and master frame. These concepts, proposed by Erving Goffman (1974) to describe the way in which individuals classify and interpret events in order to orient themselves in their own context, have been re-elaborated by Snow and his associates for the study of social movements (see Part 6: New Directions). According to this re-elaboration, actors adopt frameworks for the interpretation of the reality surrounding them and of the events they witness, de-coding experiences and relating them to their environment (Andretta, 2005; Neveu, 2001; Snow and Benford, 1992). Such frames have to be innovative and, at the same time, must be consistent with the set of beliefs of those they intend to mobilise, they must be empirically credible and connected to lived experience. Frame-bridging indicates the process leading to the interconnection between two or more frames which are congruent in relations to a specific theme (Snow et al, 1986).

The possibility for diverse actors to form a social movement depends on the elaboration of a master frame, namely a unifying frame that includes others. Master frames may be more generic than those embraced by specific organisations, but they provide a 'grammar' for the understanding of events across the world. The movement for global justice has adopted a master frame linking movements and political cultures which were previously unconnected but ideologically compatible, unifying them in the fight for human and civil rights and against neoliberalism. This master frame, by co-joining the ideas of the traditional Left, those of religion and those of new social movements, managed to involve pacifists and environmentalists, feminists, anti-capitalists and Catholics, creating the preconditions for trans-national campaigns and contributing to the formation of a shared, if plural and open, collective identity. The elaboration of a new master frame does not imply the abandonment of previous frames: it is a process, at times painful, requiring dialogue, negotiation and re-framing (Andretta, 2004).

The movement for global justice doe not oppose neoliberalism per se, but its global organisations such as the G8, economic-financial institutions such as the World Monetary Fund and the World Bank, multinational companies, superpowers (particularly the USA), inter-governmental gatherings such as the World Economic Forum, intra-national agreements such as Nafta and all other institutions characterising what movements now term Empire (Hardt and Negri, 2000). These institutions and international organisations are targeted by protest because they are the prime motors of neoliberal globalisation. They are identified as the main culprits of economic and political injustice, the exploitation of the environment, the spreading of a culture devaluing human beings in the name of profit. They are not perceived as democratic institutions, but as self-appointed interest groups pursuing their own economic and military supremacy. Only rarely do the groups involved in the movement for global justice refer to national institutions in their analysis, rather, they address world issues and their causes, while identifying the international targets for their campaigns. These are easy to single out, the difficulties arising when common solutions are proposed. However, a slogan like 'another world is possible' seems to possess a global dimension, and to incorporate a variety of solutions with which the different sections of the movement may identify.

Global campaigns

While adopting a global frame, the movement for global justice, along with its local and national nodes, has organised a number of campaigns on issues of a transnational nature. I would like to highlight four overlapping themes of these campaigns:

- social reproduction and wealth redistribution: examples are the campaigns launched by 'Attac' for a taxation of speculative financial transactions (known as Tobin Tax) and the European campaign against the Bolkenstein project to limitlessly liberalise all activities of service provision;
- access to resources, sustainability and the environment: examples are the initiatives for the reduction of the debts of developing countries (Drop the Debt), aimed at the release of resources to fight poverty; the Sem Terra and Via

Campesina movements, demanding the diversification of food resources and a moratorium on genetically modified organisms. Other examples include protests against pollution for alternative energy sources and the protection of common goods such as water and forests;

- the defence of civil society and public space: some of these campaigns are aimed at supporting national minorities and indigenous groups. Initiatives also include protest against detention centres for refugees and migrants and against legislations restricting the free circulation of people across Europe. Under this rubric groups engaged in economic activity outside the market logic should also be included;

- the establishment of transparent democratic rules: initiatives around this theme include campaigns addressed at transnational institutions such as the World Bank, the International Monetary Fund and the World Trade Organisation, whose decisions affect national governments.

Through these campaigns, the movement for global justice has developed a new and alternative political agenda challenging intergovernmental transnational organisations in a global perspective (Correa Leite, 2005). An example is the mobilisation for the Tobin Tax which targets capital speculation and demands a stricter regulation of international finances (Chesnais, 2001). The promoters of such campaigns offer a global analysis of issues (the volatility of financial markets and currency speculations), they identify responsibilities and propose solutions which may produce global outcomes.

Globalisations of movements and political opportunities

This section deals with three aspects related to political opportunity: globalisations processes, the growing internationalisation of politics, and the establishment of a global social sphere. While the movements of the past emerged simultaneously with the establishment of nation-states and parliamentary democracies (Tilly, 1982; 2004), contemporary global movements emerge concomitantly with the opportunities mentioned above.

Globalisation processes

The role of globalisation in providing a system of political opportunities for national and transnational movements has been highlighted by a number of scholars (della Porta, Kriesi and Rucht, 1999). On the one hand, globalisation provides numerous reasons for protest and, in fact, offers a master frame for action shared by diverse groups and movement cultures. On the other hand, it makes mobilisation easier in that it offers the possibility for information to travel and protest to organise internationally.

Globalisation as a process affects social relations as a whole. This process is not only economic in nature, but also social, cultural and technological: it implies wider circulation of capital and goods affecting the North and the South of the world and involving those who would be unwilling to be involved (Beck, Giddens and

Lash, 1998; Bauman, 1998). Sociologists have analysed globalisation through the categories of 'space' and 'time', interpreting it as a fundamental change in the way in which physical space is experienced (Harvey, 1989; Beck, 2000). Globalisation reduces geographic distances, forcing people to adopt certain life styles which may not be wanted and to accept events which may not be understood. Globalisation is 'distance action', it is the result of the war of independence from space, namely a process which de-links political and economic decision centres and individuals in general from territorial limits (Giddens, 1990; Robertson, 1992; Bauman, 1998).

This compression of space has a number of implications for social movements. First, it generates economic, environmental and financial crises which affect human and labour rights on a global level, crises that become the focus of social movements who act, in their turn, on the global level. Moreover, globalisation offers the possibility to speed up communication, favouring exchange and contacts between local and national actors located in different places in the planet (della Porta and Kriesi, 1998). Global processes of cultural and economic integration make social movements modify their aims and nature, because they affect the way in which people perceive problems and organise to pursue possible solutions (Smith and Johnston, 2002). At the same time, they widen political spaces and the channels for the spreading of protest. For these reasons, it could be argued that the movement for global justice is a global actor who manages to utilise the technological, cultural and economic resources activated by globalisation 'from above', while turning such resources into opportunities for mobilisation and globalisation 'from below'. This process gives globalisation a different direction, notably towards participation and inclusion.

The transnationalisation of politics

One of the effects of globalisation, as the overcoming of spacio-temporal limits and the growth of opportunities for action, is the transnationalisation of politics. Today, governments are constrained by local, national and international systems of governance which they can scarcely control (Held et al, 1999). World politics has become poly-centric, and a growing number of individuals who act on the global level are taking part in international decision making. In this sense, the internationalisation of politics does not only involve official state actors, but also a variety of other actors. It entails growing horizontal density in relations between state and non-state actors, growing vertical relations between local national and transnational actors, and growing formal and informal networks involving non-state, state and transnational actors (Tarrow, 2005).

The internationalisation of politics does not imply the disappearance of state sovereignty and national identities. For example, the widespread opposition to the European Union shown in the rejection of the European Constitution in France and the Netherlands, testifies to the fact that people identify with national interests more than they do with international symbols or political entities. Rather, the effectiveness and autonomy of decisions taken by nation-states have been considerably reduced by the resistance of new actors, including social movements. In other words, state sovereignty has not disappeared, but has changed. Decision-making processes are now negotiated, directly or otherwise, with non-state transnational actors, which include NGOs and international institutions such as the EU and the UN.

A transnational public sphere

The third novel element is the existence of a transnational public sphere, which may be regional, continental or global, and to which movements refer when mobilising against governments or international institutions. A public sphere is a space where citizens discuss their objectives and where a public opinion influencing governments may take shape. A transnational public sphere, in its turn, is a space in which practices and discourses are shared by people who are located in different areas of the world, namely by people who constitute a transnational entity whose action reaches beyond national boundaries (Guidry, Kennedy and Zald, 2000). This sphere is distinct from the private and the state spheres, as well as from the economic sphere: it is a locus where critical discussions are carried out, between citizens of different countries, with a view to starting collective action. The public transnational sphere may be influenced by the action of the media, but its capacity to function also depends on access to the media themselves. Its ability to create mobilisation is associated with its social capital and the organisational structures it relies upon. In brief, its capacity to mobilise is irregular and erratic in space as well as in time.

Over the last years attempts by movements to gain the solidarity of the transnational public sphere have multiplied. The success of several campaigns has depended, indeed, on the capacity to activate such a public sphere. At times such attempts have failed to stop state repression against movements or to trigger democratisation processes, notably in the case of the Chinese students in Tiananmen in 1989. In other cases, the mobilisation of the transnational public sphere has played an important deterrent role against government repression. See for example the mobilisation which led to the fall of the Berlin wall and the collapse of the Soviet block, and more recently, the 'Orange' revolution in Ukraine or that in Beirut in the Lebanon. In both cases, along with domestic and international factors such as the threat of sanctions or the use of force, the transnational public sphere has played a crucial role. On the one hand, it has put pressure on the respective regimes, while on the other it has made the participants feel less isolated. The most important example, however, is that of the insurgency of the Zapatistas in Chiapas against the Mexican government, which was dissuaded from adopting large-scale repressive measures by international public pressure (Castells, 1997; Olesen, 2003; 2004; Tarrow, 2005). The movement for global justice has also tried to build a transnational public sphere. Its campaigns to boycott certain products or to promote fair trade and consumers' awareness would have been impossible had they not been supported by individuals who, not necessarily linked with specific organisations, nevertheless engaged in global discussion and action (Tosi, 2006).

References

Andretta M. (2004), "Movimenti e democrazia tra globale e locale: il caso di Napoli", paper presentato alla *Conferenza nazionale della SISP*, Università di Padova. 15–17 Settembre.

Andretta M. (2005), Il framing del movimento contro la globalizzazione neoliberista, *Rassegna Italiana di Sociologia*, 54(2), pp.249–274.

Bauman Z. (1998), *Globalisation. The human consequences*, Polity Press, Cambridge.

Beck U. (2000), *What is Globalization?* Polity Press, Oxford.

Beck U., Giddens A. and Lash S. (1998), *Reflexive modernization: politics, tradition and aesthetics in the modern social order*, Polity Press, Cambridge.

Brecher J. and Costello T. (1998), *Contro il capitale globale. Strategie di resistenza*, Feltrinelli, Milano.

Castells M. (1997), *The power of identity*, Blackwell, Oxford.

Chesnais F. (2001), *Tobin or not Tobin. Una tassa internazionale sul capitale,* Sankara, Roma.

Correa Leite J. (2005), *The World Social Forum: strategies of resistance,* Haymarket Books, Chicago.

della Porta D., Andretta M., Mosca L. and Reiter H. (2006), *Globalization from below. Transnational activists and protest networks,* University of Minnesota Press, Minneapolis.

della Porta D. and Kriesi H.-P. (1998), Movimenti sociali e globalizzazione, *Rivista italiana di scienza politica*, 28, pp. 451–482.

della Porta D., Kriesi H. and Rucht D. (ed.) (1999), *Social movements in a globalizing world*, Macmillan, London.

Feld W.J., Jordan R.S. and Hurwitz L. (1994), *International organizations: a comparative approach*, Praeger, Westport.

Giddens A. (1990), *The consequences of modernity,* Polity Press, Cambridge.

Goffman E. (1974), *Frame analysis: an essay on the organization of experience,* Northeastern University Press, New York.

Guidry J.A., Kennedy M.D. and Zald M.N. (2000), *Globalizations and social movements: culture, power, and the transnational public sphere,* University of Michigan Press Ann Arbor.

Hardt M., and Negri, A. (2000), *Empire*, Harvard University Press, Cambridge.

Held D., McGrew A., Goldblatt D. and Perraton J. (1999), *Globalization,* the Foreign Policy Centre, London.

Harvey D. (1989), *The condition of postmodernity*, Blackwell, Oxford.

Keane J. (2003), *Global civil society?* Cambridge University Press, Cambridge.

Montagna N. (2007), "Rappresentanza ed autorganizzazione: il welfare dal basso dei Centri Sociali Autogestiti del Nord-Est", in Vitale T. (eds), *Partecipazione e rappresentanza nelle mobilitazioni locali*, Franco Angeli, Milano.

Murphy G.H. (2004), "The Seattle WTO protests: building a global movement", in Taylor R. (eds) *Creating a better world: interpreting global civil society*, Kumarian Press, Bloomfield.

Olesen T. (2003), *International Zapatismo: the construction of solidarity in the age of globalization*, ZED Books, London.

Olesen T. (2004) The transnational Zapatistas solidarity network: an infrastructure analysis, *Global Networks*, 4 (1), pp. 89–107.

Neveu E. (2001), *I movimenti sociali*, il Mulino, Bologna.

Pianta M., and Silva F. (2003), *Globalisers from below. A survey on civil society organizations*, GLOBI research report, Roma.

Robertson R. (1992), *Globalisation: social theory and global culture*, Sage, London.

Rucht D. (1999), "The transnationalization of social movements: trends, causes, problems", in della Porta D., Kriesi H. Rucht D. (eds), *Social movements in a globalizing world*, Macmillan, London, pp. 206–222.

Sikkink K. and Smith J. (2002), "Infrastructures for change: transnational organizations, 1953-93", in Khagram S., Jamev V.Riker, Sikkink K., (eds), *Reconstructing world politics: transnational social movements, networks and norms,* University of Minnesota Press, Minneapolis, pp. 24–44.

Smith J. (2001), Globalizing resistance: the battle of Seattle and the future of social movements, *Mobilisation*, 6 (1), pp. 1–19.

Smith J. (2005), "Exploring connections between global integration and political mobilization", in Podobnik B., Reifer T. (eds), *Transforming globalization. Challenges and opportunities in the post 9/11 era*, Brill, Leiden, pp. 29–50.

Snow D.A. and Benford R. (1992), "Master frame and cycles of protest", in Morris A., Mueller C. (eds), *Frontiers in social movement theory*, Yale University Press, New Haven, pp. 133–155.

Snow D.A., Rochford B., Worden S. and Benford R. (1986), Frame alignment processes, micromobilization and movement participation, *American Sociology Review*, 51, pp. 464–481.

Tarrow S. (2001), Transnational politics: contention and institutions in international politics, *Annual Review of Political Science*, 4, pp. 1–20.

Tarrow S. (2005), *The new transnational activism*, Cambridge University Press, Cambridge.

Tilly C. (1982), "Britain creates the social movement", in Cronin J., Schneer J. (eds.), *Social conflict and the political order in modern Britain*, Croom Helm, London, pp. 21–51.

Tilly C. (2004), *Social movements, 1768–2004.* Paradigm publisher, Boulder-London.

Tosi S. (2006), *Consumi e partecipazione politica. Tra azione individuale e mobilitazione collettiva,* Franco Angeli, Milano.

Chapter 45

Vincenzo Ruggiero

DICHOTOMIES AND CONTEMPORARY SOCIAL MOVEMENTS

THE DEBATE ON SOCIAL MOVEMENTS seems to revolve around a number of conceptual and practical dichotomies. Along with the traditional dyad 'reform–revolution', which constantly accompanies the perception and evaluation of collective action, dichotomies include views of movements as producers of identity versus movements as pursuers of resources, movements as expressions of the local versus movements as the result of the global, movements as expression of rationality versus movements as the outcome of passion, and so on. The dyad 'recognition-redistribution' provides yet another dichotomy along with a relatively new analytical angle. This paper discusses some of the dichotomies now faced by contemporary social movements (CSMs). By CSMs, also referred to as new global movements (della Porta, 2003), I mean the large array of groups and organizations engaged in political protest in Seattle, Washington, Prague and Genoa; the groups involved in the European Social Forum and in the Porto Alegre World Social Forum; and finally the movement contesting neo-liberalism during the world economic summits (Tilly, 2003; Wallerstein, 2003).

Originally published by Taylor and Francis Journals (UK), 'Dichotomies and Contemporary Social Movements', by Vincenzo Ruggiero, *City*, Vol 9, No. 3, December 2005, pp 297–306 (Taylor and Francis Ltd, http://www.informaworld.com), reprinted by permission of the publisher.

Identities and resources

[. . .]

Attempts at resolving the dichotomy identity–resources have multiplied along the expansion of the study of social movements. The emphasis on 'networks', for example, is consistent with the analytical framework of advocates of resource mobilization and theorists of new social movements alike. Both, in effect, would accept that participants in collective action are embedded in social networks which make the adoption of an 'activist identity' likely, on the one hand, and political mobilization possible, on the other (Melucci, 1989; McAdam *et al.*, 1996).

CSMs, or new global movements, are faced with a similar challenge, namely the search for a synthesis of their multiple characteristics. Theoretically, such synthesis would require the identification of a variety of common elements such as: shared beliefs and solidarity, action focused on conflicts, and use of protest as part of an ever-expanding 'repertoire of contention' (Traugott, 1995). According to Tarrow (1994), the identity–resources dichotomy can be superseded if movements mount collective challenges, draw on social networks, common purposes and cultural frameworks, and finally, build solidarity through structures and identities to sustain collective action. However, the diversity of the groups and individuals participating in CSMs may require more. The different components of the movement have extremely diversified needs and these relate to identity and resources in a number of specific manners. For some components it is access to resources that determines a strong affirmation of identity, whereas for others identity is forged because access to resources is denied. Finally, other components may prioritize minimum standards of resources while postponing the issue of blending their identity with that of other participants. In brief, CSMs are faced with the task of changing the system while changing the individuals involved. As Breton's famous formula goes: 'Marx said "Change the World", Rimbaud said "Change Life": for us these two watchwords are one' (Trebitsch, 1992, p. xx).

The social as mobility

The emergence of CSMs raises general sociological issues and, simultaneously, demands some rethinking of the categories elaborated within the specific field of the sociology of social movements.

The cross-national nature of these new movements, for example, echoes the contemporaneous mobility of goods, people, information and images, which reconstructs the 'social as society' into the 'social as mobility'. The flows of people beyond national territories are also described as explosions of desires, and as such they are deemed central to sociological scrutiny. Because of its proximity to social movements, sociology has always attempted to make sense of collective desires, and 'it is unlikely that it will survive if it does not again embody the ambitions of one or more of such social movements' (Urry, 2000, p. 18).

According to Bourdieu (2001), history teaches us that there is no meaningful social policy without movements capable of imposing it, and that it is not markets but, again, social movements that are able to civilize the economy. Against economic fatalism, governments should interfere with the laws governing the economy, because these are by no means natural laws. CSMs mobilize against these alleged natural laws and produce new leaderships, new types of organizations inspired by self-management, and 'characterized by a structural lightness allowing agents to re-appropriate their role as active subjects' (Bourdieu, 2001, p. 59). These new organizations are said to adopt forms of action of high symbolic content, to pursue concrete objectives, to be internationalist in nature, to require strong personal engagement from participants and finally to shape themselves as loosely co-ordinated networks.

Some of these characteristics may well be present in CSMs, particularly if we consider that they require non-delegate, strong, personal engagement and are shaped as loosely co-ordinated international networks. However, in response to 'liberals' who preach that all must be left to the market, these movements are faced with the choice of confining their role to that of victims denouncing the market, or actively proposing alternative economic strategies (Touraine, 1999; Ruggiero, 2002).

Impacting on choice

Is it paradoxical that a movement should advocate a global 'public sphere' and an international 'civil society', when both concepts derive from national state formations, and could therefore be described as inherently non-global? Civil society, the public sphere and, for that matter, sovereignty were conceived by national states and referred to limited territories (real or imagined): these concepts made sense only when applied to the relationship those limited territories had with the outside.

> "Early modern social theorists, from Hobbes to Rousseau, understood the civil order as a limited and interior space that is opposed or contrasted to the external order of nature. The bounded space of civil order, its place, is defined by its separation from the external spaces of nature." (Hardt and Negri, 2000, p. 187)

However, this paradox may well reflect the character of new movements, for while staging struggles that are rooted in local conditions, they attempt to leap immediately to the global level. Because of their potential ability to supersede this dichotomy, it has triumphantly been suggested that contemporary struggles 'are at once economic, political, and cultural—and hence they are bio-political struggles, struggles over the form of life ... creating new public spaces and new forms of community' (Hardt and Negri, 2000, p. 56). On the contrary, participants in CSMs appear to more prudently stress that the new struggles may just constitute a step forward in relation to the ritualistic gatherings staged as symbolic oppositional displays against the gatherings of the elites. In other words, struggles may simply aim at affecting political and economic choice. This leads to some further considerations.

Reform or change?

CSMs have been tentatively distinguished into three broad types. Movements of the first type are said to adopt strategies of 'de-linking', in that participants formulate radical alternatives to the global economy by withdrawing from official markets altogether. The second types of movement are denoted by attempts to achieve 'globalization from below' (della Porta, 2003), namely they are guided by traditional internationalism encouraging unity among victims of economic and political oppression from around the world. The third types are described as movements of 'contestation and reform', as they 'attempt to recover the authority of the state to regulate corporations, constrain their abuses and deliver social benefits' (Starr, 2000, p. xi). In brief, the movements of the third type are said to utilize existing democratic channels, and to seek new legislation while protesting and boycotting.

CSMs successfully use existing democratic channels for the mobilization of a large number of diverse individuals, a success that perhaps could hardly be achieved if those channels were ignored (see the participation in these movements of sections of official parties, trade unionists and local or national politicians). However, whether they can be described as mere 'reformative' movements rather than 'transformative' ones is difficult to assess (Wilson, 1973). A typology recognizing these two types of movement unwarrantably separates movements aiming to 'change the social structure' from movements 'aiming at partial change to try to offset current injustices and inequalities' (Cohen and Rai, 2000, p. 2). The history of social movements, in contrast, proves that reformative efforts may trigger unpredictable transformative processes, and that a neat separation between 'reform' and 'change' is fruitful less to collective action than to institutional agencies attempting to segment and dismember it (Lefebvre and Scalzone, 1999). Moreover, while movements are forced to move away from specifically national forms of opposition and confrontation, they are also encouraged 'to build transnational cooperation around shared goals that include social change' (Smith et al., 1997, p. 59).

While becoming more transnational, social movements inevitably alter their 'repertoires of action' and are compelled, therefore, to expand beyond their own localized space (Tilly, 1986). What forms of identity, no longer coinciding with space, are likely to be fostered by this expansion remains to be debated.

Social equality and cultural difference

Concerns about the possibility for progressive social change arise from a number of features characterizing the present condition. In Fraser's (1997) diagnoses such features include the absence of credible alternatives to the current order, the predominance of demands for *recognition of difference* rather than for *social justice*, and finally, the resurgence of economic liberalism and the related growth of social inequality. In the present context, CSMs are faced with the choice of advocating either social equality or cultural difference. Here is, supposedly, yet a new dichotomy. However, the politics of redistribution and the politics of recognition are not mutually exclusive, and critical theorists as well as movements 'should aim instead to identify the emancipatory dimensions of both problematics and to integrate them into a single, comprehensive framework' (Fraser, 1997, p. 4).

Documents released and practices put in place by contemporary movements seem to implicitly endorse this project, combining claims for recognition with demands for redistribution. For example, these movements link up with their counterparts in developing countries, where analyses of the relationships between 'centre and periphery' of the world give rise to specific political strategies (Brandford and Rocha, 2002; Brandford and Kucinski, 2003). The recognition of the cultural differences found in developing and developed regions, respectively, intensifies rather than hampers attempts to identify common economic objectives. The centre and the periphery are seen as suffering from the consequences of similar, though symmetric, global policies.

> "What is striking is that from Mali to England, from Canada to Brazil, from France to Thailand, and from the United States to Russia, we are faced with profound similarities and a high degree of complementarity between policies defined as structural adjustment at the periphery and those baptised as austerity at the centre." (Attac, 2000, p. 15)

This process has been equated to a shift from solidarity to fluidity, in the sense that collective action emerging and intensifying in the 1990s is deemed to typically reflect social formations that increasingly take the form of networks, scapes and flows (McDonald, 2002). Hence a concept of identity as a field of tensions, one determined by various sources and multifaceted experiences, a notion of identity as a process shaped by the multiple relationships in which social actors are involved (Diani, 2000). Echoing Simmel's (1955 [1908]) analysis of the social structure as the result of multiple linkages to different primary and secondary groups, CSMs are said to develop their identity while diversifying their affiliation. In other words, where traditional movements established loyalty, and therefore identity, through contacts provided by *concentric circles* of affiliation, in new social movements *intersecting circles* of affiliation prevail.

A master frame

Although it may be problematic to analyse CSMs from the standpoint of social psychology, some tenets of this discipline may prove helpful. For example, let us consider that identity is located in a specific social space and shaped by relationships both *within* and, as claimed above, *among* intersecting groups. In a related formulation, collective identity transcends pure role or group identity, in that it refers to shared self-definitions and common efforts towards the production of social change. Assuming that CSMs are formed by a variegated alliance of groups pursuing change in social values and life styles, variables such as values and value systems may help bring our analysis further. 'The value domain as the locational context for identities places a greater emphasis on culture than on social structure, and on the moral context of identities' (Gecas, 2000, p. 94). Collective identity, in other words, offers orientation in a moral space, gives rise to a sense of self-esteem and self-efficacy, and, finally, prompts 'what is worth doing and what is not', leading individuals to appreciate their capacity to change the surrounding environment (Taylor, 1989, p. 27). The network of CSMs faces a similar task, namely conferring this type of collective identity on its members, whereby members feel that their action can impact on the present economic and political situation, and that global developments are not ineluctable. While restoring some sense of subjectivity in participants, CSMs attempt to highlight the crucial role of human agency. On the other hand, they are faced with the task of advocating economic development and, simultaneously, contrasting its unwanted effects. Collective action, however, may lead to the persuasion that the 'laws' of the economy are not universal laws after all. Participants in CSMs, in brief, are required to revise the manner in which they view some features of contemporary life, seeing them no longer as part of misfortune, but of injustice (Snow *et al.*, 1986).

Some notions of frame analysis may help elaborate this point further (Goffman, 1974). Groups and organizations read and respond to problems while framing that reading in a definition of their situation (Crossley, 2002). For example, they frame individual and collective disadvantage in terms of broader system failings rather than in terms of personal failings. This amounts to a form of 'cognitive liberation', whereby groups turn into movements capable of shaping strategies for change (McAdam, 1982). This process engages individual social movements, whose specific cognitive liberation takes place in the limited context in which they operate, but also involves groups mainly focused on demands for recognition. CSMs, which are composed of a number of different movements, are forced to align the diverse frames of participating groups and organizations, therefore to draw a 'master frame' able to accommodate a large variety of demands, including demands for recognition as well as redistribution. This master frame may take shape thanks to the growing inequality both between countries and within specific national contexts. Global cities, for example, reproduce inequality internally and externally: there are forms of peripheralization at the very centre of global cities in developed countries (Sassen, 1994). As opposed to segmentation, the concept of peripheralization entails a form of apartheid whereby archaic work forms and conditions coexist with advanced financial valorization, and both are engaged in mutual reproduction (Ruggiero, 2001). The social apartheid experienced at the international level by developing countries, framed as such by social movements there, finds points of contact with that experienced by some groups in developed contries. The effectiveness of this master frame is to be associated to the degree of change shown by the system against which action is directed (Diani, 1996), in other words, to the extent that advocates of globalization are prepared to amend some of its unjust effects.

It has been argued that the term globalization has spread like wildfire, 'mainly as legitimation for the deregulation of financial markets', and that it has justified the decline of state powers to regulate capital flows. This process seemed as inevitable as the disempowerment of social movements, who were consequently advised to circumscribe their political possibilities. 'The only politics left was a politics of conserving and in some instances downright conservative resistance' (Harvey, 2000, p. 13). Here is yet another dichotomy. CSMs are faced with the challenge to prove that other types of resistance are possible.

It would appear that, to a degree, transnational social movement organizations 'have been able to articulate strategic frames that motivate global level organizing and collective action' (Smith, 2002, p. 505). Their 'master frame' has emerged alongside increasing communication among diverse groups, and together with the development of new skills for understanding and managing the differences characterizing them. It is not easy to predict to what extent, and for how long, such master frames will be able to incorporate these differences.

The free city and the end of Jerusalem

Organizational models put in place by contemporary social movements rest upon a final dichotomy: should they converge their energy on structured organizations and parties or should they, instead, opt for informal interaction among participants? The adoption of network forms of organization, and the notion that contemporary movements can better be described with terms such as *multitude*, seem to provide an implicit response to this dilemma.

A mythological exemplification of contemporary notions of network and multitude can be found in the contrast between Kreon, the dictator of Thebes, and a citizen of the 'free city'. When Kreon's messenger asks to see the top authority of the city, he is told that not a man, but a crowd is in charge in that city (Savater, 1996). CSMs will have to combine structured organizations, which are among their components, with the organizational model of the free city, a model embraced by others of their components. The task, here, is to resolve the dichotomy between rigid leaderships and horizontal structures, between decisions derived from the strength of collective motivation and decisions resulting from effectiveness of representatives. Put differently, CSMs may have to choose between a vertical and a horizontal type of organization. Vertical organizations have characteristics of economic enterprises and bureaucracies. Their concept of mobilization is linked with the professional efficiency that their leaders promote. The growth of the organization coincides with a greater strength of its leadership and the overall anonymous strength of its membership. As partners of an economic-type consortium, the members provide an indirect resource, whose role is less to influence decisions than to strengthen the leaders' capacity to implement them. Vertical organizations require a delegated participation which gives the leaders a symbolic support (and often a financial one) and strengthens their bargaining power, both public and private. Transparency and democracy will come in the future, but only if they are renounced in the present. Another world may be possible, but only as a future reward for current deprivation. By contrast, horizontal organizations draw their strength from the participatory intensity of their members and from the breadth of the networks that activists construct. These organizations depend on the decisions, values and lifestyles adopted by those who participate. Non-delegated action shapes and consolidates their choices, values and lifestyles. Such organizations take shape while trying out practices; their participants' identity is not pre-set but rather is shaped through action. Liberation is simultaneous with action: to change the world and to change oneself are coexisting aims.

Finally, CSMs are only partly 'open-ended', in the sense that some of their components refuse to engage in building up a superior representative entity, such as a party or an all-embracing organization. These components do not rely on a precisely identifiable set of ideologies which, in some traditional movements, help endure the present while postponing happiness to a future Jerusalem (Foa, 1982). In this sense, these sectors within CSMs are *new* social movements, exemplifying some of the features identified by Etienne Balibar (1998) in contemporary social conflicts, which, 'after the failure of utopias finally take inspiration from imagination'. In Balibar's analysis utopias belong to traditional social movements that use them as an imaginary compensation for reality. Traditional movements, in other words, are inspired by the pursuit of a final stage in society, characterized by definitive harmony. CSMs, on the other hand, do contain some traditional elements, and while some sectors see conflicts as leading to yet other conflicts, other sectors pursue harmony. In other words, CSMs are faced with the dichotomy between adopting a teleological stance or endorsing *the end of teleology* (Ruggiero, 2001).

Rationality versus emotions

With 'the decline of Jerusalem', action produced by social movements need not be measured in terms of final achievements. Conversely, according to some components of CSMs, action is to be gauged through the degree of rational pursuit of a predetermined end-stage. Does participation in social movements need to be related to the cognitive belief that final, millennarian, success is likely? Echoes of another dichotomy can be heard here.

Some previous analyses conceive of social movements as business activity, whereby movements seem to be led by leaders-entrepreneurs competing for the allegiance of participants and employing calculated oppositional strategies (Dobbin, 2001). Such analyses are the result of a process turning passions motivating social behaviour into 'interest', namely into calculative behaviour (Hirschman, 1977). CSMs include groups who express defiance, but also pleasure, emotions, passions, indignation and fury, and incorporate them all in their action. Their asserting agency may respond to the mere need to reclaim dignity; protest itself may be the goal (Goodwin *et al.*, 2001).

In this respect, their action may be regarded as lacking rationality when measured against potential realistic achievements, or even as irrational when confronted with the inescapable 'reality' of globalization. However, it is the very official notion of 'the real' that sectors of contemporary movements appear to challenge. This notion implies that 'reality' is both the object of our knowledge and the fulcrum of our actions. 'We reach out to it, we try to grasp it, either to observe it, or to transform it. The real demands realism' (Lefebvre, 2002, p. 194). The real, however, reveals its profundities to those who wish to penetrate it in order to transform it, and while sometimes it appears to be 'the sole reality, the reality of realists, dense, weighty and solid', at other times it seems that 'its weight is artificial, that its denseness is insubstantial: unreality incarnate'. Lefebvre suggests that, along with dispelling these obscurities and clarifying our terminology, we should distinguish between the actual and the real, or again, between the present and the real.

> "Let us begin by reintegrating the possible within the real ... The possible is seen as abstract and vague, while the real is seen as thick and weighty, as 'being' or 'existing'. But the possible enters the real. It appears there: it

announces and invokes its presence within it, and then sets about destroying it and negating it". (Lefebvre, 2002, pp. 194–195)

It remains to be seen whether CSMs will be able to resolve the dichotomy between real achievement and contestation of the official notion of the 'real'.

[. . .]

References

Attac (2000) *Les peoples entrent en résistance*. Paris: Centre Europe-Tiers Monde.

Balibar, E. (1998) *Droit de cité. Culture et politique en démocratie*. Paris: Editions de l'Aube.

Bourdieu, P. (2001) *Contre-feux 2: Pour un movement social européen*. Paris: Raisons D'Agir.

Brandford, S. and Kucinski, B. (2003) *Politics Transformed: Lula and the Workers' Party in Brazil*. London: Latin American Bureau.

Brandford, S. and Rocha, J. (2002) *Cutting the Wire: The Story of the Landless Movement in Brazil*. London: Latin American Bureau.

Cohen, R. and Rai, S.M. (eds) (2000) *Global Social Movements*. London: Athlone.

Crossley, N. (2002) *Making Sense of Social Movements*. Buckingham and Philadelphia: Open University Press.

della Porta, D. (2003) 'Democracy in movement: organizational dilemma and globalization from below', paper presented at 'Les Mouvements Alter/Anti-Mondialisation', Paris, 4 November.

Diani, M. (1996) 'Linking mobilization frames and political opportunities', *American Sociological Review* 61, pp. 1053–69.

Diani, M. (2000) 'Simmel to Rokkon and beyond: towards a network theory of (new) social movements, *European Journal of Social Theory* 3, pp. 33–47.

Dobbin, F. (2001) 'The business of social movements', in J. Goodwin, J.M. Jasper and F. Polletta (eds) *Passionate Politics: Emotions and Social Movements*, pp. 74–80. Chicago and London: University of Chicago Press.

Foa, V. (1982) *La Gerusalemme rimandata*. Turin: Rosenberg & Sellier.

Fraser, N. (1997) *Justice Interruptus: Critical Reflections on the Postsocialist-Condition*. New York and London: Routledge.

Gecas, V. (2000) 'Value identities, self-motives, and social movements', in S. Stryker, T.J. Owens and R.W. White (eds) *Self, Identity and Social Movements*, pp. 93–109. Minneapolis: University of Minnesota Press.

Goffman, E. (1974) *Interaction Ritual*. Harmonsdworth: Penguin.

Goodwin, J., Jasper, J.M. and Polletta, F. (eds) (2001) *Passionate Politics: Emotions and Social Movements*. Chicago and London: University of Chicago Press.

Hardt, M. and Negri, A. (2000) *Empire*. Cambridge, MA: Harvard University Press.

Harvey, D. (2000) *Spaces of Hope*. Edinburgh: Edinburgh University Press.

Hirschman, A.O. (1977) *The Passions and the Interests*. Princeton, NJ: Princeton University Press.

Lefebvre, H. (2002) *Critique of Everyday Life*, Vol II. London: Verso.

Lefebvre, H. and Scalzone, O. (1999) *Du contract de citoyenneté*. Paris: Syllepse/Périscope.

McAdam, D. (1982) *Political Process and the Development of Black Insurgency, 1930–1970*. Chicago: University of Chicago Press.

McAdam, D., McCarthy, J.D. and Zald, M.N. (1996) *Comparative Perspectives in Social Movements*. Cambridge: Cambridge University Press.

McDonald, K. (2002) 'From solidarity to fluidarity: social movements beyond collective identity: the case of globalization conflicts'. *Social Movement Studies* l(2), pp. 109–128.

Melucci, A. (1989) *Nomads of the Present: Social Movements and Individual Needs in Contemporary Society*. London: Hutchinson Radius.

Offe, C. (1985) 'New social movements: challenging the boundaries of institutional politics', *Social Research* 52(4), pp. 817–868.

Ruggiero, V. (2001) *Movements in the City*. New York: Prentice Hall.

Ruggiero, V. (2002) 'Attac: a global social movement?', *Social Justice* 29(1–2), pp. 48–60.

Sassen, S. (1994) *Cities in a World Economy*. Thousand Oaks, CA: Pine Forge Press.

Savater, F. (1996) *Dizionario filosofico*. Rome/Bari: Laterza.

Simmel, G. (1955 [1908]) *Conflict and the Web of Group-affiliations*. Glencoe, IL: Free Press.

Smith, J. (2002) 'Bridging global divides? Strategic framing and solidarity in transnational social movement organizations', *International Sociology* 17(4), pp. 505–528.

Smith, J., Chatfield, C. and Pagnucco, R. (1997) *Transnational Social Movements and Global Politics*. Syracuse, NY: Syracuse University Press.

Snow, A.D., Rochford, E.B., Worden, S.K. and Benford, R.D. (1986) 'Frame alignment processes, micromobilization, and movement participation', *American Sociological Review* 561, pp. 464–481.

Starr, A. (2000) *Naming the Enemy: Anti-corporate Movements Confront Globalization*. London and New York: Zed Books.

Tarrow, S. (1994) *Power in Movement: Social Movements, Collective Action and Politics*. Cambridge: Cambridge University Press.

Taylor, C. (1989) *Sources of the Self*. Cambridge, MA: Harvard University Press.

Tilly, C. (1986) 'European violence and collective violence since 1700', *Social Research* 53, pp. 159–184.

Tilly, C. (2003) 'Social movements enter the twenty-first century', paper presented at 'Contentious Politics and the Economic Opportunity Structure', University of Crete, 17–18 October.

Touraine, A. (1999) *Comment sortir du libéralisme*, Paris: Fayard.

Traugott, M. (1995) *Repertoires and Cycles of Collective Action*, Durham, NC: Duke University Press.

Trebitsch, M. (1992) 'Preface', in H. Lefebvre, *Critique of Everyday Life*, Vol. I, pp. ix–xxviii. London: Verso.

Urry, J. (2000) *Sociology Beyond Societies*. London: Routledge.

Wallerstein, I. (2003) 'Cancún: la fine dell'offensiva neoliberista'. *Carta* 39, pp. 50–55.

Wilson, J. (1973) *Introduction to Social Movements*. New York: Basic Books.

Index

page references followed by f indicate an illustrative figure; n indicates a note; t indicates a table

Aaronson, Susan A. 318
Action Party (Risorgimento) 42, 56, 57–8
advocacy groups *see* Khagram, Riker and Sikkink
Africa, rural mobilization 101
agitation 67–8, 80, 82, 304
alliances 149; North and South 316
America 8, 15, 93, 192, 193, 215, 216; 1960's
    riots 97, 100; civil rights movement 107,
    109, 110, 120, 122, 148, 174, 189, 202,
    204, 228, 230, 273; 341 *see also* Evans; Civil
    War 84; Eisinger on protest 140; Evan's
    Personal Politics 140–1, 152–6;
    "exceptionalism" 288; McAdam on Black
    insurgency 141–2, 177–85; Medicare 107;
    Montgomery bus boycott 98; Mueller on
    women's liberation 198, 226–34; NAFTA
    318, 340, 343, 351; poverty and insurgency
    172–8; response to coup d'état 100–1;
    Sanctuary movement 343; school
    desegregation 99; Seattle *see* Khagram, Riker
    and Sikkink, Montagna, Smith; Shay's
    rebellion 81; student movement 275, 276,
    300, 341; Three Mile Island disaster 123;
    Tocqueville, *Democracy in America* 139–40;
    Whiskey rebellion 81; withdrawal
    movements 112
anarchy 10, 34, 61, 215
Anderson, Benedict 344
Andretta, M. 350
Angola 107
anomie 3–4, 9
antislavery movement 341

Appadurai, Arjun 297; *Grassroots Globalisation*
    298, 303–6
apathy 75
Apter, David, *Ideology and Discontent* 147
Argentina 342
Aristotle 170
Attac 351, 361
Audley, John J. 318
Ayres, Jeffry M. 318

Badiou, Alain 6
Baglioni, Simone 345
Bailis, L. 123
Balibar, Etienne 364
Banaszak, L. A. 166
Banfield, Edward 162n
bargaining 2
Bauman, Z. 353
Beck, Giddens and Lash 352–3
Beck, U. 353
Belgium 341
beliefs 242, 333; belief amplification 258;
    deprivation and 106–7; generalized 80, 83,
    85, 106, 155; shared beliefs and solidarity
    268–9, 358; *see also* values
Bell, D. 216
Bennett, W. Lance 341
bloc recruitment 182
Blumer, Herbert, expressive movements 71–2;
general social movements 64–6; *Social Movements* 4,
    42–3, 64–72; specific social movements 66–71
Boli and Thomas 327

Bolkenstein project 351
Bookchin, Murray, *Our Synthetic Environment* 276
Boulanger adventure 59
Bowen *et al.* 106
Brandford and Kucinski 361
Brandford and Rocha 361
Brazil 240
breakdown theorists 45
Brecher and Costello 351
Breton 358
Breton and Breton 113n
Brinton, Crane 98, 99
Britain 8, 15, 81, 84, 85, 100, 101, 191, 341;
    industrial communities 123; mass
    marches 189
Bunch *et al.* 310, 311, 312
Bush and Simi 342
Butler and Savage 90

Calhoun, Craig 127; dualism 245, 290, 292–3;
    perception 243, 291, 292, 293;
    psychoanalysis 291–2; *Putting Emotions in
    Their Place* 242–3, 289–95;
Camisards 188, 189–90
Canada: Saskatchewan farmers 98, 185; Seattle
    protest 299, 318, 319
Cantril, H. 112
Castells, M. 354
castes 214; Durkheim's view 21, 22, 23
Central Europe, collapse of socialist system 310
Chabanet, Didier 342, 345
charismatic movement 83
charities, funding 131
Chatfield, Charles 324
child-care and women at work 227
Chile 335
China 84, 85, 304; Tiananmen 354
cities 134–6, 209; Appaduri on Shack/Slum-
    Dwellers International (SDI) 298, 304–5;
    distribution of power among social classes in
    medieval Italian city 50–1; Eisinger on protest
    in American 140, 157–62; global 362;
    relationship between countryside and 101–4,
    120; patrician monopolies in Venice 47–9;
    patrician monopolies outside Venice 49;
    popolo 49–51 classical notion of 'free city'
    363; Simmel's view 10; Weber's view 41–2,
    47–51
Civil Rights Acts 1964 and 1965 122; Title VII
    154, 229
civil rights movement 107, 109, 110, 120, 122,
    174, 189, 202, 204, 341; Evans 140–1,
    152–6; Morris 148; women's movement and
    228, 230
civil society 17, 139–40, 174, 196, 197, 206,
    207, 208, 244, 349, 351, 359; defence of 352;

neoconservative view of 207; utopian
    view 303
Clark, Hochstetler and Friedman 323
class 21, 22, 23, 98–9, 214, 275; alternatives to
    traditional middle class–protest 202–4; class
    and market economics 52–4; communal
    action and class interest 53–4; communal
    action and class interest 53–4; concept of
    class struggle 8; definition of 52; excluded
    groups 158–9, 197, 217; Marx and Engels
    Communist Manifesto, The 13–16; people
    outside core industrial working class 196,
    211; *see also* poverty and insurgency;
    totalitarianism and class movements 76–7;
    types of class struggle 54; Weber, *Class, Work,
    Party* 1, 52–4
Cleary, Seamus 318
cognitive change 298, 344–5 for more general
    discussion of cognitive factors; *see* Calhoun,
    perception; Eyerman and Jamison
Cohen, I. J. 42
Cohen and Rai 360
Cold War 344
collective action 3, 4, 5, 6; 44–5; conflict and
    7–39; Calhoun 244, 289, 290, 294; Diani
    269–71; Eisinger 140, 158; Escobar and
    Alvarez 198, 240; Evans 140–1; Jenkins 119,
    126, 127; Marwell and Oliver 90–1, 128–38;
    McAdam, McCarthy and Zald 106, 107;
    McCarthy and Zald 89; Melucci 198, 223;
    Mueller 198, 228, 233; Oberschall 88; Olson
    87–8, 93–4; Ruggiero 357, 358, 360, 361,
    362, 363; Smith 299, 323; Tarrow 139, 140,
    145, 146–50; *see also* transnational collective
    action
collective behaviour, hegemony and 41–85
collective goods 130, 131, 137, 241, 250, 254
collective identity *see* identity, collective
collective interests 212, 365
collective will 42, 59
Colombia 101
colonisation of everyday life 196, 204
Commission on Global Governance 328
communal action and class interest 53–4
communal modes of production and
    distribution of goods 209
communication 44; communicative action 196;
    communication network 182–3; *see also*
    information; internet; media; newspapers
communism 75, 215 *see also* Marx, *Communist
    Manifesto*, Communist party; Russia; USSR
Communist party 76, 84; in Hungary 99
Comte, Auguste 7, 8
Congress of Racial Equality (CORE) 109
conscience adherents 111
conscience constituents 111, 121, 122

consciousness raising 141, 153, 155, 227–8
contagion, crowd behaviour 38, 149
contemporary social movements (CSM) 301, 357–65; failure of utopias 364; identities and resources 358; impacting on choice 359–60; master frame 361–3; notion of 'free city' 363; rationality versus emotions 368–9; reform or change 361; social as mobility 358–9; social equality and cultural difference 361–3
conversion potential 181
conviction 69
countermovement 109
Country Life movement 82
coup d'états: 1960 100; USA and 100–1
Crawford and Naditch 106
craze 79, 80, 81
critical mass and problem of collective action 128–33
Critical Mass Bulletin 112n
Crossley, N. 43, 244, 362
crowds, 10, 34–9, 79, 155, 244; dancing 71–2; mind of 36–9; power of 34–5
Crusades 27
cultural contexts 195, 196, 198, 199, 201–5, 217, 237, 240, 268, 277; counterculture 209, 216, 217; cultural patterns 213
cultural difference and social equality 360–1
cultural trends, new 64–5
Cunningham, Hilary 343
Curtis and Zurcher 182
cycles 274; of protest 262–3

Daly, Mary, *Church and The Second Sex, The* 154
Darwin, Charles 7
DAWN (Development Alternatives for Women) 298, 309–14; contribution of 313–14; North and South alliance 312; Seattle 313
De Angelis, Massimo 5–6
debt reduction 351
decentralized movements 125–6
deep democracy 298, 304
Delanty, G. 9
Della Porta, Donatella 342, 345, 360
Della Porta, Kriesi and Rucht 352
Della Porta and Diani 241
Della Porta and Kriesi 343, 345, 353
Della Porta and Tarrow, cognitive change 300; environmental change 300; relational change 300 *Transnational Protest and Global Activism* 300, 339–46;
Della Porta *et al.* 349
Deutsch-Französische Jahrbücher 17
development *see* DAWN; Mayo on women and development; Shack/Slum-Dwellers International (SDI)

Diani, Mario 10, 361, 362; action outside institutional sphere and routine social life 270–1; collective action and conflictual issues 269–70; *Concept of Social Movements, The* 243, 266–72;
diffusion 298, 340–1
direct action 74
Direct Action Network 320t, 321
division of labour, Durkheim 1, 9, 21–4
Dobbin, F. 364
doge, power of the 47–9
domestic nongovernmental organizations 329
Dorsey, Ellen 328
Downes and Spilerman 159, 161
Downs, A. 105
dramaturgy 323
dualism, Calhoun's view 245, 290, 292–3
Durkheim, Émile 1, 2, 6; anomie 3–4, 9; collective consciousness 27n; collective effervescence 9, 10; collective force 26; *Division of Labour in Society, The* 9, 21–4; *Elementary Forms of the Religious Life, The* 9, 25–8; 'right of combat' 6, 9, 23; solidarity 8–9, 22–3

Eastern Europe, collapse of socialist system 310
Edelman 184
Eder, Klaus 342
EEOC 154
Egret, J. 148
Eisinger, Peter K 162n; characteristics of protest 159–60 *Conditions of Protest in American Cities, The* 140, 157–62, 179
election survey, National Election Studies, University of Michigan 227
electoral systems: as a structuring institution 173–4; national states 191–2; Switzerland 143, 163–70; voting opportunities, USA 157, 158, 161n
electronic activism 323–4
elites 5, 6, 61, 76, 89, 103, 107, 110, 122, 126, 172, 217; discussion of elite model political system 178; Marxist view 178
Elson, D. 307
Elster, J. 88
Engels, Frederick: *Articles on Britain* 16n; *Communist Manifesto, The* 8, 13–16; *Critique of Political Economy* 8, 17–18; 'English Ten Hours Bill, The' 16n; *German Ideology, The* 3
England *see* Britain
entrepreneurs, role of 89–90, 122, 364; entrepreneurial model 120
environmental factors 198, 203, 236, 273, 274, 276; Earth Day 276; globalisation 299, 300, 319, 344, 351; Green party 215
Epictetus 290

Epple-Gass 163
Equal Employment Opportunities Commission 229
Equal Rights Amendment 154, 156, 231
ERAP 155
Escobar and Alvarez, *Theory and Protest in Latin America Today* 198–200, 235–40
esprit de corps, development of 68–9, 72
Etzioni, A. 113n
Europe 81, 191, 335, 340, 341–3, 345, 351, 352; opposition to EU 353; strike against Renault 342
Evans, Sara, *Personal Politics* 140–1, 152–6; preconditions for insurgent collective identity 155
evolution and progress 7
experts, role of 323
externalisation 342–3
extreme action *see* totalitarianism
Eyerman and Jamison 44; *Social Movements: A Cognitive Praxis* 242–3, 272–77

fair trade 354
Falk, Richard 327, 328
fascism 75, 76, 85, 247
Federal Advisory Council Act, USA 323
Feld, Jordan and Hurwitz 350
feminism *see* women's movement
Fifty Years Is Enough campaign 318, 321t, 322
Finnemore, Martha 331, 332
Flanders 101
Fleishman, John A. 249
Florini, Ann 329
Foa, V. 364
Fogelson, Robert 162n
Foster, J. (1974) 123
Foster, J. (1999) 320
Fox and Brown 320, 342
framing processes 244; CSMs 361–3; frame alignment (Snow *et al.*) 255–65; frame amplification 242, 257–8, 264; frame analysis (Goffman) 5, 242, 259, 260, 261, 263; frame bridging 242, 256–7, 262; frame extension 242, 258–9, 264; frame transformation 259–61, 264; framing work 142–3, 147; global factors 264, 300, 350–1; McAdam, McCarthy and Zald's view 279, 281–2, 285–6, 287; norms and framing 331–4
France 8, 9, 15, 75, 76, 148, 216, 341; 1848 99, 100, 192; attacks on McDonald's 345; compared to Switzerland 164, 166, 167; Mouvements Altermondialistes 297; Poujadists 74; Protestants of Cévennes 188, 189–91; revolution 19–20, 27, 58, 84, 85, 97–8, 189; rural areas 102; Tocqueville's comparison with America 139–40; wine growers movement 188

Franco-Prussian War 9
Fraser, N. 364, 365
Freeman 183
free-riding 88, 90, 91, 123, 129, 130, 131, 182, 253
free speech movement, Berkeley 182
Freud 294
Friends of the Earth 320t, 321

games *see* models
Gamson *et al.* 260
Gamson, W. A. 105, 124, 147, 180–1, 182, 249, 319
Garibaldi 56, 58
Garner and Zald 149
gender issues *see* women's movement
Gerhards and Rucht 322
Gerlach and Hine 124, 181
Germany 8, 48, 75, 85, 100, 164, 166, 191, 215, 247; fall of Berlin wall 354; Globalisierungskritische Bewegungen 301; guilds in the Middle Ages 49, 50; Schleswig-Holstein 98; student movement 275, 300, 341
Ghana 100
ghettos: migration to 174; riots 159, 161, 172
Giddens, A. 353
Gitlin, Todd 275
Giugni and Passy 341
global factors 5, 216; campaigns 351–2, 354; frame analysis 260, 263, 300, 350–1; networks 329, 330, 333–4, 349–50; organisational forms 300; political opportunities and globalisation of movements 352–4; women's movement 221, 298, 307–14, 335; utopian 297, 298, 303, 306; *see also* Appadurai; contemporary social movements; Mayo; Smith; transnational collective action
Global Justice Movement (GJM) 297, 298, 300, 340, 349, 350, 351, 352, 353
Goffman, E. frame analysis 5, 242, 259, 260, 260, 262, 281, 350, 362
Goldstein and Keohane 333
Goodwin, Jasper and Polleta 244
government, responsibility for 60
grammar of forms of life 195, 196, 201
Gramsci, Antonio 4; *Modern Prince, The* 42, 59–63; *Notes on Italian History* 42, 55–8
Greenpeace 320t, 321
Group of Eight 344, 351
Guarnizo, Portes and Landolt 344
Guidry, Kennedy and Zald 354
Gurr, T. R. 106, 113n, 162n

Habermas, Jürgen, *New Social Movements* 195–6, 201–5

Hardin, R. 147, 148
Hardt and Negri 351, 359
Hare Krishna 256, 259
Harrington, A. 8
Harrington, M. 113n
Harris Survey 156
Harvey, D. 353
Heberle, Rudolf 98, 113n, 187, 194n
Hegel 17, 18n, 19
Heirich, Max 261
Held *et al.* 353
hereditary transmission of wealth and power 23, 47, 48
HEW 154
Hill and Rothchild 149
Hirschman, Albert 146, 364
Hobbes 359
Hooghe, Liesbet 345
Huber, Joan 227
humanitarian movement 81
human rights 298, 303, 343, 351
Human Rights for Women 230
Hungary 88, 99, 100
Hypothesis 4 88, 97–8

ideas, IR definition of 333
ideology, role of 147
identities and resources 358
identity 213, 222, 224; collective 332, 361–2; collective, Latin America 238–9; collective, of women 227, 229–33; Diani's view 243, 268–9, 270, 271; Montagna's view 302; Smith's view 319
Imig and Tarrow 341, 342
Independent Media Center, Seattle (IMC) 324
India: Bhopal 323; Shack/Slum-Dwellers International (SDI) 298, 304–5
indigenous groups 198, 236, 303, 335, 345
Indonesia 84, 85
industrial conflict and size of population 120
information: information societies 221–3; production of 197, 218–20, 222; *see also* internet; media; newspapers
intergovernmental organization 331
internalization 341–2
International Confederation of Free Trade Unions (ICFTU) 322
International Conference on Population and Development, Cairo 1994 311
International Monetary Fund (IMF) 340; protests against 235, 300, 316, 317, 318, 327, 342, 351, 352
international nongovernmental organizations (INGOs) 329
International Relations (IR), study of 328
internet 299, 323–4, 341

Italy 76, 85, 240, 345; concept of Italy descended from Rome 59; fascism 75; Patrician dominion in 41–2, 47–9; *popolo* 49–51; rural areas 101, 102, 345; Tarrow's work on social movements 142; unification 42, 56–8
I.W.W. 75, 76

Japan 102, 216
Jasper, J. 89
Jenkins, Craig 123, 124; *Social Mobilisation Theory and Social Movements* 90, 118–27; formation of social movements 119–20; organization of social movements 124–6; *see also* resource mobilisation
Jenkins and Perrow 113n, 119
Jewish culture 217
Joas, H. 43, 45
Jubilee 2000 318

Kane, Anne 293
Kanter, R. M. 112
Katz and Gurin 181
Katzenstein, Peter J. 332
Katzenstein, Keohane and Krasner 328
Keane, J. 350
Keck and Sikkink 303, 318, 324, 327, 329, 332, 343
Keohane, Robert O. 328
Kertzer, D. 146
K. K. K. 75
Khagram, Riker and Sikkink, *From Santiago to Seattle: Transnational Advocacy Groups Restructuring World Politics* 299–300, 327–36; domestic and international opportunity structures 334–6; forms of 328–30; norms and framing 331–4
Klandermans, Bert 45, 232, 331, 332, 334; collective benefits 249–50, 254; mobilization 251–2, 254; *Mobilization and Participation: Social-Psychological Expansions of Resource Mobilization* 241–2, 247–54; motives 250, 256; research method 252–3; selective costs and benefits 250, 254; willingness to participate 249–51
Klein, Ethel 227–8
Klein, N. 297
Knight, W. Andy 328
Koopmans, R. 165
Kornhauser, William 4, 43–4, 141, 174; on leaders 43–4; *Politics of Mass Society, The* 43, 73–8, 179, 244
Krasner, Stephen D. 33
Kriesi and Wisler, *Social Movements and Direct Democracy in Switzerland* 143, 163–70; action

repertories 165–8; chances of success 165; 'entry price' in cantons 166, 167t, forms taken by protest events in cantons 168, 168t

Kriesi *et al.* 146, 166, 168

Kriesi, Hanspeter 330

labour movement, definition of 81, 216

Latin America 100, 101, 198–9, 235–40, 300, 349; Southern Cone countries 237

Laver, M. 88

lawyers groups 323

leadership 43–4, 97, 98, 183; agitator 67; contention and 146; cult of sainthood 69–70; general social movements and 65–6; political parties and 60, 61; power of the doge 47–9; problems of political leadership and modern Italy 56–8

Lebanon 354

Le Bon, Gustave, 4; *Crowd, The* 10, 34–9, 244

Lefebvre, H. 364–5

Lefebvre and Scalzone 364

Legal Defense Fund 230

Leites and Wolf 112, 113n

Lenel, Walter, *Die Enstebung der Voberschaft Venedigs an der Adria* 48, 51n

Levine, D. H. 148

Levy, S. 113n

Lieberson and Silverman 158, 162n

Lineberry, Robert 162n

Lipschutz, Ronnie 327, 328

Lipset 98, 183

Lipset and Wolin 182

Lipsky, M. 105, 146

local government 157–8; reform government 158, 162n

Lupsha, Peter 162n

McAdam, Doug 334, 335; cognitive liberation 186; *Freedom Summer* 148, 332; generation of insurgency 178–9; indigenous organizational strength 181–3; *Political Process and the Development of Black Insurgency 1930–1970* 141–2, 177–85, 184f, 331, 362; structure of political opportunities 179–81

McAdam, McCarthy and Zald 328, 332; *Comparative Perspectives on Social Movements* 243–4, 279–88; framing process 279, 281–2, 285–6, 287; linking opportunities 282–6; mobilizing structures 279, 280–1, 286–7; political opportunities 279–80, 283, 284, 286; using the perspective comparatively 286–8

McCarthy and Zald 119–20, 121–2, 192, 257; Diani on 268, 269, 270; *Resource Mobilisation Theory and the Study of Social Movements* 89–90, 105–13; *see also* resource mobilisation

McCarthy, John D. 256, 257, 318, 320t, 332

McCarthy, John *et al.* 5

Machiavelli, *Prince, The* 59

Mahila Milan 304

Mannheim 77

Marcuse, Herbert 215, 275

market economics and class 52–4

Marks and McAdam 334

Martin and Ross 345

Marullo, Pagnucco and Smith 318

Marwell and Oliver, critical mass and problem of collective action 128–33; *Critical Mass in Collective Action* 90–1, 128–38

Marx and Wood 113n

Marx, Karl 1, 2, 3, 93, 95, 106, 134, 141, 155, 178, 362; *Articles on Britain* 16n; *Capital*, 3; *Communist Manifesto, The* 8, 13–16; *Contribution to the Critique of Hegel's Philosophy of Law* 17, 18n; *Critique of Political Economy* 8, 17–18; *Eighteenth Brumaire of Louis Bonaparte, The* 8, 19–20; *German Ideology, The* 3

Marxism, abandonment of 198

Marxism, post 239

mass behaviour 43, 73–8, 217, 244; mass following 61, 62; mass participation in political action, fear of 4, 10

Mayo, Marjorie, *Globalisation and Gender, New Threats, New Strategies* 298, 307–14

Mazey and Richardson 343

McDonald, K. 361

Mead, Herbert 43

media, role of 287, 299, 324; *see also* information

Melder 183–4

Melucci, Alberto 147, 268, 269; defining newness 220–1; Escobar and Alvarez' view 241–2; Mueller's view of 226, 228, 231, 232, 233–4; *Strange Kind of Newness: What's New in New Social Movements? A* 197, 218–25

Mendelson and Glenn 344

Mertes 297

messianic movement 83

Merton, Robert 4

Mexico 240, 324, 343; debt crisis 233; Zapata rebellion 99, 101, 322, 354

Meyer and Tarrow 329

micromobilization 255, 257, 267, 268

migration 348; Mexican border crossing 343

millennial movement 77, 83

Mittelman, James H. 327

mob 10, 75, 244

Mobilization for Youth and the Community Action Program 122

mobilizing structures: McAdam, McCarthy and Zald 279, 280–1, 286–7 models 132–8; 334–5, 363; bipolar model of latency and visibility 224–5; elite model 178; political process model 141, 145, 177–85; political process model of movement emergence 184f

Moderates, the (Risorgimento) 56–7, 58

Montagna, Nicola, *Social Movements and Global Mobilisations* 300, 351–4

morale, development of 69–70

Morocco 102

Morris, Aldon 148

Morrison, D. E. 113n

Moser 308, 309

Mueller, Carol, *Conflict Networks and the Origins of Women's Liberation* 198, 226–34

Mueller, E. 106

Murphy, G. H. 349

mystics 290

myth and morale 70

Naidoo, Kumi 328

Naim, M. 318, 327

Nairobi 310, 311, 314

Narbonne 189

National Association for the Advancement of Coloured People (NAACP) 109

national conflicts, definition 213

nationalistic movement 80, 83, 84, 85

National Organization for Women (NOW) 126, 154, 229–30

National Slum Dwellers Federation 304

national social movement 193, 194, 244; definition 188; rise of 186–7, 191–2

National Welfare Rights Organization (NWRO) 123

neocommunitarianism 213

neoconservatives 196, 205, 206–7

neocorparatism 126

neoliberalism 300, 351

Netherlands 164, 166, 242, 252–3

networks 133–8, 257, 343; activist 303–4; DAWN 312; Diani 243, 267–8, 271; global 297, 305; informal 243, 267–8, 271, 304, 340; Melucci 224, 226, 231; Mueller 198, 226–34; submerged 226, 228–32; transnational 329, 330, 333–4, 349–50, 362, 363; variables 134–8

Neveu, E. 351

New Left, USA 141, 155–6, 228, 230

new social movements (NSMs) 351; actors 211; autonomy 240; compared to traditional social movements 214–17, 273–4, 276–7; CSMs 368; definition of 195, 197, 208–11, 220–1, 237, 239–40, 273; mode of action 210; symbolic challenges 223–5; *see also* individual authors, part five

newspapers 60, 322–3

Nichiren Shoshu 256, 259, 260

Noble, T. 8

nongovernmental organizations (NGOs) 298, 304, 308–9, 312, 313, 314, 331, 332, 340, 342–3, 345, 352, 353; definition of 329; former Soviet Union and East Central Europe 344; newspapers 322–3

norm-orientated movements 80–3; collective outbursts and 81; framing and norms 300, 331–4; more general social movements and 81–2; normative innovation 80; structural conduciveness 82–3; types of organizations and 82; value-added sequence of 82

North American Free Trade Agreement (NAFTA) 318, 340, 343, 351

Notes from the Second Year 231

Nussbaum, M. 308

Oberschall, Anthony 119, 249, 334; *Social Conflicts and Social Movements* 88–9, 95–104, 105, 107, 109, 112, 181, 182; *see also* resource mobilisation

O'Brien *et al.* 327, 328

Offe, Claus, new paradigm 208–11; *New Social Movements: Challenging the Boundaries of Institutional Politics* 196, 206–11; old paradigm 207–8

official templates 323

Olesen, T. 354

Olson, Mancur, comparison of Marwell and Oliver's view of free riding to Olson's 129–30, 137; *Logic of Collective Action, The* 87–8, 93–4, 107, 122–3, 127, 146, 148, 253, 254

outbursts, collective 81; hostile 80

Palley and Palley 159

panic 79, 80, 81, 155

Parsons, T. 44, 174

participation in social movements, *see* resource mobilisation, participants; Klandermans; Snow *et al.*

Passy, Florence 350

peace movement 81, 203, 215, 318, 340, 351

Pearson and Jackson 307

People's Global Action (PGA) 320t, 321–2

personal change movements 125

Peterson, M. J. 327

Petras and Zeitlin 101

Philippines 323

Pianta and Silva 349

Pianta, Mario 300, 345

Piven and Cloward, institutional limits on the incidence of mass insurgency 170–2; limited impact of mass defiance 175–6; patterning of insurgency 172–5; *Poor Peoples' Movements* 140, 170–6

Plato 290

Poland 100

political force, aims of 213

political opportunities: globalisation of movements and 352–4; McAdam, McCarthy and Zald's views 279–80, 283, 284, 286

political parties, *Modern Prince, The* 60–3; historical necessity for 62–3

political process, definition of 139; model of 141, 145, 177–85; *see* part four for full discussion

politics, transnationalisation of 353

popolo 49–51

postmodernists 290

Poujadists 74

poverty 98; globalisation and 300, 305; insurgency and 140, 170–6; women in the South 311

pressure groups 93

professions, free, role in opposition and protest 102–4, 122; business groups 103–4

Promotion of Area Resource Centres 304

propaganda 44, 60

proximate objects, sphere of 73–4

psychological factors 43, 44–5, 57, 126, 281; cognitive approach (Eyerman and Jamison) 242–3, 272–77; dancing crowd 71–2; emotions *see* Calhoun; indefinite images and behaviour 65; 'inner demons' 244; Klandermans 241–2, 247–54

Public Citizen 320t, 321

public sphere, global 354, 359

Putnam, Robert 334

Quarantelli and Hundley 106

race, factor of *see* civil rights movement; ghettos; McAdam on black insurgency; riots, race

Rancière, Jacques, *On the Shores of Politics* 6

rationalist theories 88, 89, 90, 94, 129, 202, 203, 216, 219, 244; emotion versus rationality 290, 291, 295, 364–5; participation 249

Reader's Digest 156

reality and responsibility 74

referendum 163, 170n

Reformation 83

reform movements 66, 70–1

Reinicke and Deng 328

Reising, Uwe 341

relational change 300, 345–6

relations of production, view of Marx 17–18

religious movements 71–2, 80, 83–4, 215, 262, 271, 355; Anabaptists 77; change and value-orientated movements 84–5; creed and sacred literature 70; cult of sainthood 69–70; dissenting women 148, 154; divisions of wealth and power 44; fundamentalism 223; Hare Krishna 256, 259; Jewish culture 217; Nichiren Shoshu 256, 259, 260; Protestants of Cévennes 188, 189–90; 'spiritualization of politics' 77; transnational church affiliations 322; *see also* Durkheim, *Elementary Forms of the Religious Life, The*

remote objects, response to 73, 74–5

repertoires 194n, 261; changes to 189; globalisation and 299, 300, 322–4; of contention 146; social movements, collective action and 165–6, 193–6; studying 189–91

resource mobilisation theory 4–5, 88–90, 96–27; compared to political process 139; compared to traditional social movements 108, 119–20; demobalisation 96; deprivation and beliefs 106–7; emergence of 118–19, 286; focal points 89, 100–1; future of 126–7; identities and resources 362; Latin America 238, 239; loosening of social control 98–100; mobilisation compared to social control 96; participants 97–8, 118 *see also* Klandermans, Snow *et al.*; process of 121–4; recruitment strategies 124, 182; relationship between city and countryside 101–4, 120; social-psychological factors *see* Klandermans; theoretical elements 109–11

revolution 45, 79, 149–50; 1848 99, 100, 190; Bolsheviks 112; French Revolution 19–20, 27, 58, 84, 85, 97–8, 189; Hungary 88, 99, 100; Italian 47, 57; Mexico 99, 101; "passive" 57; religious revolution 83–4; revolutionary movements 66, 70–1, 83–5

Rich, Bruch 318

'right of combat' 6, 9, 23

Rimbaud 362

riots 45, 75, 79, 97, 100, 132, 140, 157, 174, 175, 217; IMF 235, 300; New Haven and Detroit 161; race 159, 161, 162n, 170

Risorgimento 56–8

Risse and Sikkink 334, 335

Risse-Kappen, Thomas 327

Risse, Ropp and Sikkink 327, 331

Risse, Thomas 331

Robertson, R. 353

Rochon, T. R. 147

Rogers 121

romantics 290, 292

Rootes, Christopher 341

Rose, A. 107

Rothman and Oliver 318
Rousseau 292, 359
Rucht, Dieter 330, 341, 350
Rudé 97, 98
Ruggiero, Vincenzo 241, 297, 359, 362; 364, *Dichotomies and Contemporary Social Movements* 300–1, 357–65
Rule and Tilly, "Political Process in Revolutionary France, 1830–1832" 177
rural areas 101–4, 112, 123, 124; urbanization of southern black population, USA 120
Russia 75, 81, 84, 85, 101; Bolsheviks 112
Rwanda 99

Salisbury, R. H. 113n
Sarachild, Kathie 152, 153
Sassen, S. 362
Savage, M. 89
Scheler, Max 242, 272, 273
Scholte, J.A. 318
Schumpeter 73–4
Schwartz, Michael 249
science 275, 277; *see also* technology
Seattle *see* DAWN; Khagram, Riker and Sikkink; Montagna; Smith, Jackie
Seattle Post Intelligencer 324
sect formation 83
self control 8, 9
self-interested behaviour 87, 93–4, 122
Selznick 74–5, 76
Sem Terra movement 351
Sen and Grown 310
Shack/Slum-Dwellers International (SDI) 298, 304–5
Shaw, Timothy M. 328
Sikkink and Smith 318, 350
Simmel, George 4, 95, 361; *Conflict (On Individuality and Social Forms)* 10–11, 29–33; 'Conflict and the Webb of Group-Affiliation' 10; conflict as an integrative force in the group 31–3; 'Metropolis and Mental, The' 10; *Philosophy of Money* 1–2; sociological relevance of conflict 30; unity and discord 31
Smelser, Neil J. 4, 106, 155, 174; *Theory of Collective Behaviour* 44–5, 79–85
Smith, Adam 245, 290–1
Smith and Johnston 352, 353
Smith, C. 322
Smith, Chatfield and Pagnucco 327
Smith *et al.* 360
Smith, Jackie 328, 346, 363; accounting for needs in North and South 319; *Globalizing Resistance: The Battle of Seattle and the Future of Social Movements* 299, 316–24, 349; mobilizing structures 320t; movement origins 317–22;

movement tactics and political processes 234–6
Smith, Pagnucco and Lopez 319
Smith, Pagnucco and Romeril 346
Snow and Benford 147, 350
Snow and Machalek 261
Snow *et al.* cycles of protest 262–3; *Frame Alignment Processes, Micromobilization, and Movement Participation* 242, 255–65, 281, 350, 366; micromobilization 255, 256
Snyder and Tilly 10
social conflict, characteristics of 212–13
social location and forms of defiance 174–5
social movement industry (SMI) 109–10, 112
social movement organization (SMO) 109–10, 121–2, 125, 165, 267, 271, 285–6; potential beneficiaries 111; resource mobilization task of 110–11; *see also* Snow *et al.*
social movements: compared to new social movements 214–17, 273–4, 276–7; compared to political process 177–8, 179–80; compared to resource mobilisation 108, 119–20; concept of 265–71; countermovement 109; definitions of term 89, 109–10, 142, 177, 187–8, 196–7, 212, 239, 273; emergence of *see* McAdam, McCarthy and Zald, resource mobilisation theory, emergence; national social movement 186–7, 191–2, 193, 244; new social movements, definition of 195, 197, 208–11, 220–1, 237, 239–40 *see* new social movements for more detail; repertoire and 191–4; rise of 186–99; trends in Latin American social movements theory and research 238–40; *see also* contemporary social movements; cultural sphere; individual authors; social movement organization
social movement system (SMS) 267
social order, creation of a new 213
social-psychology *see* psychological factors
social networks *see* networks
sociation 10
solidarity 8–9, 22–3, 24, 90, 98, 123, 253, 322; shared beliefs and 268–70, 358; spontaneous solidarity 22, 23, 57–8; *see also* esprit de corps
Sorel 75
Soule, Sarah A. 341
South Africa 341
Southeast Asia 100
Southern Christian Leadership Conference (SCLC) 109
Spain 76
Spencer, Herbert 3, 7–8; compared to Durkheim 8–9
Spilerman 160–1, 162n
Stallings, R. A. 106

Starr, A. 360

State Commissions on the Status of Women 228

states 125, 213; dichotomy of civil society and 206, 208; direct democracy in Switzerland 143, 163–70; framing issues 147; history of subaltern classes 42, 55–6; leadership and development of the nation and modern state of Italy 56–8; *Modern Prince, The* 59–63; national states and rise of national social movement 191–2, 194; Tocqueville 139–40

states and international norms 333

states and non states, relations between 300, 305, 339–40, 353

Stienstra, D. 310, 312, 314

Stiles, Randall W. 327

strain 180; Smelser's theory 44–5, 155

strategic social construction 332

Strickland and Johnston 113n

strikes 132, 140, 175, 231, 232, 342

Structural Adjustment Program Review Initiative 312

structural-functionalist perspective *see* Blumer; Smelser

structural theories 106, 113n, 118, 119, 216, 244; electoral system as a structuring institution 175–6; framing work 142–3, 147; horizontal 331, 345, 350, 353, 363; limits of 228; local government structures and protest 158–9; mobilizing structures 147–8; opportunity structures 334–6; political opportunities 179–81, 184; post-structural theories 239

student movements 109, 126, 153, 275–6, 300, 321, 324, 341

Student Nonviolent Coordinating Committee (SNCC) 109, 153, 155, 230

Students for a Democratic Society (SDS) 153, 230

subaltern classes 42, 55–6

subjectivity 141, 142; Marxist view 180

submerged networks *see* Mueller, Carol

Switzerland: social movements and democracy 143, 163–70; Zurich guilds 49–50

symbolic factors 244; interactionist tradition 43

Tarrow, Sidney 328, 329, 332, 335, 349, 354; contention, cycles of 149–50, 262; contention, repertoire of 146; *Democracy and Disorder* 142, 345; dynamics of movements 148–50; framing work 142–3, 147; mobilizing structures 147–8; opportunities and constraints 145–6; outcomes of movements 150; *Power In Movement* 142–3, 145–50, 330, 334, 358; religious communities 148

Taylor, Charles 291, 362

Taylor, V. *Marketisation of Governance* 313

tax rebellion 188, 189, 190

technology 216, 219, 256, 300; division of labour and 227; *see also* internet; science

Ten Hours Bill 14, 16n

terrorist organizations 268

Third World debt 318

Third World Network 320t, 321

Tilly, C. 98, 105, 106, 119, 125, 149, 194n, 257, 262, 265, 341, 349, 360; collective action repertoires 165–6, 170n; Diani on, 268, 269, 270; *Social Movements and National Politics* 142, 186–94

Tilly, Tilly and Tilly 105

Tobin Tax 351, 352

Tocqueville, Alexis de 95; *Democracy in America* 139–40

Tönnies and Pareto 4

totalitarianism 44, 60, 75–7, 78

Touraine, Alain 239, 267, 268, 269; *An Introduction to the Study of Social Movements* 196–7, 212–17; social movement and structural conflict 3; struggle for historicity 274

transnational associations 322–3

transnational coalitions (campaign) 299, 329, 330, 333–4, 343, 345

transnational collective action, definition of term 343; Della Porta and Tarrow 300, 339–46; Khagram, Riker and Sikkink 299–300, 327–36; Montagna 300, 349–54; *see also* contemporary social movements; global factors

transnationalisation of politics 353

transnational networks 329, 330, 333–4

transnational public sphere 354, 359

transnational social movement organizations (TSMOs) 318–22, 320t, 329, 350, 362

transnational social movements 330

transparency 352, 363

Traugott, M. 358

Trebitsch, M. 358

Tullock, G. 113n

Turner and Killian 106, 107, 269

Turner, Brian 3

Turner, Ralph 110, 162n

Turner, Vincent 294

Ukraine, 'orange' revolution 354

unemployment 173–4

unions 53, 183, 193, 271, 299, 318, 319, 322, 345, 360; Dutch industrial workers 252–3; farm workers 123; funding 131; Philippines 323; women's movement and 229–30

United Nations 343, 345, 353

United Nations Centre for Human Settlements 305

United Nations Decade for Women 310
United Nations Development Programme
  (UNDP), *Development Report* 1999 308
United Nations Third World Conference,
  Nairobi 1985 310
Urry, John, *Sociology Beyond Societies* 3, 358
USA *see* America
USSR, collapse of 310, 344, 354
utilitarian tradition 215, 294
utopian movement 83; global 298, 303, 306
utopias, failure of 364

value-orientated movement 80, 83–5; definition
  of 83; major lines of variability 83–4;
  religious change and 84–5; revolution and 85;
  violence and 85
values 2, 64; amplification 257–8, 262; new
  values 2, 9, 65; post-materialist values 5,
  122; 195, 208–11, 222; shared 9, 42; *see also*
  beliefs
Venice, patrician monopolies in 47–9
Via Campesina 351–2
Vietnam 112, 275, 276
volunteer labor 110

Walsh, E. J. 123
Walton, John 342
Walton and Seddon 318
Waltz 328
Wapner, Paul 328
Waterman, Fairbrother and Elger 327
Weber, Max 4; *City, The* 41–2, 47–51; *Class, Work,*
  Party 1, 52–4; *Economy and the City* 41
Weber-Michel theory 126
welfare rights organizations 122, 123, 126
welfare state, constitutional arrangements
  of 207

Wilkinson 187
Wilson, J. 105, 113n, 360
Wilson, Q 162n
withdrawal movements 2, 111, 112
Women in the New University Conference 154
Women's Caucus 313
Women's Equality Day Strike 233, 234
Women's Equity Action League (WEAL) 229
Women's International League for Peace and
  Freedom 318
women's movement 64, 65, 81–2, 110, 111,
  122, 126, 148, 182, 183, 202, 209, 228,
  230, 276, 288, 345, 351; Evans 141, 152–6;
  global aspects of 221, 298, 307–14, 335;
  Latin America 240; Mayo 298, 307–14;
  Mueller 198, 226–34
World Bank 305, 316, 317, 318, 327, 340, 341,
  351, 352
World Economic Forum, Davos 344, 345, 351
World Social Forum, Porto Alegre 2001 297,
  312, 344
World Summit on Social Development,
  Copenhagen 1995 311
World Summit on Social Development, Geneva
  2000 311, 313
World Trade Organization (WTO) 299, 319–22,
  320t, 327; 1994 316, 340, 344, 352; GATS
  321; internet site 324; Quad 316–17
World Women's Conference, fourth, Beijing
  1995 311, 345

Yashar, Deborah J. 345
Young, B. 307
Young, K. 309, 310
youthful protest groups 203, 204

Zald and Ash 125